Best Places
to Stay
in the South

The Best Places to Stay Series

Best Places to Stay in America's Cities
Kenneth Hale-Wehmann, Editor

Best Places to Stay in Asia
Jerome E. Klein

Best Places to Stay in California
Anne E. Wright

Best Places to Stay in the Caribbean
Bill Jamison and Cheryl Alters Jamison

Best Places to Stay in Florida
Christine Davidson

Best Places to Stay in Hawaii
Kimberly Grant

Best Places to Stay in Mexico
Bill Jamison and Cheryl Alters Jamison

Best Places to Stay in the Mid-Atlantic States
Kent Steinriede

Best Places to Stay in the Midwest
John Monaghan

Best Places to Stay in New England
Christina Tree and Kimberly Grant

Best Places to Stay in the Pacific Northwest
Marilyn McFarlane

Best Places to Stay in the Rockies
Roger Cox

Best Places to Stay in the South
Carol Timblin

Best Places to Stay in the Southwest
Anne E. Wright

Best Places to Stay in the South

Carol Timblin

Bruce Shaw, Editorial Director

Fourth Edition

HOUGHTON MIFFLIN COMPANY

BOSTON • NEW YORK

For information about permission to reproduce selections from this book, write to Permissions, Houghton Mifflin Company, 215 Park Avenue South, New York, New York 10003.

Fourth Edition

ISSN: 1060-7757
ISBN: 0-395-86940-4

Printed in the United States of America

Maps by Charles Bahne
Design by Robert Overholtzer

This book was prepared in conjunction with Harvard Common Press.

QUM 10 9 8 7 6 5 4 3 2 1

To my family—George, Justin, Alison, and Brandon

Acknowledgments

A book of this scope and magnitude would not be possible without the support and help of travel professionals and the understanding of family and friends. I am deeply indebted to the state travel directors and their staffs who helped plan itineraries; to cooperative innkeepers and restaurateurs who have given generously and graciously of their southern hospitality; to the publisher who continues to provide the necessary support for such a project; and to others out there who extended their encouragement and friendship during my travels and research. Thanks to all of you.

I am especially grateful for the following people and organizations who provided special assistance on this edition: Carol Godwin, an Alabama-based travel writer; Lynn Edge, travel columnist for the *Birmingham News*; Starr Smith, travel columnist for the *Montgomery Advertiser*; Alabama Bureau of Travel and Tourism; Kerry Ann Kraus and Tyler Hardman, Arkansas Department of Parks & Tourism; Bill Schemmel, author of *Georgia Off the Beaten Path* and *Country Towns of Georgia*; Georgia Department of Industry, Trade and Tourism; Brook and Barbara Elliott, Kentucky freelance travel and outdoor writers; Kentucky Department of Travel Development; Susan Morris, president of Bed & Breakfast Reservation Services World-Wide, Inc.; Louisiana Office of Tourism; Mississippi Department of Economic and Community Development; Emily Sarah Linebeck, publisher and editor of *Southern Inns and Bed & Breakfasts* magazine; Bill Hensley; travel editor of *North Carolina Magazine*; North Carolina Travel & Tourism Division; Cherie Had and Carol Mullis, South Carolina Department of Parks, Recreation, & Tourism; Ardi Lawrence, coauthor of *Natural Wonders of Tennessee—A Guide to Parks, Preserves & Wild Places*; Barbara Parker, Tennessee Department of Tourism.

Special appreciation also goes to publisher Bruce Shaw and editor Dan Rosenberg and their staff at the Harvard Common Press. I also wish to acknowledge Patricia Cheatham, who researched the history and attractions of Alabama, Arkansas, Georgia, Kentucky, Louisiana, Mississippi, North Carolina, South Carolina, and Tennessee.

A very special thanks goes to my husband George, who's always there for me; to my daughter Alison and my son Brandon; and to my little grandson Justin, who lights up my life and continues to amaze me as he discovers the world.

Contents

Introduction

Working on this edition of *Best Places to Stay in the South* has been enlightening and encouraging. I continue to be amazed at the number and variety of new places to stay in the South. They just get better and better. I also enjoy having the opportunity to meet new innkeepers and get reacquainted with ones that I've known for a few years through the book. They and the readers who write letters keep me up to date on how well the book is doing, who's reading the book, and whether a lodging deserves to be counted among the "best places to stay."

Though I try to visit as many inns as possible between revisions of *Best Places to Stay in the South* it is becoming increasingly difficult to stay current on what is happening in the nine-state region the book covers. For that reason, in updating this edition I relied on the expertise and knowledge of travel writers and editors and people associated with lodging associations and reservations services who have first-hand knowledge of accommodations in the South. They suggested some wonderful places that I might have never discovered on my own. I really believe their research efforts have made this a better book.

Thinking back over the initial odyssey I took through the South in 1991 in preparation for the first edition, as well as more recent trips through certain states, my mind is still crowded with pleasant memories of luxurious and comfortable rooms in historic plantations, city hotels, farmhouses, mountaintop inns, and other retreats; of sumptuous breakfasts around elegant tables, shared with travelers from around the world; of warm, hospitable innkeepers in love with people, life, and what they do; of travel professionals and volunteers proud of their cities and regions and eager to have visitors; of beautiful sunrises over the ocean, golden sunsets beyond the mountains, and myriad colors of day lilies in all their summer glory.

As a southerner, I had preconceived notions about the type of people I might encounter and the hospitality they would offer, and I was almost afraid I would be disappointed. My odysseys confirmed my highest expectations, and I was not disappointed at all. The South is still the most culturally rich region in the country. People still count, values are important, and traditions are to be cherished. People still practice southern hospitality with a sincerity, grace, and charm that are unparalleled anywhere in the world. Southerners are not caught in a time warp, as evidenced by the progressiveness of our cities—Atlanta (where the world came calling in the summer of 1996), Charlotte, Columbia, Nashville, Memphis, Jackson, New Orleans, Louisville, Little Rock, Montgomery, and others.

This book is intended to introduce you to the richness of the South and its people, to guide you to the best places to stay, to provide inside information about the history of the region, as well as things to see and do.

Best Places to Stay in the South is intended for all types of travelers—families looking for a place they can enjoy together; couples in search of romance; disenchanted travelers who are tired of the run-of-the-mill motel.

Each chapter in this edition focuses on a particular state and includes a general introduction, sometimes a more detailed account of a particular region within the state; maps and illustrations; descriptions of each lodging selected for the book; and highlights about the inn or the place. The Appendix helps you select the places that offer what you may be looking for in the way of special activities such as skiing, hiking, gourmet dining, and other interests. It also notes places that are accessible to the physically challenged.

The Choices

After months of research and investigation of places in North Carolina, South Carolina, Georgia, Alabama, Mississippi, Louisiana, Arkansas, Tennessee, and Kentucky, we selected those we felt were the best. In selecting these places, several things are considered—comfort, cleanliness, hospitality, ambiance, and uniqueness, regardless of whether the lodging is a five-star resort or a rustic mountaintop cabin. The inns are not rated, but each is judged on its own merits.

Most of the inns selected for the book were either visited by me or a research associate. In a few cases, where a personal visit was not possible, information was exchanged by letter, fax, and telephone. None of the entries is a paid advertisement.

Not everyone will agree with the choices. Some great places may have been excluded, not because of their quality, but by necessity (the property may have been temporarily closed or in the process of changing owners, for example). Chains have been excluded for the most part, but some were included because they are in fact the places to stay in a certain town or region.

Rates and Taxes

The stated rates were in effect at press time and subject to change without notice. Taxes are not included, so the total costs may be slightly higher than listed. Taxes differ by region and may range as high as 11 percent. Unless otherwise indicated, rates listed are for one night and are usually the double rate, the cost for two. Please keep in mind that weekend and corporate rates are usually lower, but no attempt has been made to list them in the book. However, some seasonal rates are included.

Meals

Breakfasts are described as full or Continental. Most innkeepers insist that they served a Continental-plus breakfast, meaning that they offer more than just toast, juice, and coffee, but this designation has not been included. A full breakfast in the South usually includes eggs with sausage, bacon, or ham, almost always grits (yummy with cheese and butter) juice and/or fresh fruits, homemade biscuits, homemade jams and jellies, real butter, and coffee and tea. A Continental breakfast will usually feature Aunt Nellie's homemade banana bread or apple fritters, sometimes cereal, fresh fruit, juice, coffee, and tea. A few hosts place a lot of emphasis on "healthy" breakfasts—fresh foods that are low in fat and cholesterol.

Booking a Room

When booking a room, be specific about your wants and needs. If you prefer a private bath, need a quiet room, or desire the lowest rate possible, convey these wishes to the innkeeper. If they aren't met, you can always request a change. You don't have to accept a room or conditions you don't like. Rare will be the southern innkeeper who isn't willing to bend over backwards to please you.

The information in this guidebook is as up to date and accurate as possible, but changes inevitably occur. It's always a good idea to check on rates and policies before you go to an inn and to make reservations as far in advance as possible. Reservation services usually include a fee in the rate, but they can locate lodgings in private homes that are not advertised.

Best Places to Stay in the South is the most comprehensive compilation of outstanding lodgings for this region. I hope you find the selections to your liking and enjoy traveling throughout my homeland as much as I do. If you don't get royal treatment, please let me know. Godspeed.

Carol Timblin
Charlotte, North Carolina

Alabama

Best Bed-and-Breakfasts

Best City Stops

Best Country Inn

Best Gathering Places

Best Parks

Fort Payne
De Soto State Park Resort, 17
Guntersville
Lake Guntersville State Park, 20

Best Plantations

Talladega
Orangevale, 35
Valley Head
Winston Place Mansion c. 1851, A Bed and Breakfast, 37

Best Resorts

Orange Beach
Perdido Beach Resort , 27
Point Clear
Marriott's Grand Hotel, 28

Alabama reveals astonishing diversity in its 51,718 square miles. In lively Mobile and the Gulf Coast Delta, an aura of bygone days hovers about stately antebellum mansions, and brooding forts guarding Mobile Bay are reminders of a devastating war that almost broke our nation's spirit. In the central region, gracious Montgomery, among the South's most picturesque capital cities, evokes the memory of the Deep South as it flourishes with contemporary vitality.

Alabama's largest metropolis, Birmingham, perhaps best known as an iron and steel center, has burgeoned into one of those bold New South cities that's a sparkling buckle on the Sunbelt. In prosperous Huntsville, the United States space program was born, spearheaded by German scientists after the end of World War II. In the north there are also dramatic caves and caverns to explore, along with some of the oldest Indian habitations in the United States. Forest-clad mountains and shimmering recreational lakes also stretch across the northern portions of Alabama, abounding in opportunities for outdoor adventure.

Mobile, with a population of 204,490, dreams along quiet, tree-shaded streets and bustles beside its broad bay. Portions of its downtown area are preserved in such historic districts as Church Street East, de Tonti Square, Old Dauphin Way, and Oakleigh Garden —the latter showcasing the 1833 Oakleigh Period House; nearby is the Museum of Mobile, where you can explore the city's history. Another era is reflected at U.S.S. *Alabama* Battleship Park, a one-hundred-acre site that is home to the famed World War II "battlewagon" and the U.S.S. *Drum* submarine.

Just outside Theodore on the western edge of Mobile Bay lies Bellingrath Gardens, notable for brilliant displays of spring azaleas, which give way to late spring's roses followed by autumn's vibrant splashes of yellow, bronze, and russet chrysanthemums. Dauphin Island, south across Mississippi Sound, includes an Audubon bird sanctuary with walking trails; with its broad white sandy beaches, it is a pleasant spot for swimming, picnicking, fishing, and boating. Fort Gaines, on the island's eastern tip, guards the western shore of Mobile Bay. Captured by Union land forces in 1864, it houses a Confederate museum along with the anchor of the U.S.S. *Hartford*, flagship of Union Admiral David Farragut, who attacked Fort Morgan across the bay with his famous command "Damn the torpedoes . . . full speed ahead!"

A scenic auto/passenger ferry ride leads across the bay to the massive, star-shaped Fort Morgan, which has been restored and renovated. Stretching eastward for 32 miles, the shimmering white sandy beaches of "Alabama's Riviera" encompass the popular Gulf Coast resorts of Gulf Shores, Orange Beach, and Perdido Key. Anglers can choose fresh- or saltwater fishing nearly year-round. You can also go for mackerel, redfish, trout, and bluefish from the 825-foot Gulf State Park pier. (Year-round programs at the 6,000-acre park feature bike hikes, beach and nature walks, guided canoe trips, and crafts classes, and children's activities.) Alabama's deep sea fishing charter fleet is located in Orange Beach, and sailing charters are also available. Fresh Gulf seafoods are specialties of many restaurants, plain or fancy, in the area. Don't miss a coastal delicacy — crab claws — either steamed in the shell or fried, served with zesty ketchup-horseradish sauce. About halfway up the eastern shore of Mobile Bay at Point Clear is one of the South's splendid old resorts, the storied Grand Hotel.

Montgomery, with a population of 195,471, became the Confederacy's first capital when Jefferson Davis was sworn in as its president in February 1861. Legacies of the era remain in such historic structures as the First White House of the Confederacy; the imposing 1851 state capitol, which also served as the first capitol for the Confederate States of America; and Old Alabama Town, preserving historic pioneer and antebellum structures.

A striking presence on the Montgomery scene is Alabama Shakespeare Festival, which moved from Anniston in 1985 to occupy the dramatic Renaissance-style Carolyn Blount Theatre. It has blossomed into one of the nation's top professional theaters, presenting classics year-round. The Montgomery Museum of Fine Arts next door, notable for its American works, includes the Blount collection of paintings and watercolors and showcases Artworks, a hands-on gallery and studio for youngsters and the young at heart.

Northward, linked to Montgomery by I-65, Birmingham is set against the backdrop of gentle mountains. It is Alabama's largest city, with a population of 264,527 (881,761 in the metro area). Iron and steel built the "Magic City," which has undergone an impressive downtown renaissance in recent years. Its trademark, the mammoth Red Mountain statue of Vulcan, Roman god of the forge, symbolizes Birmingham's past, which is also celebrated at Sloss Furnace National Historical Landmark, site of an early ironworks. Now among the South's major medical and educational centers, Birmingham is a cultural hub as well, boasting such major attractions as the Birmingham Museum of Art and the Birmingham Civil Rights Institute, a state-of-the-art facility chronicling the role the city played in the civil rights struggle and present-day racial progress. In April, the colorful Birmingham Festival of Arts. And in a state where football reigns, perhaps many Alabamians' most cherished repository is the Alabama Sports Hall of Fame, honoring famous state athletes and the legendary Crimson Tide football coach Paul "Bear" Bryant, who brought the University of Alabama at nearby Tuscaloosa to national attention. Tiger football fans are equally fervent at Auburn, home of Alabama's largest institution of higher learning — Auburn University.

At nearby Talladega, east of Birmingham, equally rabid stock car racing fans have their heyday at the Talladega Superspeedway. Heralded as the world's fastest speedway, it is home to such major events as the Winston Select 500 and the DieHard 500. Nearby on Speedway Boulevard, the International Motorsports Hall of Fame and Museum showcases a multimillion-dollar collection of automobiles and racing memorabilia.

North Alabama is the heartland of the Tennessee Valley Authority, a picturesque domain of sparkling blue lakes and gently rolling Appalachian foothills. The recreational lakes Wheeler and Guntersville, which stretch like a necklace across northern Alabama, offer wonderful opportunities for houseboating, swimming, water skiing, sailing, boating, and fishing, and various recreational sites are scattered about the heavily wooded shorelines. Several state parks have facilities rivaling luxurious private resorts, some with golf courses and tennis courts.

Northern Alabama's largest city, Huntsville, which has a population of 170,984, rose to prominence when Dr. Wernher von Braun and a German scientific team developed the Saturn V moon rocket, which boosted the U.S. space program. At the U.S. Space and Rocket Center, hands-on exhibits bring space explorations to life, and you can view the nation's only full-size space shuttle exhibit and tour the U.S. Space Camp training center.

More surprises await you throughout northern Alabama. You can explore vast limestone caves (Rickwood Caverns in Jefferson County and Sequoyah Caverns at Valley Head) and view 8,000-year-old prehistoric Indian relics at Russell Cave National Monument outside Bridgeport. On a contemporary note, head for Fort Payne, hometown of the renowned country-and-western group Alabama. Their fan club and museum are open daily. Outside town, 5,000-acre DeSoto State Park Resort stretches along Little River Canyon atop Lookout Mountain. DeSoto Falls, plunging 110 feet, is a favorite spot for picnicking, swimming, and fishing. The park includes a lodge, cottages, campsites, picnic areas, and hiking trails.

For more information, contact the Alabama Bureau of Tourism and Travel, P.O. Box 4927, Montgomery, Alabama 36103-4927, 334-242-4169 or 800-ALABAMA.

Anniston

The Victoria: A Country Inn & Restaurant

1604 Quintard Avenue
P.O. Box 2213
Anniston, AL 36202
205-236-0503
Fax: 205-236-1138

> A Victorian inn known for its wonderful food

Innkeepers: Fain and Beth Casey. **Accommodations:** 56 rooms and 4 suites (all with private baths). **Rates:** $64–$219. **Included:** Continental breakfast. **Payment:** Major credit cards. **Children:** Welcome. **Pets:** Not allowed. **Smoking:** Allowed. **Open:** Year-round.

➤ **Also located on the property is a one-bedroom guest house with a wet bar, whirlpool bath, and private patio — an ideal honeymoon retreat. Wildlife artist Larry K. Martin's gallery, the Wren's Nest, is in the old carriage house.**

This Alabama landmark was built in 1887 on the highest hill on Quintard Avenue by John McKleroy, a Confederate veteran, gubernatorial candidate, and partner in the Anniston Land Company. After his death in 1894, his son William lived in the house for twenty-five years. The property then changed hands twice before being purchased in 1984 by South Carolina developers Terry Powell and John Hipp. During the restoration, Earlon McWhorter, the general contractor, and his wife, Betty, fell in love with the house and bought it.

The three-story Queen Anne Victorian structure remains the centerpiece of the property, which takes up an entire block. The building houses the restaurant downstairs and three suites upstairs and is decorated in antiques, some of them original to the house and some purchased in Europe by the owners. A 43-room addition behind the house has been coordinated to blend with the architecture of the main house and is tied to it by covered walkways. Between the main house and the addition is a large swimming pool.

Food is a very important part of an experience at the Victoria. Everything on the menu is à la carte, and selections vary with the season. Choices may include escargot sautéed with artichoke hearts, Canadian blue mussels in cream sauce, Victoria's seafood chowder, Caesar salad with anchovy dressing, and various entrées such as fresh Gulf shrimp grilled with honey mustard, roast pork tenderloin with raspberry sauce, and breast of chicken with Emmenthal Swiss and asparagus. The Victoria is considered the place to eat in Anniston.

Auburn

Auburn University Hotel & Conference Center

241 South College Street
Auburn, AL 36830-5400
334-821-8200, 800-2-AUBURN
Fax: 334-826-8746

> A conference center in the middle of a university town

Management: Richfield Hospitality Services. **Accommodations:** 248 rooms (all with private baths). **Rates:** $64–$100 (2-night minimum on home football game weekends). **Included:** Use of recreational facilities. **Payment:** Major credit cards. **Children:** Free in room with parents. **Pets:** Small, well-behaved pets allowed. **Smoking:** Smoking and nonsmoking floors. **Open:** Year-round.

➤ **Regardless of being a fan of the War Eagles, it's not hard to get in the spirit, especially when Auburn whips Alabama. You'll know when Auburn has won by the noise and revelry near Toomer's Drugstore. (The corner gets rolled when Auburn wins.)**

Your group won't have to contend with traffic in this village setting, and you needn't worry about not having the latest in technology. Everything is state of the art at the Auburn University Hotel & Conference Center, built in 1988 with meetings in mind. Does your group need computer access? The instructional computer lab has computers and printers, programmed for stand-alone operation or group networking to external systems. What about teleconferencing? That's available through Auburn University's Satellite Uplink facility and its Educational Television Center; in addition, the conference center has a full array of audiovisual equipment for rent. The day's events can be viewed on television sets throughout the center.

There's also plenty of space in the large meeting halls and breakout rooms, and the center has been planned so that traffic flows easily from one room to the other. In addition to the large auditorium (about 5,400 square feet) are two ballrooms, eight break-out rooms, an executive board room and a seminar room. The latter features tiered seating, large-screen projection, and an interactive audio system. All the conference facilities are on the ground floor, along with the hotel lobby, the registration desk, restaurants, offices, and the gift shop. The center is conveniently located in the village within view of the campus clock tower. Directly across the street is R. B. Draughon Library, one of the largest research libraries in the Southeast.

For groups, the hotel offers full catering services. Soups and sandwiches are offered in the Deli, and Ivy's Restaurant serves three meals a day, with entrées such as grilled scallops, pecan catfish, pork loin, and prime rib. You can also walk to restaurants in the village.

The six-story brick hotel is designed in contemporary Georgian architecture. It has a classic, traditional look inside, with heavy round columns and hardwood floors covered in Oriental rugs in the lobby. Guest rooms have dark cherry furniture, including broken-pediment headboards, complemented by the artwork of Alabama artists and draperies and bedspreads made of rich fabrics. The center offers an outdoor pool and a fitness center. The Auburn Links golf course offers 18 holes and Links on the Lakes has 54 holes, 18 of which are lighted for night play.

In addition to the many services offered to groups, the center provides transportation to and from the Auburn.

Birmingham

The Tutwiler: Grand Heritage Hotel

Park Place at 21st Street North
Birmingham, AL 35203
205-322-2100, 800-845-1787
Fax: 205-325-1183

| **A Birmingham tradition for decades** |

Owner: Grand Heritage Hotels. **General Manager:** Danny Hiatt. **Accommodations:** 95 rooms and 52 suites (all with private baths). **Rates:** $125–$650 weekdays; $69–$139 weekends. **Included:** Complimentary airport transportation, shoeshines, and newspapers; nightly turndown and chocolates; use of health club. **Payment:** Major credit cards. **Children:** Welcome. **Pets:** Allowed. **Smoking:** Smoking and nonsmoking rooms. **Open:** Year-round.

➤ **Those who stay on the Heritage level (accessible by key only) are given extra amenities — plush terry robes, monogrammed towels, hairdryers, bathroom scales, newspapers, magazines, complimentary hors d'oeuvres, and concierge service in the Club Lounge. Some suites even have fireplaces.**

The reflection of lighting fixtures and brass accents on the marble floors casts a golden glow over the lobby of the Tutwiler — a symbolic statement of the hotel's class and position in Birmingham. The original hotel was constructed in 1914 and named for Major E. M. Tutwiler, a primary investor in the property who had made his fortune in railroads, coal mining, and real estate. For sixty years it was the hotel in Birmingham, attracting such luminaries as Charles A. Lindbergh, Tallulah Bankhead, Will Rogers, Eleanor Roosevelt, Nelson Eddy, and others.

Gradually losing its luster, the structure was finally imploded in 1974 to make room for a bank building. Nine years later Temple Tutwiler III, the major's great-grandson, led the movement to convert the Ridgely Apartment Building, which had been designed to have similar architectural features by the same architect, into a hotel.

In late 1986, the Tutwiler was reborn in its old neighborhood near the Convention Center, Museum of the Arts, public library, and Linn Park. Original art from the museum is often displayed in the hotel. The hotel is a Birmingham tradition and a National Historic Landmark, with a Presidential Suite for visiting dignitaries. Its new owner is Grand Heritage Hotels International of Annapolis, Maryland. The company has already completed renovations on the lobby and is currently updating the guest rooms. It will add 20 luxurious suites and a new ballroom in the spring of 1998.

The Tutwiler is like a European hotel, with emphasis on service and amenities. Guests are given a complimentary newspaper, turn-down service with chocolates in the evening, and a complimentary shoeshine. Each guest is entitled to complimentary airport limousine service, and guests may use the downtown YMCA to exercise. Christian's Restaurant, under the direction of Chef Bernard Axel, features American and Continental cuisine with regional influences. It was named one of the top twenty-five restaurants in the country in 1995. Room service is available at the hotel. A favorite gathering place for guests is Bernard's Pub.

The hotel offers a number of weekend packages focused on horseracing, football, and romance. Packages include a welcome cocktail and a Continental breakfast.

Fairhope

Bay Breeze

742 South Mobile Street
(Scenic Highway 98)
Fairhope, AL 36533
Mailing address:
P.O. Box 526
Fairhope, AL 36533
334-928-8976
Fax: 334-928-0360
http://www.bbonline.com/al/baybreeze/

> **This bayside B&B, once a
> fishing cottage, is an ideal
> place to kick off your shoes**

Innkeepers: Bill and Becky Jones. **Accommodations:** 4 rooms and 1 cottage
(all with private baths). **Rates:** $95 for rooms; $105 for cottage; 7th night free
when you stay 6 nights. **Included:** Full breakfast. **Payment:** Major credit cards.
Children: Check with innkeepers. **Pets:** Check with innkeepers. **Open:** Year-
round.

➤ **Becky, a retired schoolteacher, is the ultimate hostess who goes out
of her way to provide special favors for her guests. It may be a special kind
of breakfast jelly, a popular recipe, or a favorite coffee.**

Guests have a ringside seat to all the activities of beautiful Mobile
Bay at this unique bed-and-breakfast inn owned by Becky Jones, a
retired schoolteacher, and her husband Bill, who directs the pharmacy at Thomas Hospital. With its glass windows and lush, shaded
three-acre garden, its antique furnishings and family heirlooms, the

stucco house is a far cry from its humble beginnings as a four-room summer fisherman's cottage that Becky's parents built in the 1930s. The house has been remodeled many times to suit the changing needs of the family, but today it serves as a very comfortable bed-and-breakfast inn. It was named the best bed-and-breakfast in Baldwin County in 1995 and 1996. (The couple also operate Church Street Inn a short distance from Bay Breeze.)

Becky and Bill have their own private quarters upstairs at Bay Breeze, but guests have the full run of the downstairs which includes a sitting room with a fireplace, a wicker-furnished glassed-in porch (great for watching sunsets), living room, and kitchen. A full breakfast is served in the kitchen overlooking the Bay or on the pier during the summer. One of the most popular dishes is Eggs Benedict. The two large guest rooms have iron and brass beds, and the cottage suite (which can accommodate four) includes a living room and mini-kitchen. Decorated with antiques and Oriental and hooked rugs, the inn has brick floors and pickled white pine paneling.

Some guests prefer to stay on the property and relax on the beach or go fishing or crabbing on the long private pier. Other guests, tempted by Fairhope, a summer haven for artists and writers, enjoy exploring the shops, museums, art galleries, and restaurants. Golf and tennis are also optional activities.

Church Street Inn

51 South Church Street
Fairhope, AL 36533
Mailing address:
P.O. Box 526
Fairhope, AL 36533
334-928-8976
Fax: 334-928-0360
http://www.bbonline.com/al/churchstreet/

> **An interesting family home that's now a delightful B&B**

Innkeepers: Bill and Becky Jones. **Accommodations:** 3 rooms (with private baths). **Rates:** $85; 7th night free when you stay 6 nights. **Included:** Full breakfast. **Payment:** Major credit cards. **Children:** Check with innkeepers. **Pets:** Check with innkeepers. **Open:** Year-round.

➤ **Upon departure, one guest said that staying at the Church Street Inn was better than reading a novel, because of all the family pictures, scrapbooks, and mementos left by Becky's mother, a talented opera singer who had three husbands.**

Totally different from its sister inn (Bay Breeze Guest House), Church Street Inn represents "early 1920s Fairhope." On the National Register of Historic Places, the two-story tile-stucco cottage features an inviting front porch where you can enjoy summer nights. Becky Jones herself spent many summers on the porch when her mother, a talented opera singer, lived in the house. Most of the antique furnishings, including knickknacks and family pictures and scrapbooks, belonged to her. A special book that Becky put together focuses on her mother's interesting life.

The guest rooms are named for the Joneses' granddaughters — Laura Leigh, Ellen Elizabeth, and Ashley Anne. Ellen Elizabeth's room features her great-grandmother's Jenny Lind bedroom suite, and the bath in Ashley Anne's room has the original clawfoot tub and turtleback-beaded board ceilings.

A full breakfast is served in the formal dining room, which has a Tiffany stained glass chandelier. Sitting in the highback rockers on the porch or relaxing in the courtyard, named in honor of the Joneses' grandson Clark, are also favorite pastimes.

Located in the middle of the quaint seaside village that is known for its flower boxes and brick sidewalks, the inn is convenient to shops, restaurants, gardens and parks, and the municipal pier, which juts out over Mobile Bay.

Fort Payne

DeSoto State Park Resort

Blaylock Drive
265 County Road, Box 951
Fort Payne, AL 35967
205-845-5380, 800-568-8840
Fax: 205-845-3224

A Civilian Conservation Corps project that lives on

Owner: State of Alabama. **Accommodations:** 25 motel rooms, 11 cabins, 11 chalets (all with private baths). **Rates:** $59–$72, March–November; $53–$78, December–February; $5 for each additional person and rollaway beds (two-night minimum on weekends; 3-night minimum on certain holidays; discounts offered Monday–Thursday). **Payment:** American Express, MasterCard, Visa. **Children:** Welcome. **Pets:** Not allowed. **Smoking:** Allowed. **Open:** Year-round.

➤ **Little River Canyon is one of the deepest canyons east of the Rockies, 400–600 feet deep and 16 miles long. The park also has the distinction of containing the only river in America that flows its entire length on top of a mountain. Classified as an Alabama Wild and Scenic River, Little River runs its course across Lookout Mountain.**

Located on Lookout Mountain, which extends from Chattanooga, Tennessee, into northeast Alabama, DeSoto State Park offers some spectacular mountain scenery and wildlife. Named for the Spanish explorer Hernando DeSoto, the DeSoto State Park Resort was built by the Civilian Conservation Corps (CCC) during the Depression. It covers approximately 5,000 acres and is 35 miles long. The park is perhaps best known for its many waterfalls, the most spectacular being the 100-foot DeSoto Falls, and Little River Canyon, something of a mini–Grand Canyon.

The park has a large owl population, and a full-time naturalist is on duty. In addition to the park's natural beauty, visitors enjoy the Olympic-size swimming pool, tennis courts, picnic area, playground, and eight miles of hiking trails, many of which follow the Little River.

Guests have a choice of cabins, chalets, or motel rooms — all recently renovated. The cabins, constructed by the CCC from hand-hewn logs and stone found in the area, are furnished with hand-crafted furniture made on site and include everything needed for light housekeeping. Each cabin has a screened porch, and most have a working fireplace. The chalets also have fireplaces and kitchens; the motel rooms have cable television. Three meals a day are offered in the lodge, remodeled from the original building using stone and wood to have a more contemporary look.

Greensboro

Blue Shadows Bed & Breakfast Guest House

Box 432, Route 2
Greensboro, AL 36744
205-624-3637

A country B&B where the art of southern hospitality is practiced religiously

Innkeepers: Thaddeus and Janet May. **Accommodations:** 1 suite and 2 rooms (private bath in suite, 2 rooms share a bath). **Rates:** $65. **Included:** Continental breakfast, beverages, and desserts. **Payment:** Cash or checks. **Children:** Welcome. **Pets:** Not allowed. **Smoking:** Allowed on outside balcony. **Open:** Year-round.

➤ **The Mays have a two-mile nature trail, with offshoots (named for their daughters — Allison, Emily, Melissa, and Roxanne) that are blazed with**

**different colors of ribbons. Their property includes a "treasure forest" of
hundreds of plantation pines.**

After traveling all over the world as a pilot for thirty-four years,
Thaddeus May decided to retire with his wife Janet to his family
home in Alabama — a spot near Greensboro where his parents had
lived for more than half a century. Janet had first visited the home
shortly after their wedding. (At the time she was a professional
model in New York.) "I thought how I would love to live here one
day, " she recalls.

The name Blue Shadows is derived from the blue and green
shadows that are cast over the house when the sun comes up. Built
in 1941 on the site of a Gothic-style house that had been on the
320-acre property since 1855, the Cape Cod house is a rambling
structure that seems to go on forever. Some of the materials in the
old house were incorporated into the new one. The Mays added
guest quarters over the garage in 1981 as quarters for their five
children, their spouses, and fourteen grandchildren when they
came to visit. (Actually, the space was added for Mrs. May's elderly
mother, but she never lived there.) Since the space was not always
occupied, however, the Mays decided to turn their home into a
bed-and-breakfast inn in 1987. Though they had never been involved in such an occupation before, they knew plenty about it,
having stayed in many inns in England, Ireland, Scotland, and New
Zealand.

The spaciousness of Blue Shadows makes it ideal for guests. The
guest house is a three-room suite, which includes a large living
room with fully stocked kitchenette, a bedroom, and a
bath/dressing room. The house has a private balcony that overlooks the fruit orchards and cultivated fields. It is furnished in antiques and contemporary pieces and memorabilia from all over the
world. There's also a VCR, plus a video library with more than 100
movies. The Mays have two guest rooms in the main house.

Mrs. May doesn't cook breakfast for guests but provides plenty of
cereal, milk, juice, muffins, and coffees; no one ever goes hungry.
In the afternoon she serves tea and scones, often on the back lawn
under the huge towering trees. The B&B doesn't offer dinner, of
course, but nearby restaurants serve heaping plates of chicken, ribs,
steak, and catfish.

Though guests love the house, they are even more fascinated
with the grounds at Blue Shadows. There's a ten-acre catfish pond
(actually a commercial venture for Captain May), where you can
throw in a hook for a while. A fishing boat stays tied up at the

dock, waiting for someone to use. Also on the property is a 20-acre horse barn, painted a lovely hyacinth color with white trim.

Blue Shadows is off the beaten path (three miles from town via Highway 14 West), but it's the kind of place that many people are looking for — truly one of the best-kept secrets in the South. The Mays have entertained guests from all over the United States and several foreign countries.

Guntersville

Lake Guntersville State Park Lodge & Convention Center

1155 Lodge Drive
Guntersville, AL 35976-9126
205-571-5440, 800-548-4553
Fax: 205-571-5459

> An excellent spot for fishing and relaxing

General Manager: Joe Evelsizer. **Accommodations:** 94 rooms and 6 suites in lodge (all with private baths); 18 chalets and 16 cabins (all with private baths and fully equipped kitchens). **Rates:** $56–$108, March–October; $54–$108, November–February. **Included:** All recreation except camping and greens fees. **Payment:** MasterCard and Visa. **Children:** Welcome. **Pets:** Not allowed. **Smoking:** Smoking and nonsmoking rooms. **Open:** Year-round.

➤ **With close to 6,000 acres, the park is also a natural habitat for the American bald eagle. January is designated as eagle awareness month.**

Built in 1974 when George Wallace was governor, Lake Guntersville State Park overlooks one of the largest lakes in the Tennessee Valley. The 66,470-acre lake is Alabama's premier spot for fishing, boating, and water skiing, with boat docks and launches, rental equipment, and a tackle shop. Within walking distance of the lodge is an 18-hole championship golf course plus tennis courts, swimming pool, and nature center. The park has a trained park naturalist who conducts regular programs.

Guests have several options for lodging — rooms in the main lodge, newly renovated cottages, or chalets, many of which have wonderful views of the lake. Situated on the bluffs, the main lodge is a 1970s contemporary building with sixteen huge wrought-iron chandeliers and massive stone fireplaces. Stained Alabama pine is used throughout. The chalets continue to be popular with guests because they feature fireplaces.

Breakfast is served in the Bluffside Coffee Shop; lunch and dinner, in the Chandelier Dining Room. Both are located in the lodge and offer lakeside views. The lodge was designed with meetings in mind, and several large rooms and the outdoor plazas easily accommodate groups.

Huntsville

Huntsville Marriott

5 Tranquility Base
Huntsville, AL 35805
205-830-2222, 800-228-9290
Fax: 205-895-0904

| The only hotel on the grounds of the Space and Rocket Center |

Owner: Azar, Inc. **General Manger:** Kevin Latone. **Accommodations:** 290 rooms (all with private baths). **Rates:** $69–$130. **Payment:** Major credit cards. **Children:** Welcome. **Pets:** Not allowed. **Smoking:** Allowed. **Open:** Year-round.

➤ **The hotel is often used by parents dropping their kids off at Space Camp as well as business people attending a meeting or conducting business in the space-oriented city.**

At this hotel you're about as close to space as you're going to get on earth. Within view of rockets and modules that have been used in the U.S. space program, the Huntsville Marriott is the only hotel located on the grounds of the Space and Rocket Center, Alabama's number one tourist attraction. The hotel provides a courtesy van to and from the airport.

You'll have a choice of three types of rooms — cabana rooms with private balconies or patios, suites, or regular rooms with king-size beds. Whatever the configuration, all the rooms have sitting areas, large working desks, two telephones, and facilities for modems and teleconferencing. On the concierge level guests get a complimentary Continental breakfast and afternoon hors d'oeuvres.

The spacious lobby is a good place to meet friends and associates. There are two restaurants — Cortlands and Seasons — plus a high-energy lounge, Otters. Every Tuesday evening the area residents gather for a big party at the hotel. You can swim anytime of the year here, either in the outdoor or the indoor pool. The hotel has an exercise room, sauna, whirlpool, and game room.

Radisson Suite Hotel

6000 Memorial Parkway South
Huntsville, AL 35802
205-882-9400, 800-333-3333
Fax: 205-882-9684

A city hotel known for its service and luxurious accommodations

Owner: Enterprise Lodging LLC. **General Manager:** Malinda S. Haynes. **Accommodations:** 153 suites (all with private baths). **Rates:** $80–$200. Included: Coffee. **Payment:** Major credit cards. **Children:** Welcome. **Pets:** Damage deposit required. **Smoking:** Smoking and nonsmoking rooms. **Open:** Year-round.

➤ **The Living Room Lounge features a fireplace, and the Plantation Restaurant, famous for its chocolate praline dessert, has an intimate feeling. On weekdays a breakfast buffet is served.**

Built in 1989, this Neoclassical building has a contemporary look, with large open spaces that unify the public rooms and make them conducive to gathering. When the weather is warm, guests gather around the heated pool in the center of the complex. There's also a whirlpool exercise room.

Nothing has been omitted in the guest rooms, either. Each has a desk, dining table, sleeper sofa, coffeemaker, wet bar, and refrigerator. The King Penthouse, Room 2002 (one of two such accommodations in the hotel), is the most elaborate, with its large parlor, dining area, kitchen, master bedroom, and Jacuzzi. It is decorated in rich green, brown, and rust and features traditional mahogany furniture. The king-size bed is covered with plush, dark paisley bedding and a mountain of pillows. Extra-large towels are provided. The Plantation Restaurant serves three meals a day, and the Living Room Lounge is open every evening.

The Radisson Suite Hotel is convenient to the Redstone Arsenal and NASA and only seven minutes from downtown. A complimentary shuttle runs between the hotel and the Main Street South Shopping Boutiques and Parkway Shopping Mall.

Mobile

Radisson Admiral Semmes Hotel

251 Government Street
Mobile, AL 36602
334-432-8000, 800-678-8946 or
800-333-3333
Fax: 334-405-5942

> **A historic city hotel noted for its cuisine and ambiance**

General Manager: Kashi Misra. **Accommodations:** 170 rooms (all with private baths). **Rates:** $89–$240. **Included:** Complimentary coffee, health club privileges. **Payment:** Major credit cards. **Children:** Welcome. **Pets:** Not allowed. **Smoking:** Allowed. **Open:** Year-round.

➤ **Elegant and opulent, the hotel is furnished in Chippendale and Queen Anne pieces, and each room has a writing desk, an armoire, and a comfortable chair with an ottoman. The lobby has marble floors, crystal chandeliers, and a grand staircase.**

The Radisson Admiral Semmes Hotel, Mobile's premier hotel property, was built in 1940. It was renovated in 1985, during which time the 250 rooms were reduced to 170, creating larger spaces. Located in downtown Mobile, the hotel has served as a social center since its beginning. In 1992 it became a member of the prestigious Historic Hotels of America of the National Trust for Historic Preservation. With its emphasis on service and its meeting space, the Admiral Semmes is a good place for business conventions.

Fine dining is offered in Oliver's, with cocktails in the Admiral's Corner. On Friday evenings, Chef Henry stages the Cajun Buffet in addition to the soup and salad buffet that's offered every night. Oliver's has developed a separate menu for low-calorie consumers and added more vegetable and fish entrees on the regular menu. All selections, including the seafood Newburg and the émincé of lamb, are cooked with cholesterol-free olive oil. With Mobile's mild weather, the heated outdoor pool and whirlpool may be used year-round, as can the courtyard and gazebo. Guests also have health club privileges.

Montgomery

Red Bluff Cottage

551 Clay Street
Montgomery, AL 36104
Mailing address:
P.O. Box 1026
Montgomery, AL 36101
334-264-0056
Fax: 334-262-1872

A city B&B offering
gracious southern
hospitality

Innkeepers: Mark and Anne Waldo. **Accommodations:** 4 rooms (all with private baths). **Rates:** $55–$65. **Included:** Full breakfast. **Payment:** Major credit cards. **Children:** Welcome. **Pets:** Not allowed. **Smoking:** Not allowed. **Open:** Year-round.

➤   **Mark served as an Episcopal priest in a local parish for twenty-eight years, while Anne was kept busy raising their six children.**

Guests can enjoy breakfast in the dining room or on the verandah overlooking the Alabama Plain at this capital city B&B, built in 1987 on the bluffs as a retirement home and inn by Mark and Anne Waldo. They have entertained all their lives, so innkeeping is just a continuation of what they have been doing all along.

The raised cottage is located a block from Interstate 65 in the historic Cottage Hill District, which affords great views of the city and the capitol. It is light and airy and furnished in antiques, some dating to the eighteenth century. Guest rooms are located on the first floor, entered from the parking lot at the back, and the public rooms are upstairs. The great room, with a fireplace, is often used for watching television. The music room/library has a harpsichord and a piano, plus lots of books, of course. A crib and a cot are available for little ones, and one guest room has an adjoining room that is ideal for a child.

Orange Beach

The Original Romar House

23500 Perdido Beach Boulevard
(Highway 182)
Orange Beach, AL 36561
334-974-1625
800-48-ROMAR (76627)
Fax: 334-974-1163
original@gulftel.com
http://www.bbonline.com/al/romarhouse/

> **A beach house on the Gulf that's the ultimate in lodging**

Owner: Jerry M. Gilbreath. **Innkeeper:** Darrell Finley. **Accommodations:** 6 rooms and one cottage (all with private baths). **Rates:** May–Labor Day, $129–159; Labor Day–mid-November and March–April, $89–$109; November–February, $79–$99. Cottage: $109–$189. Two-night minimum required on weekends. **Included:** Full southern breakfast, afternoon wine and cheese, use of whirlpool spa, private beach, and honor bar. **Payment:** Major credit cards. **Children:** 12 and older welcome. **Pets:** Not allowed. **Smoking:** Allowed in the bar and on the deck. **Open:** Year-round.

➤ **The owner has refurbished the front of the house to give it a more elegant look, adding an eleven-foot mahogany front door from Australia and two New Orleans–style arched stained glass windows on either side of it. One of the original pieces of furniture inside is a twelve-foot-long heart pine table, built in one night by one of the first owners of the house and an Italian craftsman.**

Surprised will be the guest who thinks this is an ordinary beach cottage. Established in 1924 by Spurgeon Roach and Carl Martin (Romar is a combination of their surnames), this place never looked so good or had so much character. Thanks to owner Jerry M. Gilbreath, a Mississippi attorney, Romar House was Alabama's first seaside bed-and-breakfast inn. It officially opened in the spring of 1991.

The casual charm of the 4,200-square-foot beach house on the Gulf of Mexico has been retained on the upper level, but the ground floor, where most of the guest rooms are located, is nothing short of luxurious. Stained glass windows add light and beauty in unexpected places, marble tiles have been laid, and the bedrooms, named for local festivals, are decorated in art deco motifs. Favorites are Number 2, the Red Snapper Room, which features mahogany furniture and large stained glass windows; Number 3, the International Song Writer's Festival Room, known for its masculine hunter green motif and blond art deco bedroom suite; and Number 4, the Mardi Gras Room, which has the most colorful stained glass in the house. The latest addition to the inn is the Parrot House Cottage, a Caribbean villa with parrot decor. Ideal for romantic celebrations, the unit has a color television, stereo, full kitchen, and dining room.

Guests are treated to complimentary wine and cheese every evening except Sunday in the upper-level Purple Parrot Bar, named after Gilbreath's bar in Belize. On the ground level, left partially open to the outside, is another retreat for guests, where they may enjoy the whirlpool spa, hammock, and sitting area. A wraparound covered deck is a great spot for having morning coffee and reading the newspaper. By design, none of the rooms has a telephone or television, but these are available in the common area.

Guests are served a complimentary full southern breakfast that features egg casserole, grits, homemade muffins and biscuits, fruits, juices, coffee, tea, or hot chocolate. Then they're free to do whatever they please for the rest of the day — relax on the beach, shop for souvenirs, go fishing in the Gulf or boating in Perdido "Lost " Bay (named by Spanish explorers in 1693), or explore historic sites such as Fort Morgan, several miles west of Orange Beach.

The inn doesn't offer lunch or dinner, but the innkeeper will gladly offer dining suggestions and make reservations at a local restaurant.

Perdido Beach Resort

27200 Perdido Beach Boulevard
Orange Beach, AL 36561-3299
334-981-9811, 800-634-8001
Fax: 334-981-5672

A luxurious family resort on the water

Resident Manager: Tom Rasinen. **Accommodations:** 345 rooms and suites (all with private baths). **Rates:** $125–$295, May–early September; $99–$259, September–October; $69–$215, November–February. **Payment:** Major credit cards. **Children:** Welcome. **Pets:** Not allowed. **Smoking:** Allowed. **Open:** Year-round.

➤ **The primary attraction at this resort is the beach. Guests can soak up the sun on the white sugary sand, go fishing in Cotton Bayou, sail a catamaran, or watch the boat traffic pass by. They can also team up for a tennis match, work out in the health club, swim in the indoor/outdoor pool surrounded by palm trees, roam around the 32 acres of dunes, or play golf at Cotton Creek Club or Perdido Bay.**

The twin towers of the Perdido Beach Resort stand out from all the other buildings as you head toward the arched bridge over Perdido Pass, just 30 minutes west of Pensacola, Florida. Opened in 1987, the Mediterranean-style high-rise hotel is the premier property in Orange Beach, an up-and-coming resort area on the Gulf Coast that is sometimes called America's Riviera.

Each of the 345 luxurious rooms and suites has a balcony overlooking the Gulf. Sitting areas, writing desks, wet bars, and extra-long tubs are standard in the well-designed rooms. Guests enjoy cable TV and in-room movies. The lobby is decorated with mosaics by R. Gregorin, an Italian who was commissioned to do artwork for the hotel.

Voyagers features many Gulf Coast Creole dishes prepared tableside. Under the direction of Chef Gerhard Brill, the restaurant has received several distinctive awards — including AAA's four diamonds, Gourmet Diners Society of North America's Golden Fork Award, International Restaurant Rating Bureau's Best of the Best Award, the Best American Traditional Restaurant Award, and One of America's Best Chefs Award. A native of Germany, Brill has practiced his cuisine all over the world, including Zurich, Peking, and New Orleans. Casual fare is available at Café Palm Breeze and Splash; the latter is poolside.

In the evenings guests gather around the piano bar in the Sandpiper Lobby Lounge; for the high-energy set, there is Night-Reel. The hotel prides itself on its large, friendly staff — about 350 in all — making the guest to staff ratio at least two to one.

The Perdido Beach Resort is a place you can take the kids and not feel out of place. The hotel provides activities for its "Perdido pals," children ages six to twelve; nannies are available for those five and under. A number of packages are offered, including some designed especially for families.

Point Clear

Marriott's Grand Hotel Resort and Golf Club

Scenic Highway 98
Point Clear, AL 36564
334-928-9201, 800-544-9933
Fax: 334-928-1149
MHRS.PTLAL.DOS@marriott.com
http://222.marriott.com/marriott/PTLAL

> **A beautiful old resort brimming with gentility**

General Manager: Reed Pullan. **Accommodations:** 306 rooms and 16 cottages (all with private baths). **Rates:** $99–$219. **Payment:** Major credit cards. **Children:** Welcome. **Pets:** Not allowed. **Smoking:** Allowed. **Open:** Year-round.

➤ **Some members of the staff have been serving guests for more than thirty years. Bucky Miller has been tending bar in the Birdcage Lounge**

since 1941 — he's famous for his mint juleps, which contain mint leaves he picks personally.

If ever stars fell on Alabama, they must have fallen here, on this magnificent old southern queen — Marriott's Grand Hotel. Since 1847 there has been a hotel on this peninsula, which juts out on the east side of Mobile Bay. And if ever romance has blossomed, it most assuredly has done so here — the site of antebellum balls, debutante parties, and other soirées attended by the South's first families. But what counts more these days is that the resort has maintained the highest standards in the hotel industry and today continues to garner accolades, just as it did in the early days.

The Grand Hotel is a four-diamond property, the Grand Hotel recently won the 1997 Southern Living Readers' Choice Award for being one of the top five resorts in the South. It has also been rated as one of the world's best golf resorts by *Golf* magazine. Marriott bought the property in 1981 but has adhered to long-held traditions, to the delight of guests. The Grand Hotel remains a resort committed to service. The ratio of staff to guests is one to one. In addition to golf, the resort offers tennis, croquet, bicycling, horseback riding, swimming, fishing, sailing, yachting, and other activities. The 750,000-gallon pool, one of the largest in the world, was made from the hull of a ship. If you desire, the staff will cook your catch of the day for dinner. Moms and dads can relax and enjoy themselves while the kids stay busy with activities at Grand Fun Camp. The hotel is surrounded by summer homes at Point Clear, but with 550 acres of property, there's plenty of room to get lost.

After a full day of recreation, you can join your friends for afternoon tea at four o'clock or get together for cocktails before dinner at Bay View restaurant or the Grand Dining Room, known for its continental cuisine and European service. For those who are inclined to dance, there's a band. Of course, not everyone wants to eat in the formal dining room every night, so the resort offers light fare in the Birdcage Lounge. Lunch is also available at the Lakewood Golf Club. Restaurants in the nearby village of Fairhope and Mobile, a 45-minute drive away, are always an option.

Families have been returning to the Grand Hotel for generations, often requesting the same rooms year after year. It's not uncommon to celebrate Thanksgiving, Christmas, and New Year's at the resort, and Valentine's Day is always special. Stays are also built around special seminars on computers, wine, gardening, and Big Band music. Golf and honeymoon/anniversary packages are also available.

The history of the Grand Hotel is rich and varied. The first hotel was a two-story, forty-room wooden structure built by F. H. Chamberlain out of materials he hauled to Point Clear in a boat. In a separate building was the Texas Bar, which was extremely popular until 1940, though it suffered hurricane damage in the 1890s. Gunnison House, added in the early 1850s, was used for social events. The hotel survived the Civil War, sustaining a hit from a Yankee ship, and served as a hospital for Confederates, three hundred of whom are buried near the Azalea Golf Course. Fire hit the hotel in 1869 and 1871. Then, in 1875, Captain H. C. Baldwin, a steamboat master, built the first Grand Hotel on the site. During World War II the United States Air Force used the property as a training site. Marriott completely renovated the property in 1981, adding 176 rooms and a conference center. All the rooms were refurbished in 1990.

Selma

Grace Hall Bed & Breakfast Inn

506 Lauderdale Street
Selma, AL 36701
334-875-5744
Fax: 334-875-9967

| A bed-and-breakfast tour home that's a showplace in every sense of the word |

Innkeeper: Joey Dillon. **Accommodations:** 6 rooms (all with private baths). **Rates:** $79–$125. **Included:** Full breakfast, afternoon refreshments, and turndown service. **Payment:** Major credit cards. **Children:** 6 and older welcome. **Pets:** Check with innkeeper. **Open:** Year-round.

➤ **Completed in phases, the restoration is Mrs. Dillon's tenth. Her husband, Coy Dillon, a consultant, has assisted her on each project.**

Owner Joey Dillon thought of every detail when she restored this lovely antebellum Italianate home and turned it into a bed-and-breakfast inn. A historic designer by profession and lover of history and architecture, she took great care to document everything she did. Her work was certified and approved by the U.S. Department of the Interior, and Grace Hall is on the National Register of Historic Places.

In the heart of Selma's historic district, Grace Hall was built around 1857 by Henry Ware and occupied by the Evans, Baker, and Jones families for over a century. The front of the two-story white clapboard structure features five groups of large windows, including two bay windows on each side of the front door and a Palladian window over the portico. It also has bracketed eaves and New Orleans–style galleries that connect the main house to the annex and open onto a lovely courtyard. The brick-paved walk in front of the house is lined with boxwoods, and there is a beautiful garden behind the house. All the guest rooms have fireplaces, air conditioning, telephones, cable TV, and HBO, and private baths (though a little on the small side). Grace Hall is filled with antique furnishings, much of it original to the house.

Mrs. Dillon offers evening refreshments, ice with turndown service, assistance with dinner reservations, and a complete tour of Grace Hall. She serves a full breakfast of eggs and bacon, French toast, pancakes, or crêpes and will prepare lunch or dinner for groups of ten or more if requested in advance. Honeymoon, anniversary, and holiday packages are available. Since opening the B&B in 1986, Mrs. Dillon and her husband have entertained guests from all over the world.

Sterrett

Twin Pines Resort and Conference Center

1200 Twin Pines Road
Sterrett, AL 35147
205-672-7575
Fax: 205-672-2103

> **A favorite lakeside retreat
> for families and groups**

President/Owner: Robert L. (Bob) LeRoux. **General Manager:** Paul J. Watry.
Accommodations: 46 rooms (all with private baths). **Rates:** $105–$190; Getaway Package, $165 per day, including meals, for two people. **Included:** All recreational amenities. **Payment:** Major credit cards. **Children:** Welcome (3 and under free). **Pets:** Not allowed. **Smoking:** Allowed. **Open:** Year-round.

➤ **The resort has a "seven-sacker" moonshine still built by Alabama native John Higgins, a former moonshiner. A seven-sacker holds seven sacks of sugar at a time and produces a gallon of moonshine.**

The lakeside setting is so serene it's hard to believe that Twin Pines Resort and Conference Center is only 30 minutes from metropolitan Birmingham. But if you need a place for your group's next meeting or just want a quiet getaway by yourself, this retreat may fill the bill.

Built in 1987, the resort is geared to providing a relaxing atmosphere with all the necessary support services to conduct business meetings. The land chosen for the resort is a 200-acre tract with a 46-acre lake; its name comes from twin pine trees on the property. Great care was taken not to detract from the natural beauty of the area. A fifty-foot-long covered bridge built of old materials was erected on the property to link the roadway around the lake, and it is now listed on the official state map. Central to the facility is the registration, dining, and meeting hall — originally a restaurant that was moved to the site.

The resort and conference center has meeting rooms, banquet and reception areas, meals featuring old-fashioned country cooking (light fare available), and every type of recreation imaginable. You can enjoy the Aqua cycles on the lake, ride a bike, play Ping-Pong, try your hand at shuffleboard or horseshoes, go on a hay ride, or fish for bass, bream, crappie, and catfish (no license required). There are softball fields, deep-sand volleyball courts, a party barn and arcade, and table games. The staff at Twin Pines will set up your entire meeting — from meals to audiovisual aids to organized sports. The resort hosts all kinds of groups, from business meetings to family reunions to weddings.

Guests are housed in five rustic but elegant lodges. Each deluxe room has a lake view and includes two double beds, an individual refrigerator, coffee maker (with coffee provided), remote controlled color televisions, clock radios, hair dryers, massage shower heads, flashlights, and ceiling fans. Firewood and outdoor grills are also provided.

Talladega

The Governor's House

Exit 165 off I-20
Embry Cross Rd.
Lincoln, AL
Mailing Address:
500 Meadowlake Lane
Talladega, AL 35160
205-763-2186 or 205-763-7272
Fax: 205-362-2391

> **A B&B in a tranquil country setting**

Innkeepers: Ralph and Mary Sue Gaines. **Accommodations:** 3 rooms (one with private bath, two with shared bath). **Rates:** $70–$80 per room; $210 for entire house. **Included:** Full breakfast. **Payment:** Cash or checks. **Children:** 12 and older welcome. **Pets:** Not allowed. **Smoking:** Allowed on porch. **Open:** Year-round.

➤ **Guests may also fish from the lake stocked with bass and bream, play tennis on the Plexipave court, enjoy a picnic, pet the goats, admire Hereford cattle, feed apples to the horses, play with the cats, help with gathering eggs, and watch hay making during cutting season. The Gaineses' two Weimaraners love to accompany guests on walks around the farm.**

Ralph and Mary Sue Gaines couldn't bear to see this old Talladega house torn down, so they had it moved to their farm near Lincoln and restored it as a bed-and-breakfast inn. Now it sits on a knoll overlooking Logan Martin Lake and the rolling hills — a beautiful sight from the front porch or the side terrace. Guests may rent the entire house or a room.

Built in 1850, it once served as the home of Alabama Governor Lewis Parsons. It contains the original windows and wood floors. The house gleams with fresh paint and wallpaper and is cooled by central air conditioning and ceiling fans. Mary Sue, an antiques dealer for many years, has filled it with beautiful family treasures, including quilts made by her mother. The kitchen curtains are hung on tobacco sticks that came from her great-grandparents' farm. Guests are welcomed with fresh flowers and complimentary wine.

The Gaineses can provide just about any experience guests might want — from a typical overnight stay with breakfast to an elegant dinner at sunset served on their patio-boat. (Guests may bring their own boat if they wish.) The hosts will prepare special meals for guests, given advance notice.

Mary Sue's Horse Barn Galleries antiques shop is always open for browsing; her husband, Ralph, is a practicing attorney. The couple has five grown children and several grandchildren.

Orangevale

1400 Whiting Road
Talladega, AL 35160
205-362-3052
Fax: 205-761-1800

A B&B on an old plantation

Innkeepers: Dr. Richard (Dick) and Billy Bliss. **Accommodations:** 6 rooms (all with private baths). **Rates:** $95. **Included:** Full breakfast. **Payment:** Cash or checks. **Children:** 12 and older welcome. **Pets:** Not allowed. **Smoking:** Allowed on grounds. **Open:** March–December (closed Christmas).

➤ **This antebellum plantation is still a working farm, where you can stroll through the fields, look at the livestock, go fishing, and pick berries and fruits in season. Restored dependencies include log cabins, the old kitchen, well house, and smoke house.**

Orangevale had stood vacant for many years when Dick and Billy Bliss bought the property in the late 1960s and began an extensive restoration of the main house and outbuildings. After bringing up four children, they decided to open their home to guests.

Listed on the National Register of Historic Places, the Greek Revival plantation house was built during 1852–54 by Levi Lawler on the historic Jackson Trace Road. He is said to have lived in the double pen log cabin while the big house was under construction.

Guests have a choice of two guest rooms in the main house, the old kitchen, a log cabin dating to the 1830s, or Lawler's cabin. All are beautifully furnished and come with a private bath. The cabins and the old kitchen each have a fully equipped kitchen, a working fireplace, and a television. All accommodations have central heat and air.

The Blisses lead busy, active professional lives (he's a physician; she's an interior designer), so they make every effort to provide a quiet, stress-free atmosphere. Guests are welcome to sit on the patio with a mint julep in the summertime, take walks, go fishing, pick berries, or relax with a good book. Or they may visit nearby attractions — including Cheaha State Park, Logan Martin Lake, the Talladega Superspeedway, and the International Motorsports Hall of Fame.

Guests are treated to fresh fruit upon arrival. A full breakfast featuring sausage and egg casserole, muffins and sweet rolls, fruits, juices, and coffee is served at the lazy-Susan table in the kitchen or on the patio, weather permitting. If you prefer the privacy of your guest quarters, a Continental breakfast is provided. Tea and coffee are offered in all the facilities.

Valley Head

Winston Place Mansion c. 1851
A Bed and Breakfast

P.O. Box 165
Valley Head, AL 35989
205-635-6381, 888-4 WINSTON

> One of Alabama's most beautiful "big houses" now welcomes guests.

Innkeepers: Jim and Leslie Bunch. **Accommodations:** 5 rooms (all with private baths). **Rates:** $100, plus $10 for each additional person. **Included:** Continental breakfast. **Payment:** Discover, MasterCard, Visa. **Children:** 6 and older welcome. **Pets:** Not allowed. **Smoking:** Allowed on grounds. **Open:** Year-round

➤ **William Overton Winston, the builder of Winston Place, served as the first president of the Wills Valley Railroad, connecting Alabama with Tennessee. It was chartered in 1852 and consolidated with the Northeast & Southwest Railroad in 1868. Now a part of the Norfolk-Southern Railroad, Wills Valley is considered the most picturesque section of the Alabama Great Southern Railroad. Winston, who died in 1871, is buried in the family cemetery at Winston Place.**

After living in North Carolina for fourteen years, Jim and Leslie Bunch moved with their two children to her family home — Winston Place — in 1994 when Jim's company transferred him to Fort Payne, where he manages ten Hardees restaurants. Encouraged by family and friends, the Bunches turned the twenty-room mansion into a bed-and-breakfast inn. (The Bunches live in another house on the property.) Renovation included new wiring, paint and wallpaper, heating and air conditioning, and a modern kitchen with a vaulted ceiling. Interior designers from Alabama, Tennessee, and Georgia redecorated the mansion as the Designer Showcase Home of Fort Payne in 1995.

On the National Register of Historic Places, the inn offers five beautifully decorated rooms, just recently redone by Michael Berstein of Crown Craft to showcase their textile lines, which include the Williamsburg Foundation, Bob Timberlake, Raymond Waites, and Emmanual Urgano. Guests are served a full breakfast in the formal dining room on vintage linens and family china. As you might expect, Winston Place is a popular spot for weddings and parties. The recreation room in the basement commemorates Jim's illustrious career as a University of Alabama lineman under the legendary coach Paul "Bear" Bryant during 1978 and 1979 and his being named an All American.

Though guests may be perfectly satisfied to remain on the property during their entire stay, there are many local attractions and special events to enjoy — DeSoto Falls, DeSoto State Park, and Sequoyah Caverns, and the June Jam. Chattanooga, with its many attractions, is only 45 miles away.

One of Alabama's great showplaces, Winston Place has an illustrative history. It began as a crude dog-trot log house located on land at the base of Lookout Mountain that used to be a part of the Cherokee Nation. In fact, the Council often gathered under a giant red oak tree on the property. In 1835, William Overton Winston — a lawyer, state legislator, and later first president of the Wills Valley Railroad — purchased 3,000 of the surrounding acres and had 40 slaves and several Cherokees construct the magnificent mansion. Practically everything used in the 15-room house was made on site — lumber, bricks for the eight fireplaces, and glass panes for the 94 windows. The present verandah with its Doric columns was a later addition.

In 1863, Winston Place was occupied by 30,000 to 60,000 Yankee soldiers prior to their engagement in the famous Battle of Chickamauga. During their encampment one of the Winston slaves hid the family silver in a dry well in the backyard, from which it was later retrieved intact.

The mansion remained in the hands of the Winston family until 1944 when it was sold to Leslie's grandparents, Mr. and Mrs. Harry Hammond.

Arkansas

Best Bath House

Eureka Springs
Palace Hotel & Bath House, 53

Best Bed-and-Breakfasts

Eureka Springs
The Brownstone Inn, 50
Helena
The Edwardian Inn, 56
Hot Springs
Stitt House Bed & Breakfast Inn, 58
Vintage Comfort Bed & Breakfast Inn, 60
Johnson (Fayetteville Area)
Johnson House Bed & Breakfast, 62
Little Rock
Hotze House, 68
Magnolia
Magnolia Place Bed & Breakfast, 70
Mountain View
The Inn at Mountain View, 75
Pine Bluff
Margland Bed & Breakfast Inns, 78
Springdale
Magnolia Gardens Inn, 70
Texarkana
Mansion on Main, 83

Best City Stop

Little Rock
The Capital Hotel, 64

Best Country Inns

Eureka Springs
Dairy Hollow House, 51
Fort Smith
Beland Manor, 54

Best Farms and Guest Ranches

Hot Springs
 Stillmeadow Farm, 57
Little Rock
 Pinnacle Vista Lodge, 69
Mountain Home
 Scott Valley Resort & Guest Ranch, 73

Best Outdoor Retreats

Lakeview
 Gaston's White River Resort, 63
Ponca
 Buffalo Outdoor Center, 79

Best Parks

Mena
 Queen Wilhelmina Lodge, 72
Mountain View
 The Ozark Folk Center, 77

Best Romantic Hideaways

Eureka Springs
 Arsenic & Old Lace Bed & Breakfast Inn, 48
Little Rock
 The Empress of Little Rock, 66

A link between the South and the Midwest, President Bill Clinton's home state of Arkansas reflects characteristics of both regions. It covers 53,187 square miles and almost seems like two states when considered geographically and culturally.

Eastward lie the broad plains of the Mississippi River Delta, the state's richest agricultural area. The ancient, mellow Ozark Mountains, worn and rounded by time, stretch through the state's northern reaches. The Ouachita Mountains, separated from the Ozark plateau by the fertile Arkansas River valley, range farther south. Native arts, crafts, folk culture, and music are distinctive in the mountain regions, preserved originally through isolation and necessity, now proudly cherished as a connection with the past.

With good reason, Arkansas calls itself the "Natural State." Within the mountain ranges, sparkling blue lakes, formed by rivers harnessed behind massive hydroelectric dams, offer wonderful opportunities for fishing, boating, water sports, camping, and picnicking in still undisturbed settings. Arkansas boasts two and a half million acres of national forest lands and more than nine thousand miles of streams and rivers. Public waters yield 130 varieties of fish, including bass, bream, catfish, crappie, and rainbow trout.

The election of Bill Clinton to the presidency in 1992 has put Arkansas on the international map, and record numbers of visitors are converging on the state wanting to see any place associated with the president. Towns who can claim him are capitalizing on the opportunity to draw more visitors. To assist travelers, the state tourism office has produced a packet called "The Presidential Cities of Arkansas," detailing the places where you can walk in the steps of the president. They are Hope, his birthplace; Hot Springs, where he grew up; Fayetteville, where he and Hillary first lived after they were married; and Little Rock, where he served for four terms as governor of the state and where Hillary practiced law.

During the presidential campaign the little town of Hope became a household word. Today visitors are flocking to see the two homes where Bill Clinton spent his early years and to his kindergarten and elementary school.

Bill Clinton grew up in the resort town of Hot Springs (population 37,000). In the Ouachita Mountains, Hot Springs National Park is one of the nation's most unusual, since much of its 4,800 acres of woodland ridges, valley, and low-lying peaks is almost surrounded by the city. Here forty-seven hot mineral springs spew forth almost a million gallons of water daily. Some is piped into bathhouses — one in the park and four at city hotels (including the early 1920s Arlington and the Majestic) — for medicinal therapy. The park has good walking and bridle trails. Summer interpretive programs include a bathhouse tour, campfire programs, and quarry hikes. There are also limited programs during the spring blooming and fall foliage seasons.

There's a hint of earlier days along Central Avenue. The historic business district is undergoing gradual renovation. On Bathhouse Row, several original structures are being refurbished in an adaptive use program. Most elaborate of these bathhouses, the Fordyce, built in 1914, has been restored and includes the National Park Service visitor center and a museum depicting area and spa history.

Oaklawn Park, one of Arkansas' most popular attractions (where the president's mother spent a lot of time), features thoroughbred horse racing from mid-January through mid-April. A recent multi-million-dollar renovation has resulted in a renaissance for the track, where stakes reach about $3 million during the season.

West of Hot Springs and extending beyond the Oklahoma border at Mena is the Ouachita National Forest. From here you can follow the Talimena Scenic Byway, where elevations reach nearly 3,000 feet. Queen Wilhelmina State Park, atop one of the state's highest peaks, includes a modern lodge with a restaurant, built on the site of the original structure. The park also offers campsites, picnicking, a miniature railroad, a petting zoo, and miniature golf.

Little Rock, Arkansas' sprightly capital city, where the president got his experience in politics, is a made-to-order base for leisurely meanderings in every direction. But time should be allowed to discover attractions in the city that takes its name from the term "Le Petit Roche," as early French explorers called the rock outcroppings. A major Arkansas River port with a population of about 170,000, Little Rock is a handsome contemporary city with skyscrapers dotting its skyline. Yet it also offers intriguing glimpses into Arkansas' past.

The fourteen-building Arkansas Territorial Restoration reflects the state's early days. Especially notable is Hinderliter House, possibly last used as the territorial legislature's meeting site in 1835, one year before Arkansas gained statehood.

The Territorial Restoration, Old State House (now a museum of Arkansas history), and Villa Marre, an 1881 Victorian mansion, are included in the Quapaw Quarter District, a nine-mile-square area, which includes many buildings on the National Register of Historic Places.

The handsome state capitol, built of Arkansas white marble and modeled after the U.S. Capitol, has sometimes been featured as a movie stand-in for the national structure. Its gardenlike grounds include the Arkansas Vietnam Veterans Memorial.

The Arkansas Art Center, a strikingly handsome modern building in MacArthur Park, displays contemporary paintings, sculpture, prints, and ceramics and is the site of the annual Delta Art Exhibition.

Riverfront Park is a lively "people place," with a river walk, fountains, gardens, playgrounds, and an amphitheater. Here, too, is the "little rock" for which the city was named when it was settled on the Arkansas River bluffs in 1814. The park is also the site of Little Rock's gala Memorial Day Riverfest, a visual and performing arts festival. A year-round farmers' market is located here.

Lesser known Fayetteville, nestled in the Ozark Mountains in the northwest corner of the state, is the fourth presidential city. Billed as the "First Family's first home," it was here that he and Hillary were married and where they both served on the faculty of the University of Arksansas Law School. Among the points of interest are the couple's first home, Clinton's Congressional campaign headquarters, and Waterman Hall on the university campus.

Several miles northeast of Fayetteville is Eureka Springs, a resort town so picturesque it has been called "America's Little Switzerland." This quaint, charming little city tumbles up steep Ozark hillsides, its streets running in crooks and angles. It's a treasure trove of Victorian homes, with a winding main street lined with impeccably renovated buildings that house art, crafts, and antiques shops. Reflecting Eureka Springs' origins as a late-19th-century spa, the restored Palace Bathhouse offers opportunities to take the waters. The Original Ozark Folk Festival is a popular late autumn event, and several live country music and comedy shows attract visitors from early spring through late autumn. The Eureka Springs Gardens is here.

Farther southeast, near the heart of the Ozark National Forest just outside Mountain View, the Ozark Folk Center showcases the region's distinctive handicrafts and authentic music and dance. In cedar buildings on serene hillsides, friendly craftsfolk fashion tomorrow's heirlooms: white oak baskets, quilts, woodcarvings, dulcimers, corn shuck dolls, forged iron, and other distinctive wares. Evenings, well-known folk singers, dancers, and musicians perform in a modern auditorium, while impromptu jam sessions take place on the square in Mountain View (every night of the year unless it rains). The center, a state park, welcomes overnight guests; a handsome dining room offers such luscious down-home specialties as country ham, mountain trout, fried chicken, and cornbread. Northwest of Mountain View, National Forest Service staffers conduct year-round tours of dramatic Blanchard Spring Caverns, one of the century's major cave finds.

From Yellville or Marshall, you can explore a 125-mile stretch of the Lower Buffalo National River, a wilderness stream protected by the National Park Service. Buffalo Point has cabins and campgrounds; sections along the idyllic, free-flowing water course offer floating, camping, swimming, horseback and bicycle riding, hiking, and scenic drives.

With several huge blue mountain lakes formed by harnessing the White River for hydroelectric power and flood control, the Arkansas Ozarks are a haven for water sports and outdoor recreation. Popular sites include Greers Ferry Dam and Lake, northeast of Heber Springs; Lake Norfork, east of Mountain Home, with a free ferry crossing the lake; Bull Shoals, northwest of Mountain Home, one of the state's largest lakes, its cold waters an ideal environment for rainbow trout; and Beaver Dam and Lake, west of Eureka Springs. At designated sites along the lakes, you'll find facilities for swimming, picnicking, camping, boat launching, and fishing. A float trip on a flat-bottomed john boat for trout casting is considered the ultimate by fishing buffs.

An area of the state that has no presidential connection but one that has a rich, storied past is Fort Smith. From 1817, two successive frontier forts flourished here, along with the courtroom of notorious "Hanging Judge" Isaac Parker, who had jurisdiction over Oklahoma Indian Territory. Fort Smith National Historic Site includes the Barracks, Judge Parker's courtroom. A replica of the gallows stands on the grounds as a grisly reminder of frontier justice. Downtown, the Old Fort Museum depicts the city's development, and the Clayton House, a classic revival Victorian structure, is among original homes preserved in the Belle Grove Historic District. Across the river is Van Buren, a turn-of-the-century town that is being reborn. It has historic homes and stores, an opera house, and the Ozark Scenic Railroad, which offers excursions to Rudy and Winslow in the spring, summer, and fall.

For more information, contact the Arkansas Department of Parks and Tourism, One Capitol Mall, Little Rock, Arkansas 72201, 501-682-7777 or 800-628-8725; http://www.1800natural.com. E-mail: arkansas@1800 natural.com.

Eureka Springs

Arsenic & Old Lace Bed & Breakfast Inn

60 Hillside Avenue
Eureka Springs, AR 72632
501-253-5454 or 800-243-LACE
Fax: 501-253-2246
arseniclace@prodigy.net

> **A Victorian B&B that's a sure hit**

Innkeepers: Gary and Phyllis Jones. **Accommodations:** 5 rooms (all with private baths, including whirlpool tubs). **Rates:** $100–$160; 2-night minimum some holidays and weekends. **Included:** Full breakfast, afternoon refreshments. **Payment:** Major credit cards. **Children:** 14 and older welcome. **Pets:** Not allowed. **Smoking:** Allowed on verandahs and in gardens. **Open:** Year-round.

➤ **Reminders of the hit play *Arsenic & Old Lace* are scattered through the inn, and elderberry wine is served to guests.**

Surround yourself with lace and luxury at one of Eureka Spring's most luxurious B&Bs, offering the ultimate in ambiance and service. Choose a room with a whirlpool tub, a fireplace, or a private verandah opening onto the lush hillside gardens. Have refreshments and complimentary snacks while you watch a favorite movie or read a book. Feast on a three-course gourmet breakfast in the morning and then catch a trolley to other parts of the historic district. Or sign up for golf or tennis at a nearby country club.

Arsenic & Old Lace, a Queen Anne reproduction of early Victorian homes in Eureka Springs, was built by Jeanne Simpson Johnson in 1992. It features distinctive moldings and cornices, tin ceilings, antique doors, mantels, stained glass windows, and is furnished in reproduction antiques and original oil paintings (the portrait in the parlor is of Jeanne). The Treetop Suite, located in the two-story octagonal tower, has floor-to-ceiling windows that look out on the trees.

A savvy businesswoman, who realized she faced some tough competition with nearly fifty B&Bs in town, Jeanne chose the name Arsenic & Old Lace from the popular play and movie. She also instituted the tradition of serving elderberry wine to guests and used touches of Arsenic & Old Lace memorabilia in decorating. Her marketing savvy paid off, and the inn soon became a headliner. A serious illness forced Jeanne to put the inn on the market, however, and she carefully selected its heirs, Gary and Phyllis Jones of New York.

The couple stumbled upon Eureka Springs and Arsenic & Old Lace while touring the United States in his classic airplane looking for an inn to buy. After retiring from IBM, they had spent a year attending innkeeping seminars, reading about B&Bs, and talking with other professionals in the business. Phyllis is an avid gardener and gourmet cook, and Gary loves people and entertaining, so innkeeping was a natural. (Since taking over the inn, they've made several changes and plan to add a water garden and fountain to the Monet Room.)

"Eureka is mystical town," says Phyllis. "I really believe the town called us here."

Phyllis now holds a number of local offices, including the directorship of the local Preservation Society, while Gary operates Golden Age Aircraft, Inc. as a full-time business and serves as chairman of the local airport commission and director of the Arkansas Air Museum in Fayetteville. The Joneses have been featured twice in *Kiplinger's Personal Finance* magazine (in 1994 and 1996) and in IBM's *Out of the Blue* magazine.

The Brownstone Inn

75 Hillside
Eureka Springs, AR 72632
800-973-7505

A former waterworks building serves as a B&B near the railroad

Innkeepers: Marvin and Donna Shepard. **Accommodations:** 2 rooms and 2 suites (all with private baths). **Rates:** $80–$105. **Included:** Full breakfast, complimentary beverages and homemade snacks. **Payment:** MasterCard, Visa. **Children:** Not appropriate. **Pets:** Not allowed. **Smoking:** Allowed on decks and patio. **Open:** Mid-March–mid-December.

➤ **The innkeepers have a special love for the building because Donna's grand-father, W. W. Hatcher, worked here around the turn of the century when it housed the Ozarka Water Company. The company shipped bottled water by wagon or rail from Eureka Springs to markets all over the country, thus spreading the fame of the area's good water. (Water was piped in from the springs in Mill Hollow).**

Railroad buffs love this unique bed-and-breakfast inn because they have a ringside seat to the comings and goings of the Eureka Springs and North Arkansas Railroad. The inn sits on a hill looking over the railroad and the historic depot; a restored steam train takes passengers on lunch and dinner excursions through the Ozarks. The train is a big attraction, of course, but guests may also take the trolley to other area attractions or to shop in downtown Eureka Springs.

Marvin and Donna Shepard, who purchased the inn in 1993, love innkeeping and the change of pace it brings. Marvin retired after 33 years with the telephone company in Denver, Colorado; Donna formerly worked for an oil company. They get rave reviews for their sumptuous breakfasts — quiche, buttermilk pancakes with homemade hot apple cinnamon syrup, and flavored waffles, all served with bacon, ham, or sausage and juice, fresh fruit, coffee, and tea. The Shepards provide complimentary beverages and homemade cookies in the afternoon and evening.

The two-story building was constructed of native limestone around 1890 and converted to an inn by Anita Elmore, a retired schoolteacher from Fayetteville, Arkansas, in 1989. Many of the Victorian furnishings in the inn are family pieces that belong to the Shepards.

Each room and each suite has a private entrance and bath. Uncle Sam's Suite is decorated in an Americana theme; Aunt Clair's, in a Victorian theme and peach hues. Both suites have hardwood floors and open onto an outside wooden deck. The downstairs rooms were originally used to store the bottled water and have 13-foot ceilings. The Rose Room features a queen-size rice poster bed and floral wallpaper; the Ozarka Room, an Italian tapestry, crystal wall sconces, and a seven-foot mahogany bed. It opens onto the parquet brick patio facing the railroad, but its most distinctive feature is its arched window. All rooms and suites come with cable TV and radio and have ceiling fans in addition to independent heat and air conditioning.

Dairy Hollow House Country Inn

515 Spring Street
Eureka Springs, AR 72632
501-253-7444, 800-562-8650
Fax: 501-253-7223
frontdesk@dairyhollow.com

A well-known children's author and her husband play hosts at this renowned country inn

Innkeepers: Ned Shank and Crescent Dragonwagon. **Accommodations:** 3 rooms and 3 suites (all with private baths). **Rates:** $135–$185, plus $20 during holidays and October (2-day minimum on weekends, 3-day minimum on holidays). **Included:** Full breakfast. **Payment:** Major credit cards; checks preferred. **Children:** Not appropriate. **Pets:** Not allowed. **Smoking:** Not allowed. **Open:** February–December.

> ➤ **Throughout the year Ned and Crescent hold special events for guests.
> Their Murder Mystery Weekends (Crescent is the scriptwriter, of course)
> and Gardener's Weekends are very popular, and Crescent's You Can't Drive
> with the Emergency Brake writing workshops are always full.**

Wake up to the sun peeping through the trees and then sit for a while on the deck listening to the sounds of early morning as you sip your dark-roasted coffee and vicariously recall your childhood days through Crescent Dragonwagon's many books.

Expect a friendly rap at the door promptly at nine o'clock; on the other side will be a smiling breakfast cook who has come to deliver your hot breakfast in a handmade Ozark white oak basket. Inside you may find a hot German pancake, still in the skillet; fresh cinnamon apples; sautéed slices of ham; and an assortment of fresh breads served with real butter and homemade jellies. These will be accompanied by a personal note from Ned Shank that lists the contents of the basket and suggested activities for the day.

Each morning at Dairy Hollow is special because Ned, Crescent, and the staff work at making your stay a memorable occasion. It's not surprising that the unpretentious inn has been acclaimed by the *New York Times, USA Today, Conde Nast Traveler, Chocolatier, Gourmet, Southern Living,* and *Glamour* magazine. It is a three-time winner of Uncle Ben's 10 Best Country Inns of the Year.

Ned and Crescent have been innkeeping for fifteen years. They started with a three-room farmhouse that had belonged to the brothers of a friend of Crescent's. Building on their success with the three rooms, Ned and Crescent remodeled a 1940s bungalow into three suites, a reception area, and a restaurant, and became a full-fledged country inn. They plan to open a four-room luxury suite next to the farmhouse sometime in 1997. Crescent turns out delectable dishes made from farm-fresh ingredients. Ned, a historic preservationist, keeps all the records on the computer and enjoys being host.

With names such as Summer Meadow, Peach Blossom, and Spring Garden, rooms at Dairy Hollow might well have come from one of Crescent's storybooks; the decor makes you feel as if you're stepping into the land of make-believe. Summer Meadow, on the main floor of the bungalow, is decorated in blue, yellow, and pale pink; skylights bring in the sunshine. An overstuffed couch by the fireplace invites you to sit and read one of Crescent's books, or you can write in the Word Book — guests' comments sometimes show up in the *Moos-Letter.* A table for two, decorated with friendly ceramic cows, is set in the kitchen, and a jug of special iced herbal cooler awaits you in the refrigerator, as do the makings for morning tea or coffee. Guests are welcome to use the hot tub and make use of the complimentary firewood. The bed, outfitted in yellow and blue sheets and a soft antique quilt, is built into one side of the bedroom. A private deck looks over the trees and the road that leads to the farmhouse in the woods. Rooms are equipped with hair dryers, flashlights, and fire extinguishers. Though the inn is located within the Eureka Springs Historic District on the quieter end of town, it is one mile from the hustle and bustle. The tram stops by the inn.

The restaurant at Dairy Hollow is open to the public for four to six seasonal dinners a year with set seating times by reservation. Here you often find Crescent who has coauthored a cookbook featuring innovative "Nouveau 'Zarks" cuisine — dishes such as persimmon mousse, Ozark bouillabaisse, New Wave Ozark bean soup with "Arkansalsa" and crème fraîche, or poke salat.

Palace Hotel & Bath House

135 Spring Street
Eureka Springs, AR 72632
501-253-7474 (hotel)
501-253-8400 (bathhouse)
Fax: 501-253-7494
http://www.eureka_spings_usa.com/lodging/palace.html

One of the most elegant bathhouses in Arkansas doubles as a B&B

Owners: Steve and Francie Miller. **Accommodations:** 8 suites (all with private baths, including double water-jet spa tubs). **Rates:** $127–$146 (surcharge during October, winter rates during December–February). **Included:** Continental breakfast, turndown service. **Payment:** Major credit cards. **Children:** Not appropriate. **Pets:** Not allowed. **Smoking:** Allowed. **Open:** Year-round.

➤ **Said to be a house of ill repute during the Depression, the Palace Hotel & Bath House has been beautifully restored by its present owners.**

You can live it up in this elegant bathhouse just as your grandmother or great-grandmother did in the Victorian era — take a eucalyptus steam bath in an original oak barrel steam cabinet, soak in a whirlpool mineral bath, don a clay mask, and get a relaxing massage. The full treatment costs $42 to $59, depending on whether you get a half-hour's or a full hour's treatment. The experience is offered on the lower level of the Palace Hotel & Bath House, the only historic bathhouse north of Hot Springs still in operation. Without a doubt, taking the baths at the Palace is about as authentic as you can get.

The four-story brownstone building features a central domed tower with Romanesque windows and entryway with the year 1901 written at the top, awnings on the front windows, and a sign you can't miss. (Two levels of the building hang on the cliff below street level.) Owners Steve and Francie Miller have converted the top floors into luxurious suites, complete with double water-jet spa tubs and wet bars. Rooms are elegantly furnished in turn-of-the-century Victorian antiques, and each has a coffeemaker and cable television. All of the rooms are fresh and pretty, for the Millers refurbish at least one room a year.

Overnight guests are welcomed to the Palace in the afternoon with a refreshment tray. During the dinner hour, the staff turns down the beds. In the morning, a Continental breakfast of orange juice, sliced fruit, fresh muffins, and coffee is delivered to your room on a butler's tray, complete with linen napkins and fine cutlery.

Fort Smith

Beland Manor

1320 South Albert Pike
Fort Smith, AR 72903
501-782-3300
800-334-5052
belandbnb@ipa.net

A B&B known for its food

http://www.bbonline.com/ar/belandmanor

Innkeepers: Mike and Suzy Smith. **Accommodations:** 7 rooms (all with private baths). **Rates:** $65–$95, plus $14.95–$22.50 per person for dinner on weekends. **Included:** Full gourmet breakfast, beverages, desserts, turndown service. **Payment:** Major credit cards. **Children:** Older children welcome. **Pets:** Not allowed. **Smoking:** Allowed outside. **Open:** Year-round.

➤ **While staying at the Beland Manor, you may want to check out all the attractions of this Old West town, preserved for posterity at the Fort Smith National Historic Site.**

Food gets top priority at this bed-and-breakfast inn, and for good reason. Mike and Suzy Smith, the owners, were in the catering business for five years and the restaurant business for eighteen. They serve a full gourmet breakfast in the dining room, featuring three courses on Sunday. The Smiths offer an Italian dinner to guests on Friday evenings and a Continental meal on Saturdays for an additional charge, plus desserts and turndown service on special occasions. Luncheons and dinners for groups can be arranged by advance reservations.

The Smiths set up their B&B in 1992, adding several bathrooms and a commercial kitchen to the Colonial home, a Designers Showcase Restoration prior to becoming an inn. They have four guest rooms — the Presidential Room, Ruth and Louis Suite, Antoinette's Fan, Frontier Room, Golden Room, Colonial Room, and the Library — each one individually decorated. The most expensive room is the Presidential Room featuring American antiques and a double whirlpool tub, and all rooms have private baths, telephones, writing desks, and comfortable chairs. Cable TV is available in all rooms.

In the great room upstairs there are games, books, cable TV, VCR, movies, complimentary soft drinks and snacks, and an honor bar. Chrome barstools from the fifties get a lot of attention.

Helena

The Edwardian Inn

317 S. Biscoe
Helena, AR 72342
870-338-9155 or 800-598-4749
Fax: 870-572-9105

**A B&B offering choice
rooms near the Mississippi**

Innkeeper: Marjorie Hornbeck and Olive Ellis. **Accommodations:** 18 rooms and suites (all with private baths). **Rates:** $50–$85. **Included:** Continental breakfast. **Payment:** American Express, MasterCard, Visa. **Children:** Welcome. Pets: Small pets welcome. **Smoking:** Allowed on verandahs. **Open:** Year-round.

➤ **Rooms in the inn are named for prominent town citizens, including the seven Confederate generals who came from Helena. (A battle was fought here in 1863, resulting in heavy losses for the Confederacy. A museum and cemetery commemorate that event.) There are several historic homes in town.**

No expense was spared in constructing this fine Victorian home for W. A. Short, a successful cotton merchant, in 1904. He hired the Clem brothers of St. Louis to build the house high on the hill overlooking the Mississippi River in Helena, a small town in the Delta. And he spent $100,000 doing it — a goodly sum in those days. Unfortunately, the trees now obstruct the view of the river except from the third floor.

The exterior of the inn, painted yellow and white, is perfectly symmetrical, with wide curved verandahs. Inside are quarter-sawn oak paneling, wooden mantels, "wood carpets" (thirty-six different woods imported from Germany and mounted on canvas), and brass hardware — all still in excellent condition. Occupied by the Short family until 1917, the house was used for various purposes — as an apartment building, boarding house, funeral home, and alcohol rehabilitation center — before it was rescued from demolition and turned into an inn by eight partners in 1984. It is now on the National Register of Historic Places.

The inn is ideal for business travelers, as each room has its own telephone and TV with remote control. The honeymoon suite has its own private glassed-in porch. Space on the third floor is ideal for group meetings. The lack of a parlor downstairs is somewhat disappointing, but the wide verandahs serve the same function in nice weather. A Continental breakfast is served in the Sun Room, an addition to the rear of the house.

Hot Springs

Stillmeadow Farm

111 Stillmeadow Lane
Hot Springs, AR 71913
501-525-9994

A New England–style home in the woods offering southern hospitality

Innkeepers: Gene and Jody Sparling. **Accommodations:** 4 rooms and a cottage (all with private baths). **Rates:** $65–$80. **Included:** Full breakfast. **Payment:** MasterCard and Visa. **Children:** 12 and older welcome. **Pets:** Not allowed. **Smoking:** Not allowed. **Open:** Year-round.

➤ **The Sparlings chose a change of pace at mid-life (he was a process control manager and she was a special education teacher), so they purposely don't schedule events or happenings for their guests. When not busy with innkeeping, Gene enjoys wood-carving and Jody does needlework.**

The house looks old, but it was actually built in 1984. Located in the middle of 70 acres of woods, the New England saltbox is a simple house with natural wood siding and standard windows that are evenly spaced to give a feeling of balance and symmetry.

The post-and-beam construction of the house, visible in the natural wooden exposed ceilings, is quite unusual for this area. Owners Gene and Jody Sparling fell in love with the style and decided to build the inn to accommodate their collection of New

England antiques, which they sell in their Sassafras Shop on the grounds. The rooms are spacious, and their white walls show off the handsome furnishings — armoires, dry sinks, four-poster beds, woven coverlets, braided rugs, pewterware, and salt-glazed crockery. For those who want more privacy, there's a cottage. The inn has been featured in prominent publications such as *Glamour, Country Magazine, Travel South,* and *National Geographic.*

This peaceful setting offers numerous trails to hike, horses at a nearby stable to ride, and plenty of places to read a book or just sit and think. With its abundance of birds and small animals, Stillmeadow is a mecca for nature lovers. The Sparlings provide binoculars and guidebooks.

The biggest event of the day at Stillmeadow Farm is usually breakfast. It's a full meal, featuring omelettes, casseroles, fresh fruit, rolls, juice, and coffee. Since the Sparlings don't serve dinner, guests usually go to Hamilton House on the lake by the same name, about three miles away, or to Hot Springs, a little over four miles away.

Stitt House Bed & Breakfast Inn

824 Park Avenue
Hot Springs, AK 71901
Tel. & Fax: 501-623-2704
http://www.bbonline.com/aer/stitthouse

Built as a private home, this B&B was also a famous restaurant

Innkeepers: Horst and Linda Fischer. **Accommodations:** 4 rooms (all with private baths). **Rates:** $95–$110. **Included:** Full breakfast, snacks and refreshments, turndown service. **Payment:** Major credit cards. **Children:** 14 and older welcome. **Pets:** Not allowed. **Smoking:** Not allowed. **Open:** Year-round.

➤ **Samuel Stitt, who built the mansion in 1875, was one of the city's most prominent and industrious business-men, and his wife Augusta Gaines was the daughter of Major William Haney Gaines, a Civil War hero. Their son Frank Lewis Stitt carried on his parents' tradition of hospitality.**

Horst and Linda Fischer have been in the hospitality business for a long time. Linda ran the well-known Stitt House Restaurant for many years and now oversees Grady's Grill in the Majestic Hotel. Horst is general manager of the Arlington and Majestic Hotels. When the Fischers became empty-nesters, they turned their pre-Victorian home (formerly the restaurant) into a bed-and-breakfast inn in early 1995. The mansion, which they purchased from the Stitt family in 1983, sits on a hill surrounded by two acres of lush greenery in the heart of Hot Springs National Park.

Guests are welcome to use all the public rooms of the elegantly furnished house, and the outdoor heated pool is open from May through September. On the National Register of Historic Places, the Stitt House is believed to be the oldest dwelling in Hot Springs. Reflecting a mixture of Italianate and Victorian architecture, the mansion was built in 1875 by Samuel Stitt, a businessman who built the first Arlington and Eastman Hotel and was a cofounder of the Mountain Valley Water Company. The house has high ceilings, tall windows, crystal light fixtures, a hand-carved oak staircase in the foyer, and five imposing fireplaces.

The four guest rooms are named for the Fischer children. Kai's Korner is a two-room suite with a wrought iron king-size canopy bed draped with Battenburg lace. Michael's Manor is decorated in mahogany furniture. Loc's Loft features a mahogany bed, whirlpool tub, and skylights. Hong's Hideaway has a hand-carved bedroom suite from France and a clawfoot tub. All the rooms come with his and her terry-cloth robes, complimentary refreshments, and other amenities. Each night guests select the breakfast menu and where they want to have breakfast (in bed, in the formal dining room, or on the front verandah). The full breakfast includes freshly squeezed orange juice and specials such as eggs Benedict, quiches, and baked blueberry French toast.

Vintage Comfort Bed & Breakfast

303 Quapaw
Hot Springs National Park,
AR 71901
501-623-3258
800-608-4682 (reservations only)
http://www.bbonline.com/ar/vintagecomfort

> **A comfortable B&B in the national park**

Innkeeper: Helen R. Bartlett. **Accommodations:** 4 rooms (all with private baths). **Rates:** $70–$90; corporate rate $55 single (Monday-Thursday). **Included:** Full gourmet breakfast and beverages. **Payment:** Major credit cards. **Children:** 6 and older welcome. **Pets:** Not allowed. **Smoking:** Allowed on verandahs. **Open:** Year-round.

➤ **Active in the chamber of commerce, Helen Bartlett is excited about the town's comeback as a tourist destination. She is a retired board member and past president of the Bed & Breakfast Association of Arkansas.**

So intent on doing a good job of running a bed-and-breakfast inn is owner Helen Bartlett that she passes on her expertise to others with the same aspirations in an annual class she teaches through the University of Arkansas.

Encouraged by the town's participation in Main Street USA, a program to rejuvenate towns across the country, Helen bought the 1907 Victorian Queen Anne home and opened it as a bed-and-breakfast inn in 1988, retaining its architectural integrity while making it bright and cheerful. The house is decorated in excellent taste, avoiding the clutter and overstatement that are prevalent in so many Victorian homes.

The bedrooms, in soft pastel colors, are named for Mrs. Bartlett's family members, including her granddaughter, Courtney Elizabeth. A favorite with guests, especially honeymooners, is Debrah Ann's Room, with a six-foot clawfoot tub and access to the upstairs screened porch. Leah Anne's Room, which features a bay window overlooking Quapaw, is painted pale lavender with a border of large cutout roses that match the rose print of the bedspread. Lynn Helen's Room, popular with business travelers, has a large desk and a phone jack. There are no phones or television sets in the rooms, but reading material is never lacking. All of the rooms are air conditioned.

Guests are treated to a full gourmet breakfast each morning — Southwest dishes that Helen learned to make while living in Houston — and homemade muffins, breads, and jellies. High tea is served on the first Friday of the month.

The B&B is about four blocks from Bathhouse Row and other attractions in downtown Hot Springs. Hiking trails on West Mountain are also nearby.

Johnson

Johnson House Bed & Breakfast

5371 South 48th Street
P.O. Box 431
Johnson, AR 72741
(Fayetteville area)
501-756-1095

A country house where the welcome mat is always out

Innkeeper: Mary K. Carothers. **Accommodations:** 3 rooms (all with private baths). **Rates:** $70–$95. **Included:** Full country breakfast. **Payment:** Cash or checks. **Children:** Well-behaved children welcome. **Pets:** Not allowed. **Smoking:** Allowed. **Open:** Year-round.

➤ **The ceiling in the parlor is made of natural wood and was decorated by a carriage painter to look like the top of a game table — it is fascinating.**

Located between Fayetteville and Springdale just off U.S. 71, this elegant country farmhouse will remind you of visits to Grandmother's long ago. Built in 1882 of signed handmade brick, it features twelve-foot ceilings and a beautiful staircase that extends the full height of the second floor.

After running a tearoom and antiques shop in Houston, Mary K. Carothers decided to move to Arkansas and open a bed-and-breakfast inn when her youngest daughter was in college. She runs an antiques and gift shop here in the old smokehouse and pampers guests with gourmet breakfasts in the dining room overlooking the green fields or on the terrace in good weather. Mary K. has decorated the house with beautiful Victorian antiques and her own personal treasures. The bedrooms are large and have private baths with clawfoot tubs and brass showers.

Johnson House guests enjoy playing croquet, horseshoes, and shuffleboard or exploring the rural area. The two outside porches are wonderful places to read a good book and enjoy a glass of lemonade.

Lakeview

Gaston's White River Resort

1777 River Road
Lakeview, AR 72642
870-431-5202
Fax: 870-431-5216
http://www.gaston.com

A premier fishing resort where celebrities practice their favorite sport

Owners: Jim and Jill Gaston. **Accommodations:** 74 riverside cottages and lodges (all with private baths; many with fully equipped kitchens, redwood decks, and wood-burning fireplaces). **Rates:** $69–$805, plus $14 for children over 6 and each additional person; 2-for-1 winter rates often available December–March. **Included:** Complimentary boats, airplane tie-downs, landing. **Payment:** MasterCard, Visa. **Children:** Welcome. **Pets:** Allowed. **Smoking:** Allowed. **Open:** Year-round.

➤ **One of the premier fishing resorts in the country, Gaston's has been featured in numerous national magazines.**

At Gaston's White River Resort in the Ozarks, you can land on the airstrip and be fishing for rainbow and brown trout on the White River within minutes. The resort has been owned and managed by Jim and Jill Gaston and their family since 1958.

Each cottage comes with its own john boat, but there is a charge for the motor. You are free to fish anywhere you wish on the river, and the resort offers organized fishing trips on Bull Shoals Lake, float trips down the White River, and a fly-fishing school. Children have their own fishing area — a large pond on the property. In case you leave any of your equipment behind, you can buy just about any type of fishing supplies you might need at the resort. Recent additions at Lake Gaston include a new conference lodge, outdoor pool, gazebo, and dock.

Gaston's offers a number of other diversions besides fishing — tennis courts, a swimming pool, a game room, and a nearby golf course. A mile-long nature trail along the river is dotted with wild-flowers, especially in the springtime. For evening entertainment, people go to the country-and-western music hall in Bull Shoals.

Guests have the option of lakeside cottages, a four-bedroom house, two lodges, or a river villa that accommodates twenty peo-ple; the resort is ideal for families and large groups. Three meals a day are offered in the wood and glass dining room overlooking the water. The contemporary room is decorated with discarded motors and bikes suspended from the ceiling. As you might expect, fish (trout, flounder, walleye, and other varieties, prepared in a variety of ways) is a big item on the menu. The staff will cook your prize catch if you wish. Sunday brunch is quite popular.

Little Rock

The Capital Hotel

111 W. Markham
Little Rock, AR 72201
501-374-7474, 800-766-7666
Fax: 501-370-7091

A historic property frequented by government officials

General Manager: Joseph B. Rantisi. **Accommodations:** 118 rooms and 5 de-luxe suites (all with private baths). **Rates:** $127–$168 and $91–$110 weekends. **Included:** Buffet breakfast. **Payment:** Major credit cards. **Children:** Under 12 free with parents. **Pets:** Not allowed. **Smoking:** Smoking and nonsmoking rooms. **Open:** Year-round.

➤ **While serving as governor of Arkansas, President Bill Clinton was a frequent visitor at the Capital Hotel.**

History has been written within these walls since 1872, when the building was erected as the Deneckla Block for stores and apart-ments. Since then, presidents, governors, congressional representatives, and others have made the hotel their headquarters when they were in Little Rock. Two years after the hotel opened, President Ulysses S. Grant sent in federal troops to settle a dispute about the governor's race between Joseph Brooks and Eliasha Baxter. After a fire swept the block in 1876, the building was converted into the Capital Hotel — complete with a restaurant, bar, barber shop, and billiards hall. The Capital enjoyed many good years as a hotel but went into a decline during the Depression.

Restored in 1983, the Capital is a full-service, four-diamond luxury hotel. Joseph B. Rantisi, the general manager, is European-educated and trained in hospitality management and has spent more than thirty years working at hotels all over the world. Because of its convenient location to the state government complex and the convention center, the Capital is ideal for businesspeople. The hotel offers complete corporate executive services. Amenities include complimentary bathrobes, bathroom scales, overnight shoeshines, one-hour pressing and steaming service, 24-hour room service, electronic locks, and cellular telephone rental. The hotel offers five meeting rooms; it also serves as a social center for the city.

Architecturally, the Capital is a gem. The facade is cast iron, and the elegant atrium lobby exudes Old World charm with its Roman arches, Corinthian columns, mosaic tile floors, stained glass skylights, brass accents, and gold-leaf trim. The marble staircase in the lobby was made for grand entrances. The guest rooms have many windows, 15-foot ceilings, and are furnished in mahogany four-poster and canopy beds and marbletop tables. The suites and corner rooms are the most sought after. Favorites are Room 422, which has six windows, and the Grant Suite, Room 208, which has seven.

Ashley's at the Capital, named a Distinguished Restaurant of North America, features Continental cuisine all day and is reknowned for its Sunday brunch. The hotel and the restaurant are the only Arkansas establishments to hold a four-diamond rating since opening year. The Capital has been recognized as one of the Best 500 Hotels in the World by *Conde Nast Traveler.*

The Lobby Bar is a favorite gathering place for guests. Capital weekend packages such as the Basic Carefree Weekend and the Romantic Weekend are very attractive. The latter includes accommodations for two, champagne on arrival, fresh roses, a box of imported chocolates, a five-course dinner at Ashley's, a Continental breakfast in bed, valet parking, and all taxes and gratuities.

The Empress of Little Rock
A Historic Victorian Bed & Breakfast

2120 Louisiana
Little Rock, AR 72206
501-374-7966
Fax: 501-375-4537

An exquisite Victorian B&B

Innkeepers: Robert Blair and Sharon Welch-Blair. **Accommodations:** 5 rooms (all with private baths). **Rates:** $100–$140. **Included:** Full gourmet breakfast, refreshments, and clerical assistance. **Payment:** Major credit cards. **Children:** 10 and older welcome. **Pets:** Not allowed. **Smoking:** Not allowed. **Open:** Year-round.

➤ **Saloonkeeper James H. Hornibrook got the last laugh on Little Rock society, who would have nothing to do with him, when he built the most outlandish, ostentatious house in the city in 1888.**

This historic B&B is indeed "the Empress" of the capital city. Designed by Max Orlopp and Casper Kusener, the 1888 mansion is considered the best example of ornate Victorian architecture in Arkansas. It features a divided stairway, a three-and-a-half story tower, stained glass skylight, and octagonal shaped rooms. The finest Arkansas materials were used in the house, including the native woods used in the ornate wainscoting and parquet flooring. It had steam heat, plus gas and electricity and six working fireplaces, an intercom, and three water closets with tubs and running hot water. On the National Register of Historic Places, it was the home of James H. Hornibrook, a successful saloonkeeper, who was spurned by Little Rock society and got even by building the most ostentatious house in the Quapaw District and hosting illegal poker games in the tower. Unfortunately, he died of a stroke in 1890, and his broken-hearted widow passed on a couple of years later. In 1897 the 7,500-square foot house became Arkansas Women's College and later was used as a rooming house, nursing home, apartments, and a halfway house.

Robert Blair, an executive with Southwestern Bell, and Sharon Welch-Blair, a financial consultant for New York Life for ten years, bought the house in late 1993 and transformed it into The Empress in 1995. Sharon had become enamored with old houses when they had lived in New Jersey. During the costly renovation and restoration, which involved demolishing extra walls, removing an elevator, adding new heating and air conditioning, sidewalks, landscaping, and other tedious jobs, Bob encountered Mr. Hornibrook's apparition twice. The ghost advised him to "save the mansion and care about this house." Taking his advice, the Blairs have recreated the Victorian atmosphere of the Hornibrook era with all the modern conveniences (telephones, radios, TVs upon request, and copy and fax machines).

Today the Blairs pamper, coddle, and spoil guests. Sharon dresses in period costumes and gives tours of the mansion. She and Bob serve gourmet breakfasts by candlelight. The five guest rooms are named for historic Arkansas figures — James H. Hornibrook (the original owner), John Edward Murray, Eliza Bertand Cunningham, Petit Jean, and the Reverends Washburn and Welch who evangelized Arkansas. They host family reunions and mystery weekends and offer several special packages — romance and wedding packages and pampering packages which include hair styling, manicures and pedicures, and body massages and facials. Sometime in the future they plan to open a gift shop and a garden with a gazebo, and provide Victorian dressing gowns and smoking jackets for guests. The inn received earned a four-diamond rating.

Hotze House

1619 Louisiana Street
Little Rock, AR 72206
Tel.: 501-376-6563
Fax: 501-374-5393
http://www.bbonline.com/ar/bbaa/index/html

> A corporate B&B that offers
> all the extras

Innkeepers: Peggy Tooker, Steven and Suzanne Gates. **Accommodations:** 4 rooms (all with private baths and fireplaces). **Rates:** $90 (corporate rates available). **Included:** Full breakfast, snacks and refreshments, turndown service. **Payment:** Major credit cards. **Children:** 5 and older welcome. **Pets:** Not allowed. **Smoking:** Allowed on porches only. **Open:** Year-round.

> ➤ **Peter Hotze fought for the Confederate Army at Shiloh, Chickamauga, and Murfreesboro and was wounded in the Battle of Franklin and then imprisoned at Camp Chase in Ohio. He refused to take the oath of allegiance as long as the South was fighting.**

Pronounced "hote-sy," Hotze House is located in Little Rock's Historic Quapaw District, just two blocks from the Arkansas Governor's Mansion. In fact, the Neo-Classic mansion with its Ionic columns is sometimes mistaken for the chief executive's residence.

The turn-of-the-century mansion was built by Austrian Peter Hotze who made a fortune in cotton. He came to Arkansas at the age of 21 in 1857, served in the Confederate Army, and later married Johanna Krause of Little Rock. His thriving business ventures took him to New York, but he returned to his adopted city with his two grown daughters and a son after his wife died.

The house was restored to its former grandeur in 1992 by IBMers Steven and Suzanne Gates, who through their corporate travels had come to appreciate quality accommodations. They decorated the 8,500-square-foot house — which features original mahogany wood paneling, Italian tile fireplaces, and parquet floors — with a combination of antiques and traditional furnishings. They also added all the modern conveniences that corporate guests expect — private baths, in-room telephones and data ports, cable TV, copier and fax access, and other amenities.

Because the Gates are still on the road a great deal, they rely on Suzanne's mother, Peggy Tooker, to look after guests. She handles corporate parties and meetings and serves an elaborate breakfast (omelets, frittatas, or French toast) in the formal dining room or the conservatory. The inn is also popular with honeymoon and anniversary couples.

Hotze House is listed on the National Register of Historic Places and has been featured in *Country Inns, Southern Living,* and other publications. Dylan Jones of the London *Sunday Times* called the Hotze House one of the best guest houses in the South, where he found himself "devouring . . . the idiosyncratic interpretation of The Great American Breakfast."

Pinnacle Vista Lodge

7510 Highway 300
Little Rock, AR 72212
Tel. & Fax: 501-868-8905

A country bed & breakfast

Innkeepers: Chet and Linda R. Westergard. **Accommodations:** 2 rooms and 1 suite (all with private baths). **Rates:** $89–$125. **Included:** Full breakfast, snacks and refreshments, games, fishing. **Payment:** MasterCard and Visa. **Children:** 6 and older welcome. **Pets:** Not allowed. **Smoking:** Not allowed. **Open:** Year-round.

➤ **Nearby Mountain State Park offers over 40 miles of hiking trails, picnic tables and grills, and playground. It's an excellent place for bird-watching and canoeing.**

Located in the country a mile south of Pinnacle State Park near Little Rock, Pinnacle Vista Lodge is a quiet 23-acre retreat where you can leave all the worries of the world behind. You can take a walk, go fishing, relax in the hammock with a good book, play billiards, listen to the player piano, or simply enjoy the view of Pinnacle Mountain. The recreational pleasures of the state park are also available to guests, as well as horseback riding at nearby Twelve Oaks Stables.

Pinnacle Vista began as a one-bedroom log cabin well over half a century ago. As the owner's family grew, another structure was added. Many years later a building contractor restored the buildings, maintaining the original rustic style. (He also built a large horse barn.) The focal point of the 6,000-square-foot house is the great room, with its vaulted ceilings and massive stone fireplace.

Chet and Linda Westergard bought the property in 1990 after moving to the area from Florida. After extensive renovations and filling the house with their favorite antiques, they opened their home to guests in 1995. The Westergards offer three guest rooms (each with its own separate entrance), including Nana's Retreat, which has an extra bed for a child or adult. The Westergards are happy to share their two friendly dogs.

Chet is a regional estate-planning specialist, and Linda, a former travel agent and craft and floral designer, is president of the Bed and Breakfast Association of Arkansas. They plan to renovate the upper floor of the barn for group functions, convert the lower barn into an antiques shop, and possibly add a honeymoon cabin.

Magnolia

Magnolia Place Bed & Breakfast

510 East Main
Magnolia, AR 71753
870-234-6122, 800-237-6122
Fax: 870-234-1254

A fine example of
Foursquare architecture

Innkeeper: Carolyn Hawley. **General Manager:** Ray Sullivent. **Accommodations:** 5 rooms (all with private baths). **Rates:** $99. **Included:** Full breakfast, welcome refreshments, house tour. **Payment:** Major credit cards. **Children:** 14 and older welcome. **Pets:** Not allowed. **Smoking:** Not allowed. **Open:** Year-round.

➤ **The annual Magnolia Blossom Festival in the spring features the World Championship Steak Cook-Off, an event that attracts as many as fifty teams who compete for the Silver Governor's Cup.**

After standing vacant for a decade, this lovely bed-and-breakfast inn was a year in the making. Ray Sullivent, the former owner of the Best Western Coachman's Inn in Magnolia, hired the services of Ron White, a local decorator and preservationist, and some of the finest craftsmen in the area to restore the 1910 house, considered a classic example of Foursquare architecture. The symmetrical house was built by Colonel Charles McKay, a prominent attorney, and his wife Mary; several generations of the family have lived here.

The inn, featured in *Southern Living* in 1996, is truly a feast for the senses. The flower-filled garden is not only beautiful but aromatic, and the wraparound porch, with its large rocking chairs and swing, invite you to sit a spell. Upon entering the inn, you notice an Oriental table from the Ming dynasty, perhaps carved for a wedding or other festive occasion, and hear the strains of classical music through the hall. The focal point of the parlor is a baby grand piano dating to 1825. (Some of the antiques in the house were collected during the renovation, while others are family heirlooms.) Wonderful aromas waft from the kitchen, where Carolyn bakes bread and cookies for guests. She prepares a full breakfast, which is served on an 1820s table made of five different woods in the elegant dining room. According to a family legend, President Warren G. Harding dined at this table when it belonged to Carolyn's great-grandfather.

Each of the five guest rooms is unique. One displays the grace of Eastlake style; another an ornately carved Rosewood suite from France. The downstairs bedroom is Empire-style and combines with the Music Room to make a two-room suite with a fireplace. All the rooms have private baths, telephones, queen beds, and televisions.

A quick stroll from Magnolia Place will take you to the town's historic sites, antiques shops, art galleries, and craft stores. Be sure to see the Magnolia Murals that have been painted on some of the buildings downtown to depict the area's rich history. Within a short drive are other diversions — Big Boy Toys and Gallery; Lake Columbia (a favorite spot for anglers) and Logoly State Park, featuring interpreters and workshops on ecological and environmental topics; Southern Arkansas University, which offers a farm tour; and the historic Couch-Marshall House and Colonel McKay Crumpler Home.

Mena

Queen Wilhelmina Lodge

Queen Wilhelmina State Park
3877 Highway 88 W
Mena, AR 71953
501-394-2863, 800-264-2477

| A mountain lodge offering cloudtop exhilaration |

Owner: Arkansas Department of Parks and Tourism. **Accommodations:** 38 rooms (all with private baths). **Rates:** $57–$100. **Payment:** Major credit cards. **Children:** Welcome. **Pets:** Not allowed. **Smoking:** Smoking and nonsmoking rooms. **Open:** Year-round.

➤   **In appreciation of the Dutch and in anticipation of the royalty who might visit the hotel, the owners named the inn in honor of Queen Wilhelmina and prepared a lavish suite for her. The queen never came, but she did send a representative.**

Located high on Rich Mountain (elevation nearly 3,000 feet) in the Ouachita range, this lodge was named for a queen of the Netherlands. The current building is about twenty years old; the lodge that existed here before it was built in 1898. The present structure was patterned after the original one.

   A new railroad through Arkansas prompted Arthur Stillwell of the Kansas City, Pittsburgh, and Gulf Railroad to persuade a group of Dutch investors to finance the first resort hotel — a 35-bedroom inn with four bathrooms — in hopes of attracting wealthy patrons from Texas, Oklahoma, Missouri, and Louisiana. Unfortunately, the hotel, named Castle in the Sky, fell on hard times within three years, disappointing its investors and promoters. Eventually, the inn was torn down.

   The area was officially named Queen Wilhelmina State Park in 1957. A second inn was built in 1963 but burned down ten years later. A new two-story inn with 38 rooms was constructed in its place in 1975. Built of glass, stone, and wood, the inn offers panoramic views of the Ouachitas.

The park is a gathering place for families and groups looking for wholesome fun. Guests never lack for activity, especially in the summertime; the rest of the year is quiet on the mountaintop. Guests congregate around the fireplace in the lobby, play croquet and volleyball, and hike the mountain trails. The most famous trail is Lover's Leap, with its viewing platform at the leap. The park also offers miniature golf, a petting zoo, a miniature railroad (the longest 16-gauge railroad in the country) and naturalist programs.

Rooms in the inn are standard; the two queen suites are a little more luxurious and have fireplaces and sitting areas. To the delight of most guests, none of the rooms has a telephone, but all are air conditioned and feature television sets, coffeemakers, and complimentary coffee.

The inn's restaurant features standard American cuisine; it is best known for its homemade yeast bread and hot fruit cobblers. Talimena Drive, a National Scenic Byway, passes by the in and connects Mena, Arkansas, with Talihina, Oklahoma, a distance of 54 miles. A published guide directs visitors to overlooks and historic sites and offers commentary on the flora and fauna of the area.

Mountain Home

Scott Valley Resort & Guest Ranch

Highway 5, P.O. Box 1447
Mountain Home, AR 72653
870-425-5136
Fax: 870-424-5800

An Ozarks guest ranch with high national ratings

Innkeeper: Kathleen Cooper. **Accommodations:** 28 rooms (all with private baths). **Daily Rates** (3-day minimum, June–mid-August): Summer: Adults, $130; children 6–12, $110; children 2–5, $65; under 2 free. Spring and fall: Adults, $115, children 6–12, $95; children 2–5, $55. Weekly rates: Summer: Adults, $775; children 6-12, $660; children 2-5, $390 Spring and fall: Adults, $690; children 6–12, $570; children 2–5, $330. **Included:** All meals and activities; boats and canoes on White and North Fork rivers and ferry tour with three-day stays. **Pay-**

ment: MasterCard and Visa. **Children:** Welcome. **Pets:** Allowed. **Smoking:** Smoking and nonsmoking rooms. **Open:** Year-round.

➤ **The Sun Valley Resort has won *Family Circle* magazine's Family Resort of the Year award each of the three years the publication has held the contest.**

There can't be any greater place for families than Scott Valley Resort & Guest Ranch, located in the Ozarks of Arkansas. After dinner each evening, little ones come with nickels and dimes to make their big purchases at the store — usually a candy bar or a pack of chewing gum, maybe some red licorice. And before Mom and Dad pack up to head home, there's usually a last-minute stop to stock up on souvenirs, including shirts emblazoned with the ranch's name.

And there's more to the resort than the souvenirs. The ranch has a stable full of horses (70 plus) and a petting zoo that has pigs, rabbits, goats, and kittens. There's a terrific playground, and guests can go horseback riding, play tennis, swim in the pool, enjoy the spa, or look for wildflowers on the 625-acre property.

If you want to venture out, try trout fishing on the White River, take a canoe trip, or go jet skiing on Norfolk Lake. Though not located on the water, the ranch is close to several lakes and rivers. The staff will gladly cook your catch or freeze it for you to take home.

Summer evenings are devoted to hay rides, music shows, and watching the glorious sunsets. Guests are housed in simple rooms, all on ground level. They do not have televisions or phones, but they're perfect for families. Two-room family units have one room with a queen-size bed and a second room with twin beds; some even have a hide-a-bed or bunk beds, allowing room for families of six or seven. The complimentary laundromat has washers, dryers, and irons. The ranch has an excellent reputation for its food; home-cooked meals are served buffet-style in the dining room.

The ranch was built in 1953 by Gene Scott, and some additions were made in 1971. Mrs. Cooper and her late husband bought the property in 1985 following their retirement.

Mountain View

The Inn at Mountain View

307 West Washington Street
P.O. Box 812
Mountain View, AR 72560
870-269-4200, 800-535-1301
Fax: 870-269-2956
jbwilliams@motel.net
http://aros.com/theinn

> An old-fashioned mountain inn where music and hospitality blend in harmony

Innkeepers: Bob and Jenny Williams. **Accommodations:** 11 rooms (all with private baths). **Rates:** $69–$97. **Included:** Full country breakfast. **Payment:** Discover, MasterCard, Visa. **Children:** Not appropriate. **Pets:** Not allowed. **Smoking:** Allowed on verandahs. **Open:** Year-round.

➤ **There's plenty to do in Mountain View — hiking, canoeing, horseback riding, tennis, and bicycling. (Bob is an avid mountain biker.) The Ozark Folk Center State Park is the main attraction, but the White River, Buffalo River, Blanchard Springs Caverns, and Ozark National Forest are nearby.**

Every guest at the Inn at Mountain View gets to sleep under a handmade quilt, personally selected by Jenny Williams. The quilts are a few of the special touches that she and her husband, Bob, have incorporated into this 1886 inn that is on the National Register of Historic Places. Hand-embroidered linens are another trademark.

Built by Civil War veteran John Webb, who named it the Dew Drop Inn, the establishment catered to drummers (traveling salesmen), circuit riders, and weary travelers in the early days. For a while it served as a boarding house and eventually was restored to its original use.

The house is filled with Victorian treasures — some family pieces, but many gleaned by Jenny from antiques shops in the area. Rooms have romantic names like Violet's Arbor, Rebecca's Hideaway, Penelope's Chamber, Grandmother's Attic, Mallard's Rest, and Nathaniel's Study — the latter two are more masculine than the others. The Garden Suite features a king-size bed, sitting room, and kitchenette with dining area. Turndown service with bedtime mints is available on request.

The inn sits a block off the square in Mountain View, where folk musicians gather every evening to play and sing. Sometimes guests who are musically inclined bring their own instruments for a jam session on the verandah or in the parlor of the inn. This suits Jenny, who plays the piano.

In their restoration and redecoration of the inn, the Williamses have made it very inviting. Petunias line the walk, and rockers beckon guests to sit for a while. The rich, dark wainscoting in the lobby gives it a warm, cozy feeling, and the sunroom, decorated in white wicker and floral fabrics, bursts with brightness. The house is air-conditioned and all the bedrooms have ceiling fans, but don't expect to find television sets or phones in the rooms. (Guests may watch cable TV in the lobby, however.) The Williamses are planning to install a Jacuzzi.

Bob and Jenny, who moved to Mountain View from Florida, purchased the inn in 1990 and completely renovated and redecorated it. Bob, formerly in the vending business, has fast earned a reputation for his bountiful country breakfasts, which include Belgian waffles, fresh raspberry ambrosia, eggs, bacon, "real" hash browns, biscuits, sausage gravy, basil tomatoes, homemade peach butter, and other delicacies — all served family-style from the large lazy Susans in the center of the dining tables. The use of fresh products is very important, since Jenny has sold health food products for more than fifteen years. Most guests say they can easily skip lunch after one of Bob's breakfasts.

The Ozark Folk Center State Park

Spur 382 off Highway 5,
P.O. Box 500
Mountain View, AR 72560
870-269-3871
800-264-3655 (FOLK)
Fax: 870-269-2909

> **A modern inn where mountain culture comes to life**

Superintendent: Bill Young. **Accommodations:** 60 rooms (all with private baths). **Rates:** $50–$55, single or double; $5 for each additional person (discounted admission charge for crafts area and music show). **Payment:** Major credit cards. **Children:** Under 13 free with parents. **Pets:** Not allowed. **Smoking:** Allowed. **Open:** Year-round.

➤   **The Ozark Cultural Resource Center** offers opportunities to delve into the crafts, music, history, and lore of the region.

The past comes alive at the Ozark Folk Center in the heart of the Ozark Mountains. You can hear centuries-old fiddle tunes, watch woodcarvers at work, and see patches of cloth become artwork as a quilt is assembled. Arts, crafts, and music are preserved in their old forms and shared with visitors at the center.

More than twenty pioneer skills and crafts are demonstrated daily from mid-April through October (weekends only in early April), and visitors may sign up for private studies on blacksmithing, furniture building, basket weaving, and other crafts. There's even the Young Pioneers Program for kids aged 7 to 14 throughtout the season, which teaches children about pioneer life in the Ozarks through classes on such subjects as pottery and herbs, spelling bees, corn shuckings, square dances, games, and chores. There are residence Elderhostels year-round for those 55 and older dealing with folk culture, antiques, Ozarks outdoors, and more. If you don't choose to make crafts, you may buy them in the gift shop, plus wonderfully scrumptious products such as homemade peach and apple preserves.

Every evening except Sunday everyone enjoys the picking, singing, and jig dancing at the music show. Once a month on Sunday night a special gospel concert is presented. Only acoustic instruments are used to play the nineteenth- and early-twentieth-century tunes. The center, which celebrates its twenty-fifth anniversary in 1998, offers a full schedule of seminars and special events from

March through December, winding up with the Ozark Thanksgiving and Christmas.

Visitors like to hike the nature trails that fan out from the grounds (they're especially beautiful in the fall), visit the Heritage Herb Garden, and swim in the pool at the lodge, which also has a game room. The Herb Garden features herbs that would have been used by a granny woman or "yarb" doctor in the mountains, plants that contain natural dyes, plants that produce cloth, and native wildflowers. A butterfly and wildlife sanctuary allows guests in the park's restaurant to see the Ozarks "up close" as they observe raccoons, hummingbirds, perhaps an occasional bear, come to the water and food sources in full view of diners. For those who don't care to walk, a free tram whisks visitors around the grounds.

Guests are housed in hexagon-shaped buildings (two bedrooms per building), spaced a fair distance apart so that no one feels crowded in the natural wooded area. All the rooms have been totally redecorated and feature two double beds, a bathroom, coffeemaker and coffee fixings, television, and telephone. The full-service restaurant on the grounds serves three meals a day, and the Smokehouse Sandwich Shop offers sandwiches, plates, and baskets filled with old-fashioned fried pies, fudge, and other goodies from 10 A.M. until 5 P.M. during the summer season.

Pine Bluff

Margland Bed & Breakfast Inns

P.O. Box 7111
Pine Bluff, AR 71611
870-536-6000, 800-545-5383
Fax: 870-536-7941

> **A historic inn that specializes in pampering guests**

Owner: Ed Thompson. **Manager:** Wanda Bateman. **Accommodations:** 19 rooms (all with private baths, some with Jacuzzis and bidets). **Rates:** $85–$105. **Included:** Continental or full breakfast. **Payment:** Major credit cards. **Children:** Welcome. **Pets:** Not allowed. **Smoking:** Allowed. **Open:** Year-round.

➤ **The innkeepers are both active in the community. Ed Thompson has a moving company; Wanda Bateman is a realtor and owner of a consignment shop.**

With guests being "number one" at this inn, you can expect lots of pampering when you stay here. Every convenience and luxury have been considered, and the staff is always ready to serve.

The inn is made up of three historic buildings which have been meticulously restored — Margland II (the main inn), a 1903 Dutch Colonial, Margland III, a former duplex dating to 1895, and Margland IV, built in 1905. Margland II received the Historic Preservation Award for Arkansas in 1986, one year after the inn opened. Buildings are connected by brick walkways, terraces, and decks. Rooms are elegantly furnished in an eclectic style — a mixture of antiques, collectibles, wicker, and contemporary furniture — and have conveniences such as VCRs and cable television. The inn has a swimming pool, exercise room, conference rooms, and fax service.

Guests are encouraged to place their breakfast order on a card and hang it outside their door at night. The meal will be promptly delivered the next day or served in the formal dining room, whichever you prefer. (Guests may request a full meal.) The inn also serves lunch and dinner to groups of six or more by advance request and will assist guests with dinner reservations. Menu selections include crown roast of pork, beef tenderloin, or chicken, all served with rice, a vegetable, salad, dessert, and beverage. The inn is popular with businesspeople, tour groups, and families.

Ponca

Buffalo Outdoor Center

P.O. Box 1
Ponca, AR 72670
870-861-5514, 800-221-5514
boc@buffaloriver.com
http://www.buffaloriver.com

A place for nature lovers and adventure-seekers

Innkeepers: Mike and Evelyn Mills. **Accommodations:** 19 cabins (fully furnished and equipped, all with private baths). **Rates:** $80–$200. **Included:** Cabin rental; activities are additional. **Payment:** MasterCard, Visa. **Children:** Welcome. **Pets:** Not allowed. **Smoking:** Allowed. **Open:** Year-round.

➤ **One of the main attractions at BOC, of course, is the river, which meanders for 132 miles through the scenic Ozark highlands, with bluffs towering 500 feet above, cascading waterfalls, and massive boulders.**

On the scenic Buffalo National River in the Ozark Mountains at Ponca, the Buffalo Outdoor Center is one of the best places to stay in the state, according to some enthusiasts. It offers nineteen log cabins, constructed in 1985 — all of them have air conditioning, ceiling fans, a stone fireplace, barbecue grill, and porch swing. Each cabin has three double beds and sleeps six comfortably.

Guests at the Buffalo Outdoor Center are active: they enjoy canoeing, rafting, fishing, and guided john boat trips on the river, plus mountain biking, horseback riding, hiking, and hot air ballooning. Visitors are encouraged to come prepared for these activities: pack sweaters and raingear, plenty of dry clothes in case you get soaked, extra sets of vehicle keys, a camera, and lots of film.

Whether you come here for a romantic getaway, a sporting adventure, or just to get away from it all, you'll probably find what you're looking for.

Springdale

Magnolia Gardens Inn

500 North Main
Springdale, AR 72764
501-756-5744 or 800-756-5744
Fax: 501-756-2526

> A Springdale landmark, this
> B&B is an ideal home base
> for an Ozarks tour

Innkeepers: Charles and Marjorie Ryffel. **Accommodations:** 10 rooms (all with private baths). **Rates:** $100–$135, with discounts after a 7-day stay. **Included:** Full plantation breakfast, snacks and refreshments, turndown service. **Payment:** American Express, MasterCard, Visa. **Children:** Not appropriate. **Pets:** Not allowed. **Smoking:** Not allowed. **Open:** Year-round.

> ➤ **Original owner Judge Millard Berry started the first telephone company in Springdale and was influential in the construction of the Washington County Courthouse.**

Situated on 10 wooded acres in the heart of Springdale, this B&B takes its name from the 50 giant magnolia trees on the property. Built in 1883 by Judge Millard Berry for his wife and seven children, the Victorian retreat was converted into an inn by Charles and Marjorie Ryffel in 1993. Afraid of what the new owners would do to the house, Springdale residents opposed its sale at first, but now the inn is a local attraction. World travelers, the Ryffels had stayed in more than one hundred B&Bs and spent two years renovating the property (including a cottage where they now live) before opening it to the public. Prior to becoming innkeepers, the Ryffels were owners of a heavy construction firm in Newport Beach, California.

The two-story mansion features an angled roof and turret, an outside spiral staircase, and brick walkways. The antique furnishings, which include handmade quilts made in the Ozarks, blend perfectly with the new hardwood floors and wallpaper. The house has 10 beautifully decorated guest rooms with private baths, featuring restored footed tubs and pedestal sinks. The bed in the Weaver's Room was fashioned from a huge 150-year-old weaving loom; the Swingers Loft features a swinging bed and an attic sitting room that is accessible by ladder; and the red and black Boudoir has a huge metal bathtub.

Meals, under Marjorie's direction, include a full plantation breakfast and lunch, served Tuesdays through Fridays. The inn is often used for weddings, special parties, family reunions, and business meetings. Guests may stroll the gardens, relax in the spa, or read a good book from the library.

Texarkana

Mansion on Main

802 Main Street
Texarkana, AR 75501
903-792-1835
Fax: 903-793-0878

A standout in a city of B&Bs

Owners: Tom and Peggy Taylor. **Innkeepers:** Lee and Inez Hayden. **Accommodations:** 6 rooms (all with private baths). **Rates:** $60–$109. **Included:** Gourmet breakfast, afternoon desserts and refreshments. **Payment:** American Express, MasterCard, and Visa. **Children:** Check with innkeepers. **Pets:** Not allowed. **Smoking:** Not allowed. **Open:** Year-round.

➤ **Within walking distance of the inn is the historic Perot Theater, restored by native Ross Perot. From September through May, it offers classical and popular music concerts, classical ballet, and Broadway-type productions.**

Texarkana, which straddles the Arkansas/Texas border, is known for its outstanding B&Bs, and one of its newest establishments, Mansion on Main, has quickly gained a following.

Owners Tom and Peggy Taylor, who also have a B&B in nearby Jefferson, Texas, have entrusted the running of the inn to Lee and Inez Hayden. (The Haydens moved to the area from New Orleans, where Lee was a security supervisor at a shipbuilding company and Inez was an instructor chef at Cookin' Cajun Cooking School. Now she has her own cooking school in Jefferson.) Inez's culinary talents have been put to good use at the Mansion on Main. The Gentleman's Breakfast features entrees such as shirred eggs with honey-cured ham, orange pecan French toast with Vermont maple syrup, cheese blintz with fresh seasonal fruit, and chicken à la Mansion with sourdough biscuits. Lemonade is served on the balcony on warm days and hot cider in the kitchen or parlor when the weather is cool.

Built in 1895 for Confederate widow Rachel Moores, the Neoclassical mansion features fourteen Ionic columns from the St. Louis World's Fair, which were added later. The historic home has parquet flooring, oak paneling, beveled glass, brass fixtures, and crystal chandeliers. The inn has six guest rooms furnished in antiques, period pieces, and lace curtains. Victorian nightgowns and sleepshirts are provided for the enjoyment of guests. The bathroom in the Penthouse Suite has his and her oversize antique footed bathtubs. The Honeymoon Suite includes a music room/parlor with an 1890 piano that Scott Joplin, a Texarkana native, would have loved to play. The two-room Governor's Suite on the ground level is wheelchair accessible. Lady Bird Johnson and author Alex Haley each slept in the Ragland Room.

Georgia

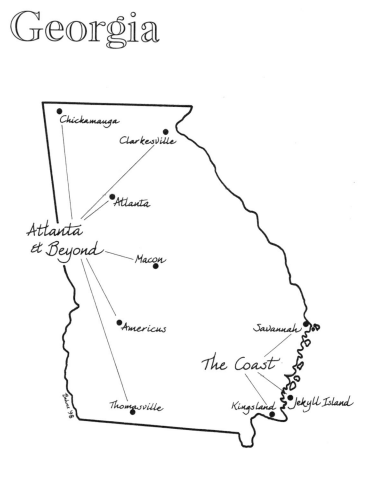

Chickamauga

Clarkesville

Atlanta

Atlanta
& Beyond

Macon

Americus

Savannah

The Coast

Thomasville

Kingsland

Jekyll Island

Bruce '98

From southern marshes and coastal plains, Georgia's terrain gradually unfolds to encompass low-lying sandy hills and the gently rolling Piedmont where, surprisingly, portions of Atlanta reach an elevation of 1,050 feet. Northward beckon the southernmost peaks of the Blue Ridge Mountains. The Appalachian Trail also begins in northern Georgia, winding and climbing its way to its terminus in Maine.

The largest state east of the Mississippi River, Georgia encompasses a surprising diversity in its 58,876 square miles. Serene old Savannah seems light years removed from the state capital, bustling, soaring Atlanta, touted as the symbol of the New South. And the state that shares with Florida the nation's last natural swamp areas, the vast 435,000-acre Okefenokee Swamp, also shelters old mountain communities, where residents cherish crafts and music.

Georgians have made the most of their differences, developing luxurious coastal resorts, preserving historic cities and towns, and pursuing agriculture, commerce, industry, and cultural achievements. From the southern coast to the northern mountains, Georgia includes almost sixty state parks. Some are day-use facilities with picnic grounds and nature trails, while others offer overnight accommodations, swimming, hiking, water sports, and camping. Two splendid national forests, Oconee, between Athens and Macon, and Chattahoochee, in northern Georgia, have well-developed recreation sites. Two rivers, the Chattahoochee, with a National Recreation Area running from Atlanta to Lake Lanier, and the Chattooga, a National Wild and Scenic River to Chattahoochee National Forest, offer challenging canoeing and rafting.

Georgia is an anglers' paradise. You can surf cast on the coastal Sea Islands, go for bass, bream, and catfish in rivers and marshlands, or take to the Piedmont and mountain lakes for boating and fishing. Spectator sports reach an art form at the Masters, one of golf's most prestigious events, held the first week in April at Augusta National Country Club.

For more information, contact the Georgia Department of Industry, Trade, and Tourism, P.O. Box 1776, Atlanta, Georgia 30301, 404-656-3590.

Atlanta and Beyond

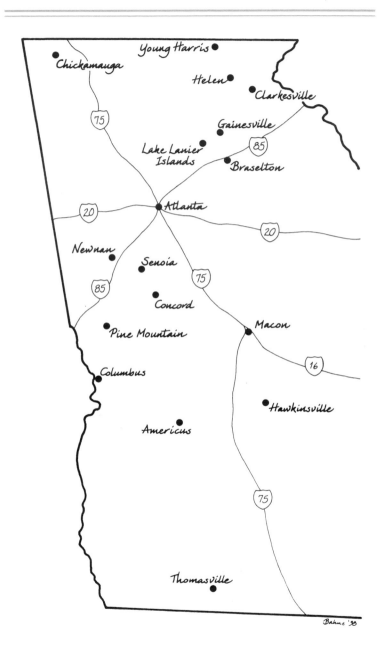

Young Harris

Chickamauga

Helen

Clarkesville

75

Gainesville

Lake Lanier
Islands

85

Braselton

Atlanta

20

20

Newnan

Senoia

75

85

Concord

Pine Mountain

Macon

Columbus

16

Hawkinsville

Americus

75

Thomasville

Bahme '93

Best Bed-and-Breakfasts

Best City Stops

Best Country Inns

Best Historic Inn

Best Meeting Places

Atlanta
Emory Conference Center Hotel, 98
Braselton
Chateau Elan, 106

Best Mountain Retreats

Chickamauga
Hidden Hollow Resort, 109
Helen
Helendorf River Inn & Towers, 118

Best Plantations

Concord
Inn Scarlett's Footsteps: a Plantation, 113
Thomasville
Melhana—The Grand Plantation Resort, 130

Best Resorts

Lake Lanier Islands
Renaissance PineIsle Resort, 100
Pine Mountain
Callaway Gardens and Resorts, Inc., 126
Young Harris
Brasstown Valley Crowne Plaza Resort, 132

Best State Park

Helen
Unicoi State Park Lodge and Conference Center, 119

Atlanta's boosters had begun calling it the "World's Next Great City" long before it was named as site of the 1996 Summer Olympics — the biggest and most prestigious event to ever come to the city. Reflecting its rising international status, hotels under German, Swiss, and Japanese ownership have opened.

Although *Gone With the Wind* memorabilia is a top seller in Atlanta shops, don't expect an Old South aura here. General Sherman took care of that when his troops torched the place in 1864. You'll still spot historic overtones, though. The gold-domed state capitol symbolizes the nation's first gold rush. On the grounds of the Swan House, home of the Atlanta Historical Society, you can visit the Tullie Smith House Restoration, a simple 1840 weatherboard homestead reflecting the "plantation plain" style of the antebellum Piedmont.

Stone Mountain Park, east of Atlanta, is highlighted by a famous 825-foot-high granite outcropping with a monumental equestrian carving of Jefferson Davis, Robert E. Lee, and Stonewall Jackson. The park also includes an antebellum plantation with a Piedmont mansion and subsidiary buildings and Confederate Hall, showcasing one of the South's most complete Civil War museums.

Several attractions add vitality to downtown Atlanta. Replacing an earlier entertainment center of the same name, Underground Atlanta includes retail shops, restaurants, lounges, nightclubs, and food kiosks. Adjacent to Underground, the three-story World of Coca-Cola pays tribute to a renowned homegrown product. It features the world's largest collection of Coca-Cola memorabilia and includes a replica 1930s soda fountain. Guests can sample free Cokes along with soft drinks made by Coca-Cola around the world.

Downtown in CNN Center, west of the capitol, you can also explore another Atlanta institution, the headquarters of Cable News Network and Headline News Network. Viewers watch news staffs in action from an overhead observation booth and can admire memorabilia of the Atlanta Braves and Atlanta Hawks.

Near the refurbished Zoo Atlanta and restored Cyclorama panoramic painting in Grant Park depicting the Battle of Atlanta, the Museum of the Jimmy Carter Library at the Carter Presidential Center also welcomes visitors. It depicts major events in the terms of the first thirty-nine U.S. presidents and displays state gifts presented to President and Mrs. Carter.

Reflecting another distinctive chapter of Georgia history, the Martin Luther King, Jr. Historic District includes the birthplace and gravesite of the Nobel Peace Prize winner and civil rights leader, along with the M. L. King, Jr. Center for Non-Violent Social Change and the Ebenezer Baptist Church, where he and his father preached.

North of Atlanta is the town of Helen, which has converted itself — lock, stock, and lederhosen — to a replica Bavarian village, with import shops, German restaurants, and entertainment ranging from oom-pah bands to bluegrass. At Dahlonega, center of Georgia's early-19th-century gold rush, the Dahlonega Gold Museum State Historic Site displays memorabilia, including gold dust and historic relics. You can pan for riches at nearby Crisson's Gold Mine and other sites.

Northwest of Tallulah Falls, a series of recreational lakes has been formed by hydroelectric dams. There are vacation cottages, marinas, and campgrounds at Lakes Rabun and Burton. Other bucolic northeast Georgia retreats include Vogel State Park, south of Blairsville, and Unicoi State Park, northwest of Helen. Both are resort-type parks, with a full array of activities and services. Hiwassee, another northern Georgia treasure, is site of the popular Georgia Mountain Fair each August. Here, too, the *Reach of Song*, Georgia's official heritage drama, is staged from mid-June through early August. It depicts the Appalachians' mountain heritage in song, dance, and theatrical vignettes. Nearby, Brasstown Bald, Georgia's highest peak, soars 4,784 feet. On a clear day one can see portions of four states.

Columbus, 108 miles south of Atlanta, is Georgia's second largest city, with a population of about 175,000. Here you can explore a 26-block historic district to visit such handsomely restored structures as the 1871 Springer Opera House, which hosted luminaries such as Edwin Booth and Oscar Wilde and is now the State Theatre of Georgia. The Columbus Iron Works, which once manufactured cannons for the Confederacy, is now the city's Convention and Trade Center. And the impressive Columbus Museum, one of the largest in the Southeast, displays nineteenth- and twentieth-century paintings and American decorative arts. South of Columbus at Plains, birthplace of President Jimmy Carter, the Jimmy Carter National Historic Site includes the railroad depot where the thirty-ninth president launched his campaign, his former boyhood homes, and his brother Billy's gasoline station.

Nestled in western Georgia's gentle Appalachian foothills are extraordinarily beautiful Callaway Gardens. Here one of the world's largest collections of azaleas — more than seven hundred varieties — usually come to peak bloom in April. The 2,500-acre garden complex is a full-scale family resort. In the gardens at the Cecil B. Day Butterfly Center, named for the founder of Days Inn of America, thousands of brilliantly hued butterflies flutter freely in the world's largest glass-enclosed conservatory.

Nearby, at Warm Springs, is the simple six-room Little White House, the only home that President Franklin D. Roosevelt ever owned. It is preserved much as it was when the four-time U.S.

president died there on April 12, 1945. You'll see the unfinished portrait Mme. Elizabeth Shoumatoff was painting when Roosevelt suffered a fatal cerebral hemorrhage.

The city of Macon, almost in the state's geographic center, is a delightful blend of Old and New South. The antebellum mansions in its older residential district were spared by Sherman on his march to the sea. The birthplace of Georgia's renowned poet Sidney Lanier is on High Street and is open to visitors. Each March, Macon stages a gala ten-day Cherry Blossom Festival, as about 16,000 Yohino cherry trees come to peak bloom — more than in Washington, D.C.!

The Cottage Inn

129 Highway 49 North
P.O. Box 488
Americus, GA 31709
912-924-9316 or 912-924-6680
Fax: 912-924-6248
http://www.americus.net~cottage

> A classic cottage in a
> secluded pecan grove

Innkeepers: Jim and Billie Gatewood. **Accommodations:** 1 room and 3 suites (all with private baths). **Rates:** $65. **Payment:** MasterCard, Visa. **Children:** Welcome. **Pets:** Check with innkeepers. **Smoking:** Allowed on verandahs. **Open:** Year-round.

➤ **You won't be bothered by hovering innkeepers at this B&B, as the Gatewoods have set this up to be a private experience. If you do need them, they are just next door.**

If you like seclusion and privacy, this quiet retreat just outside Americus is for you. And if no other guests are registered, you may have the entire cottage to yourself.

Slated to be torn down, the antebellum raised cottage was moved from Cuthbert, Georgia, to Jim and Billie Gatewood's five-acre pecan orchard next to their home. This little white house was built in 1852, and it features a lacy front porch. You enter the house from the front porch into a wide hallway that runs the length of the house; if you keep going, you'll exit at the back onto a small porch. The entire cottage has two suites — a bedroom, bathroom, and parlor to the right and the same configuration of rooms to the left.

Behind the cottage is an annex, which came from the same place in Cuthbert. It has one guest room, a bathroom, and a kitchen shared by all guests; the kitchen has a separate entrance so that guests may come and go without disturbing others. All the rooms are elegantly furnished in antiques from the area and feature twelve-foot windows that bring the outside indoors. They have central heating and air conditioning and are equipped with cable television and telephones, as well as extra towels, blankets, and pillows.

Guests are welcome to use the Gatewoods' personal tennis court next to their home but should make a formal request. Jim is an attorney, and Billie stays busy with their three children.

Windsor Hotel

125 West Lamar Street
Mailing address:
104 Windsor Avenue
Americus, GA 31790
912-924-1555, 800-678-8946
Fax: 912-924-1555, Ext. 113

> **A reborn Victorian queen offering ultimate southern hospitality**

General Manager: Frank Santoro. **Accommodations:** 49 rooms and 4 suites (all with private baths). **Rates:** $83–$107. **Included:** Full southern breakfast, newspaper, turndown service in suites. **Payment:** Major credit cards. **Children:** 15

and younger stay free with parents. **Pets:** Not allowed. **Smoking:** Allowed in designated areas. **Open:** Year-round.

➤   **A member of Historic Hotels of America, the three-star, three-diamond hotel is included in the Americus National Register Historic District.**

A queen of the South was reborn in 1991 when the castle-like Windsor Hotel reopened after a complete renovation — a project that involved more than a decade of planning, grant writing, community meetings, and public and private contributions. Three years after the Howard Dayton family donated the property to the city, Americus was certified for the Main Street Program. Grants awarded in 1978, 1979, 1980, 1983, and 1987 were used to secure the building (i.e., roof repairs, masonry work, stabilization, and other projects).

In 1986, twenty-three private citizens pledged $5,000 each to the Windsor Development Corporation, which paid for work by architects, engineers, lawyers, and accountants. And in 1989, 160 citizens of Americus invested a minimum of $1,000 each to form the Windsor Hotel Limited Partnership. This was the final step in making the dream become a reality. The total renovation costs reached nearly $6 million.

The architecture of the Windsor is officially Victorian, but the original architect Gottfried L. Norman combined several different styles — a Romanesque tower, a Flemish-stepped roof, and a three-story Moorish atrium lobby. The hotel, completed in 1893, was named for John Windsor. With its towers and arches, it is reminiscent of an elegant town hall in Europe. For seventy-five years the Windsor served as a resort hotel, closing in the mid-1970s.

The restored lobby is as grand as ever, and the Grand Dining Room offers fine dining. A Continental or traditional southern breakfast is available every day, followed by a lunch buffet. In the evening guests may order from the à la carte menu; on Tuesday and Thursday nights there is a buffet. Among the choices of entrées are Pecan Crusted Pork Loin, Salmon Cabernet, Breast of Duckling, and Veal Lindbergh. (Charles Lindbergh spent some time in Americus in 1923 prior to his solo flight across the Atlantic.) After dinner guests often unwind in Floyd's Pub, a full-service bar that is open every day but Sunday.

The Windsor offers 53 guest rooms, all furnished in period furnishings. The most elaborate rooms, located in the tower, are the Presidential Suite, named for President Jimmy Carter of nearby Plains, and the Bridal Suite. The board room, also in the tower, is named for Franklin D. Roosevelt, who made an address from the verandah next to the tower when he was Secretary of the Navy. The hotel offers honeymoon and getaway packages, murder mystery weekends, and an annual medieval madrigal dinner.

While staying at the Windsor, you should take some time to explore the restored shops surrounding the hotel — all a part of the Main Street Progam. Just a few miles away are Plains, Jimmy Carter's hometown, and Andersonville, a famous Civil War prison and site of the proposed Prisoner of War Museum. As National Historic Sites, both are interesting places to visit. (Don't be surprised if you see the former president and first lady bicycling around town.)

Atlanta

Atlanta Grand Hyatt

3300 Peachtree Road Northeast
Atlanta, GA 30305
770-365-8100, 800-233-1234
Fax: 770-233-5686

| **A thoroughly luxurious hotel with Japanese touches** |

General Manager: Peter Sahora. **Accommodations:** 438 rooms, including 22 suites (all with private baths). **Rates:** $230–$2,500. **Included:** Continental breakfast and afternoon cocktails with hors d'oeuvres on concierge floors. **Payment:** Major credit cards. **Children:** Welcome. **Pets:** Not allowed. **Smoking:** Smoking and nonsmoking rooms. **Open:** Year-round.

➤ **Business travelers love this hotel for its location and services.**

Since early 1997, this luxury hotel in Buckhead has been known as the Atlanta Grand Hyatt, but it began in 1990 as the city's first all-Japanese hotel. Though Hyatt has given the hotel a completely new look, it has kept some of its Japanese features. Kamogawa, overlooking the Japanese garden that has a 45-foot waterfall, offers authentic Japanese cuisine and private dining in its tatami rooms. (Cassis, the hotel's other restaurant, serves bistro and Continental cuisine.) One of the hotel's 22 suites is completely Japanese, and guests take off their shoes at the door, don their kimonos, and then relax Japanese style. All rooms have mini-bars, hair dryers, iron and ironing board, coffeemakers, and robes, plus a fax machine and three telephones.

There is definitely an emphasis on the business traveler here. The business center offers full secretarial service. For the exercise-minded, the fitness center and outdoor pool offer ways to relax.

Emory Conference Center Hotel

1615 Clifton Road
Atlanta, GA 30329
770-712-6000, 800-93-EMORY
Fax: 770-712-6025

| **A conference center near Emory University** |

General Manager: Paul Sthlarik. **Accommodations:** 198 rooms, including 3 suites (all with private baths). **Rates:** $110–$135. **Payment:** Major credit cards. **Children:** Welcome. **Pets:** Not allowed. **Smoking:** Smoking and nonsmoking rooms. **Open:** Year-round.

➤ **A complete meeting package includes guest accommodations, meals, breaks, conference space, audio-visual needs, and recreation.**

Set amid 30 acres of rare, pristine forest adjacent to Emory University, the Emory Conference Center Hotel combines the latest advances in executive conference center technology with the simplicity of nature. While attending a conference, you can take a stroll through the woods, take a dip in the pool, relax by the double-sided stone fireplace in the informal lobby, have a meal overlooking the beautifully landscaped Garden Courtyard, or enjoy a game of billiards in the Club Room. The Dining Room features buffets throughout the day, with a variety of hot entrees, a farmer's market, and delicious desserts. Meals may be arranged to suit your specific schedule.

The five-story hotel, owned by the University and managed by Stormont Trice Corporation, offers 198 guest rooms, over 20,000 square feet of meeting space, a comprehensive business center, and a full-service fitness center. Guest rooms are appointed with everything a person needs to carry on daily business. Amenities include oversized work desks, data ports, dual-line telephones, including personal voice mail and a direct line for computer hookup, and a dedicated in-room fax capability. Every technologically advanced service imaginable is available to guests — video teleconferencing, computers, fax machines, cellular phones, radios, pagers, and center audio-visual patching capabilities. An on-site audio-visual staff, an assisted listening system for the hearing impaired, and simultaneous interpretation systems are also available. Meeting rooms have ergonomic chairs and dedicated audio-visual equipment. The two state-of-the-art amphitheaters have built-in front and rear projection systems.

The fitness center offers a full array of amenities for relaxation — a heated lap pool, hydrotherapy pools, men's and women's sauna, coed steam room, aerobic exercise equipment, and lighted sports courts for volleyball, basketball, and tennis.

Four Seasons Hotel Atlanta

75 Fourteenth Street
Atlanta, GA 30309
770-881-9898, 800-332-3442
Fax: 770-873-4692

A European-style hotel in Atlanta's art district

Managing Director: Brian Flaherty. **Accommodations:** 242 rooms and suites (all with private baths). **Rates:** $250–$4,500. **Payment:** Major credit cards. **Children:** Welcome. **Pets:** Not allowed. **Smoking:** Smoking and nonsmoking rooms. **Open:** Year-round.

➤ **Many guests who come to the Four Seasons take advantage of its proximity to the city's art district: the hotel is within walking distance of the High Museum of Art and the Woodruff Arts Center.**

One of Atlanta's premier hotels, this five-star property opened in the midtown area in late 1992 as the Grand Hotel Atlanta. In 1997 it was renamed the Four Seasons Hotel Atlanta.

Guests enter the hotel through the European-style marble lobby, and after check-in are escorted to their rooms. Both elegant and functional, the traditionally furnished rooms feature marbled bathrooms with European fixtures, hair dryers and robes, and all the usual amenities. The top floor of the hotel has one-, two-, three-, and four-bedroom suites; executive suites are also located on most floors. All the suites have living rooms with stereos, facsimile, and computer outlets, and many feature wet bars. Each suite is unique in its decor. The most elaborate suite features a living room, a banquet dining room, a kitchen with separate entrance, and a master bedroom with a luxurious whirlpool bath. Breakfast, lunch, and dinner are served in the Cafe, and guests often relax after hours in the Bar and the Lounge.

The Four Seasons offers a private, Neoclassic design health spa with an indoor lap pool, sun terrace, whirlpool spa, weight room, and a steam/sauna bath. Other services include 24-hour valet parking, 24-hour in-room dining, concierge, safety deposit boxes, and business services.

Renaissance Waverly Hotel

2450 Galleria Parkway
Atlanta, GA 30339
770-953-4500, 800-468-6571
Fax: 770-953-0740

A suburban hotel known for its Sunday brunch

General Manager: Hermann Gammeter. **Accommodations:** 521 rooms and 24 suites (all with private baths). **Rates:** $175–$1,500; weekend rates available. **Payment:** Major credit cards. **Children:** Welcome. **Pets:** Not allowed. **Smoking:** Smoking and non-smoking rooms. **Open:** Year-round.

➤ **The hotel has a $6 million-plus art collection, established by real-estate developer and art aficionado Trammel Crow when he opened the property in 1983. The collection includes works by southeastern and Georgia artists and a group of sixteen hand-carved teakwood bells, each seven feet tall.**

Whether or not you spend the night at this luxury hotel, you should try the Sunday Brunch, the largest in Georgia and voted "Atlanta's Best" by several local publications. Every Sunday the hotel offers brunch in the upscale Waverly Grill and the more leisurely Atrium Cafe. Menu specialties include open-faced lobster omelets, peach and ricotta blintzes, plus gourmet ice creams. A musical trio provides entertainment. Children under the age of twelve are given their own space in the Lobby Bar during the Sunday event.

Every guest is awakened with a pot of fresh coffee and a newspaper, delivered to the door immediately after the wake-up call. The hotel also provides nightly turndown service upon request.

If you stay on the Club floor, a concierge staff is on hand to serve the complimentary Continental breakfast, afternoon tea with petit fours, evening hors d'oeuvres, and coffee.

Rooms on the other floors are very spacious. Each one has a sitting area and is well equipped with telephones, television options, and in-room movies. The Presidential Suite, where Ronald Reagan stayed on two occasions when he was president, has seven rooms. The master suite has a bathroom with a two-person Jacuzzi. The carpet in the foyer features the presidential seal, and space has been allocated for the Secret Service.

Recreational options at the Renaissance Waverly include an outdoor pool and an indoor pool with a whirlpool, racquetball courts, a fully equipped exercise room, steam room, sauna, aerobics studio, and health lounge with snack bar and wide-screen TV. You can also get a massage at Spa Sydell.

The hotel offers a number of special weekend packages designed around the spa, romance, and the Sunday brunch. Regular weekend rates are considerably less than the standard weekday rates.

Near Marietta, about eleven miles from downtown Atlanta, Renaissance Waverly Hotel is the focal point of the Atlanta Galleria shopping center and office complex. The Cobb Galleria Convention Centre is directly connected to the hotel for convenience.

The Ritz-Carlton Atlanta

181 Peachtree Street, N.E.
Atlanta, GA 30303
770-659-0400, 800-241-3333
Fax: 770-688-0400

> **A downtown luxury hotel that's intimate and service-oriented**

General Manager: Valerie Ferguson. **Accommodations:** 447 rooms, including 22 suites (all with private baths). **Rates:** $205–$1200. **Included:** Continental breakfast; food and beverages on the Club floor. **Payment:** Major credit cards. **Children:** Welcome. **Pets:** Not allowed. **Smoking:** Smoking and nonsmoking rooms. **Open:** Year-round.

➤ **Fresh flowers (about 2,500 daily), original art, and fine silver and china add to the ambiance of the Ritz-Carlton Atlanta.**

A sister to the Ritz-Carlton Buckhead, this downtown glass and marble property is just as impeccable in its ambiance and service. Much of the hotel's character, even its name, is patterned after the Ritz-Carlton Boston, which was purchased by W. B. Johnson Properties, Inc., in 1983, the year before this property opened.

Compared with other downtown hotels, known for their vast, multi-story atrium lobbies, the 25-story Ritz-Carlton Atlanta appears small and unassuming — but it is really the most elegant hotel around. Dark mahogany public interiors, Oriental carpets, and fine traditional furnishings create an intimate, comfortable setting, much like a quiet library where you might gather with friends.

The Ritz-Carlton Atlanta is also known for its outstanding food, including Sunday brunch, which is considered one of the city's best. The Restaurant is one of only two Four-Star, Five-Diamond restaurants in the state. Food is also available in The Cafe, which offers menu selections for the fitness conscious, and The Bar, where you may order from the Gold Medal wine list. The Lobby Lounge is the setting for the complimentary Continental breakfast, afternoon tea, and evening cocktails; a pianist entertains in the afternoon.

The hotel offers concierge and room service 24 hours a day, valet parking, safety deposit boxes, and other amenities. Special services such as secretarial help, portable typewriters, and international telex and fax are geared to the business traveler. The executive fitness center, open daily, offers massage therapy and steam and sauna rooms.

The rooms are special as well, with extras such as marble bathrooms, refreshment cabinets, plush terrycloth robes, and maid service twice a day. In keeping with the classic style of the hotel, they are furnished in eighteenth- and nineteenth-century reproductions. The 24th and 25th floors of the hotel and the Club floors are accessible by elevator key only. The concierge staff provides a Continental breakfast, light lunch, afternoon tea, evening hors d'oeuvres, and late night cordials and chocolates. The Presidential Suite and the Ritz-Carlton Suite, with its baby grand piano, are located here.

The Ritz-Carlton Buckhead

3434 Peachtree Road, N.E.
Atlanta, GA 30326
770-237-2700, 800-241-3333
Fax: 770-239-0078

> An award-winning five-diamond hotel in the heart of Atlanta's Buckhead

General Manager: Bob Warman. **Accommodations:** 553 rooms, including 29 suites (all with private baths). **Rates:** $225–$1,050. **Included:** Complimentary food and beverages on the Club floor. **Payment:** Major credit cards. **Children:** Ritz-Kids program offering special foods and services. **Pets:** Not allowed. **Smoking:** Smoking and nonsmoking rooms. **Open:** Year-round.

➤ **The company's motto is "Ladies and gentlemen serving ladies and gentlemen." Every service imaginable has been thought of and offered, from international currency exchange to concierge.**

Very few hotels have their own symphony orchestra, art curator, food and wine university, not to mention a recycling program that has been adopted by all other hotels in the company. The Ritz-Carlton Buckhead does; perhaps that's why it's the flagship of the company and keeps garnering the highest awards in the hotel industry. A Five-Diamond property, the hotel has been noted by *Conde Nast Traveler* and *Zagat Survey* and has received numerous awards and honors.

Built in 1984, the hotel is one of two Ritz-Carltons in the Atlanta area and one of several worldwide. It is also a member of Leading Hotels of the World. The entire chain takes its name from the Ritz-Carlton, Boston, purchased by W. B. Johnson Properties of Atlanta in 1983.

From the moment of arrival until departure, guests feel they are special, for service is the watchword. The company's training program stresses the importance of perfect service. Employees are trained to set and wait tables, be hospitable and friendly rather than arrogant, address guests properly by name, and say things such as "Good morning" and "My pleasure."

The public rooms of the 22-story hotel, with its tiered bay windows, are exquisitely done. The walls of the lobby feature Honduras mahogany moldings and African Sappele hardwood paneling; the floors are Italian Botticino classic white marble with inlaid continental mahogany marble from Tennessee. There are cut-crystal chandeliers from Europe and sparkling wall sconces. The rooms are furnished in classic eighteenth- and nineteenth-century style, complemented with works of art from the hotel's outstanding collection. Art tours are scheduled regularly. The Ritz-Carlton also has five Steinway grand pianos, often used for special concerts at the hotel.

Rooms at the Ritz-Carlton Buckhead are just as impeccable. Among the special features are Brunschweig & Fils fabrics used in the window treatments and bedspreads, marble baths, terrycloth robes, full toiletries, twice-a-day maid service, and other luxuries. Guests also get hair dryers, shoeshine service, and nightly turndown service. Guests also may take advantage of the 60-foot indoor lap pool, the fitness center, and the sundeck.

Guests on the Club level receive the ultimate in personal service, privacy, and security; the Club is accessible by elevator key only. Food presentations are offered five times a day, including a Continental breakfast, light lunch, afternoon tea, before-dinner cocktails and hors d'oeuvres, and after-dinner cordials and truffles. Private concierge staff and premium bar are provided.

Food is given full attention by the Ritz-Carlton Buckhead staff. In the hotel's main dining room, meals are presented on the Ritz-Carlton china, complemented by the blue cobalt glassware that has become a trademark of the hotel. The Café offers all-day dining, including "cuisine fitness vitale." Food is also available in the Bar, and afternoon tea is served daily in the Lobby Lounge. Sunday brunches are very popular.

Throughout the year the hotel stages special events for the enjoyment of guests. In July the hotel pulls out all the stops to celebrate the Fourth. Another time the focus might be on the Vidalia onion. Mozart is celebrated in March. The hotel stages cooking classes with the hotel's key chefs, monthly afternoon tea and fashions shows featuring fashions from nearby Lenox Square and Phipps Plaza shops.

Shellmont Bed & Breakfast

821 Piedmont Avenue, N.E.
Atlanta, GA 30308
770-872-9290
Fax: 770-872-5379
http://www.bbonline.com/ga/shellmont

A Victorian B&B in midtown that's one of thirty-five Atlanta historic landmarks

Innkeepers: Ed and Debbie McCord. **Accommodations:** 5 rooms and a carriage house (all with private baths). **Rates:** $90–$150. **Included:** Full breakfast, beverages, evening chocolates, morning newspaper, fresh flowers, fruit basket. **Payment:** American Express, MasterCard, Visa. **Children:** 12 and younger welcome in carriage house; 12 and older welcome in main house and carriage house. **Pets:** Not allowed. **Smoking:** Allowed on porches. **Open:** Year-round.

➤ **The most unusual architectural feature of the house is the Turkish Corner, with its inverted domed ceiling, stenciled walls, and Moorish hardware. It is similar to some of the designs you see in the famous Fox Theatre a short distance away.**

When you arrive at the Shellmont Bed & Breakfast Inn, you step back a century into the Victorian age. Built in 1892 for Dr. Perrin Nicholson, the two-story wooden home is located in Atlanta's midtown near Piedmont Park and the midtown MARTA stop. Because Dr. Nicholson held the architect Walter T. Downing in high esteem, he gave him free reign in designing the 6,000-square-foot home.

Though the house is simple and small compared with the mansions that were built on Peachtree Street and Ponce de Leon Avenue at the time, Downing added marvelous architectural details. A shell motif is used throughout, the most pronounced being on the second story of the rounded bay walls. Other motifs include fruit in the dining room, ornate garlands over the fireplace in the foyer, and musical notes in what was probably the music room — all carved of wood. Other notable features are leaded and stained glass (believed to be by Tiffany), heart pine flooring, and special moldings.

Three generations of Nicholsons lived in the house. In 1982, Ed and Debbie McCord decided to purchase it for a bed-and-breakfast inn. (Ed is a developer and city planner, and at the time of the purchase had already renovated five houses with Debbie.) The restoration took over a year, with much of the work being done by the McCords. They stripped and painted the original woodwork, jacked up the floors, replaced the foundation, roof, and shingles, removed paint and wallpaper to reveal the original detailing and removed and rebuilt the porch.

The McCords renamed the house the Shellmont, incorporating the shell motif (which symbolizes tranquillity) and the "mont" from Piedmont. They opened their inn to the public in 1984, continuing renovations on the separate carriage house until it was completed. The Shellmont is furnished with Victorian antiques and reproductions.

In 1988, the McCords received the Mayor's Award for Preservation and Adaptive Reuse, and today the Shellmont is on the National Register of Historic Places. It is one of thirty-five Atlanta structures with landmark status. The McCords continue to upgrade the house and gardens and recently reupholstered the furniture.

Upon arrival at the Shellmont, guests are welcomed with fresh flowers and a fruit basket in the room, complimentary beverages, and turndown service with chocolates. The inn has four guest rooms, plus the carriage house, which has a fully equipped kitchen. The McCords will assist guests with anything they might need — dinner reservations, sightseeing plans, picnic lunches, and concert tickets. The full breakfast features freshly squeezed orange juice, fruit, ham and egg soufflé, homemade breads, and fresh ground coffee, plus cereals. Offered at two seatings, it is served on linen with china and crystal. Guests seem to enjoy strolling through the gardens, which has three fish ponds and music piped from the inn.

Braselton

Chateau Elan

100 Rue Charlemagne
Braselton, GA 30517
770-932-0900, 800-233-WINE
http://www.chateauelan.com

| The only resort and conference center in the U.S. with a winery |

Innkeeper: Hank Evers. **Accommodations:** 307 rooms (all with private baths). **Rates:** $119–$225 in inn, $165–$225 in spa, $210–$299 in golf villas. **Payment:** Major credit cards. **Children:** Welcome. **Pets:** Not allowed. **Smoking:** Smoking and nonsmoking rooms. **Open:** Year-round.

➤ **Chateau Elan is the recipient of** *Corporate Meetings and Incentives Magazine's* **Golden Links Award and** *Meeting News'* **"Planners Choice" Award.**

Driving through the rolling North Georgia hills on I-85, you are tempted to put on the brakes and stare at the first sight of Chateau Elan. This is not the place you expect to find a French-style resort and conference center with its own winery. With more than 200 acres of wine-producing grapes, its wines have received 240 national and international awards for quality and excellence.

The remarkable, short history of this four-star property, which continues to garner national and international awards for its wine, golf courses, and conference center, began in 1981 when Dr. Donald Panoz and his wife decided to establish the winery. In the early years they brought in the winemaker Ed Frederick from the West Coast to oversee the initial process and design of the vineyard. He was followed by a second winemaker, Jean Coutois, who influenced the winemaking in a French way. In 1988, the Chateau housing the Art Gallery and Wine Market was built. In 1989 the a championship golf course and practice facility were added, followed in 1992 by the opening of the full-service European health spa. The next year, the Legends members-only golf club (designed by Gene Sarazen, Sam Snead, and Kathy Whitworth and site of the first Sarazen World Open Championship) and the 144-room Chateau Elan and Conference Center were added to the landscape. A Stan Smith tennis complex and the Equestrian Show Center opened in 1994. Two years later, more guest rooms, meeting space, and another championship golf course, the Woodlands, were added. And in 1997, an authentic Irish pub opened on the property.

Chateau Elan now offers more than 300 rooms and suites, six restaurants offering a variety of cuisines from French-Continental to casual Georgia cooking, and a 25,000-square-foot conference facility. Many guests come here just to relax, while others may be here for business concerns. Whatever the reason, they find plenty to do — golf, tennis, cycling, walking, horseback riding, swimming, pampering at the spa, or taking a tour of the winery.

The resort offers a number of attractive packages that allow guests to focus on a particular activity they wish to pursue. Basic packages include the Vintage Bed & Breakfast, Escape to Romance, and Golf Package. In addition, several overnight and day packages are designed around the spa, one of the only spas in the country to offer the Louison BOBET treatment, a form of thalassotherapy hydrotherapy using algae.

Chickamauga

Gordon-Lee Mansion

217 Cove Road
Chickamauga, GA 30707
706-375-4728
800-487-4728
GLMBB1@aol.com
http://www.fga.com/welcome/gordon-lee

| A historic inn near a Civil War battleground |

Innkeeper: Richard Barclift. **Accommodations:** 4 rooms and 1 log house (all with private baths). **Rates:** $75–$125. **Included:** Full breakfast and house tour in inn. **Payment:** MasterCard, Visa. **Children:** All children welcome in log house; 12 and older welcome in inn. **Pets:** Not allowed. **Smoking:** Allowed on verandahs. **Open:** Year-round.

➤ **Soldiers left their names and graffiti scrawled on the walls, but these writings were lost years ago.**

History was made within the walls of this 1847 antebellum mansion near the Chickamauga Battlefield. The original site was where the Cherokee nation had its courthouse before being driven from the area to Oklahoma. James Gordon, who settled here in 1836 on 2,500 acres, built the house with the help of slaves over a period of seven years. Its real claim to fame occurred in 1863, however, when it became Union headquarters for General Rosencrans and his staff and then the main hospital for the wounded from the Battle of Chickamauga. The two-day conflict was one of the bloodiest in American history, when the Confederate and Union forces combined suffered thirty-four thousand casualties. You can tour the battlefield just a short distance from the house.

The Greek Revival mansion, with its giant Doric columns, sits amid seven acres on top of a big hill at the end of an avenue of ancient oaks and maples. Under the guidance of historians, Dr. and Mrs. Frank Green restored the house.

The house is open for tours and to overnight bed-and-breakfast guests, who have the mansion to themselves. Innkeeper Richard Barclift acts as host but lives elsewhere on the property. Guests enjoy complimentary sherry in the library and a full breakfast in the formal dining room. Tours of the house are complimentary to overnight guests.

The adjacent log house has been recently restored and is now available to guests. With its king-size bed, twin beds, two baths, and full kitchen, plus fireplace, it is ideal for families. Guests who stay in the log house provide their own breakfast.

Hidden Hollow Resort

463 Hidden Hollow Lane
Chickamauga, GA 30707
706-539-2372

A secluded mountain hideaway

Innkeepers: Tommy and Bonny Jean Thomas. **Accommodations:** 2 rooms, 1 suite, and 5 cabins (all with private baths). **Rates:** $58–$78; 7th night free. **Included:** Fishing, canoeing, and use of trails. **Payment:** Cash or checks. **Children:** Supervised children welcome. **Pets:** Not allowed. **Smoking:** Not allowed in cabins. **Open:** Year-round.

➤ **Many couples tie the knot, celebrate with friends, and then honeymoon at Hidden Hollow Resort.**

This quaint retreat in the mountains of northwest Georgia is an ideal place to kick off your shoes and do nothing. Tommy and Bonny Jean Thomas offer rustic accommodations in the main inn and log cabins on a private spring-fed lake amid 140 acres. Rooms in the inn have refrigerators and coffee makers; the cabins feature fireplaces Tanglewood Cabin, the largest, offers three small bedrooms. Romancers like the coziness of the Sleepy Hollow Cabin. For groups and families who want to rough it, there are several wilderness cabins. Outdoor grills and picnic tables are convenient to all the accommodations.

Guests may enjoy a variety of activities — hiking, fishing, canoeing, and folk dancing in the Music Hall on occasion. (The Thomases are avid folk dancers.) Other diversions are whitewater rafting on the Ocoee River, a 1996 Olympic site, and visits to Chickamauga National Park, Sequoyah Caverns, and the attractions of nearby Chattanooga and Lookout Mountain.

Clarkesville

Glen-Ella Springs Inn & Conference Center

Bear Gap Road
Route 3, Box 3304
Clarkesville, GA 30523
706-754-7295, 800-552-3479
Fax: 706-754-1560

A mountain country inn offering great food and lodging

Innkeepers: Barrie and Bobby Aycock. **Accommodations:** 14 rooms (all with private baths) and 2 suites (with private baths and whirlpool tubs). **Rates:** $100–$180. **Included:** Full breakfast. **Payment:** American Express, MasterCard, Visa. **Children:** Welcome. **Pets:** Not allowed. **Smoking:** Limited. **Open:** Year-round.

➤ **The hotel was originally built by Glen and Ella Davidson in 1875 to serve guests who came to the area to "take the waters" for their health and vitality.**

Barrie and Bobbie Aycock literally brought a ghost back to life when they renovated the Glen Ella Springs Inn a few years ago.

Though it had been built originally as an inn, the building had ceased to be one around 1915 and had been victimized by weather and vandals for years. The Aycocks had passed by the old structure for years on their way from Atlanta to their vacation home on the lake. When they discovered that the building was for sale, they sold everything they had to purchase and renovate it as an inn.

The project took six months to complete. They found the structure of the old two-story wooden building to be sound, and the fieldstone stacked fireplaces required only a little work. They replaced the long porches, added another block of rooms, and built a house for themselves. While Bobby was busy with the renovation, Barrie scoured the countryside for antiques to furnish the inn. They opened the dining room in July of 1987 and sixteen rooms in the fall, just in time for the leaf season, which brings hordes of travelers to the north Georgia mountains. Since then, they've welcomed visitors from near and far, hosted wedding receptions, family reunions, and corporate groups. A conference room meets the demand for executive retreats and banquets. The inn has been named one of the top summer getaways by *Travel and Leisure* magazine and North Georgia's best gourmet inn by *Atlanta Magazine*.

The inn represents rustic elegance at its best. The great room features heart pine paneling and a stone fireplace that extends two stories; the two long, narrow dining rooms are similar, with the same type of fireplaces. The not too spacious guest rooms are paneled in the same boards, but most have been pickled or painted to give them a lighter color. Each room has a telephone. All the rooms open onto the outside verandahs, which look over the swimming pool and the meadow or the front yard. There are two suites, each with a separate sitting room and bathrooms with whirlpool tubs.

The Aycocks' philosophy of innkeeping is to provide a relaxing setting and good food for their guests, so they don't try to do much programming. Guests usually enjoy hiking the inn's 16 acres, swimming in the pool, and rocking on the verandahs. The Aycocks offer plenty of books and games, and during the winter months stage murder mysteries and special events centering on food.

Barrie, who oversees the dining room, grows her own herbs and is an excellent cook. She is assisted by Jeff and Jennifer McKenna. The inn also has a horticulturist on staff, who is responsible for the herb, perennial, and vegetable gardens. The restaurant is open to the public for dinner from June through October, and reservations are usually required. A buffet lunch is served on Easter Sunday, Mother's Day, and Thanksgiving.

Columbus

Historic Columbus Hilton

800 Front Avenue
Columbus, GA 31901
706-324-1800, 800-524-4020
Fax: 706-576-4413

| A former grist mill now serves as a spiffy city hotel |

General Manager: Rick Greenwald. **Accommodations:** 171 rooms and 6 suites (all with private baths, mini-bars, and coffeemakers). **Rates:** $70–$120. **Included:** Milk and cookies, complimentary shoeshines and turndown service on concierge floors. **Payment:** Major credit cards. **Children:** Free with parents. **Pets:** No. **Smoking:** Smoking and nonsmoking rooms. **Open:** Year-round.

➤ **On this site a mill, operating as early as 1847, was spared when Union troops marched through Georgia in 1865. By 1887, the mill was the largest cornmeal and flour mill in the South.**

Part old, part new, the Columbus Hilton combines the best of two centuries. Located downtown in the historic district across the street from the Columbus Riverwalk along the Chattahoochee River, the contemporary-style hotel uses space from a century-old grist mill. Across the street the convention center has taken the place of a Civil War cannon factory.

One wing of the hotel, housed in the old Empire Grist Mill, features brick walls and heavy exposed timbers. Hunter's Bar & Grille, a favorite gathering spot for guests, is located here. Pemberton's Café offers lunch, breakfast, and dinner amid a collection of Coca-Cola memorabilia. Guests also enjoy the outdoor pool.

Thirty-six concierge-level rooms are located on the sixth floor. Guests staying here have a few more perks: Continental breakfast, free beverages, shoeshines, and terrycloth robes, but all the rooms have coffeemakers.

Concord

Inn Scarlett's Footsteps: A Plantation

40 Old Flat Shoals Road, Route 18
Concord, GA 30206
Tel. & Fax: 770-884-9012
gwtw@gwtw.com
http://www.gwtw.com

> A B&B offering a *Gone With the Wind* experience

Innkeepers: Vern and K. C. Bassham. **Accommodations:** 5 rooms and 5 cottages (all with private baths). **Rates:** $79. **Included:** Full breakfast, tour of mansion and Gone With the Wind Museum. **Payment:** American Express, MasterCard, Visa. **Children:** 10 and older welcome. **Pets:** Not allowed. **Smoking:** Not allowed. **Open:** Year-round.

➤ **It's easy to "think about tomorrow" and dream of having an 18-inch waist while reliving the life of Scarlett at Inn Scarlett's Footsteps, a Georgia plantation home that more closely resembles Ashley Wilkes's Twelve Oaks than it does Tara.**

If you're looking for Tara, this is it — the only plantation in the world that is devoted to Margaret Mitchell's classic, *Gone With the Wind*. To help you get into character, innkeepers Vern and K.C. Bassham rent ball gowns to guests for pictures on the grand staircase. They've also decorated their 1905 white-columned plantation house, formerly known as Magnolia Farms, in the style of the book and film. Tours are given by guides dressed in Civil War costumes, and horse and carriage rides are available by reservation. Miss K.C.'s Gift Shop sells *Gone With the Wind* souvenirs. Vern, a former men's hairstylist, and K.C., a former real estate agent, bought the property in 1992, fulfilling K.C.'s girlhood dream of living in Tara someday.

Each of the five guest rooms is named for a character and decorated in a style that reflects his or her personality — Scarlett, Rhett, Melanie, Ashley, and Mr. Gerald. The Basshams recently added five upscale cottage named for other book characters — Miss Ellen, Aunt Pitty, Dr. Meade, and Mammy. The Guests awaken to the theme song of the movie and are served a full breakfast in the formal dining room. Later in the day they may sip iced tea on the front verandah and watch the horses grazing in the pasture. Guests often want to see the Basshams' private collection of *Gone With the Wind* memorabilia.

Located 35 minutes south of Jonesboro, the fictitious Tara is a popular spot for catered luncheons, afternoon teas, barbecues, balls, and weddings. Packaged as Under the Peach Tree, Dixie in Georgia, The Confederate Countryside, and Moonlight & Magnolias BBQ and Ball, they are priced from $12.95 to $49.95 and include tours of the plantation, admission to the Gone With the Wind Museum, outdoor entertainment, and parking.

Gainesville

The Dunlap House

635 Green Street
Gainesville, GA 30501
770-536-0200
Fax: 770-503-7857
b_ventress@compuserve.com
http://www.bestinns.net./

> A bed-and-breakfast inn
> that's ideal for corporate
> clients

Innkeepers: Ben and Ann Ventress. **Accommodations:** 10 rooms (all with private baths). **Rates:** $105–$155. **Included:** Full breakfast. **Payment:** American Express, MasterCard, Visa. **Children:** Not appropriate. **Pets:** Not allowed. **Smoking:** Allowed on verandah only. **Open:** Year-round.

➤ **The beautiful 1910 home was built of timber from trees on the property by the Dunlap family. Before it was totally renovated into a bed-and-breakfast inn in 1985, it had served as apartments for about forty years.**

When Ben and Ann Ventress found the Dunlap House closed and needing new owners, they knew their dream of becoming innkeepers had come true. They took possession in September of 1992 and have been enjoying their new profession ever since. Ben practiced dentistry in Atlanta and Ann was a corporate officer in a manufacturing company.

The Ventresses, true professionals when it comes to dishing out southern hospitality, have brought love and warmth back to the house. The hosts welcome visitors with refreshments at check-in time. The next morning they serve a full breakfast of cereals, hot egg dishes, fruit, freshly squeezed orange juice, hot breads, and coffee and tea — either in the common area, on the verandah, or in the guest room. They do not offer dinner, but guests only have to walk across the street to Rudolph's, a restaurant specializing in Continental cuisine.

The guest rooms at the Dunlap House are decorated in elegant fabrics and plush carpeting and furnished in period reproductions. Each room has an individual thermostat, telephone, remote-control cable television, writing desk, computer data port, built-in hair dryer, and 24-hour security. Also provided are extra-plush towels, a terrycloth robe, and bottled Georgia mountain mineral water. Fax and computer printing are available.

The inn caters to business travelers by offering every convenience and amenity that might make their stay more comfortable. Honeymoon couples and vacationers also appreciate the caring attitude of the innkeepers. Dunlap House has entertained such celebrities as Tom Cruise, Paul Newman, Charles Kuralt, and Denis Weaver.

Hawkinsville

The Black Swan Inn — Country Inn & Restaurant

411 Progress Avenue
Hawkinsville, GA 31036
912-783-4466

> A distinctive inn and restaurant in Georgia's historic heartland

Innkeeper: Mary Jean Pace. **Accommodations:** 6 rooms (all with private baths). **Rates:** $80–$85. **Included:** Continental breakfast. **Payment:** MasterCard, Visa. **Children:** Not appropriate. **Pets:** Not allowed. **Smoking:** Not allowed. **Open:** Year-round.

➤ **Since the 1920s, harness horse trainers have made Hawkinsville their winter home.**

The Black Swan Inn, a turn-of-the-century home that has been renovated into an inn and restaurant, takes its name from the steamboat era, when a vessel called the Black Swan used to carry dry goods, cotton, and passengers up the Ocmulgee River from Savannah to Hawkinsville. The town has been known since the 1920s, however, as the harness-racing capital of Georgia, because trainers use it as their winter home.

The Southern Colonial–style home was built as a family residence for James P. Brown, a prominent cotton planter, state politician, entrepreneur, hotelier, and restaurateur. Today it welcomes visitors to relax on its rocker-lined verandahs and enjoy the ambiance of its Victorian interiors. The inn has six guest rooms, each appointed with selected antiques, a fireplace, ceiling fan, color television, telephone, and private bath. The VIP room features a whirlpool bath. Two rooms are available as a suite.

A complimentary Continental breakfast with homemade pastries is served in the main dining room or on the sun porch. A full southern breakfast is available upon request. In the evening guests may enjoy Continental cuisine with a French flair in the softy-lit elegant restaurant. Menu selections include filet mignon, steak au poivre, veal scaloppini, chicken Marsala, and other selections. Reservations are required.

Helen

The Helendorf River Inn & Towers

P.O. Box 305
Helen, GA 30545
706-878-2271, 800-445-2271
Fax: 706-878-2271

> An alpine inn in an alpine
> mountain village

Innkeepers: Richard and Barbara Gay. **Accommodations:** 97 rooms (all with private baths). **Rates:** $44–$69 December–March; $54–$79 April–May, November; $74–$99 June–October. **Payment:** Diners, MasterCard, Visa. **Children:** Welcome. **Pets:** Allowed in designated rooms. **Smoking:** Allowed. **Open:** Year-round.

➤ **The transformation of Helen from a simple mountain hamlet to an alpine village in order to attract tourists has paid off. It put Helen on the map, and today the town welcomes busloads of visitors.**

The inn looks like something you might lift out of the pages of *Heidi*, and so does the entire town for that matter. Several years ago, Helen merchants and city fathers transformed their ordinary town into a Bavarian village, and today it is the biggest tourist center in the North Georgia mountains. (Oktoberfest begins on Thursday after Labor Day and is celebrated on Thursday, Friday, and Saturday evenings in September and every night except Sunday in October.)

The alpine theme, down to flower boxes and colorful flags, prevails at the Helendorf. All the rooms have a Bavarian look, and the staff dresses in costume. Built in 1973 on the site of an old sawmill, the inn overlooks the Chattahoochee River, made famous by the poet Sidney Lanier. Complimentary coffee is available all day long, and guests are treated to complimentary coffee and Danish every morning. Richard and Barbara Gay will gladly suggest restaurants and direct you to shops and attractions within walking distance.

There are several choices of rooms at the inn. All are equipped with color cable television and telephone. River rooms have in-room coffeemakers and private balconies overlooking the Chattahoochee; the suites have fireplaces, Jacuzzis, kitchens, and balconies. The Top of the Tower (in the tower) features a sitting area, kitchenette, and king-size bed. Guests enjoy the covered heated pool.

Unicoi State Park Lodge and Conference Center

Highway 356, P.O. Box 849
Helen, GA 30545
706-878-2201, 770-389-7275,
800-864-PARK
Fax: 706-878-1897
http://www.ncc44.com/ga-st-pk/frames/stinunic.htm

A resort park in the mountains

General Manager: William Bentley. **Accommodations:** 100 rooms (all with private baths); 30 cottages (with private baths, fully equipped kitchens, and fireplaces). **Rates:** Lodge rooms, $59–$89; cottages, $65–$125. **Payment:** Major credit cards. **Children:** Welcome. **Pets:** Not allowed. **Smoking:** Smoking and nonsmoking rooms. **Open:** Year-round.

➤   **One of Georgia's most popular state parks, Unicoi offers many recreational choices.**

Surrounded by the Chattahoochee National Forest of the Georgia Highlands just outside the alpine village of Helen, Unicoi State Park offers contemporary lakeside lodging amid its 1,000 acres. Groups usually prefer the lodge with its numerous gathering spots plus the full-service dining room that offers three buffet-style meals a day. Individuals and families like the privacy of the cottages, most of which are located near the lodge. Ten of the older structures are in a different area of the park. The one-, two-, and three-bedroom units are fully furnished and equipped for light housekeeping and have fireplaces.

The park's conference center offers a variety of meeting rooms that are ideal for groups of up to four hundred people. The center provides audiovisual equipment, copy and fax services, and banquet service, either buffet style or individual seating.

The lake offers canoeing, paddle boating, fishing, and swimming. Hikers enjoy the park's many trails, including one that leads to Helen. Unicoi also has a world-class mountain bike trail. There are also tennis courts, plus a year-round golf package.

Lake Lanier Islands

Renaissance PineIsle Resort

9000 Holiday Road
Lake Lanier Islands, GA 30518
770-945-8921, 800-HOTELS-1
Fax: 770-945-1024
http://www.renaissancehotel.com

| A world-class resort with recreational opportunities galore |

General Manager: Tom Marello. **Accommodations:** 241 rooms and 9 suites (all with private baths). **Rates:** $124 mid-November–mid-March, $166 mid-March–mid-November. **Included:** Coffee and newspaper with wake-up call, shoeshine, valet parking, afternoon tea, guided lake cruises, and many recreational activities. **Payment:** Major credit cards. **Children:** Welcome. **Pets:** Not allowed. **Smoking:** Smoking and nonsmoking rooms. **Open:** Year-round.

➤ **At Christmastime, Santa Claus arrives by boat. Thanksgiving and Christmas dinners are staged annually for the adults.**

Perhaps Georgia's most luxurious island resort, Renaissance PineIsle Resort is located on Lake Lanier just 45 minutes north of Atlanta. Surrounded by 38,000 acres of water, it features an 18-hole championship golf course designed by Gary Player, which was the site of the LPGA's Nestle World Championship for five years in the late 1980s. In addition to golf, guests can play tennis, go horseback riding, ride bicycles, fish for bass, enjoy the water park, and participate in numerous water-related sports. There is even a hot tub big enough for twenty-one people. Many activities and amenities are complimentary, including the weight room, aerobics classes, pontoon boat cruises, and organized sports like beach volleyball, shuffleboard, and horseshoes.

Because of its unlimited recreational offerings, the resort is ideal for families and groups. There is something for everyone. During the summer months the resort has a formal children's program, so that parents can enjoy golf, tennis, and other activities. The summer schedule is filled with organized activities from daylight to dark. Golf, tennis, water skiing, romance, fall foliage, and family fun packages are very popular.

Dining is an important feature of PineIsle as well. The resort has three restaurants, plus a lounge with live entertainment during peak seasons, and 24-hour room service. Breezes Restaurant, overlooking the lake, features American regional cuisine with an emphasis on prime aged beef and fresh seafood; the less formal Clubhouse offers light breakfasts and lunches; and the outdoor Marina Grill is known for its hamburgers and sandwiches.

The resort offers 213 rooms, 28 spa rooms, and 9 suites — all recently refurbished and upgraded. All have cable TV, private balconies or terraces, safes, and refreshment centers. The spa rooms all have an individual hot tub spa on a private, enclosed patio. Established in 1975, Renaissance PineIsle Resort has earned Mobil's four stars and AAA's four diamonds for twenty consecutive years.

Macon

1842 Inn

353 College Street
Macon, GA 31201
912-741-1842, 800-336-1842
Fax: 912-714-1842, Ext. 41

> An elegant vintage inn

Vice President and General Manager: Phillip T. Jenkins. **Accommodations:** 21 rooms (all with private baths). **Rates:** $95–$165. **Included:** Continental breakfast, hors d'oeuvres, shoeshines, fresh flowers, newspaper. **Payment:** American Express, MasterCard, Visa. **Children:** 10 and older welcome. **Pets:** Not allowed. **Smoking:** Smoking and nonsmoking rooms. **Open:** Year-round.

➤ **Amenities that really count have been incorporated into this elegant inn in the heart of Macon — from fresh flowers to shoeshine service to assistance with dinner reservations. The inn has been awarded a four diamond and a four star rating.**

Phillip T. Jenkins, a management consultant, had been looking for an inn for a long time when he happened upon the 1842 Inn. Fortunately for him, it was just the type of place he had dreamed of owning, and it was for sale. Since taking over the Greek Revival mansion and the adjoining Victorian cottage, which had served as an inn since 1985, Jenkins has been sprucing them up — adding new fabrics, paints, and wallpapers. The inn is furnished in period antiques and quality reproductions.

Jenkins has retained some of the traditions established by the original owners, and he's also added an evening cocktail hour, open to guests and local residents. Hors d'oeuvres are complimentary, and drinks are offered through the cash bar. Through a special arrangement, guests may dine at the exclusive Macon City Club, or they may opt for local restaurants. Turndown service with imported chocolate mints is offered while guests are out to dinner, and shoes are shined while they sleep.

In the morning a Continental breakfast of fresh juice, fruit, breads, pastries, tea, and coffee is delivered on a silver tray to the room, along with the morning newspaper and fresh flowers. Some of the rooms have whirlpool tubs and gas-lit fireplaces.

Newnan

The Old Garden Inn

51 Temple Avenue
Newnan, GA 30263
770-304-0594
Fax: 770-304-9003

A B&B created with comfort in mind

Innkeepers: Ron and Patty Gironda. **Accommodations:** 5 rooms (all with private baths). **Rates:** $75–$99. **Included:** Full gourmet breakfast, afternoon refreshments, chocolates with turndown service. **Payment:** American Express, MasterCard, Visa. **Children:** Check with innkeepers. **Pets:** Not allowed. **Smoking:** Not allowed. **Open:** Year-round.

➤ **Though the Old Garden Inn was built many years after Sherman marched through Georgia, he spared the antebellum mansions of Newnan because so many of them were used as hospitals during the war.**

Ron and Patty Gironda have gone out of their way to provide every comfort a guest might need or want at their turn-of-the-century Greek Revival bed-and-breakfast, one of many beautiful mansions in Newnan. The white Adirondack furniture with its linen pillows invites guests to relax on the spacious white-columned porch (the inn's most popular gathering spot), as does the overstuffed furniture found in all the public rooms. All of the guest rooms are designed to appeal to the special tastes of individual guests. The king and queen beds are covered in custom-made bed covers, summer quilts, and high-count cotton sheets. The bathrooms feature hair dryers, English toiletries, and fluffy towels. The music room has antique art and the music of Enya, DiBlasio, and other New Age artists. The Hazelnut Cappuccino machine is available 24 hours a day. Guests are welcome to help themselves to whatever they find in the well-stocked refrigerators on each floor, as well as the kitchen.

Patty's talents as an interior decorator are evident everywhere in the house, but she's also an excellent cook, thanks to her Louisiana upbringing. Mornings begin with award-winning coffee, blended juices with fruited ice cubes, and a strawberry-banana and red grapefruit compote with blackcurrant cream sauce. This is followed by a hot plate of banana dumplings with raspberry sauce, crepes with raspberry cream and peaches, Monte Carlo breakfast sandwiches, eggs Benedict, or Georgia Peach Breakfast Taco (a crisp shell filled with fruit, homemade crème fraîche, and raspberry syrup from Germany).

The Girondas continue to make improvements at the inn. In anticipation of Olympic guests in 1996, they added a picket fence with a rose arbor, replaced the front walkway with brick, and added a small knot garden. The gardens of the one-and-a-half-acre estate include a wisteria arbor, herb garden, and pecan grove. Dee Keller, an internationally known stencil artist, has decorated hallways in a garden theme.

Parrott-Camp-Soucy Home and Gardens

155 Greenville Street
Newnan, GA 30263
770-502-0676
Fax: 770-502-0139

**A B&B that's a beautiful
Greek Revival home**

Innkeepers: Rick and Helen Cousins. **Accommodations:** 4 rooms (all with private baths). **Rates:** $105–$165. **Included:** Full breakfast, afternoon refreshments, turndown service. **Payment:** MasterCard and Visa. **Children:** Not appropriate. **Pets:** Not allowed. **Smoking:** Allowed on grounds. **Open:** Year-round.

➤   **Newnan, located 45 minutes southwest of Atlanta, contains some of the state's most prized architectural treasures, including the Parrott-Camp-Soucy Home and Gardens. Passersby call it a "traffic stopper."**

After searching for two years in five states, Rick and Helen Cousins, both computer consultants, purchased their dream B&B in 1994 — the Parrott-Camp-Soucy Home and Gardens in Historic Newnan. The Cousins' consulting work has taken them all over the world, and they got hooked on the idea of owning a B&B while living in San Francisco. Helen has since given up her profession to run the inn full-time, while Rick, working as a "lone eagle," telecommutes from their residence in the pre–Civil War carriage house.

Set amid four acres of formal gardens, the Greek Revival home was built in 1842 and assumed its Second Empire Victorian character in 1886 when it was renovated by Charles Parrott, the president of a local bank. Years later it fell into disrepair but was meticulously renovated again in 1989 by Chuck and Doris Soucy, who received a number of prestigious awards for their efforts — including the Great American Home Award from the National Trust for Historic Preservation. The home boasts 14-foot ceilings; elaborately carved mantles, staircase, and alcoves; original stained glass windows; reproduction wallpapers and elegant hand-sewn fabrics; fireplaces in every room; and quarter-sawn oak, black walnut, cherry, and maple paneling in the entry hall, ladies parlor, formal dining room, and library. Wide verandahs with kitty-cat cut-outs on the railings make a whimsical statement.

The four guest rooms are elegantly furnished with canopy and half-tester beds and coverlets fashioned by Helen and her mother. Each room has a working fireplace, comfortable sitting area, and a vintage bathroom. The Regency Room, the most elaborate room in the house, features a clawfoot slipper tub in front the fireplace, an 1890s ribcage shower, and a private verandah leading to the garden where there is a hammock for two.

Guests are served a French aperitif upon arrival, and then they may do whatever they like: take a dip in the pool, stroll in the garden, watch a black and white film classic from the library, or read a good book. The innkeepers will turn down the bed and light the fire for you while you're out to dinner. The full breakfast, served in the dining room, comes with freshly squeezed juices, homemade granola, fruit, muffins, quiche, French toast, and cappuccino.

The inn is a good home base for touring nearby attractions such as Callaway Gardens, the Little White House at Warm Springs, and all the sights of Atlanta.

Pine Mountain

Callaway Gardens

U.S. Highway 27
Mailing address: P.O. Box 2000
Pine Mountain, GA 31822-2000
706-663-5136, 800-282-5068
Fax: 706-663-5004

A beautiful resort offering some unusual attractions

President: George P. Fischer. **Accommodations:** 350 rooms, 155 cottages, 49 villas (all with private baths). **Rates:** Inn rooms, $90–$120; villas, $140–$675; cottages, $120–$550. **Included:** Gardens admission and attractions. **Additional:** Golf, tennis, and other sports fees. **Payment:** American Express, MasterCard, Visa. **Children:** Welcome. **Pets:** Not allowed. **Smoking:** Allowed. **Open:** Year-round.

➤ **Come summer, the big top goes up and Florida State University students stage the Flying High Circus. Every day there are water skiing shows, and the Masters Water Ski Tournament is held in May.**

If you want to get in touch with nature, Callaway Gardens is the ideal setting. There are hundreds of spots for quiet reflection, including a two-hundred-year-old log cabin and the Ida Cason Callaway Memorial Chapel, named for the founder's mother.

Nestled in the Georgia pines between Atlanta and Columbus, the 14,000-acre gardens were the dream of Carson J. Callaway and his wife, Virginia — a dream that rose out of the Depression to become one of the South's showplaces. Here, amid the azaleas, chrysanthemums, hollies, and pines, live more than 230 species of birds and other wildlife and 50 varieties of butterflies (which have their own 7,000-square-foot glass habitat). Mr. Carson's Vegetable Garden is a model garden that doubles as a setting for the PBS *Victory Garden* show, and the John A. Sibley Horticultural Center is a showcase of exotic and native plants and flowers. Many of the products grown in the gardens are offered for sale in the Country Store on top of Pine Mountain.

But Callaway Gardens is more than a lush, beautiful, green garden. It is a resort and conference center that offers every recreational amenity you can imagine: golf (63 holes in all), tennis, racquetball, a fitness center, fishing, boating, trap and skeet shooting, water skiing, swimming, hiking, jogging, and bicycling (more than seven miles of paved trails wind through the woods). Also, workshops on gardening, home horticulture, natural history, and wildlife are offered throughout the year.

Guests have their choice of three different types of lodging — the inn, cottages, or villas. The inn is designed like a typical motel, but the rooms have been refurbished recently with natural pine headboards and armoires, floral print bedspreads and drapes, and delicate butterfly prints. Bathrooms have been retiled and rewallpapered. Fully equipped cottages and villas in a secluded woodsy setting have one to four bedrooms. The cottages (the most rustic accommodations) have fireplaces and screened porches; the villas (the most luxurious) have fireplaces; screened porches, patios, and sundecks; washers/dryers; and separate baths for each bedroom.

The resort offers several dining options — from casual eateries such as the Beach Pavilion to fine dining in the Georgia Room. General dining is available in the Plantation Room, which serves three meals a day and Sunday brunch.

Callaway Gardens is also one of the largest resort conference centers in Georgia, with thirty-seven meeting rooms, a 10,000-square-foot ballroom, and all types of office support services.

The Veranda

252 Seavy Street
P.O. Box 177
Senoia, GA 30276-0177
770-599-3905
Fax: 770-599-0806

> An inn that gets rave
> reviews for its food

Innkeepers: Jan and Bobby Boal. **Accommodations:** 9 rooms (all with private baths). **Rates:** $99–$130, plus $25 per person for lunch and $40 per person for dinner. **Included:** Full breakfast or brunch buffet. **Payment:** Major credit cards. **Children:** Welcome if supervised by parents. **Pets:** Not allowed. **Smoking:** Allowed on verandah. **Open:** Year-round.

➤ **The Boals are always doing special things for guests, such as giving them flowers and leaving goodies on the pillow at night**

The Veranda calls itself a bed-and-breakfast inn, but it's really a country inn because of the emphasis on food. Guests rave about it and entice other people to have the same experience. Everything on the menu is made from scratch — from the fruit soup to twenty different desserts. A typical five-course candlelight dinner might include onion soup, shrimp mousse, broccoli and chicken casserole, salad (sometimes prepared with edible flowers), and raspberry layer cake. Favorite breakfast dishes include fresh fruit with home-churned sherbet, omelets with assorted fillings, or poached eggs on roast beef hash, grits or potatoes with bacon or ham, homemade sourdough bread, hot cinnamon rolls, and waffles with whipped cream and strawberries. A brunch buffet is offered several days a week.

As you might suspect, innkeepers Jan and Bobby Boal love to entertain. Jan was a professor at Georgia State University in Atlanta before he retired; his wife, Bobby, is an artist, lover of children's books, and wonderful cook. They're always doing special things for guests, such as giving them flowers and leaving goodies on the pillow at night.

The inn's other claim to fame is its kaleidoscope collection. You can examine them, twirl them to change the shapes and formations, and buy them in the Veranda's gift shop. They sell for as little as $2.50 and as much as $7,000. The Boals have other collections you can also enjoy — walking sticks, antiques, musical instruments, books, and games. The Boals have used their antiques collection to furnish the rooms, each in a different way. Some feature brass beds and oak dressers. The Rainbow Room has a whirlpool tub.

The Veranda, formerly the Hollberg Hotel, was built in 1906. For a number of years it hosted the annual reunions of Georgia's Confederate veterans and welcomed such distinguished guests as William Jennings Bryan. The inn is located in Senoia's historic district.

After the movie producer Jon Avnet and his wife Barbara treated Jessica Tandy and Kathy Bates to dinner at the Veranda, production of *Fried Green Tomatoes* was delayed for about twenty minutes the next morning while Avnet described the Veranda's food. Now fried green tomatoes are a frequent item on the menu.

Thomasville

Melhana — The Grand Plantation Resort

301 Showboat Lane
Thomasville, GA 31792
912-226-2290, 888-920-3030
Fax: 912-226-4585

> A beautifully resorted
> southern plantation now
> serves as an inn

Owner: Charles E. Lewis. **Accommodations:** 20 rooms; 10 more rooms to be added in 1998 (all with private baths). **Rates:** $150–$450. **Included:** Full plantation breakfast. **Payment:** Major credit cards. **Children:** Welcome. **Pets:** Not allowed. **Smoking:** Allowed outside. **Open:** Year-round.

➤ **During the 1930s, the movie *Gone With the Wind* was first screened in the Showboat, Melhana's private theatre.**

Plantation living at its best is offered at this historic plantation, located four miles south of Thomasville, just a few miles from I-10 and I-75. More than 40 landscaped acres provide the perfect backdrop for relaxation — whether it be strolling the gardens, playing tennis, receiving a massage, or working out in the fitness center. Horseback riding, skeet, bird and duck hunts, golf, antiquing, moonlight carriage rides, and touring neighborhood plantations are other options.

Developed by the industrialist Howard Melville Hanna, the antebellum Main House, with its heated indoor pool and English gardens, has been restored to its original grace and luxury. Guests are housed in the elegant guest rooms in the Main House, Special Occasion Cottage, Carriage House, Barns, and Stable. Other out buildings are currently being converted into accommodations, and at least ten more rooms will be available by the end of 1998. Some suites overlook the gardens, others have fireplaces, and many have Jacuzzi tubs for two. All have king/queen beds, cable TV, and a mini-bar. Every suite has a sitting area and is fully stocked with an assortment of personal amenities. Fresh flowers and terrycloth robes welcome each guest, and turndown service includes treats prepared in Melhana's kitchen. A newspaper is delivered daily.

Guests are served a full plantation-style breakfast featuring homemade breads in the main dining room, on the garden loggia, or in the privacy of their rooms. Light lunches are available to guests, and afternoon tea is served daily in the Hanna Room, followed by wine at 6 P.M. Dinner in the main house features southern regional cuisine and selected wines. In addition, 24-hour room service is available.

Melhana, one of Thomasville's renowned hunting plantations, is adjacent to Pebble Hill, a museum that is open to the public. The movie star Joan Crawford, the Duke and Duchess of Windsor, and other luminaries were guests at these opulent, private estates.

Young Harris

Brasstown Valley Resort

Young Harris, GA 30582
706-379-9900, 800-201-3205
Fax: 706-379-9999
jjohnson@brasstownvalley.com
http://www.brasstownvalley.com

> A new resort in an ancient
> Indian land

General Manager: Carol Simon. **Accommodations:** 102 lodge rooms (all with private baths) and 8 cottages (with private baths, wood-burning fireplaces, and kitchenettes). **Rates:** $89–$250. **Included:** Many recreational activities. **Payment:** Major credit cards. **Children:** Welcome. **Pets:** Not allowed. **Smoking:** Allowed in designated areas. **Open:** Year-round.

➤ **With its focus on the environment and cultural roots, Brasstown Valley has the blessings of the Georgia Department of Natural Resources, the U.S. Fish and Wildlife Service, and the Council on American Indian Concerns.**

Opened in the spring of 1995, Georgia's newest resort resembles some of the grand old resorts of yesteryear. It is built of fieldstone, glass, and wood in keeping with the beautiful Blue Ridge Mountains surrounding it — Brasstown Bald (which at 4,784 feet is the highest point in Georgia) and Three Sisters Mountain. The resort is located in the middle of 503 acres of forests and meadows in "The Enchanted Valley" of the former Cherokee Nation in what is now a natural habitat for bald eagles, peregrine falcons, red fox, and black bear.

At the center of the Brasstown Valley is the hexagon-shaped lodge with a 72-foot stone fireplace and vaulted ceiling with exposed pine beams. It offers over a hundred rooms and suites with fireplaces, some with balconies. In addition, there are eight secluded log cabins, each boasting four guest rooms, a grand parlor with a fireplace, a kitchenette, and a verandah. Colors, fabrics, and accents used in the interiors convey the feeling of earthiness and mountain culture.

Just about every recreation option a guest might want is offered at the resort. You can go hiking, trout fishing, horseback riding, rock climbing, and whitewater rafting. There is an 18-hole Scottish links style championship golf course, named by *Golf Digest* as one of the five best public golf courses in Georgia. In addition, the resort has tennis courts, a health club offering a plethora of amenities and activities, indoor and outdoor swimming pools, and more. The resort provides a seasonal children's program for kids aged 3 to 12, and the game room is available year-round. Guests may dine on North Georgia cuisine in the Dining Room or in the less formal McDivots, and most visitors enjoy cocktails in the Fireside Lounge. The resort has a huge conference center, complete with high-tech equipment and adventure and team-building programs. Guests may buy gifts and crafts, plus groceries and sundries, at the General Store and take care of all their golf and tennis needs at the pro shop on the property.

The Coast

Best Bed-and-Breakfasts

Brunswick
Brunswick Manor—A Historic Bed & Breakfast Inn, 140
Darien
Open Gates Bed & Breakfast, 143
Savannah
The Ballastone Inn & Townhouse, 150
East Bay Inn, 151
The Eliza Thompson House, 153
Foley House Inn, 154
The Gastonian, 155
The Kehoe House, 157
Lion's Head Inn, 158
Magnolia Place Inn, 159
President's Quarters, 162
River Street Inn, 163

Best City Stop

Savannah
Planters Inn, 161

Best Island Getaways

Cumberland Island
Greyfield Inn, 142
Little St. Simons Island
Little St. Simons Island, 148

Best Resorts

Jekyll Island
Jekyll Island Club Hotel, 145
Sea Island
The Cloister, 165

Best Seaside Retreat

Kingsland
The Lodge at Cabin Bluff, 147

Georgia was founded in 1733 by an aristocratic British philanthropist, General James Edward Oglethorpe. He settled a colony on bluffs overlooking the Savannah River. Planned as a haven for the insolvent and those seeking religious freedom, Savannah was laid out with public and residential buildings surrounding public squares. Remarkably, it escaped the Civil War destruction that ravished much of the state and was presented untouched and untorched as a "Christmas present" to President Abraham Lincoln by Union General William T. Sherman at the end of his march to the sea in December 1864.

Today, twenty-one tree-shaded squares, the "signatures of Savannah," remain in the historic district, dotted with fountains and statues. Downtown on Factors Walk and on Riverfront Plaza, overlooking the Savannah River, lively restaurants, lounges, and shops occupy warehouses and offices of long-ago cotton merchants (factors). Many historic Savannah house museums also welcome visitors. Among them are the Owens-Thomas House, one of the finest Regency structures in North America; the Juliette Gordon Low House, childhood home of the founder of the Girl Scouts of America; Federal-style Davenport House; the Green-Meldrim House, where Sherman briefly resided; and the Telfair Academy of Arts and Sciences, reputedly the South's oldest public art museum, housed in a splendid 1818 mansion. Of late, there's a keen interest in the privately-owned Johnny Mercer house, where the murder that is the focus of *Midnight in the Garden of Good and Evil* took place.

Savannah celebrates with green beer, green grits, and a rip-roaring St. Patrick's Day parade that is said to be second in size only to New York City's. Anytime you visit, be sure to sample a Savannah specialty — hoppin' john — black-eyed peas and rice seasoned with bacon drippings. It's reputed to bring you good luck.

Southward from Savannah, Georgia's Sea Islands — the storied Golden Isles — dot the coastline between the Atlantic and the Marshes of Glynn. They encompass one of the South's finest coastal playgrounds. State-owned Jekyll Island is a vacationer's paradise with golfing, tennis, bike trails, picnic facilities, unspoiled beaches, and numerous motor inns and campgrounds. It was once a retreat for millionaires, and some of their lavish "cottages" may be visited on a narrated tram tour.

On St. Simons, both a resort and a residential island, you can visit the remains of Fort Frederica, a National Monument commemorating General James Oglethorpe's 1742 victory over Spanish invaders at the Battle of the Bloody Marsh, ensuring British control of Georgia. St. Simons is connected by causeway to Sea Island, an idyllic residential retreat that's also home to one of the nation's premier luxury resorts, The Cloister.

Little St. Simons Island, once a private hideaway, is now accessible by a twenty-minute boat ride from St. Simons. Visitors can explore untouched beaches, go horseback riding, fish, canoe island creeks, and just relax in the unspoiled island wilderness. The largest and most southerly of Georgia's Sea Islands, Cumberland, has been protected as a National Seashore. Access is only via ferry from St. Mary's. A land of lonely beaches and slowing migrating sand dunes, it offers solitary beach basking, shelling, and campgrounds in shaded seaside areas. John F. Kennedy Jr., and his bride married in a chapel on Cumberland Island in 1996.

Brunswick

Brunswick Manor — A Historic Bed & Breakfast Inn

825 Egmont Street
Brunswick, GA 31520
912-265-6889

> A luxurious B&B with many amenities and excellent service

Innkeepers: Harry and Claudia Tzucanow. **Accommodations:** 9 rooms (6 with private baths, 3 with shared bath). **Rates:** $65–$100. **Included:** Full gourmet breakfast, high tea, homemade snacks and refreshments, fresh flowers, wake-up calls, turndown service, newspaper. **Payment:** MasterCard, Visa. **Children:** Supervised children welcome. **Pets:** Not allowed. **Smoking:** Not allowed. **Open:** Year-round.

➤ **A monument in a small park near the Old City Hall honors Major Columbia Downing, the original owner of Brunswick Manor. A prosperous businessman, he was the first president of the National Bank of Brunswick, now the Trust Company of Southeast Georgia.**

B&B pioneers in Brunswick, Harry and Claudia Tzucanow invite you to "step back in time" to their high Victorian B&B inn, which they purchased and renovated in 1988–89. (Both retired, they had lived on the coast of Connecticut, where he was a sales manager and she taught school. Their love of sailing brought them to Brunswick.)

Built in 1886 by Columbia Downing, the inn served as a family residence until World War II, when it became a rooming house for shipyard workers. After that, it was converted into an apartment house and then rescued from condemnation in the 1970s and eventually restored.

Avid collectors of antiques (and British cars), the Tzucanows filled the large house with their own personal collection of furniture, Oriental carpets, and art. The grand mansion features 14-foot ceilings, a carved oak stairway, antique lighting fixtures, and full floor-length windows topped with stained glass "eyebrow" windows.

Each guest room could be the feature of an interior design magazine. Canopied queen-size beds are dressed in designer linens and down pillows, and the bathrooms have sandalwood- scented toiletries and terrycloth robes. The Romance of the Sea room won a national award from *Country Inns* magazine, as well as Waverly Fabrics' "Room of the Year" contest. Two rooms in the house have kitchen areas. All are air-conditioned and have ceiling fans. Television sets and VCRs are available in some rooms. (The innkeepers ask that parents supervise their children at all times because of the glass greenhouse and a deep fish pond on the property.) The main house has six guest rooms; the annex, four.

Providing every comfort for their guests, Harry and Claudia place seasonal nosegays and African violets in the rooms, as well as bottled water, a fruit and cheese tray, and sherry. They serve a full gourmet breakfast featuring local dishes and have high tea every afternoon at four o'clock. They offer wake-up calls and message service, van or Jaguar limousine on request to and from the airport and local restaurants, dinner reservations, newspapers, and local maps. The house library, table games, and lawn croquet are available to guests, as are cold beverages and homemade snacks. They often give tours of the house. They also offer private day sails aboard their two boats — *China Doll* and *Alamar* — and bicycles with van delivery and pickup to nearby barrier islands. On holiday weekends the innkeepers offer special activities and meals. Their honeymoon package ($349, plus tax) includes two nights in the Savannah Gardens Suite, chilled champagne and fresh fruit upon arrival, a gourmet breakfast served in the formal dining room, Victorian High Tea, and a three-hour cruise and lunch aboard the *Alamar.*

Cumberland Island

Greyfield Inn

Cumberland Island, GA
Mailing Address:
P.O. Box 900
Fernandina Beach, FL 32035-0900
904-261-6408

> **An elegant inn on a secluded island**

Innkeeper: Brycea Merrill. **Accommodations:** 13 rooms, including 2 suites (5 with private baths, 8 with shared baths). Rates: $275–$350, plus 17% service charge (two-night minimum on weekends). **Included:** Breakfast, picnic lunch, and gourmet dinner; canapes at the bar; bicycles; guided island tour or historical outing; private ferry transportation. **Payment:** MasterCard, Visa. **Children:** 6 and older welcome. **Pets:** Not allowed. **Smoking:** Allowed in bar. **Open:** Year-round.

➤ **Accessible only by ferry, much of Cumberland Island is included in the National Seashore, and the National Park Service only allows 300 visitors at one time.**

Though the Greyfield Inn prides itself on protecting the anonymity of guests, it's no secret that John F. Kennedy, Jr., and his bride Carolyn, along with their close relatives and friends, celebrated here following their wedding in a simple chapel on the island.

The inn was built in 1901 as a private home for Margaret Ricketson, the daughter of Thomas and Lucy Carnegie. Lucy R. Ferguson, the Carnegie's granddaughter, and her family opened it to guests in the 1960s. Furnished at the turn of the century with family heirlooms and antiques, Greyfield is considered the ultimate getaway.

Guests have a choice of rooms in the main inn or cottages on the 1,300-acre estate. Many rooms overlook the salt marshes or the ancient moss-draped oaks. Ceiling fans in the rooms provide cooling breezes in the summertime, and fires in the fireplaces provide warmth in the winter. A favorite room is the Master Suite, with an antique king-size bed and a private sitting room.

Breakfast consists of fresh fruit, freshly squeezed orange juice, homemade muffins, bacon or sausage, eggs or pancakes, or the chef's special of the day. Picnic-style lunches are packed in baskets or knapsacks and may be picked up after breakfast. The candlelight dinner is served in the formal dining room and features fresh seafood, Cornish game hen, lamb or beef tenderloin, homemade breads, fresh vegetables, desserts, and wines. Hors d'oeuvres are served in the bar, an old gun room, during the evening cocktail hour, and drinks are on the honor system. Attire is usually casual, except for dinner.

Island outings may be arranged with the staff naturalist, and you may explore the island on your own. Birding, shelling, fishing, clam digging, swimming, hiking, beachcombing, or hunting for shark's teeth are favorite pastimes. Bicycles may be rented for a half-day or full-day, but they are not allowed on the beaches. Visitors should bring all essentials with them, as there are no stores on the island.

Darien

Open Gates Bed & Breakfast

Vernon Square
Darien, GA 31305
912-437-6985

An interesting inn that is off the beaten path

Innkeeper: Carolyn Hodges. **Accommodations:** 4 rooms (2 with private baths, 2 with shared bath). **Rates:** $55–$63, plus $15 for each additional person (10 percent discount with stay of four nights or more, two-night minimum on most weekends); tours, $30–$60. **Included:** Full breakfast. **Payment:** Cash or checks. **Children:** Check with innkeeper. **Pets:** Check with innkeeper. **Smoking:** Allowed on porches and in gardens. **Open:** Year-round.

➤ **Carolyn Hodges conducts tours of historic rice plantation canals in a 16½-foot blue and white canopied runabout. She also provides birding tours in remote areas.**

Located on the square in Darien, a town that seems to have stood still for years, is a bed-and-breakfast inn that is interesting and fun. Innkeeper Carolyn Hodges withdrew from urban life and is the force behind this unique operation. Recently recognized by the Georgia Bed & breakfast Council for her outstanding efforts in the hospitality field, she's an avid environmentalist who is equally at ease cooking sumptuous breakfasts or offering boat tours of the surrounding barrier islands and the Altahama River, the largest east of the Mississippi.

Carolyn's home is a two-story simple plantation house, built in 1876 by timber baron Isaac Means Aikens, with a front porch and wonderful surrounding gardens. She offers four guest rooms, each special in its own way. The Timber Baron's Room is the only one in the house with private bath. The Quilt Room, which has a private entrance, features quilts stitched by three generations of family quilters. The Botanical Room focuses on botanical prints and nature books and has heart pine flooring. The Nanny's Room, ideal for children because of its twin beds, features antique children's books. An extensive library covers the Gullah culture, black history, nature, and coastal history.

Breakfast includes plantation pancakes, shirred eggs, baked apples, oatmeal, lots of fresh fruit, a collection of jams served in special jam pots, coffee, and other dishes. On arrival, guests are served fresh lemonade or Harvey's Bristol Cream sherry.

Carolyn offers a land tour of Butler Island, where Pierce Butler had a vast plantation that was the subject of his wife Fannie Kemble Butler's journal (written in 1838–1839). She also conducts tours of the Altamaha River delta rice islands, Blackbeard Island, and the marshes.

For such a small town, Darien has figured prominently in history. The Spanish established the first European settlement in North America here in 1526. The town was burned by black troops during the Civil War, an event that was the subject of the film *Glory. Praying for Sheetrock,* a nonfiction work that told of the coming of civil rights to the county, also featured Darien.

Jekyll Island

Jekyll Island Club Hotel

371 Riverview Drive
Jekyll Island, GA 31527
912-635-2600, 800-535-9547
Fax: 912-635-2818

A historic retreat for the elite now serves all

General Manager: Kevin Runner. **Accommodations:** 114 rooms and 20 suites (all with private baths, 8 suites with large Jacuzzis; 24 rooms with wood-burning fireplaces). **Rates:** $109–$250, March–late August; $95–$229, late August–late November; $80–200, late November–mid-March; $20 for rolla-ways. **Payment:** Major credit cards. **Children:** 17 and under free with parents. **Pets:** Not allowed. **Smoking:** Smoking and nonsmoking rooms. **Open:** Year-round.

➤   **At least two historic events of national importance occurred at Jekyll Island — the Federal Reserve Act was drafted here in 1910 and the first transcontinental telephone call was made from here in 1915.**

Jekyll Island Club was once the elite of the elite, *la crème de la crème*. From 1888, when it opened, until 1942, when it was abandoned, the club was a winter hunting retreat for the Rockefellers, Goulds, Morgans, Astors, Macys, Pulitzers, and their friends who had mansions in the major cities of the Northeast as well as homes in Newport, Rhode Island. "There is just one spot in the United States that affords the seclusion from the public gaze, the surcease from business, the freedom from social demands, and the complete relaxation from nervous tension that the millionaire seeks . . . a veritable retreat for all millionaires . . . Jekyll Island, Georgia," wrote Samuel M. Williamson in *Munsey's* magazine in 1904.

At first there was a 60-room clubhouse, then a 6-unit apartment building called Sans Souci (actually the first condo structure ever built), an annex, and finally several cottages (some of them measuring 8,000 square feet). The club had several golf courses, tennis courts, a swimming pool, stable, casino, bocci and croquet courts, and a marina to handle the arriving and departing yachts. In those days the only way to get to the island was by boat; today there is a causeway to Brunswick, which lies between Jacksonville and Savannah.

The state of Georgia has owned Jekyll Island since 1947, and the clubhouse was returned to its original splendor after a $20 million restoration. Several of the cottages are open for tours, and the area is a designated historic district. The hotel itself has been designated a Historic Hotel of America by the National Trust for Historic Preservation.

Guests who stay at the clubhouse have access to all the amenities the first club members enjoyed — golf, tennis, croquet, and swimming. J. P. Morgan's tennis court is still in use, as is the Oceanside Golf Course, built in 1898. In all, guests have access to 63 holes of golf and nine tennis courts. The island has ten miles of open beach, shaded by live oaks, and plenty of level terrain (about 20 miles of trails) for bicycling. The beach is about a mile away from the club, and complimentary transportation is provided to all areas of the island. A water park, and miniature golf are also available. The hotel offers a children's program during the summer months.

Rooms in the clubhouse have been decorated to reflect Victorian opulence. They featured shuttered windows and two-poster mahogany beds and armoires set off by rich fabrics. Some of the rooms have whirlpool tubs and/or fireplaces. The public rooms, also of the period, include extraordinary woodwork. The Grand Dining Room, with its fluted columns, shuttered windows, wall sconces, and fireplace, is an elegant setting for gourmet dining. Food is also available in the deli and at the beach club, and poolside cookouts are held when the weather permits. The club is ideal for small meetings.

Kingsland

The Lodge at Cabin Bluff

Kingsland, GA 31568
912-729-5960
Mailing address:
P.O. Box 30203
Sea Island, GA 31561
912-638-3611, 800-732-4752

A fishing and hunting retreat for groups and families

Owner: Sea Island Company and Mead Corporation. **General Manager:** Bill Miller. **Accommodations:** 16 rooms (all with private baths). Rates: $250–$400. **Included:** All meals and beverages, day trip to Cumberland Island, golf, and tennis. **Payment:** Major credit cards. **Children:** Welcome. **Pets:** Not allowed. **Smoking:** Not allowed. **Open:** Year-round.

➤ **Hunting is carefully regulated to preserve the quality of each outing, with knowledgeable guides to lead parties to the best spots. Deep sea and river fishing opportunities are excellent.**

Buffered by expansive forests and the Cumberland River, the Lodge at Cabin Bluff is a unique hunting and fishing retreat that is available for groups and individuals at specified times. One hour south of Sea Island, it sits at the edge of the Intracoastal Waterway amid 50,000 acres of woodlands and marshes. It provides the perfect setting for endless recreational pursuits — hiking, boating, river and deep sea fishing, hunting, kayaking, tennis, golf, billiards, swimming, exercising, aiming at sporting clays, and taking day excursions to the nearby Cumberland Island National Seashore aboard the vintage yacht *Zapala*.

Owned by the Sea Island Company and the Mead Corporation, the Lodge at Cabin Bluff, an Orvis-endorsed fly fishing and wing shooting facility, offers sixteen rustic yet elegant rooms in the Main Lodge and six cabins — ideal for family and group getaways. Meals, included in the rate, are a hearty fare with home-style breakfasts, midday meals, riverside oyster roasts, and open-air cookouts. A day trip to Cumberland Island, plus golf and tennis, are also included in the rate. Offshore fishing, golf instruction, and shooting lessons are extra.

One of the earliest hunting and fishing clubs in America, the Lodge at Cabin Bluff is steeped in history. The Camden Hunt Club was organized here in 1827. A century later, Howard Coffin, the founder of the Sea Island Company who made a fortune with the Hudson Motor Car Company, purchased the property. Coffin hosted some of the most influential people of the times here, including President Calvin Coolidge. The property was sold in 1942, but recently the Sea Island Company became involved through a joint ownership arrangement with Mead Corporation.

Little St. Simons Island

Little St. Simons Island

P.O. Box 21078
St. Simons Island, GA 31522
912-638-7472
Fax: 912-634-1811
lss@mindspring.com

| An island paradise where encounters with nature are routine |

General Managers: Kevin and Debbie McIntyre. **Accommodations:** 15 rooms (all with private baths; 2 rooms in Hunting Lodge have wood-burning stoves) **Rates:** $300–$525 (two-night minimum); use of entire island, $3,400–$4,600. **Included:** Three meals a day, cocktail receptions, transportation, use of boats and canoes, all activities. **Payment:** MasterCard, Visa. **Children:** 8 and older welcome during high season, all ages during summer. **Pets:** Not allowed. **Smoking:** Limited to outside areas. **Open:** Year-round.

➤ **The lodge has a small library with some obscure titles. Have you ever heard of *Journal of a Residence on a Georgia Plantation,* written around 1838 by Frances Anne Kemble?**

The only way you can get to Little St. Simons Island is by boat (a 20-minute trip from Hampton River Plantation on nearby St. Simons Island) — and you need a reservation. (The only vehicles on the 10,000-acre island belong to the staff.) When you arrive at Little St. Simons Island, you will be personally greeted by Debbie McIntyre, who manages the island retreat with her husband, Kevin. She gives you an orientation to the island, informs you about the meal schedule, and then escorts you to your room.

Your accommodations may be rustic if your room is in the 1917 Hunting Lodge, where everyone congregates for meals and parties. The River Lodge and Cedar House overlooking the marsh are a little more upscale, with contemporary furnishings and carpeting. Honeymooners and families enjoy the privacy of Michael Cottage, which has a porch and an outdoor shower in addition to the bath inside.

Meals are served family-style in the Hunting Lodge at 9:00 A.M., 1:00 P.M., and 7:30 P.M.; cereal and coffee are provided for early risers at 6:30 A.M. Guests meet for cocktails in the main lobby every night at 6:30. The home-cooked meals are hearty and delicious, with specials such as Lowcountry boil, featuring healthy portions of shrimp, sausage, corn, potatoes, and carrots. Picnic lunches can also be ordered.

After your initial encounter with other guests, you'll be on a first-name basis with everyone for the duration of your visit. There's no formal entertainment to speak of after dinner, unless there's a special slide show. Everyone seems content to retire early and listen to the cicadas through the open windows. Forget the TV, newspaper, and telephone; you can escape them here.

Little St. Simons teems with numerous species of birds, raccoons, opossums, alligators, loggerheads, armadillos, fallow deer, and snakes, including eastern diamondback rattlers. Guests go on nature walks and bird watches, take canoe trips, and go horseback riding, swimming, fishing, and crabbing.

Visitors to the island consider themselves quite lucky since Little St. Simons is the only remaining privately owned barrier island on the East Coast. Rice was grown on the island originally, but in 1908 the Berolzheimer family purchased the island to use the cedar trees in the manufacture of Eagle pencils. Finding the wood too gnarled for that purpose, they built a hunting lodge and have been enjoying the island ever since. No one hunts anymore, but family members return every November and December to celebrate the holidays.

Savannah

The Ballastone Inn

14 East Oglethorpe Avenue
Savannah, GA 31401
912-236-1484, 800-822-4553
Fax: 912-236-4626

| An elegant, luxurious B&B |

Innkeeper: Jean Hagens. **Accommodations:** 18 rooms (all with private baths, 6 with whirlpool tubs, 14 with fireplaces). **Rates:** $100–$225. **Included:** Full breakfast, afternoon tea, valet parking, turndown service, newspaper. **Payment:** American Express, MasterCard, Visa. **Children:** 16 and older welcome. **Pets:** Not allowed. **Smoking:** Allowed in bar. **Open:** Year-round.

➤ **This Savannah inn has an illustrious history — it was a private home, a bordello, apartments, and an inn.**

The Ballastone Inn was built in 1838 as a private residence for Major George Anderson, the commander of Fort McAllister. In 1864, it fell to General Sherman, and in 1892, Captain Henry Blum, president of the Germania Bank, enlarged it. In the 1920s it served as the Lester House apartments, only to become a bordello, frequented by many of the city's prominent citizens the following decade. In the early 1970s it gained respect because of its association with the Girl Scouts. And in the early 1980s, it was converted to an inn. Jean Hagens has recently refurbished the inn, giving it a fresh look.

A stay at the Ballastone begins with a beverage and an opportunity to talk with the concierge to map out what you want to do in Savannah. At night you get turndown service with chocolates and a cordial, and a terrycloth robe is provided for your comfort. If you want to watch a movie or read a book, you can check one out from the inn's library. Jean serves a full breakfast. She has also added valet parking as an amenity.

East Bay Inn

225 East Bay Street
Savannah, GA 31401
912-238-1225, 800-500-1225
Fax: 912-232-2709

A comfortable historic inn near the water

Innkeeper: Susan Steinhauser. **Accommodations:** 28 rooms (all with private baths). **Rates:** $109–$129 (10% discount with AAA and AARP cards). **Included:** Continental breakfast, afternoon reception, turndown service, parking. **Payment:** Major credit cards. **Children:** Welcome. **Pets:** Under 30 pounds allowed with $25 fee. **Smoking:** Smoking and nonsmoking rooms; not allowed in public rooms. **Open:** Year-round.

➤ **Guests usually congregate in the parlor between five and seven o'clock for wine and sherry and then browse through the collection of**

menus before deciding on a restaurant. Or they may compare notes on where they ate the night before and what they've seen that day.

One of Savannah's most delightful inns, the East Bay Inn is located in the city's Historic Waterfront District across from Emmett Park, within walking distance of great restaurants and quaint shops. As with most Savannah inns, parking is limited. Built in 1853, it was first used as a cotton warehouse and trading center. Later on, it housed J. S. Pihncussohn's Cigar and Tobacco Company. In the early 1980s it became the East Bay Inn. It is owned by the same investors who own Olde Harbour Inn, located on East Factors Walk.

East Bay offers 28 beautiful rooms, furnished with four-poster rice beds, armoires, and Oriental carpets. The rooms have all the modern conveniences, including private baths, direct dial telephones, cable television, and coffeemakers, with all the makings for coffee or tea. While guests are having dinner, the staff freshens the room, fills the ice bucket, turns down the covers, and leaves handmade chocolates on the pillow. They will also arrange carriage rides and tours.

The complimentary Continental breakfast buffet of fresh fruit, assorted cereals, muffins, juice, coffee, and tea is served in the quaint café. Skyler's Restaurant offers soups, sandwiches, wok dishes, and gourmet seafood, lamb, and beef dishes, all of which are moderately priced.

The inn offers fax and copy services for business travelers, as well as a small meeting room for corporate groups, weddings, and parties.

The Eliza Thompson House

5 West Jones Street
Savannah, GA 31401
912-236-3620, 800-348-9378
Fax: 912-238-1920
http://www.bbonline.com/ga/savannah/elizathompson

> **An inn that offers book tours**

Innkeepers: Steve and Carol Day. **Accommodations:** 23 rooms (all with private baths). **Rates:** $89–$189. **Included:** Full breakfast, wine and cheese reception, dessert and coffee, turndown service with chocolates. **Payment:** American Express, MasterCard, Visa. **Children:** Over age 12 welcome. **Pets:** Not allowed. **Smoking:** Allowed in designated areas. **Open:** Year-round.

➤ **Guests often wander down to Mrs. Wilks' Boarding House for a hearty lunch. The restaurant is a Savannah institution.**

An overnight stay here may provide some insight on *Midnight in the Garden of Good and Evil,* John Berendt's 1994 book that rocked Savannah. According to the innkeeper Carol Day, the book was written on Jones Street within a block of the Eliza Thompson House, and Mr. Berendt sometimes stays at the inn. As might be expected, the inn offers book tours.

Carol and her husband Steve purchased the Eliza Thompson House in the fall of 1995 and have totally refurbished the property, reclaiming hardwood floors and installing Oriental carpets. The inn consists of two homes, an 1847 three-story mansion and a carriage house. It has 23 guest rooms, all furnished in antiques.

The Days serve a deluxe full breakfast, created by one of the city's best chefs, in the courtyard or garden room. They also offer hors d'oeuvres and wine from 5:30 until 7:30 each evening, followed by desserts and coffee from 8:30 until 10 P.M. Lunch is available at several nearby restaurants, including the famous Mrs. Wilks Boarding House, a block away. The courtyard, with its three fountains and Ivan Bailey sculpture, is the site of catered parties, weddings, and receptions.

A three-diamond, three-star property, the Eliza Thompson House is named for its original owner, a hostess known for her southern hospitality.

Foley House Inn

14 West Hull Street
Savannah, GA 31401
912-232-6622
Fax: 912-231-1218
http://www.bbonline.com/ga/savannah/foley

A premier inn with every amenity and convenience

Innkeeper: Inge Moore. **Accommodations:** 19 rooms (all with private baths). **Rates:** $120–$225. **Included:** Continental breakfast, wake-up calls, afternoon tea, evening cordials, turndown service with chocolate mints upon request, shoeshine service, concierge, local telephone calls. **Payment:** American Express, MasterCard, Visa. **Children:** 12 and younger free with parents. **Pets:** Not allowed. **Smoking:** Allowed in designated rooms and areas. **Open:** Year-round.

➤ *Vacations* magazine rated Foley House Inn as one of the ten "most romantic inns" in the country.

Overlooking famous Chippewa Park, the Foley House Inn is one of Savannah's premier inns, and B&B connoisseurs, especially Europeans, love it.

Just about every amenity is provided here. Leave your quarters for street parking with the staff and ask them to feed the meter for you. Have your shirts laundered and ready to wear the same day. Request a videotape from the tape library and it will be delivered to your room. If you have a craving for popcorn, that can be arranged as well. These are but a few of the many services the inn offers. In the evening, wine, sherry, and port are offered in the parlor, and the staff will make dinner reservations and arrange tours. The Continental breakfast is served on silver service to the room or in the courtyard. Fax services are also available for a slight charge. The list goes on and on.

Danish-born owner Inge Svensson Moore has renovated the inn, which includes two Victorian townhouses and a carriage house, to reflect the rich heritage of Savannah and the house itself. Each room is a perfectly restored masterpiece, an interior designer's dream. Painted in Savannah's historical colors, the rooms are filled with antiques and Persian rugs, reflecting an English motif, and each door has an English name printed on it. Some rooms have hand-carved fireplaces that are used during the cooler months; some have large Jacuzzis. All have cable TV and video cassette players.

The Gastonian

220 East Gaston Street
Savannah, GA 31401
912-232-2869, 800-322-6603
Fax: 912-232-0710

> **An opulent, well-managed inn in the historic district**

Innkeeper: Anne Landers. **Accommodations:** 13 rooms and 3 suites (all with private baths, including 12 whirlpool tubs). **Rates:** $185–$350. **Included:** Full gourmet breakfast, afternoon tea, wine and cordials, concierge, turndown service. **Payment:** Major credit cards. **Children:** Over age 12 welcome. **Pets:** Not allowed. **Smoking:** Allowed on porches and decks. **Open:** Year-round.

➤   **The most innovative bath in the house is located in a closet in the Chief Tomochichi Room, named for the Indian chief who ruled the area when Savannah was settled. Round and deep, the tub has a seat.**

Lavish is the best way to describe this inn. The Gastonian has enjoyed a four-diamond rating eleven consecutive years. It is impeccable in its total presentation — from food to service to ambiance.

The inn makes its mark in its elegance, service, and cuisine. Each of the seventeen guest rooms is large and has its own working fireplace. The Gastonian is best known for the Caracalla Suite, named for the emperor who brought bathing into the home. The suite consists of two rooms, one dedicated to bathing and the other to sleeping. The eight-foot Jacuzzi for two, with polished brass fixtures, is located in the middle of the room. Nearby are two monogrammed terrycloth robes and a CD player with a selection of romantic music. To one side of the tub is a working fireplace; directly in front is the king-sized rice bed. Just a few steps away is a comfortable front porch where breakfast can be served under a slowly turning fan. Live oaks draped in Spanish moss screen the porch from the beautiful historic street.

Opened in 1997, the Garden Suite has direct access to the lovely walled garden. A splashing fountain in the small pond right outside the door may lull you to sleep, and there is also a side garden with another fountain.

The honeymoon suite is located by itself in the carriage house, which is decorated in an Oriental red and has a Chinese wedding bed with canopy. It has a private deck and a Chinese red Kohler birthday bath as well. Guests who stay here get a rose on the pillow at night.

Anne Landers has been an innkeeper for more than ten years, and she knows how to run a luxury inn. She is assisted by a professional staff who can provide details on Savannah's well-known attractions and perhaps tell you where to go for the freshest shrimp and seafood.

Iced tea and lemonade are offered to guests upon arrival, and bottled water is always available in the rooms. Hot coffee and a morning newspaper are delivered to each guest room daily. Guests may opt for breakfast in the room but most enjoy the company of other travelers in the dining room or the sunny kitchen. Chef specialties at The Gastonian include grits with tasso ham and poached eggs or crab quiche with fresh corn muffins. Afternoon tea always includes fresh ginger cookies that are baked right after breakfast. Guests may also enjoy a selection of complimentary wines with delicacies such as smoked salmon and homemade pate.

Hugh and Roberta Lineberger created the Gastonian in 1986. They brought two adjacent Regency Italianate houses, built in 1868, and renovated them as a unit. (A curved iron bridge, spanning the gardens, joins the two buildings.) They bought all the antique furnishings in England and decorated the houses in Savannah colors. Since purchasing the inn from the Linebergers, Anne has painted the inn and redecorated it with fresh fabrics, replanted the garden, and added a new phone system.

The Kehoe House

123 Habersham Street
Savannah, GA 31401
912-232-1020, 800-820-1020
Fax: 912-231-1587

A luxury inn that has won accolades

Innkeeper: Maureen Horvath. **Accommodations:** 15 rooms (all with private baths). **Rates:** $150–$250. **Included:** Full gourmet breakfast, hors d'oeuvres (with cash bar), nightcap, 24-hour concierge service. **Payment:** Major credit cards. **Children:** Welcome. **Pets:** Not allowed. **Smoking:** Allowed on verandahs only. **Open:** Year-round.

➤   **The Renaissance Revival mansion was built in 1892 by Irishman William Kehoe, the owner of a successful iron foundry. He often used the cupola on the roof to survey his thriving businesses.**

The Kehoe House opened to guests in early 1993 and quickly earned AAA's four-diamond rating. The inn is owned and managed by Consul Court Property Management, L. P., an Atlanta-based company that specializes in small luxury inns, with an emphasis on European-style service.

The Kehoe House, a restored, five-story Victorian townhouse on Columbia Square in the historic district, offers thirteen guest rooms, two suites, and a small meeting room. (Business meeting services are available.) The guest rooms are named for counties in Ireland. Constructed of brick, terra cotta, and iron, the house features projecting bays, porches, and balconies on the outside and high ceilings, marble mantels, a dozen fireplaces, and wainscoting on the inside. Consul Court restored the home and filled it with the finest antiques and accessories, including four-poster beds and armoires. It is on the National Register of Historic Places.

Unlike many Savannah inns that serve just a Continental breakfast, the Kehoe House serves a full meal. The inn also offers private, off-street parking.

Lion's Head Inn

120 East Gaston Street
Savannah, GA 31401
912-232-4580
800-355-LION
Fax: 912-232-7422
Lionshead@sys.conn.com
http://www.bbonline.com/ga/savannah/lionshead

> **An inn that's truly an elegant home**

Innkeeper: Christy Dell'Orco. **Accommodations:** 6 rooms (all with private baths). **Rates:** $95–$190; corporate rates available. **Included:** Continental breakfast, afternoon wine and cheese, turndown service, parking. **Payment:** Major credit cards. **Children:** Welcome. **Pets:** Not allowed. **Smoking:** Allowed on porches and courtyard. **Open:** Year-round.

➤ **The Dell'Orcos are always available to assist guests with dinner reservations and tour plans.**

Unlike many of Savannah's inns, which have a resident innkeeper, the Lion's Head Inn is a real home, occupied by a young, energetic family. And that's what makes this inn stand apart from all the rest. Many of Savannah's lodging establishments do a professional job, but they can't create the type of family atmosphere that you experience in an inn like the Lion's Head.

Seeking a lifestyle change in a warmer climate, owners John and Christy Dell'Orco moved to Savannah from Michigan in the spring of 1992. They spent months restoring the townhouse in the historic district before opening the inn to the public in the fall. Managing it and taking care of Jonathan and baby Gabrielle occupy most of Christy's time, while John practices law. Guests enjoy the children so much they often include messages to them in letters they send to Christy and John.

The 9,200-square-foot Federal-style home, with its wraparound porch and side courtyard, was built by J. R. Hamlet for the Wade family in 1883. Mr. Wade died before the house was completed, so his wife decorated it as she thought her husband would have wanted it. Knowing that he liked lions, she had a terra cotta lion's head placed in the steps; later a lion's head doorknocker was added.

Located north of Forsyth Park, the inn is furnished in Federal and Empire antiques, which Christy collected over a ten-year period throughout the East Coast. Among the collection are hand-carved furniture by Antoine Quervelle, a marble sculpture by F. Romanelli, and exquisite nineteenth-century light fixtures. The guest rooms are furnished with four-poster beds and Oriental carpets and have private baths. All the rooms have working fireplaces (except for the Natchez Suite on the second floor), cable TV, VCR, HBO, and telephones.

Wine and cheese are served in the late afternoon. The evening turndown service includes sherry and chocolate mints. The Continental breakfast features fresh fruit, homemade muffins, croissants, bagels, sweet rolls, granola, juices, tea, and coffee, served in the formal dining room. The inn is available for small weddings, receptions, and parties.

Magnolia Place Inn

503 Whitaker Street
Savannah, GA 3140
912-236-7674, 800-238-7674
Fax: 912-236-1145

| A Victorian inn where romance is guaranteed |

Innkeepers: Rob and Jane Sales and Kathy Medlock. **Accommodations:** 13 rooms (all with private baths, 6 with Jacuzzis, 11 with fireplaces). **Rates:** $110–$215. **Included:** Continental breakfast and afternoon beverages, evening desserts and coffee. **Payment:** Major credit cards. **Children:** Welcome. **Pets:** Not allowed. **Smoking:** Allowed on verandah only. **Open:** Year-round.

➤ **On display in the "collector's cabinet" in the parlor is a wonderful butterfly collection, including now extinct species. Hand-colored prints of butterflies complement the decor in the room.**

Even the name suggests soft summery breezes, moonlit nights, and romance. And when you stay at Magnolia Place Inn on Forsyth Park in Historic Savannah, you'll find an atmosphere made for romance.

Tea or complimentary wine are served every afternoon in the soft pink parlor with its many floor-to-ceiling windows. At night you get pralines and cordials with turndown service. For breakfast homemade muffins, hot baked croissants, and coffee are delivered on a silver platter to your room, or you may join other guests in the parlor or the patio. The concierge can always suggest things to do and places to go in Savannah.

Built for Guerrard Hayward, a local cotton merchant, in 1878, the two-story High Victorian inn features wraparound verandahs on two levels, parquet floors and inlaid marquetry, original hand-painted fireplace tiles and mantels, high ceilings, and antique furnishings purchased in England. Several of the beds are four-posters, dressed in canopies and side draperies. The house has served a number of different functions, and one of its most famous residents was Pulitzer Prize–winning poet Conrad Aiken.

Planters Inn

29 Abercorn Street
Savannah, GA 31401
912-232-5678, 800-554-1187
Fax: 912-232-8893

**A small hotel offering
personal service**

Innkeeper: Natalie Almon. **Accommodations:** 56 rooms (all with private baths). **Rates:** $99–$135. **Included:** Continental breakfast, afternoon tea, turndown service, shoeshine service, newspaper in lobby. **Payment:** Major credit cards. **Children:** Welcome. **Pets:** Not allowed. **Smoking:** Smoking and nonsmoking rooms. **Open:** Year-round.

➤ **Opening as the John Wesley Hotel in 1912, it was renamed the Planters Inn in 1984 after an extensive renovation.**

This small hotel, a landmark building, overlooks historic Reynolds Square and is but a short walk to Savannah's busy waterfront. The lobby is a center of activity, where guests check in and enjoy an evening wine reception. Service is a high priority here, and the staff are well trained. The inn has a three-diamond and a three-star rating.

All the rooms are furnished in the finest fabrics, and all have travertine marble baths with plush towels, cable TV, and telephones with modem ports. A large conference room accommodates groups.

Many of the services you find in a large hotel are available here. Staff members freshen the room at night, providing turndown service with chocolates. Valet service and in-room dining from the Pink House Restaurant are available. Small fees are charged for garage parking and the use of cribs and rollaway beds.

Presidents' Quarters

225 East President Street
Savannah, GA 31401
912-233-1600, 800-233-1776
Fax: 912-238-0849

A historic inn that's fit for presidents

Innkeeper: Stacy Stephens. **Accommodations:** 9 rooms and 7 suites (all with private baths). **Rates:** $137–$200. **Included:** Continental plus breakfast, afternoon tea, fruit basket and chilled bottle of wine, turndown with cordial and chocolates, newspaper, private parking. **Payment:** Major credit cards. **Children:** Welcome. **Pets:** Not allowed. **Smoking:** Allowed in restricted areas. **Open:** Year-round.

➤ **Since Presidents' Quarters opened, it has welcomed the actor Karl Malden, the federal judge Jack Camp, President Phillip Hillary of Ireland, and other famous guests.**

The two townhouses used in 1985 as a backdrop for the filming of a slave scene in Alex Haley's *Roots* look nothing like they did then. Restored and renovated in 1987, they're now an elegant hotel. The Greek Revival structures were built in 1855 by John Scudder for the Andrew Gordon family.

Using history and the presidency as the theme of this four-diamond inn, the property owner has created a luxury hotel around a unique concept. The rooms are furnished in pieces from the Thomasville Reproduction Heritage Collection, not the usual museum-type antiques found in many bed-and-breakfast inns around the city, and are decorated with framed prints and memorabilia relating to twenty U.S. presidents who have called on the colonial city. (These include Presidents George Washington, Theodore Roosevelt, Franklin D. Roosevelt, Woodrow Wilson, Calvin Coolidge,

Harry S. Truman, John F. Kennedy, Lyndon B. Johnson, Jimmy Carter, and others. President Bill Clinton has also visited the city, but he has not been honored by the inn yet.)

All the rooms have plush carpeting, gas log fireplaces, ceiling fans, standard-size Jacuzzi tubs, and terrycloth robes. Some have balconies or loft bedrooms. No modern convenience has been overlooked. Outdoors, guests enjoy the beautifully landscaped courtyard and a Jacuzzi splash pool. Oglethorpe Square across the street offers other diversions. Private walled parking is also provided. There is elevator access for the disabled.

River Street Inn

115 East River Street
Savannah, GA 31401
912-234-6400, 800-253-4229
Fax: 912-234-1478

A bed-and-breakfast inn overlooking the Savannah River

General Managers: Mike Brandon and Pamela Bradshaw. **Accommodations:** 44 rooms (all with private baths). **Rates:** $85–$145. **Included:** Continental breakfast, morning newspaper, afternoon reception, turndown service with homemade chocolates. **Payment:** Major credit cards. **Children:** Under 18 free with parents. **Pets:** Allowed with prior approval. **Smoking:** Allowed. **Open:** Year-round.

➤ **Casual dining is offered in Huey's Café, as well as Mates, the lounge. Both are located on River Street, along with other restaurants such as Riverhouse, Chartes House, and the Shrimp Factory.**

You have a bird's-eye view of the Savannah River from many of the rooms in this unique inn between Factor's Walk and River Street. You're also just steps away from restaurants, shops, and attractions.

Built in 1817, the building was first used as a warehouse for storing, sampling, grading, and exporting raw cotton, and when more space was needed, more floors were added. Cotton operations long terminated, the building was converted to another use in 1987 — a 44-room inn, complete with dining spaces, a lounge, and meeting rooms. Everything in the building has been modernized, but care has been taken to retain its charm, leaving brick walls, heavy timbers, and catwalks intact (a key factor in creating the five-level atrium).

The main entrance to the inn is from Factor's Walk, a series of alleys and walks on the bluffs. The reception area is used for guest check-in and the afternoon wine reception. Guest rooms are furnished in queen-size four-poster and canopy beds, large writing desks, and Oriental rugs. All the rooms have hardwood floors and polished brass bath fixtures; some feature balconies and floor-length windows. Thirty-three rooms offer river views; the rest overlook the park.

The hotel caters to individuals and business travelers. Guests are served a complimentary Continental breakfast accompanied by a morning newspaper in Huey's, and a wine reception is held on weekdays. In the evening homemade chocolates accompany turn-down service. The hotel has satellite television and direct-dial telephones and offers secretarial assistance and fax and copy services. Guests may play pool in the Billiard's Room and use the Downtown Athletic Club a block and a half away. A number of special packages are available.

Sea Island

The Cloister

Sea Island, GA 31561
912-638-3611
800-SEA-ISLAND
Fax: 912-638-5159

> **A seaside resort that caters to its guests**

Managing Director: Ted Wright. **Accommodations:** 262 rooms and suites (all with private baths). **Rates:** $147–$290 per person, double occupancy, mid-March–November and Christmas weeks; $124–$183, double occupancy, December–mid-February; $134–$220, double occupancy, mid-February–mid-March; single rates also available. **Payment:** Cash or checks. **Included:** All meals (recreational fees extra). **Children:** Welcome; children's program and babysitting services available. **Pets:** Not allowed. **Smoking:** Smoking and non-smoking rooms. **Open:** Year-round.

➤ **The Cloister is a wonderful honeymoon destination — listed in its 1945 guest register are George and Barbara Bush.**

Do you want to get in shape? Have a makeover? Learn to play golf via the latest instruction techniques? Ride a horse on the beach? If so, then the Cloister, consistent winner of Mobil's five stars and an endless list of other accolades (including *Zagat Survey*'s Travel Excellence Award), is the place to go. Located just off the coast of Georgia, the island resort offers tennis, croquet, bicycling, boat cruises, nature tours, skeet shooting, sunbathing, and a host of other activities. With the temperature on Sea Island hovering between 59 and 76 degrees year-round, you can participate in most activities even on the coldest winter days.

The Golf Learning Center, a joint venture of *Golf Digest* and the Sea Island Company, is one of the biggest draws to the Cloister. The center can simulate every swing, every play, every facet of the game of golf, providing endless practice opportunities for novices while also challenging advanced players. The center is a four-part facility with indoor and outdoor practice areas. The indoor area features swing training studios and a library including books, videos, conference rooms, and review areas; the outdoor area offers full swing and short game practice. The center holds golf clinics, intensive training sessions, junior sessions, corporate diversions, and a golf fitness program. The Cloister offers 54 holes of golf — 36 at the Sea Island Golf Club and 18 at the St. Simons Golf Club.

The Spa is also a state of the art facility, designed to address the total needs of guests, from makeup to hair to exercise. On staff are three estheticians, four massage therapists and a nutritionist — all professionally trained to give total fitness evaluations and suggest proper fitness programs.

The Cloister is also a great place for socializing. There are wine tastings, cooking classes, bridge rounds, dance clinics, and other special events. A children's program for kids aged three to eleven is available during the spring and summer and over the winter holidays.

The Spanish Mediterranean-style resort, built in 1928 by Howard Coffin, offers a variety of accommodations facing the ocean or the lush landscaped grounds. Guests receive nightly turndowns with chocolates, fresh towels twice a day, terrycloth robes, and other extras. Food at the Cloister is legendary, so dining can be quite an experience. Jackets and ties (black ties preferred on Wednesday and Saturday evenings) are required for men and boys over twelve in the main dining room and club rooms; elsewhere, casual attire is acceptable. Guests have their choice of dining options, all included in the Full American Plan — The Cloister Main Dining Room, Sea Island Beach Club, St. Simons Island Golf Club, and Sea Island Golf Club.

Kentucky

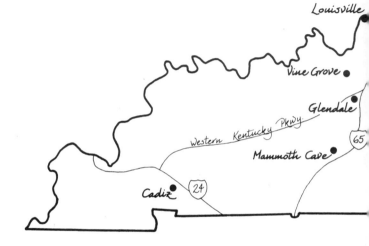

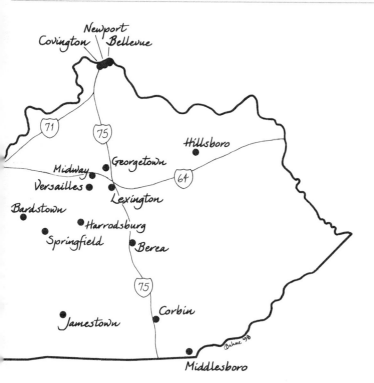

Best Bed-and-Breakfasts

Best City Stops

Best Country Inns

Best Farms and Guest Ranches

Harrodsburg
Canaan Land Bed and Breakfast, 191
Hillsboro
D. H. Resorts, 195

Best Historic Inn

Harrodsburg
Shaker Village of Pleasant Hill, 193

Best Parks

Cadiz
Lake Barkley State Resort Park, 181
Corbin
Cumberland Falls State Resort Park, 182
Jamestown
Lake Cumberland State Resort Park, 196
Mammoth Cave
Mammoth Cave Hotel/Lodge-Cottages, 203
Vine Grove
Otter Creek Park, 213

Best Plantation

Springfield
Glenmar Plantation, 208

Best Resort

Lexington
Marriott's Griffin Gate Resort, 198

Its western and northern flatlands bordered by the Mississippi and
Ohio rivers, Kentucky changes dramatically as one drives eastward. Vast Kentucky Lake and Lake Barkley, impounded by hydroelectric dams on the Tennessee River, surround the Land Be-

tween the Lakes, a pastoral 170,000-acre wooded peninsula managed by the Tennessee Valley Authority. In the south central region of this compact 40,395-square-mile state, the underlying limestone base is dotted with the world's longest known cave system, including the giant of them all — Mammoth Cave.

Northward beckons the picture-postcard bluegrass country, its gently rolling landscape dotted with magnificent thoroughbred horse farms. Here, too, are the state's largest cities, Lexington and Louisville. The limestone soil that nourishes the bluegrass is also responsible for another distinctive Kentucky product. Pure local spring waters, leached by the limestone, are used in the production of fine bourbon whiskey.

In eastern Kentucky, rimmed by tall sheer cliffs and rugged mountains, Daniel Boone passed through the Cumberland Gap with a hunting party in 1769 and returned to blaze the Wilderness Road in 1775. The passage became the major corridor for the westward movement, and many pioneers chose to settle in Kentucky rather than push farther into the interior. Kentucky became a county of Virginia, and by 1784 its population had zoomed to 30,000.

An independent lot, Kentucky frontier settlers petitioned Congress for admission to the Union, and statehood was granted in 1792. Ironically, this border state, which provided troops to both the Union and the Confederacy, also contributed each faction's president. Hodgenville was the birthplace of Abraham Lincoln, and Jefferson Davis was born at Fairview.

Kentucky boasts a state park system that's often called "the nation's finest." Facilities are so well distributed that a visitor is never more than a few hours' drive from one of the forty-seven resort or recreational parks and historical sites. Nine resort parks have golf courses and tennis courts and three — Lake Barkley, Kentucky Dam Village, and Rough River Dam — have their own airstrip.

In western Kentucky, the Tennessee River flows into the Ohio at Paducah, a major shipping port for more than 150 years. The historic river city is gradually undergoing a downtown transformation. Major catalysts of renovation were Market House Square, now lined with restaurants, shops, and restored 19th-century homes, and the refurbished 1905 Market House, now including a city museum, art center, and the Market House Theatre, which stages year-round community productions.

Also downtown, the Alben Barkley Museum, an 1852 Greek Revival house, displays memorabilia of the native son who served as vice president during the Truman administration. On Jefferson

Street at the I-24 loop, the splendid Museum of the American Quilter's Society exhibits hundreds of historic and contemporary quilts in a modern 30,000-square-foot structure. Guest quiltmakers present workshops and seminars year-round. Just across the river at Metropolis, Illinois, is entertainer Merv Griffin's Players riverboat gambling complex.

The 52,000-acre Mammoth Cave National Park lies northeast of Bowling Green and south of Elizabethtown, in a rugged woodland cut by the Green River. The caverns, among the great natural wonders of North America, include huge rooms highlighted by fantastic formations, accessible to the disabled. Historic attractions also beckon at every turn throughout central Kentucky: The little log cabin believed to be the birthplace of President Abraham Lincoln is preserved three miles south of Hodgenville, and memories of the Great Emancipator linger at Lincoln Homestead State Park north of Springfield, where you can see reproductions of his grandmother's home and his father's blacksmith-carpentry shop.

My Old Kentucky Home State Park at Bardstown is the site of one of the nation's most famous houses, Federal Hill, where Stephen Foster wrote "My Old Kentucky Home" while visiting his cousin, the owner. *The Stephen Foster Story,* by noted outdoor dramatist Paul Green, is presented here during the summer months. Reminders of stalwart Daniel Boone and the courageous pioneers also touch the region. At Old Fort Harrod State Park in Harrodsburg, Kentucky's oldest town, a reconstruction memorializes the first permanent English settlement west of the Alleghenies. "The Legend of Daniel Boone" outdoor drama is presented in the park on summer evenings.

Don't miss Shaker Village of Pleasant Hill, a beautifully restored 19th-century village of the Shaker religious sect, seven miles northeast of Harrodsburg. Its original buildings include a crafts shop with reproductions of graceful, clean-lined Shaker furniture; craftsfolk demonstrate in various houses. Dining rooms of the Trustees' Office Inn serve luscious Shaker and regional specialties, and overnight accommodations are offered in the restored buildings.

Berea, south of Lexington just off I-75, is the home of famed Berea College. A major crafts center, the college trains students in weaving, ironwork, woodcraft, and other traditional skills. Many of their works are sold in the school's Log Cabin Sales Room. The Appalachian Museum, also on campus, depicts the region's distinctive heritage, and artisans demonstrate their skills. Many students work at the Boone Tavern Hotel while studying hotel management.

In the rolling green heartland of bluegrass country, fast-growing Lexington, with a population of about 210,000, the site of Kentucky's first racetrack, offers many reminders of the Sport of Kings. At Keeneland Race Course there's thoroughbred racing in April and October. At the Kentucky Horse Park, visitors are greeted by a huge bronze statue marking the gravesite of the famed horse Man O' War. You can see the International Museum of the Horse and the American Saddle Horse Museum; experience the sights, sounds, and smells of a working horse farm on walking tours; explore the park in horse-drawn vehicles; and even opt for a horseback or pony ride.

Several historic homes welcome visitors: Ashland, the site of Henry Clay's home; Waveland State Historic Site, an 1847 Greek Revival mansion where Daniel Boone's great-nephew lived; and the Mary Todd Lincoln House, where Abraham Lincoln's wife spent her childhood.

It's just a short drive westward along I-64 to Frankfort, Kentucky's capital for almost two hundred years. The Kentucky River flows through the picturesque little city, and visitors can get a good view of it from the site of Daniel Boone's grave on a hill overlooking it. The Capitol, among the nation's loveliest, has its rotunda and dome patterned after the Hôtel des Invalides above Napoleon's tomb. Seasonal plantings are arranged in the face of the famous floral clock on the grounds.

Louisville's greatest glory comes the first Saturday each May, with the running of the Kentucky Derby, "the most exciting two minutes in sports." But Kentucky's largest city has much to offer other days as well. The lively, lavish Kentucky Derby Festival, ten days of fun and entertainment prior to the race, is an exciting range of parades, parties, picnics, balloon and steamboat races, country music concerts, and a mini-marathon. Churchill Downs Museum, at the historic track where the Derby is run, is open daily except during race seasons. It exhibits fascinating photographs, drawings, and memorabilia of Derby winners.

A bustling Ohio River port, Louisville combines genuine charm and friendliness with big-city verve. Major in-town restorations include Old Louisville, a refurbished Victorian residential neighborhood, and the West Main Street Historic District, which has one of the largest collections of 19th-century cast-iron storefronts outside New York City. In the heart of downtown, many old buildings and warehouses have been transformed into shops, lounges, and restaurants. The historic Brown and Seelbach hotels have also been impeccably restored. From Riverfront Plaza, a floating restoration, the 1914 *Belle of Louisville* sternwheeler offers sightseeing cruises on the Ohio River. You may also visit several historic houses year-round: Locust Grove, the magnificent 1809 retirement home of the city's founder, George Rogers Clark, and Farmington, built from a Thomas Jefferson design.

The Greater Louisville Fund for the Arts has been a catalyst for the city's cultural development. At downtown Riverfront Plaza, the Kentucky Center for the Arts is home to the Louisville Ballet and Orchestra, Kentucky Opera, and Stage One: Children's Theatre. The Tony Award–winning Actors Theatre of Louisville is internationally acclaimed for its Humana Festival of New American Plays, many of which go to Broadway. The splendid Museum of Art and Science reflects the history of Kentucky and Ohio River Valley and includes hands-on science displays, the Apollo 13 space capsule, and an IMAX theater with four-story screen. The J. B. Speed Art Museum has displays of modern and Old Masters paintings, African and Indian art, and works of contemporary Kentucky artists.

Upriver from Louisville lies Covington, linked to Cincinnati by Ohio River bridges and actually part of the city's metropolitan area. Downtown, its MainStrasse Village, a revitalized old German neighborhood, is a lively gathering place, with restaurants, shops, pubs, and fun-filled events, including a gala Oktoberfest. There's thoroughbred racing at outlying Turfway Park, where the Jim Beam Stakes is run.

In Kentucky's southeastern corner is the 20,280-acre Cumberland Gap National Historic Park, shared with Tennessee and Virginia. The states' borders converge at Tri-State Park, near the saddle of the gap. Along the way are glimpses of the sheer white rock cliffs that even Dan'l Boone found fearsome as he led an expedition through the pass before returning in 1775 to blaze the Wilderness Road.

For further information, contact the Kentucky Department of Travel, Department MR, P.O. Box 2011, Frankfort, Kentucky 40605, 502-564-4930 or 800-225-TRIP, extension 67.

Bardstown

Beautiful Dreamer B&B

440 E. Stephen Foster Avenue
Bardstown, KY 40004
502-348-4004, 800-811-8312

> **A B&B with all the charms of yesteryears**

Innkeepers: Dan and Lynell Ginter. **Accommodations:** 4 rooms (all with private baths). **Rates:** $79–$109. **Included:** Full breakfast, evening snacks and refreshments. **Payment:** MasterCard, Visa. **Children:** 12 and older welcome. **Pets:** Not allowed. **Smoking:** Not allowed. **Open:** Year-round.

➤ **The inn is literally a stone's throw from My Old Kentucky Home State Park, the site of Stephen Foster's home. My Old Kentucky Dinner Train, which travels the L&N's Historic Bardstown Branch line, is a popular attraction.**

Lynell Ginter fell in love with Bardstown as a child and visited here often with her parents from Ohio. After she and Dan were married, they began pondering the idea of opening a bed-and-breakfast in the popular tourist town. They had thought they would renovate an older home, but decided to build the brand-new Beautiful Dream when the property, located across from Stephen Foster's My Old Kentucky Home, became available. The result is a two-story Federal-style home featuring verandahs on each level, but with all the modern conveniences, including whirlpool tubs. Prior to opening the B&B, Lynell received on-the-job training at Brick House, a corporate inn in Lewisburg, Ohio.

The Ginter home features a formal parlor, where guests often gather around the grand piano after seeing *The Stephen Foster Story* outdoor musical drama nearby. A hearty breakfast is served in the formal dining room, and on cold days a blazing fire in the fireplace makes people linger. The inn has three guest rooms: Beautiful Dreamer, a favorite with honeymooners because of its canopied bed and double whirlpool bath; the Captain's Room, which has a fireplace and a single Jacuzzi; and the Stephen Foster Room, which is accessible to the disabled and on the ground level.

Bellevue

Weller Haus

319 Poplar Street
Bellevue, KY 41073
606-431-6829
800-431-4287

| A family home turned B&B |

Innkeepers: Vernon and Mary Weller. **Accommodations:** 5 rooms (all with private baths, one with a Jacuzzi for two). **Rates:** $75–$145. **Included:** Full breakfast. **Payment:** Major credit cards. **Children:** Welcome. **Pets:** Not allowed. **Smoking:** Allowed in designated areas. **Open:** Year-round.

➤ **It's not uncommon for the table to be dressed in vintage linens, china, crystal, and silver appropriate for the season — the perfect backdrop for Mary's home-baked goodies.**

Since the Weller Haus opened in 1989, this bed-and-breakfast inn has received nothing but praise. Located in the Historic Taylor Daughters District of Bellevue, a short distance from Cincinnati, it is listed with the National Trust. Owners Vernon and Mary Weller, who brought up their six children in the house, have received awards for their preservation efforts and are always receiving fan mail from satisfied guests.

The Wellers decided to open up their home when they became empty-nesters with lots of room to spare. The first things they did were give the house a facelift and build an addition in the back — a wonderful room overlooking the backyard garden in which guests often gather. After being in the business for three years, the Wellers purchased and renovated the house next door, yielding three additional rooms and a common kitchen for guests. From the second story you can see the church steeples and rooftops of the neighborhood, so rooms have names like Roof Top, Margaret's Porch, Church Steeple, and Nancy's Garden.

The original house is a two-story dwelling with gray siding, shuttered windows, and blue-gray striped awnings. The second property is a two-story brown-brick home with a tin roof and the same awnings. (The most elaborate room in this building features a Jacuzzi for two.) Both date to 1880 and have wrought-iron fencing surrounding them. Avid collectors of antiques, the Wellers have furnished the inn with period furnishings as well as some contemporary pieces.

Breakfast specialties are cinnamon bread and rolls and peach coffee cake, served with fresh fruits, juice, and coffee. The Wellers offer complimentary beverages to guests and often leave surprises such as cookies, fruit, and candy in the rooms. "Vernon and I truly enjoy meeting visitors and attending to their needs," says Mary. "We have a genuine interest in people."

Berea

Boone Tavern Hotel of Berea College

C.P.O 2345 Main at Prospect
Berea, KY 40404
606-986-9358, 800-366-9358
Fax: 606-986-7711

A historic hotel known for its spoon bread and friendly wait staff

General Manager: David van Dellen. **Accommodations:** 58 rooms (all with private baths). **Rates:** $55–$90. **Payment:** Major credit cards. **Children:** Welcome. **Pets:** Not allowed. **Smoking:** Limited. **Open:** Year-round.

➤ **The dining room, staffed mainly by students, serves such delicious specialties as southern peanut soup, spoon bread, chicken flakes in a bird's nest, and Jefferson Davis pie. There's a recipe for spoon bread — made of cornmeal, baking powder, salt, butter, and milk — in the** *Look No Further* **cookbook.**

There are three things you must do during your visit to Berea: sample some hot spoon bread in the dining room of the Boone Tavern Hotel, stroll the grounds of Berea College, and take time to get acquainted with the rich craft heritage of the area. Though the idea may seem a little far-fetched, all are related activities.

The Boone Tavern Hotel, which dates to 1909, is owned and operated by Berea College, a four-year institution whose unique mission is to provide educational opportunities to mountain youth who might not otherwise go to college. Students work in the dining room and the hotel to pay for their schooling and at the same time get on-the-job training in the hotel industry. (The college charges no tuition but requires that each student work ten to fifteen hours per week.) The antebellum-style hotel, with its Corinthian columns, was built originally as a guest house for college visitors. It has since become a major stop for travelers passing through Kentucky.

A stay at the hotel is an experience different from the norm because most of the staff are young college students just learning the ropes of working in a hotel. You'll find them to be bright-eyed, friendly, and eager to please (in essence, real people) — a refreshing change indeed from the veneer you sometimes find in hotels. No tipping is allowed, so you know they have no ulterior motives in providing good service. Guest rooms and public areas, totally refurbished recently, feature Berea College woodcraft, handcrafted furniture of cherry, walnut, and mahogany. The hotel can accommodate groups of one hundred or fewer.

The dining room offers three meals a day. Entrées are set with the menu. Lamb, chicken flakes in a bird's nest, roast turkey, and fried or broiled haddock are offered daily. Homemade desserts may include Kentucky chess pie, chocolate cake, or fruit crisp served with ice cream.

The hotel's location in the heart of the village makes it convenient to the college and the shops. Guests can take advantage of the wealth of cultural activities and sporting opportunities on campus and can browse and shop for handmade crafts in the local shops. Handcrafted furniture and hand-woven linens by Churchill Weavers are the most prized, but small, less expensive items can also be found. The college has a new gym with a swimming pool, track, exercise equipment, and tennis courts available to guests. Students conduct daily tours of the academic buildings and various industries.

The Doctor's Inn of Berea

617 Chestnut
Berea, KY 40403
Tel. & Fax: 606-986-3042
doesinn@mis.net

A family home that now welcomes guests

Innkeepers: Dr. Bill and Biji Baker. **Accommodations:** 3 rooms (all with private baths). **Rates:** $125. **Included:** Full country breakfast, wake-up beverages, newspaper, afternoon refreshments, and turndown service. **Payment:** Cash or checks. **Children:** Not appropriate. **Pets:** Not allowed. **Smoking:** Allowed in designated areas. **Open:** Year-round.

➤ **As Kentucky's "Folk Art and Crafts Capital," Berea has been welcoming tourists for decades. Just a short walk from the B&B are shops that sell hand-crafted furniture, pottery, jewelry, blown glass, hand-woven goods, and other beautiful treasures.**

Cocoa, a chocolate Labrador whose official title is "Hound of the Inn," welcomes guests at this lovely bed-and-breakfast, located in the heart of Berea, the Kentucky capital of folk arts and crafts. Then, owners Bill and Biji Baker take over, dishing out Southern hospitality as it is meant to be at the lovely Greek Revival home that Bill's parents built in 1949.

Bill and Biji gave their home a facelift before opening it to overnight guests. The guest rooms are furnished in Berea College handcrafted furniture and period antiques and Oriental rugs. Deep jewel tones used in the color schemes compliment the stained glass windows in some of the rooms.

Bill and Biji have retired from their professional life to devote themselves full-time to innkeeping — which they say was the "best decision" they ever made. Bill was an orthodontist; Biji, a bookkeeper. Biji enjoys making pottery and doing pen-and-ink drawings, some of her favorites being sketches of the B&B.

Bill is known for his full country breakfast, which include country ham and red-eye gravy, eggs, potatoes or grits, and biscuits. Other specialties of the house include strawberry sundae waffles, country breakfast casserole, spinach cheese grits, breakfast fruit soup, homemade granola, and other delicious dishes. Regardless of the menu, every day begins with coffee or tea and a newspaper being delivered to each guest room.

There's a plethora of activities at the inn — stereo music, the grand piano, satellite television, stereo music, or the library. Craft shops, featuring handmade items made in Berea, are a short walk from the inn. The Bakers can also arrange tee times at a nearby golf club.

Cadiz

Lake Barkley State Resort Park

Highway 68 West,
P.O. Box 790
Cadiz, KY 42211-0790
502-924-1131, 800-325-1708
Fax: 502-924-0013

An outstanding full-service state resort on the lake

Park Superintendent: John H. Rufli. **Accommodations:** 120 rooms and 4 suites (all with private baths). **Rates:** $38–$150. **Included:** All recreation except greens fees, horseback riding, and fitness center. **Payment:** Major credit cards. **Children:** Welcome. **Pets:** Not allowed. **Smoking:** Limited. **Open:** Year-round.

➤ **Most people drive their cars or boats to Lake Barkley, but you can also fly here. The park is one of three in Kentucky that has an airport. Guests can land on a 4,800-foot-long paved, lighted strip just three miles from the lodge.**

From the air, Lake Barkley State Resort Park looks like a giant wheel. The main lodge, a circular shape, is the largest wooden building constructed in the past half century. Built in 1970 of

Douglas fir and western cedar, Barkley Lodge is the center of this resort park, named by *Money* magazine as one of the top ten family vacation resorts in the country. The park honors the memory of Vice President Alben W. Barkley, a native of Paducah, who served under President Harry Truman.

Most of the guest rooms are located in Barkley Lodge, which features a large rock fireplace in the dining room and panoramic views of the water. Meals and meetings take place here. There is an Olympic-size outdoor pool just outside. Little River Lodge, tucked away in a little cove of the lake, has ten rooms. The rooms on the top level of Barkley Lodge are preferred, as they have cathedral ceilings and give the illusion of more space, though the square footage is about the same in all rooms. Each room has two double beds, a bath, and an outside deck overlooking the lake.

Fishing for largemouth, smallmouth, white, and Kentucky bass, bluegill, catfish, crappie, and sauger is a favorite pastime at the 52,000-acre lake, which runs parallel with Kentucky Lake and helps form Land Between the Lakes. The marina, one-half mile from the lodge, has 112 covered slips, 60 open slips, a launching ramp, and rental fishing, pontoon, and ski boats. The resort is not restricted to fishing and boating, however. You can also play golf at the Boots Randolph Golf Course, work out in the fitness center (which also has a spa and a Jacuzzi), play shuffleboard or tennis, or practice trapshooting. The park offers a summer recreation program, nature trails, and a playground — appealing to families and senior citizens.

Corbin

Cumberland Falls State Resort Park

7351 Highway 90
Corbin, KY 40701-8814
606-528-4121, 800-325-0063
Fax: 606-528-0704

A resort park where watching moon bows is a favorite pastime

General Manager: Danny Brown. **Accommodations:** 71 rooms (all with private baths) and 10 cottages (with private baths and fully equipped kitchens). **Rates:** $67.70–$135.39, plus $5 for each additional person. **Included:** Taxes. **Payment:**

Major credit cards. **Children:** Welcome. **Pets:** Not allowed. **Smoking:** Allowed. **Open:** Year-round.

➤ **The Big South Fork Scenic Railroad, located about 25 miles from the state park, begins its three-hour, 6.5-mile historic journey in Stearns and travels through the mountains to Blue Heron Historical Outdoor Museum.**

The only place in the Western Hemisphere where you can see moon bows, this state park is one of Kentucky's most popular. Moon bows, created by the mist of Cumberland Falls ("Niagara of the South") when the moon is full, appear four or five nights a month when the weather is clear. (Check with the park office for specific dates.)

In addition to being awed by this natural phenomenon at the resort park, you can go down the Cumberland River on a guided raft trip, ride a horse, fish, or cool off in the swimming pool. The park has more than 17 miles of hiking trails, plus tennis courts, horseshoe pits, shuffleboard, a campground, and a picnic area with a children's playground. Year-round interpretative programs focus on native plants, animals, and local history. The history of Cumberland Falls, including information on Indians who lived in the area, is told in the Bob Blair Museum in DuPont Lodge.

DuPont Lodge, overlooking the Cumberland River, is the center of park activity. It offers guest rooms, fine dining, and meeting space for small groups. Lodging is also available in the adjacent Woodland Lodge and the one- and two-room cottages, with fireplaces and fully equipped kitchens. The park also has gift and coffee shops. Extensive renovation of the lodges and cabins continues and new ones are to be added within the next two years.

Covington

The Amos Shinkle Townhouse

215 Garrard Street
Covington, KY 41011
606-431-2118, 800-972-7012
Fax: 606-491-4551

A charming small-town B&B

Innkeepers: Don Nash and Bernie Moorman. **Accommodations:** 3 rooms in main house and 4 rooms in carriage house (all with private baths). **Rates:** $77–$130. **Included:** Full country breakfast. **Payment:** Major credit cards. **Children:** Welcome. **Pets:** Not allowed. **Smoking:** Allowed. **Open:** Year-round.

➤ **At the time of its construction in 1867, John A. Roebling's bridge across the Ohio River was the longest suspension bridge in the world and served as the prototype for the Brooklyn Bridge, also a Roebling project.**

Owners Don Nash and Bernie Moorman, retired scientists, have been innkeeping at the Amos Shinkle Townhouse for over a decade. They have built up quite a following of guests and at the same time preserved a very important house.

The Greco Italianate structure was built in 1854 by Amos Shinkle, who was president of the company that hired John A. Roebling to build a suspension bridge across the Ohio River. When it was built, the townhouse had a perfect view of the bridge, as it is only a block or so away, but tall buildings now obstruct the view.

The townhouse's location in the Licking Riverside Historic District of Covington makes it convenient to the Main Strasse Village of Covington, a street famous for its quaint shops, and to Covington Landing on the river, an area of numerous restaurants and shops. The inn is also the closest lodging facility to the Cincinnati Stadium. Guests may stay in the main house or the carriage house. Families with children usually prefer the latter. The public rooms and guest rooms are furnished in antiques from local estates. Two valuable pieces date to around 1815 — a corner cupboard in one of the two formal parlors at the front of the house and a four-poster bed in one of the guest rooms.

Bernie and Don serve a full country breakfast consisting of eggs, pancakes, homemade sau-sage or bacon, pastries, fresh fruit, and goetta, a sausage-like dish made of pork, pinhead oats, onions, and spices that has been encased, sliced, and fried. Unique to Covington, it is a little like scrapple. Conversations at mealtime are usually quite interesting, especially when the topic turns to local politics. Bernie serves on the Kenton County Commission. The innkeepers also provide complimentary beverages. They have a well-stocked library of books and current magazines as well as games.

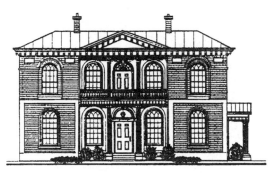

The Carneal House Inn

405 East Second Street
Covington, KY 41011
606-431-6130
Fax: 606-581-6041

Covington's most historic home, now a lovely B&B

Innkeepers: Peter and Karen Rafuse. **Accommodations:** 6 rooms (all with private baths). **Rates:** $80–$120. **Included:** Full southern breakfast, complimentary beverages. **Payment:** American Express, MasterCard, Visa. **Children:** 12 and older welcome. **Pets:** Check with innkeepers. **Smoking:** Allowed. **Open:** Mid-February–mid-December.

➤ **The house has a friendly resident ghost — that of a young woman who committed suicide because Lafayette would not dance with her.**

General Marquis de Lafayette, Senator Henry Clay, President Andrew Jackson, and perhaps John Audubon have been guests at this historic home, located at the confluence of the Licking and Ohio rivers in the Licking-Riverside National Register Historic District of Covington. And since 1992, when owners Peter and Karen Rafuse, completed their restoration of the house and opened it as a bed-and-breakfast inn, the historic home has had a steady stream of visitors. Its proximity to Riverfront Stadium and downtown Cincinnati makes it very much in demand.

The Rafuses first lived in the house when it was divided into apartments. After owning the house for several years, they decided to try their hand at innkeeping. Combining their knowledge of art and antiques, the couple set out to return the house to its original grandeur. The two-story stately brick Palladian home was completed in 1815 for Thomas Carneal, one of Covington's founders. Peter, who is a practicing architect, has added some wonderful features to the house — a glassed-in sunroom with black and white marble tile flooring, a bathroom with an antique stained glass window as the suspended ceiling, a brick-paved courtyard, and Chippendale-style railings on the upper verandahs which overlook the gardens and Licking River. Karen has used art and antiques in decorating the house in the period of its construction.

Natural entertainers, the Rafuses are known far and wide for the bountiful breakfasts they serve guests — Karen is a professional caterer. Favorite dishes include blueberry pancakes, French toast, bluegrass scrambled eggs, Kentucky scrapple made with chicken, country ham or sausage, boneless Fancy Farm country ham, and other delicacies. In 1993, *Cincinnati Magazine* voted Corneal House's breakfast as the best in Kentucky. The Rafuses often make dinner reservations for their guests and arrange carriage rides to local restaurants.

Georgetown

Log Cabin Bed & Breakfast

350 North Broadway
Georgetown, KY 40324
502-863-3514

| A quiet reprieve that takes you back in time |

Innkeepers: Clay and Janis McKnight. **Accommodations:** Two-bedroom cabin (with private bath and fully equipped kitchen). **Rates:** $84 per couple, plus $15 for each additional adult and $10 for each child under 12 and each pet. **Included:** Continental breakfast. **Payment:** Cash or checks. **Children:** Welcome. **Pets:** Welcome. **Smoking:** Allowed. **Open:** Year-round.

➤ **The furnishings are simple antiques of the period, accented with dolls, wooden toys, and handmade quilts hung as works of art.**

You can close out the world and pretend it's two hundred years ago in this 1809 authentic log cabin. But don't worry about having to chop wood and carry water; innkeepers Clay and Janis McKnight have provided all the modern conveniences, including cable TV and phones, plus kindling and wood for building a roaring fire. You needn't worry about the bears and wolves outside either, as the cabin sits on a lot directly behind the McKnights' home. Clay, who is an attorney with a penchant for history, had always wanted a cabin of his own and moved this one, piece by piece, and then reassembled it, assisted by the couple's two sons.

The first level of the cabin has a sitting room with a fieldstone fireplace, a master bedroom and bath, and a lean-to modern kitchen and family area that was added on. Upstairs is a large loft that will easily sleep two, more if the trundle bed is used. The dividers on the stairs are stenciled in a log cabin pattern. A number of celebrities, including Alex Haley, Art Linkletter, and others, were charmed by it.

The McKnights, who are avid gardeners, often share flowers and fruits with their guests. They always stock the refrigerator with an assortment of breakfast goodies, including homemade breads, coffee cake, and other pastries. As you might have guessed, Janis is quite a cook and enjoys being a hostess.

With a well-stocked refrigerator and plenty of firewood, you can forget your worries for a while.

Glendale

Petticoat Junction Bed & Breakfast

223 High Street
Mailing address:
P.O. Box 36
Glendale, KY 42740
502-369-8604, 800-308-0364

> **An old-fashioned B&B in an old town**

Innkeepers: Jack and Rachel Holman. **Accommodations:** 6 rooms (4 with private baths, 2 with shared bath). **Rates:** $65–$80. **Included:** Full breakfast, fresh flowers, and snacks. **Payment:** Major credit cards. **Children:** Welcome. **Pets:** Not allowed. **Smoking:** Not allowed. **Open:** Year-round.

> ➤ **The attention grabber in the suite is the tin tub that Jack decorated with stenciling and hooked into the plumbing. The honeymoon room also offers a nice option — a Jacuzzi for two.**

The inn is as pretty and charming as its name. You can watch the cows graze, listen to the birds, or ride the bicycle built for two to the old-fashioned general store or the antiques shops in tiny Glendale, one of the state's best-preserved old towns. And when you return from your trip, you can relax on the porch or enjoy the comforts of your room, including fresh flowers, fresh fruit, and candy.

Jack and Rachel Holman restored the 1876 farmhouse in 1988 and 1989, adding plumbing, heating, and wiring, which it had never had. Jack teaches plumbing and heating at the community college in Elizabethtown; Rachel is a former real-estate agent and now runs the inn full-time. The guest rooms are furnished in Victorian pieces, wicker, and antiques. The property contains several outbuildings, including an outhouse that has been converted into a storage building. One of the buildings has been made into guest quarters — one guest room and a two-bedroom suite, which has a sitting area, microwave, and refrigerator.

The Holmans serve a full breakfast, as well as complimentary beverages and desserts. The town has a number of good restaurants.

Harrodsburg

The Beaumont Inn

638 Beaumont Inn Drive
Harrodsburg, KY 40330
606-734-3381, 800-352-3992
Fax: 606-734-6897
http://www.beaumontinn.com

A classic country inn with a wonderful past

Owner: T. C. Dedman. **Innkeepers:** Chuck and Helen Dedman. **Accommodations:** 33 rooms (all with private baths). **Rates:** $85–$125, plus $25 for each additional person and $15 for each child under 12; discounts for extended stays. **Included:** Continental breakfast. **Payment:** Major credit cards. **Children:**

Welcome. **Pets:** Not allowed. **Smoking:** Smoking and nonsmoking rooms.
Open: March–December.

➤ **In the main inn hang portraits of General Robert E. Lee, President Jefferson Davis (a Kentuckian by birth), President George Washington, and other historical figures.**

For more than seventy years the buildings of this inn, located in the heart of Kentucky's Bluegrass region, served as one of the South's most prestigious girls' schools. Today some of the few surviving graduates return for reunions and reminisce about their school days. The property was purchased in 1917 for sentimental reasons by Mr. and Mrs. Glave Goddard, who turned it into an inn, first to accommodate returning alumnae and then to serve the traveling public. Today the inn is operated by members of the fourth generation, and it celebrated its 75th anniversary in 1993. Throughout the years the three-diamond, three-star inn has received many awards, including Uncle Ben's Award and *Innsider* magazine's Best of the Year.

You can expect the very finest of accommodations, food, service, and amenities at the Beaumont Inn. Guests are housed in the main inn, a Greek Revival structure supported by six white Ionic columns; Goddard Hall, an addition built in 1935; Greystone Hall, a private residence; and Bell Cottage, a small frame dwelling built in 1921. Most of the furnishings used in the various buildings belong to the family, as do the framed pictures, memorabilia, and collections that are so attractively displayed in glass cases in public rooms and hallways. Goddard Hall has been refurbished to complement the classic decor used in the main inn.

Today the old school library houses the inn's office; across the wide central hall are double parlors, where the students at Beaumont College used to receive their beaus. A shop on the main level sells Kentucky crafts and food. The Harrod Room is the site of the inn's annual Kentucky Derby party. The guest rooms are furnished with two-poster beds, spool beds, high Victorian beds, or cannonball beds, along with marble-top dressers, chairs, and tables crafted from cherry, walnut, mahogany, pine, or maple. At night guests receive a "Beaumont cocktail" (ice water) at their bedside.

The dining room is a large rectangular room papered in a fruit pattern, an appropriate setting for the linen-covered tables, which groan with platters of Beaumont country ham, yellow-legged fried chicken (premium corn-fed chicken), Kentucky-grown rainbow trout (usually a special), corn pudding, fresh vegetables, and Robert E. Lee orange-lemon cake. Dinner begins with the traditional ring-ing of the dinner bell. (Overnight guests receive a ten percent discount on dinner.) Gentlemen are expected to wear jackets in the dining room in the evening. Breakfast, served only to house guests, is southern-style — usually eggs, grits, bacon or sausage, and the inn's famous cornmeal batter cakes with brown sugar syrup. Thanksgiving and Christmas holidays are very special at the inn, as you might expect.

The grounds of the inn are immaculately kept and contain a variety of huge hardwood trees — ginkgoes, maples, oaks, and others — which put on a brilliant display of color in the fall. In all, there are 33 acres to roam. Guests also enjoy the outdoor swimming pool and tennis courts.

Canaan Land Farm Bed and Breakfast

700 Canaan Land Road
Harrodsburg, KY 40330
606-734-3984, 888-734-3984

A historic B&B where love abounds

Innkeepers: Fred and Theo Bee. **Accommodations:** 6 rooms (all with private baths). **Rates:** $75–$125, plus $10 for extra person in room. **Included:** Full country breakfast. **Payment:** Cash or checks. **Children:** 12 and older welcome; younger children with prior arrangement. **Pets:** Not allowed. **Smoking:** Not allowed. **Open:** Year-round.

➤ **Theo gets her wool for spinning from the Polypay and Border Leicester sheep she raises on the farm. Her goats are her pride and joy, and each has a special name — Rhapsody, Savannah, Phoebe, and Fancy.**

You can sleep in a historic farmhouse or a restored log cabin, feed the lambs or help with other chores at this farm near the restored

Shaker Village of Pleasant Hill, one of Kentucky's major attractions. During lambing season in the spring and fall, guests are welcome to help. Guests may enjoy the swimming pool or the hot tub, hike to the Kentucky River (about three fourths of a mile away), or relax in the hammocks.

Owners Fred and Theo Bee named the farm Canaan Land because it is their "promised land." The couple moved here from the Florida Keys with their five children over eighteen years ago in search of a simpler lifestyle. Fred, who grew up in Florida, practices law in Frankfort; Theo, a Virginian by birth, is a hand-spinner and artist. Both had always wanted to restore an old house and to live in the country. They opened their home in 1989 after their children grew up and moved away.

The house, located on 189 acres, built of Flemish-bond brick about 1795, with restorations and additions that date to 1895 and the present. It has the original front door and ash flooring plus tin light fixtures. The house is furnished throughout with period furniture, handmade bedspreads, featherbeds, and family heirlooms. Private baths have been added to each guest room. The restored log cabin, which dates to 1815, has two working fireplaces. It has been completely restored, with a hand-split cedar shake roof and two large stone chimneys. Made of massive hand-hewn poplar logs, the two-and-a-half-story cabin stands as a reminder of life in the frontier days.

Theo's crafts and watercolors are for sale, as well as two cookbooks.

Shaker Village of Pleasant Hill

350 Lexington Road
Harrodsburg, KY 40330
606-734-5411
Fax: 606-734-5411

> A historic country inn
> where the Shaker religion
> once flourished

Owners: ShakerTown at Pleasant Hill, Kentucky, Inc. **Accommodations:** 70 rooms and 10 suites (all with private baths). **Rates:** $50–$100. Additional: Meals and admission fees. **Payment:** MasterCard, Visa. **Children:** 17 and under free with parents. **Pets:** Not allowed. **Smoking:** Allowed everywhere except dining room. **Open:** Year-round except Christmas.

➤   **The United Society of Believers in Christ's Second Appearing, as they were called, were famous for their sometimes frenzied, but worshipful, dances — a practice that gave them the name Shakers.**

You can eat, sleep, and breathe history as it unfolded in this unique religious utopia that flourished in the first half of the 19th century and is now a historic inn — the only one of its kind in the country that accepts overnight guests. It was built by the Shakers, an off-shoot of the Quakers, who practiced celibacy and communal living for a time in this part of the country. (A handful of Shakers continue to practice the faith in New England, but none currently live in Kentucky.) At its zenith, Shaker Village was a community of five hundred people with holdings of more than 4,000 acres.

The group was industrious and self-sustaining; they built furniture and houses, raised and grew their own food, and made their own clothes. They were credited with inventing the flat broom, wooden clothespin, washing machine, and circular saw, and they often sold their seeds and herbs to the public. Today the restored complex of thirty buildings and 2,700 acres is owned by a nonprofit corporation.

No cars are allowed in the village, so you must park in one of the designated lots and walk a short distance to your room, usually located in one of the family dwellings. Don't expect bellhops here; everyone carries his or her own luggage. The rooms are furnished in beautiful, handcrafted Shaker reproduction furniture, known for its simple lines. Sparsely furnished, the rooms feature hand-woven draperies and bedspreads. Decorations consist of pegs that encircle the room, used in the old days to hang clothes, and wrought-iron wall sconces. The bathrooms are clean, modern, and utilitarian. The only things that seem out of place are the telephone and the television. (You can even get a wake-up call if you need it.)

Kentucky country fare is served in the Trustees' Office (dining room) by the costumed wait staff. Breakfast is buffet-style; lunch and dinner are served individually. During the summer and fall a light menu is also available at the summer kitchen.

You'll certainly want to tour the village and learn about the people who lived here long ago. Costumed guides are available in all the buildings and on the grounds, but a tour is self-guided for the most part. You should allow at least two hours. All the buildings are noted for their uncluttered architectural lines and dual outside doors. One of the most interesting buildings is the Meeting House, where an interpreter sings selections of Shaker music several times a day.

The village is made up of limestone, brick, and clapboard buildings facing one another across a tree-lined gravel road. It's enclosed by rows of neatly stacked stone fences, which corral the grazing black Angus cattle and Border Leicester sheep. There are several garden spots in the village to admire.

Prior to your tour, you might check out some of the complimentary videos relating to Shaker images. Throughout the year special events are scheduled, demonstrating all types of crafts and daily life activities practiced by the Shakers. A shop in the village carries many Shaker crafts. The village also operates an authentic sternwheel riverboat, the *Dixie Belle,* at Shaker Landing on the Kentucky River a short distance from the village. Several one-hour excursions are offered daily from mid-April through late October.

Hillsboro

D. H. Resorts

Western Village & Mountain Lake Manor
Route 1, Box 219-A1
Hillsboro, KY 41049
800-737-RIDE
Fax: 606-876-4006

A private resort in the eastern hills of Kentucky

Owners: Steve and Charlotte Dobson, D.H. Resorts, Inc. **Accommodations:** 5 rooms (all with private baths). **Rates:** $30 for cabins; $75–$95 for Manor House; $25–$120 recreational fees. **Included:** Amish Continental breakfast, use of recreational facilities. **Payment:** Major credit cards. **Children:** Welcome. **Pets:** Not allowed. **Smoking:** Allowed in designated areas. **Open:** Year-round.

➤ **Eventually, the resort owners plan to build an Old West–style town. They already have a good start.**

Steve and Charlotte Dobson "roughed it" in tents back in 1988 when they started building D. H. Western Village resort by Indian Creek in the Eastern Highlands of Kentucky. Today they offer horseback riding, overnight camping and lodging, hiking, swimming, fishing, and boating. There's a full program of equestrian activities — trail rides, lunch and steak rides, overnight camp rides, horseback riding lessons, and horse camps — and every May the resort stages the Spring Roundup and Ride. Other special weekends are the Ladies Getaway in August and Frost on the Pumpkin Weekend in October.

The resort has several secluded unfurnished cabins and primitive camping sites for guests who enjoy camping. Covered stalls are provided for campers who want to bring their own horses with them. Groceries and camping supplies are available in the Camp Store.

The D. H. Mountain Lake Manor offers five luxurious guest rooms: The Suite, Plantation Room, Field and Stream Room, and the Shaker Room. All have queen or king beds and private baths. Guests may gather in the common sitting room on the first floor, the upstairs game and television room, and on the outdoor deck. A Continental breakfast is included in the rate.

Jamestown

Lake Cumberland State Resort Park

5465 State Park Road
Jamestown, KY 42629
502-343-3111, 800-325-1709
Fax: 502-343-5510

A state resort park in the mountains offering varied recreational opportunities

Park Manager: Larry Totten. **Accommodations:** 76 lodge rooms (all with private baths); 30 cottages (all with private baths and fully equipped kitchens; 10 with fireplaces). **Rates:** Lodge rooms $72, mid-May–late September; cottages $81–$120, April–October; lower rates at other times. **Payment:** Major credit cards. **Children:** Welcome. **Pets:** Not allowed. **Smoking:** Smoking and nonsmoking rooms. **Open:** Year-round.

➤ **Especially popular are the Wildwood Cottages, contemporary allwood cabins with fireplaces and large decks that almost touch the trees.**

You can catch bass, bluegill, crappie, rainbow trout, rockfish, and walleye at this Kentucky resort park on Lake Cumberland, a 50,000-acre lake formed by the Cumberland River due south of the Cumberland Parkway. The park offers 100 boat slips and launching ramps for those who bring their own boats plus all kinds of rental watercraft — fishing boats, pontoon boats, houseboats, and ski boats. During spring the park sponsors fishing packages, complete with concluding award ceremonies.

When you tire of fishing on the lake, you can play golf on the nine-hole, par three course, enjoy shuffleboard, go swimming year-round (the park has indoor and outdoor pools), enjoy horseback riding in season, or take a walk on the nature trail around the lake. The resort also has an exercise room and hot tub, and children especially enjoy miniature golf, the game room, and the playground. Of course, the sighting of a deer, raccoon, or rare bird brings great delight to the young and old.

The 3,007-acre park offers different types of accommodations', all renovated recently. Luxurious Lure Lodge, with its glass elevator and atrium, overlooks the lake and has 63 rooms. An alternative is the smaller Pumpkin Creek Lodge (13 rooms) on a knoll overlooking the lake. Guests have the most privacy in the cozy cottages nestled deep in the woods. Groceries are available in the park store, and breakfast, lunch, and dinner are served in the Lure Lodge dining room. The park can accommodate groups of 200 or less.

Lexington

The Camberley Club at Gratz Park

120 West Second Street
Lexington, KY 40507
606-231-1777, 800-227-4362
Fax: 606-233-7593

> **A city hotel that pampers and pleases**

General Manager: Jonathan Miller. **Accommodations:** 38 rooms and 6 suites (all with private baths). **Rates:** $120–$260. **Included:** Continental breakfast, airport transportation, 24-hour coffee and tea, sherry, fresh fruit, and bathrobes. **Payment:** Major credit cards. **Children:** Welcome. **Pets:** Not allowed. **Smoking:** Smoking and nonsmoking rooms. **Open:** Year-round.

> ➤ **Gratz Park is an important social center of Lexington. Advance reservations are always advised during University of Kentucky sporting events and the horse racing season.**

No comfort or amenity has been overlooked at this small luxury hotel whose name includes the prestigious Gratz Park neighborhood, where the city actually began. (Henry Clay had his law office here, Confederate soldiers used Gratz Park as their headquarters, and Transylvania University, the oldest college west of the Alleghenies, is located here.) Built around the turn of the century, The Camberley Club at Gratz Park originally served as a hospital called the Lexington Clinic.

The hotel serves a complimentary Continental breakfast in the café, and sherry, fresh fruit, and bathrobes are provided in the rooms. Of special importance to business travelers are the availability of telephone, 24-hour fax services, 24-hour coffee and tea service, and airport transportation. Guests also have privileges at a local health club.

The entire building is elegantly furnished in twentieth-century reproductions. Rooms have four-poster beds, and baths are outfitted in marble and brass. Each room has remote control cable television with movie channels and a clock radio.

Marriott's Griffin Gate Resort

1800 Newtown Pike
Lexington, KY 40511
606-231-5100, 800-228-9290
Fax: 606-255-9944

| A city hotel built around a golf course and a historic mansion |

General Manager: Bruce Smith. **Accommodations:** 388 rooms and 21 suites (all with private baths) **Rates:** $135–$950. **Included:** Complimentary coffee, newspaper, health club, business center, use of all recreational facilities (greens fees extra), and complimentary airport van. **Payment:** Major credit cards. **Children:** Welcome. **Pets:** Allowed with deposit. **Smoking:** Smoking and nonsmoking rooms. **Open:** Year-round.

➤ **The mansion is said to have a ghost, that of a young girl who committed suicide when she learned of the death of her boyfriend.**

It isn't often that you find a resort of this caliber in the heart of a city. Marriott's Griffin Gate Resort is unique in several ways; it features an 18-hole championship golf course, a pre–Civil War mansion, and guest rooms that were once used as corporate offices for the Coca-Cola company.

The hotel, which dates to 1985, overlooks the Rees Jones golf course. Voted one of top seventy-five courses in the nation by *Golf Digest*, it hosted the PGA Senior Tour for several years. The pro shop was rated one of America's one hundred best golf shops in 1996. In addition to the golf course, the resort offers tennis, indoor and outdoor swimming pools, a hydrotherapy pool, a health club, massage therapy, and special activities for children, including tours of nearby horse farms.

The Mansion, which serves as the hotel's most elegant restaurant, adds another interesting dimension to the property. Built in 1854 for the Coleman family, it was destroyed by fire in 1872. The following year a new house was built on the site and named Highland Home. It was acquired years later by the Eveleth family, who added the front columns. Alfred Marks, the next owner, changed the name to Griffin Gate.

Under the direction of Chef Robert Hall, the Mansion offers entrées such as strawberry poached salmon, veal Oscar, steak au poivre, Chateaubriand, and seafood à la Mansion. There is a Sunday brunch every week. You may also order mint juleps, bread pudding, and pecan-chocolate chip pie — all Kentucky favorites. The resort's other restaurants are J. W.'s, which offers steaks and seafood, and Griffin Gate Gardens, a family-style restaurant.

Rooms have been recently renovated, and those, are located in the former corporate offices, indeed luxurious. The Heartland Suite, for example, features oak paneling, oak-carved doors, and grasscloth wallcovering. It has cherry furniture, brass lamps, a sitting area with a glass-top coffee table, a king-size bed, and a writing desk. The spacious bathroom is equally elegant. In the closet you'll find an iron, a full-size ironing board, and a shoe polisher. Distinguished guests have included Queen Elizabeth's entourage and members of President Reagan's staff.

The public rooms in the hotel are inviting, offering plenty of space for conversation and relaxing. The hotel has an outstanding collection of equestrian art.

Louisville

The Camberley Brown Hotel

335 West Broadway
Louisville, KY 40202
502-583-1234, 800-555-8000
Fax: 502-587-7006

A classic hotel known for its traditions and service

General Manager: Marcel Pitton. **Accommodations:** 292 rooms and suites (all with private baths). **Rates:** $119–$700. **Included:** Continental breakfast, hors d'oeuvres, and beverages on Camberley Club level. **Payment:** American Express, MasterCard, Visa. **Children:** Welcome (free with parents). **Pets:** Not allowed. **Smoking:** Smoking and nonsmoking rooms. **Open:** Year-round.

➤ **Famous patrons of the Brown have included the Duke of Windsor, Lily Pons, Al Jolson, Queen Marie of Romania, Harry Truman, Elizabeth Taylor, and others. Victor Mature was an elevator operator for a short time.**

When the Brown was built by Louisville millionaire J. Graham Brown in 1923, the grand opening celebration lasted a week and attracted such luminaries as David Lloyd George, former prime minister of England. Since that time, the Brown has figured prominently in the life and history of Louisville. At Derby time, the Brown has been likened to a "Who's Who." Considered one of the state's richest men, Brown lived in a one-bedroom suite in the hotel for forty-six years until his death in 1969.

Like many hotels, the Brown went through a decline, closing its doors in 1971 to become an administration building and school for the Louisville Board of Education. In the early 1980s, the Broadway Group acquired the property and returned the hotel to its former status, spending $22.2 million on the renovation. The hotel is owned and managed by the Camberley Hotel Company of Atlanta and is a charter member of Historic Hotels of America. Adjacent to the Brown is the Macauley Theater, a replica of New York's Music Box Theater.

The sixteen-story Greek Revival building is faced with brick and trimmed in stone and terra cotta. The style of the interior is English Renaissance with Adam detail. The grand lobby is opulent, with Bottocino marble walls, plaster friezes, bronze chandeliers with twenty-four-karat gold wash, and custom-designed carpets and fabrics. Guests have a choice of three restaurants — the English Grill, fine dining in a pub setting; J. Graham's Café and Bar, which serves breakfast and lunch; and the Thoroughbred Lounge, which is decorated with oil paintings of thoroughbreds. At the four-star, four-diamond English Grill, Chef Joe Castro is garnering accolades for entrées such as fillet of Shenandoah trout with Kentucky cider and sage sausage and medallion of venison with braised endive poivrade sauce. The famous "hot brown," a cheese, turkey, tomato, and bacon sandwich, originated at the Brown.

Guest rooms and suites feature custom-designed carpeting, eighteenth-century mahogany reproductions, and art depicting hunting scenes. Those who stay on the Camberley Club level receive extras such as oversize terrycloth robes, complimentary newspaper, shoeshine, and pressing service. The hotel has a 24-hour fitness center and several meeting rooms.

Old Louisville Inn

1359 South Third Street
Louisville, KY 40208
502-635-1574
Fax: 502-637-5892

An elegant B&B in the city's oldest neighborhood

Innkeeper: Marianne Lesher. **Accommodations:** 10 rooms and 2 suites (all with private baths). **Rates:** $75–$195. **Included:** Full breakfast, afternoon tea. **Payment:** MasterCard, Visa. **Children:** 12 and under free. **Pets:** Not allowed. **Smoking:** Limited to designated areas. **Open:** Year-round.

➤ **Innkeeper Marianne Lesher runs a well-organized house, and she's aware of extra niceties that make a big difference in a guest's stay — fresh flowers, cheese and fruit trays, home-baked goods, and daily copies of the Wall Street Journal.**

The homemade popovers are among the many pleasures and comforts that await guests at the Old Louisville Inn, located in the city's first suburb. You can take a bubble bath in the deep soaking tubs that are original to the turn-of-the-century Victorian house and perhaps enjoy breakfast in bed the next day. Or you might play cards with a friend, work on a puzzle, or watch television in the game room. Other options are the murder mysteries or bridge parties that are scheduled at regular intervals.

Before she decided to take up innkeeping, Marianne Lesher worked in sales and marketing. She got hands-on experience at the Point Way Inn on Martha's Vineyard and the Truckee Hotel in California. Her bent for gourmet cooking comes in handy as well. (She also occasionally enjoys hot air ballooning and flying stunt kites.)

The house was designed and built for entertaining and thus lends itself to the bed-and-breakfast concept. When it was built in 1901 as a private home for John Armstrong, president of the Louisville Home Telephone Company, it featured many luxuries not common in most homes of the day — twelve-foot ceilings with murals, ornately carved mahogany columns, an etched glass chandelier and built-in buffet in the dining room, fireplaces, and marble baths. On the third floor was a large ballroom that now serves as the Honeymoon Suite. It has a king-size canopy bed, sitting area, fireplace (though not operable), and a whirlpool tub for two. The suite is certainly the most popular room in the house, but if you're traveling alone or not feeling particularly romantic, any of the other guest rooms is more than adequate.

The Seelbach Hotel

500 Fourth Avenue
Louisville, KY 40202
502-585-3200, 800-333-3399
Fax: 502-585-9239

A social center of the city
for decades

General Manager: David Nichols. **Accommodations:** 321 rooms and 33 suites (all with private baths). **Rates:** $95–$500, slightly higher during Derby days. **Payment:** Major credit cards. **Children:** Welcome. **Pets:** Allowed. **Smoking:** Allowed. **Open:** Year-round.

➤ **The hotel has executive suites and one- and two-bedroom suites, but the Seelbach Suite is the grandest, with its bilevel parlor, oak paneling, fireplace, built-in bookshelves, bay window, and marble bath.**

Billed as Louisville's Grand Hotel, the Seelbach made its debut in 1905. Over the years it has hosted major social functions for the city's elite; in fact, F. Scott Fitzgerald is said to have gotten the inspiration for *The Great Gatsby* while attending a party in the Rooftop Ballroom. Another famous room in the hotel is the Rathskeller on the basement level — a room made entirely of Rookwood pottery.

The two-story-high dark marble lobby, with brass accents, is noted for its wide stairwell. Several of the meeting rooms have built-in fireplaces and china cabinets. Guests can enjoy fine dining in the four-star Oak Room, formerly the Gentlemen's Billiards Room, and casual dining in the Café. The perfect place for cocktails is the speak-easy atmosphere of the Seelbach Bar.

Furnishings, fabrics, and wallpapers in the beaux-arts hotel are turn of the century, and the bathrooms are marble. The seventh floor is devoted to concierge service.

The Seelbach is ideal for business travelers because of its central downtown location. The on-site business center offers computers, fax machines, telephones, and other services. The hotel doesn't have a health club, but guests have privileges at the nearby Louisville Athletic Club. Guests who are staying here on business receive a complimentary Continental breakfast.

Mammoth Cave

Mammoth Cave Hotel/Lodge-Cottages

Mammoth Cave, KY 42259-0027
502-758-2225
Fax: 502-758-2301

A National Park offering a variety of activities and lodging options

General Manager: Robert P. King. **Accommodations:** 108 rooms (78 with private baths, 30 with shared baths). **Rates:** $40–$65. **Payment:** Major credit cards. **Children:** Welcome. **Pets:** Kennels provided. **Smoking:** Allowed. **Open:** Year-round.

➤ **Used by American Indians for shelter over 4,000 years ago, Mammoth Cave was named a World Heritage Site in 1981 and became the core area of an International Biosphere Reserve in 1990. It is home to the world's most diverse cave ecosystem.**

Spelunkers love this National Park, offering 350 miles of charted passages (three times longer than any other known cave). Tours at Mammoth begin at the Visitor Center with an orientation, but it's a good idea to call ahead for reservations and find out the schedule and whether any special clothes or equipment are required. Another must-do at Mammoth is the scenic boat ride on the Green

River, which winds through high limestone cliffs and passes by cave entrances. The park also has a vast trail system for hiking, walking, and horseback riding, as well as miles of waterway for fishing and boating. Camping, picnicking, tennis, and shuffleboard are also options. Handmade crafts made by Southern Highland Craft members and other skilled craftsmen are sold in the gift shops.

Visitors have several options in all price ranges when it comes to lodging — secluded cottages, a motor lodge, and Mammoth Cave Hotel. Connected to the Visitor Center by a concrete bridge, the hotel overlooks a scenic ravine and is near the motor lodge. Hotel rooms feature all the modern conveniences, plus private patios and balconies. All are accessible to the disabled. Southern regional cuisine is offered in the hotel dining room and coffee shop.

Middlesboro

The RidgeRunner B&B

208 Arthur Heights
Middlesboro, KY 40965
606-248-4299

A Victorian B&B overlooking the Cumberland Mountains

Innkeeper: Susan Richards. **Accommodations:** 4 rooms (2 with private baths, 2 with shared bath). **Rates:** $55–$65. **Included:** Full breakfast, refreshments, turndown service. **Payment:** Cash or checks. **Children:** 14 and older welcome. **Pets:** Not allowed. **Smoking:** Not allowed. **Open:** Year-round.

➤ **RidgeRunner guests may enjoy visits to nearby Cumberland Gap National Historic Park, as well as tours of the Wilderness Road.**

This 22-room restored Victorian mansion was built in 1890 for John Cary, secretary/treasurer of Middlesborough Town Company, an English company that developed the Cumberland Gap area. It features a 60-foot front porch which overlooks the town and the Cumberland Mountains, a hand-carved walnut staircase, stained glass windows, pocket doors, and hardwood floors. The house is decorated in the style of the Victorian era.

Innkeeper Susan Richards, who loves to share stories about the house and its furnishings, describes the inn as "a home filled with antiques, love and comfort, with a feeling of 'a visit to Grandmother's house.'" As a retired teacher who spent 40 years working in one-room schools and a community center in Appalachia, she knows the area well, as does her associate Irma Gall, formerly an educational assistant and staff member of the community center that served "Stinking Creek."

Guests are served a hearty breakfast of eggs, meat, homemade breads and muffins, homemade jams and jellies, fresh fruit in season, and coffee and tea. Refreshments are served in the evening, and turndown service includes candy on the pillows.

Midway

Scottwood: Bluegrass Bed & Breakfast

Leestown Road
Midway, KY 40347
Mailing address:
Route 1, Box 263
Versailles, KY 40383
606-873-3208

A historic B&B offering elegant service and accommodations

Innkeepers: Dr. D. Gordon and Ann Knight Gutman. **Accommodations:** 3 rooms (1 with private bath, 2 with shared bath), guest cottage (with private bath). **Rates:** $125 (2-night minimum; 3-night minimum during Kentucky Derby). **Included:** Full breakfast. **Payment:** MasterCard, Visa. **Children:** 6 and older welcome. **Pets:** Not allowed. **Smoking:** Not allowed. **Open:** Year-round.

➤ **Dr. Gutman's biggest culinary claim to fame is his chocolate passion pie — and he'll share the recipe on request.**

You get to sleep between crisp, ironed sheets at this early Federal-style bed-and-breakfast home, furnished with period antiques. You'll also enjoy a beautifully prepared breakfast, served on an antique table dressed with linens, candles, and fresh flowers.

Owners Dr. D. Gordon and Ann Gutman have thought of every detail in creating the nineteenth-century ambiance of this lovely house. He has a dental practice in Cincinnati, and she's an antiques collector and dealer. Their shared interest, however, is American and historic preservation. They're also natural entertainers.

Built in 1795, the house features high ceilings, original hardwood floors, and seven fireplaces that still work. A screened-in porch overlooks South Elkhorn Creek and an adjoining horse farm. Guests may sleep in the main house or the very private guest cottage, which is equipped with a fireplace, refrigerator, and microwave. The immaculate grounds include a formal rose garden. Guests may use the Gutmans' canoe on the creek.

The innkeepers both love to cook, and their presentation of food is equal to anything you might experience in an elegant restaurant. China, silver, and linens are used at every meal.

Newport

Gateway Bed & Breakfast

326 East Sixth Street
Newport, KY 41071-1962
606-581-6447, 888-891-7500
Fax: 606-581-6447

> The city's first B&B and one
> of its most outstanding
> restorations

Innkeepers: Ken and Sandy Clift. **Accommodations:** 3 rooms (all with private baths). **Rates:** $85. **Included:** Full breakfast. **Payment:** Major credit cards. **Children:** Welcome. **Pets:** Not allowed. **Smoking:** Not allowed. **Open:** Year-round.

> ➤ **Based on their research on the house, the Clifts decided to turn the parlor into a music room. Guests now enjoy the 1904 Edison fireside phonograph, the old player-piano, and Ken's grandmother's 1910 Adler organ.**

The Gateway Bed & Breakfast, Newport's first inn, opened in 1992. Though the restoration project on the 1876 Italianate-style town house required much hard work and determination, it was a dream come true for owners Ken and Sandy Clift. They were awarded a National Trust for Historic Preservation Great American Home Award in 1993. (Of 223 applicants, they won third place in the bed-and-breakfast category.)

Rather than hiring professional renovators, the Clifts did most of the work themselves, except for installing the heating and air conditioning. They peeled off eight layers of wallpaper, removed old linoleum and carpet, installed new wiring and fixtures, reopened fireplaces that had been bricked in, installed new plumbing, refinished all the pine flooring, repaired the windows (reproducing plaster cornices that had been removed), and painted the house inside and out. Sandy took a leave from her job with the Newport Board of Education to work on the house, while Ken's flexible hours as a firefighter and paramedic gave him large blocks of time. The couple bought the house for $31,000; when they completed the restoration, it was appraised at $155,000.

The Clifts learned much about the house from former occupants. Built originally for John J. Hay, an Adams Express Company cashier, it passed through several owners, including the Carniel and Joerg families. The house survived a fire, a tornado, conversion to a multifamily residence, and years of neglect.

Gateway offers three guest rooms, each furnished with period pieces. The Clifts serve a full breakfast and offer afternoon beverages, turndown service, assistance with dinner reservations, and information on things to see and do in historic Newport and in nearby Cincinnati. Gateway is next door to the Water Tower Square and a block from Pompilio's restaurant, where a segment of *Rain Man* was filmed.

Springfield

Glenmar Plantation

2444 Valley Hill Road	**An authentic plantation in**
Springfield, KY 40069	**the country offering elegant**
606-284-7791, 800-828-3330	**accommodations**
Fax: 606-284-7791	

Innkeeper: Kenny Mandell. **Accommodations:** 6 rooms (4 with private baths, 2 with shared bath), 1 suite, and 1 cottage (both with private baths). **Rates:** $85–$175. **Included:** Full breakfast and evening desserts. **Payment:** MasterCard, Visa (cash or checks preferred). **Children:** Welcome. **Pets:** Accommodations provided outside. **Smoking:** Not allowed. **Open:** Year-round.

➤ **Virginia statesman Patrick Henry gave Samuel Grundy 5,000 acres of land as a gift. Grundy and his wife, Elizabeth, settled here and built the brick house around 1785.**

As soon as Kenny Mandell bought this 200-acre colonial estate outside Springfield in the summer of 1991, he started making improvements to enhance the beauty and ambiance of the house. He has replaced all the beds, mattresses, and bedding, upgraded the kitchen, made significant changes in the public rooms, and added new carpet, built a gazebo on the hill overlooking the valley, and opened the adjoining coach house.

Kenny is not finished with the restoration by any means, though. Work continues on the two log barns, considered by local historians to be far more significant than the two-story Georgian manor house built around 1785 — the oldest brick house in Washington County and the oldest Flemish-bond brick house in the state. The barns, believed to have housed slaves at one time, contain hand-hewn timbers measuring up to 60 feet in length. The larger of the two log structures is three stories high and measures about 45 by 65 feet.

The history of Glenmar is fascinating. The original owners grew tobacco and corn and would have needed about 200 slaves to take care of the vast acreage. Much in the manor house is original — woodwork, mantels, windows, doors, and fireplaces. The plantation is a Historical Landmark and has won the Kentucky Historical Farm Award.

Soon after guests arrive at Glenmar in the afternoon and have a complimentary beverage, Kenny conducts a house tour. The 1810 giraffe piano (an upright baby grand that stands about seven feet tall) always gets attention. After the tour, guests are shown to their rooms — furnished in antiques and decorated with handmade quilts and crochet work. Afterward, they may walk in the formal gardens, inspect the barns, or admire the llamas and horses. Other pastimes are riding the bicycles built for two and horseback riding.

Kenny doesn't serve dinner but is happy to direct people to local restaurants and attractions. He always keeps the coffeepot on and the refrigerator open for those who want a midnight snack when they return. Breakfast at Glenmar might include fried potatoes, fried apples, sausage gravy, homemade biscuits, grits casserole, ham quiche, fruit, juices, jams, jellies, and coffee.

When Kenny decided to open the bed-and-breakfast inn, he retired from a management position in Cincinnati and moved to Glenmar.

Versailles

Polly Place: Bluegrass Bed & Breakfast

Route 1, Box 263
Versailles, KY 40383
606-873-3208

| A one-of-a-kind private
| home in Bluegrass Country

Innkeepers: Ben and Toss Chandler. **Accommodations:** Three-bedroom house.
Rates: $115 per couple; $175 for four; $225 for six; 2-night minimum. **Included:**
Pantry of breakfast items, soft drinks, coffee, tea. **Payment:** Cash or checks.
Children: Not suitable for small children. **Pets:** Not allowed. **Smoking:** Allowed.
Open: Year-round.

➤ **It's quite obvious that Polly Place is well loved. Flowers line the
walkways and the grass is well trimmed, but not to the point of getting in
nature's way or detracting from the country setting.**

You can leave the windows and doors open and turn the music up
loud. Ben and Toss Chandler's dream home and art studio is located at the end of a winding country lane off the main road in the
Pisgah Rural Historic District; the closest neighbor is miles away.
The bluegrass setting is a perfect escape form the everyday world,
so revel in it for the short while that it is yours. The Chandlers
vacate the house after they welcome the guests.

Toss inherited the 200-acre farm from her father a few years ago
and designed the two-story stone and wood house herself. Downstairs are a great room with a wood stone fireplace, a dining room,
kitchen, half bath, and screened porch; two bedrooms with open
balconies and a bathroom with a Jacuzzi are on the second level;

and one bedroom is in the attic. The master bedroom opens onto a deck over the entrance.

The single most interesting aspect of the house is its spiral staircase, made of crude wood and encased in a silo-like structure, with lighted miniature rooms spaced at various levels. The house is furnished in family pieces, and Toss's artistic touches are everywhere — from whimsical artwork to her own sketches. Her easel is kept in the master bedroom.

The Chandlers provide everything you need to make breakfast as well as a good supply of soft drinks, coffee, and tea. Guests usually go to area restaurants for lunch and dinner. The house is stocked with a good library of books and magazines, plenty of tapes, and a television. You won't be expected to do any farm chores here, but you can enjoy looking at the cows in the pasture.

Shepherd Place

U.S. 60, 31 Heritage Road
Versailles, KY 40383
606-873-7843, 800-278-0864
SylviaYawn@MSN.com
Http://www.bbonline.com/ky/shepherd/

A historic B&B in the suburbs — a remnant of the past

Innkeepers: Marlin and Sylvia Yawn. **Accommodations:** 3 rooms (all with private baths). **Rates:** $65–$75. **Included:** Full breakfast. **Payment:** Cash or checks. **Children:** 6 and older welcome. **Pets:** Not allowed. **Smoking:** Not allowed. **Open:** Year-round.

➤ **The two-story home is located in the heart of Bluegrass country, near all the horse farms, the Kentucky Horse Park, and downtown Lexington. (Horseback riding is available nearby.)**

Sylvia Yawn isn't about to part with Abigail, Victoria, or any of her other pet sheep, but you can order a custom-made sweater fashioned out of their wool. Sylvia shears, washes, spins, and knits the natural fibers into lovely one-of-a-kind sweaters. But don't get the idea that this is production knitting; she makes only about three sweaters a year, and each one takes several months to complete. In addition to the sheep on the 5-acre spread, part of a much larger farm that is now an adjoining subdivision, there are ducks and geese to enjoy.

Sylvia, a former math teacher, and her husband, Marlin, who works for Federal Express, share their renovated 1820s Federal home with guests. Guests never feel crowded. The house has windows that go all the way to the wood floors, crown moldings, and fireplaces (the one in the dining room works very well). The rooms are large, and the outside offers plenty of space for roaming. Both of them grew up on farms and enjoy hard work and entertaining.

The Yawns serve a full breakfast to guests in the dining room and assist with dinner reservations at local restaurants.

Vine Grove

Otter Creek Park

850 Otter Creek Park Road
Vine Grove, KY 40108
502-583-3577
Fort Knox area: 502-942-3641
Fax: 502-583-3577

> **A resort park dedicated to
> nature and team building**

Director: John G. Rowe. **Accommodations:** 23 lodge rooms (all with private baths), 12 cabins (with private baths, fireplaces, and kitchens). **Rates:** Lodge rooms: $34–$44 Sunday–Thursday; $48–$124 Friday–Saturday. Cabins: $44–$150 Sunday–Thursday; $78–$134 Friday–Saturday. **Additional:** $8 for cribs and rollaways; recreational fees. **Payment:** American Express, MasterCard, Visa for lodge rooms; cash or checks for cabins. **Children:** Welcome. **Pets:** Allowed. **Smoking:** Smoking and nonsmoking rooms. **Open:** Year-round.

➤ **The park stages three great annual events — the Memorial Day/Bluegrass Festival; Nightmare Forest, a haunted fright hike; and Autumnfest, an October celebration of early American life with craft demonstrations and music.**

No otters live at this beautiful park overlooking the Ohio River, but there's a healthy colony of muskrats, beavers, raccoons, deer, and other wildlife — fitting company and entertainment for visitors. (Some of the park animals also live in the protected environment of the nature center.)

Owned by the city of Louisville, thirty miles to the north, the 3,600-acre park caters to groups. In fact, it's the fifth largest provider of Elderhostel programs in the country, but youth organizations, families, and various companies find it suits their needs for getaways as well. A former church that has been totally renovated is used for receptions, banquets, and parties.

The park administration has been innovative and aggressive in its approach to programs, according to director John G. Rowe. A 12-acre team course, well known in the area, offers fourteen different challenges that engage participants in such team-building activities as the trust fall, in which a participant stands with his or her back to another person and then falls into that person's arms, or the Mohawk walk, in which the team members climb a cable, one at a time, assisted by one another. The park offers half-day, all-day, and three- or five-day workshops around the teams course.

In addition to these challenges, Otter Creek offers picnicking, camping, hiking, swimming, fishing, rappelling, Frisbee golf, miniature golf, and bike rentals. There are facilities for tennis, volleyball, softball, and basketball, and the 2-mile Ped Trail includes several river overlooks. Spelunking at nearby Morgan's Cave and hayrides are other options. Buffet-style meals are served in the contemporary wood-and-glass Otter Creek Park Restaurant, offering majestic views of the river from the bluffs. The restaurant is open from 8:00 A.M. until 9:00 P.M.

Several lodging options are available at Otter Creek, many of them with river views. The 23-room Otter Creek Park Lodge offers rooms with balconies, lofts, and kitchenettes. Haven Hill Lodge and Van Buren Lodge, both log structures, come equipped with kitchens and fireplaces. Each one accommodates six to thirty people. Eight cabins on the property will accommodate one family each; two cabins are large enough for two families each.

Otter Creek Park has an interesting history. It was used by various Indian tribes for hunting and fishing. The French explorer La Salle visited the area in 1669 on his trip down the Ohio to the Mississippi. Around 1780, George Rogers Clark visited the area; about the same time Squire Boone, a brother of Daniel Boone, lived here for a while. The park was built by Civilian Conservation Corps workers during the Depression, and in 1947 the federal government gave the park to the city of Louisville.

Louisiana

Louisiana, with its piquant mélange of Spanish, French, African, British, and German heritages, is quite unlike any other state in the nation. In its southern reaches Louisiana is laced with bayous, sloughs, and lakes. Cypress trees and giant live oaks draped with Spanish moss line these waterways and riverbanks, sometimes lending almost surrealistic overtones to the landscape. The early French and Spanish heritages are apparent in the culture, cuisine, and architecture of New Orleans and Baton Rouge, the capital. And some of the fine old mansions that line both banks of the Mississippi River between the two cities also reflect the architectural influences of the antebellum American South.

In southern Louisiana, incomparable old New Orleans sprawls on a point of land almost surrounded by a deep crescent of the Mississippi River. Its heart is the seventy-block French Quarter (Vieux Carré), with iron-trimmed balconies, narrow streets, colorful buildings, antiques shops, lounges, nightclubs, hotels, and internationally famed restaurants.

Every day may seem like a festival in New Orleans, but undeniably, Mardi Gras lends an unequaled spirit of exuberance to the "City That Care Forgot." Although revelry reaches peak frenzy on Fat Tuesday, the day before Ash Wednesday, parties, parades, and musical entertainment take place virtually nonstop for the previous two weeks. Throughout Louisiana, many communities, large and small, also celebrate their own versions of Mardi Gras.

South central Louisiana became a haven for French Acadian ("Cajun") settlers after the British banished them from Nova Scotia in the 1700s. Today twenty-two parishes (counties) surrounding Lafayette make up one of the nation's most unique cultural enclaves. It's a laid-back, welcoming land where the motto "Let the good times roll" reflects a genuinely heartfelt sentiment that never fails to captivate visitors.

Only in northern Louisiana does one sense a similarity with the more typical Deep South culture, which has predominantly British roots. In great measure, this is a rural area of forests, rivers, and cotton plantations. Gently rolling pine-clad uplands link the region between the Red and Ouachita rivers. The major urban centers are Monroe and Shreveport/Bossier City, which prospered mightily when King Cotton reigned supreme in northern Louisiana.

For more information, contact the Louisiana Office of Tourism, P.O. Box 94291, Baton Rouge, Louisiana 70804-9291, 504-342-8119 or 800-33-GUMBO.

Northern Louisiana

Best Bed-and-Breakfasts

Lecompte
Hardy House, 225
Mansura
Victorian House, 226
Monroe
Boscobel Cottage Bed & Breakfast, 227
Natchitoches
Levy-East House Bed & Breakfast Inn, 228
Shreveport
Fairfield Place, 230

Best City Stop

Alexandria
Hotel Bentley, 222

Best Plantations

Cheneyville
Loyd Hall Plantation Home, 223
Monroe
Boscobel Cottage Bed & Breakfast, 227

Natchitoches (pronounced nak-a-tush) is Louisiana's oldest city. Founded in 1714 by early French traders, it was the oldest permanent settlement in the Louisiana Purchase. Many of its fine old plantation homes and townhouses are open during annual historic tours in October. Among the loveliest is Beau Fort Plantation Home, a cottage-style home on a working plantation; it's elaborately furnished with old French Creole furniture, china, and decorative items. Natchitoches was featured in the movie *Steel Magnolias*, which accurately captured the ambiance of this charming town and is based on a true story written by a native.

Alexandria lies 50 miles south of Natchitoches. Kent House showcases a French-Spanish colonial plantation house, impeccably restored. It's furnished in period furniture, with rare pieces by Creole cabinetmakers. The Alexandria Museum of Art, housed in the old Rapides Bank Building, showcases an outstanding collection of contemporary Louisiana art, and the River Oaks Square Arts and

Crafts Center on Main Street is known for its juried shows. Near Alexandria, a branch of Kisatchie National Forest includes the 31-mile Azalea National Recreational Trail, where blooms usually peak in April. In this region, too, follow the Old Texas Trail along Bayou Rapides, site of vigorous Civil War activity.

Shreveport, northern Louisiana's largest city and a major Red River port, has virtually transformed its waterfront at Shreve Square, restoring handsome Victorian warehouses and opening a pedestrian mall. Performing arts are showcased in the restored 1925 Strand Theater. Year-round, you'll discover an impressive array of museums in Shreveport. R. W. Norton Art Gallery houses American and European paintings, sculpture and decorative art, along with a stunning collection of works by two master Old West artists, Frederic Remington and Charles M. Russell. The Meadows Museum of Art displays Indo-Chinese paintings and drawings, and the imposing doughnut-shaped Louisiana State Exhibit Museum is notable for Louisiana murals and dioramas.

Shreveport is also headquarters for the American Rose Society, which operates the American Rose Center, with 118 acres showcasing the United States' national flower in numerous varieties. The American Rose Festival is staged here in late April. Two other regional festivals draw large crowds. For ten days in April, Holiday in Dixie commemorates the Louisiana Purchase with gala festivities for the whole family. And in October, the eight-day Red River Revel is an exciting annual celebration of the visual and performing arts along the waterfront. It's cosponsored with Shreveport's sister city, Bossier City.

Bossier City, across the Red River, is the area's industrial and entertainment center. There's thoroughbred horse racing from late April through early November at Louisiana Downs, one of the nation's largest tracks. Its major race, the September Super Derby, encompasses a gala seven-day festival, along with ten racing events.

Outdoor lovers will be lured by the fine fishing streams and lakes of nearby 595,000-acre Kisatchie National Forest, which also offers swimming, boating, skiing, nature trails, and campsites at Caney Lakes. Farther west, the Cypress-Black Bayou Recreation Area provides nature trails, camping, picnicking, fishing piers and a marina along with a stretch of white sandy beach.

Alexandria

Hotel Bentley

200 Desoto Street
Alexandria, LA 71301
318-448-9600, 800-356-6835
Fax: 318-448-0683

A queen of northern Louisiana is still the place to stay

Acting General Manager: Judy Emory. **Accommodations:** 168 rooms (all with private baths) and 10 suites (with Jacuzzis and wet bars). **Rates:** $59–$225. **Payment:** Major credit cards. **Children:** Under 12 free with parents. **Pets:** Not allowed. **Smoking:** Smoking and nonsmoking rooms. **Open:** Year-round.

➤ **Grand indeed is the Neoclassical structure. Its facade is made of Bedford limestone and terra cotta, with classic columns supporting a long verandah across the front. The inside lobby is dazzling, with a domed ceiling with stained glass highlights, gray marble columns, tile floor, grand staircase, and flowing water fountain.**

When the Hotel Bentley was built by wealthy lumberman Joseph A. Bentley in 1908, it was called the "Waldorf of the Red River" and the "Biltmore of the Bayous." It quickly became the political center of this part of Louisiana. Huey Long was a frequent visitor, and his brother Earl Long suffered a heart attack here shortly before being sworn in as a U.S. representative. During the two world wars, the Bentley welcomed soldiers of all ranks — Generals George Patton, Omar Bradley, Dwight D. Eisenhower, George C. Marshall, and Matthew Ridgway. In fact, it is said that some of the top brass formulated the plans for several campaigns in the red, black, and silver art deco Mirrors Lounge, now one of the liveliest night spots in northern Louisiana. In recent years the hotel has hosted many military reunions.

In 1983, the Tudor Construction Company purchased the hotel and spent the next two years renovating it to its former grandeur. Recently purchased by Rick Hartley and David Vey, the hotel will undergo another complete renovation in 1998.

The Bentley Room serves fresh fish from the Gulf of Mexico, as well as prime steaks. At Christmastime the hotel is decorated with magnificent trees, greenery, and poinsettias.

Cheneyville

Loyd Hall Plantation Home

292 Loyd Bridge Road
Cheneyville, LA 71325
318-776-5641, 800-240-8135
Fax: 318-776-5886
loydhall@linknet.net

> A plantation experience
> you'll always remember

Innkeepers: Frank and Anne Fitzgerald. **Accommodations:** 6 rooms (with baths and fully equipped kitchen). **Rates:** $95–$145 per couple, plus $20 for each additional person. **Included:** Continental breakfast, refreshments, house tour. **Payment:** Major credit cards. **Children:** Under 6 free with parents. **Pets:** Not allowed. **Smoking:** Not allowed. **Open:** Year-round by reservation.

➤ **The three-story modified Greek Revival brick home, with its double verandahs on the front and back of the house, was built between 1810 and 1820 for the Loyd family, a branch of the famous Lloyds of London. When the Fitzgerald family bought it in 1949, the house had stood vacant for eighteen years and was shrouded in vines.**

A cast of spirits lives on this Louisiana plantation. A red-haired, red-bearded ghost of a Union soldier killed on the property has been seen several times. Another lies buried under the house. One who died in the attic and appears occasionally as a violin player on the second-floor balcony is believed to be mourning the suicide death of Inez Loyd. The spirit of a black nanny has appeared to young children. On the brighter side, the plantation is also inhabited by cattle, horses, chickens and roosters, dogs, and more than a dozen cats.

The house had been abandoned for many years when the Fitzgerald family decided to buy it. Finding it to be structurally sound, they renovated it to its present condition. They often host plantation breakfasts, Christmas parties, and high teas.

Guests do not sleep in the plantation house but have several choices of accommodations. The recently-restored 1800s carriage house features suites with open fireplaces, high ceilings, a private kitchen and bath; each suite opens onto the front porch overlooking the pool, patio, and pavilion. The restored 1800s commissary, formerly used as a store, overlooks the pasture and farmland and features a new kitchen and bath. Minda's House is almost a carbon copy of the commissary. The McCullough house has two bedrooms, kitchen, washer/dryer, and a deluxe private bath with a garden Jacuzzi for two. Aunt Fanny's house offers one bedroom, a kitchen, and bath.

All rooms include a cable television, VCR, and ceiling fans. Guests are provided a Continental-style breakfast (including homebaked muffins and Louisiana coffee), complimentary wine and soft drinks upon arrival, and a tour of Loyd Hall.

Lecompte

Hardy House

1414 Weems Street
P.O. Box 1192
Lecompte, LA 71346
318-776-5178
Fax: 318-776-5103

A B&B where the word "hunger" is never mentioned

Innkeeper: Ann Johnson. **Accommodations:** 3 rooms (all with private baths). **Rates:** $75–$80; discount rates for stays longer than one night. **Included:** Full breakfast, afternoon beverages, desserts. **Payment:** Major credit cards. **Children:** Welcome. **Pets:** Not allowed. **Smoking:** Not allowed. **Open:** Year-round.

➤ **Ann Johnson enjoys sharing information about local history and characters, including her father, Lea Johnson, who once appeared on *The Tonight Show* with Johnny Carson. (Lecompte was named for a famous racehorse in 1854.)**

Dishing out southern hospitality is nothing new to Ann Johnson. She grew up in Lea's Lunchroom nearby and is now the third-generation owner. And since 1991, she's been playing the role of innkeeper and loving every minute of it — she's even saved a mound of thank you letters from the guests who have stayed at her house.

When Ann bought the planter's-style house, it was boarded up. She set about restoring it, relying on the memory of the grandson of the original owner, Dr. Humphrey Hardy, for details on its original look. Windows and fireplaces that had been covered up were relocated and included in the design. The verandahs of the one-story long house, built in 1888, were restored and the gingerbread trim put back in place. Fresh coats of white paint and dark green shutters were added. The white picket fence and brick walkway give the house a finished look.

Inside, Ann spared no expense, and the influence of her study of commercial art can be seen all over the rambling 7,000-square-foot house. But there is warmth and tradition here, as evidenced by the use of family antiques and other pieces that have belonged to friends in the community.

Guests rave about Ann's food, and it's no wonder. They have a choice of a full breakfast at Hardy House or at Lea's Lunchroom, featuring ham and eggs with grits, homemade biscuits, toast, or biscuits with cream gravy, served with homemade jellies and dark-roasted coffee. In the evening guests feast on the world-famous homemade lemon, chocolate, coconut, apple, pecan, blueberry, cherry, peach, and banana cream pies from Lea's. Lunch and dinner are also available at Lea's. There are no printed menus, but patrons always know what to expect — a choice of entrées, rice and gravy, two vegetables, homemade cornbread, and beverages. The buttermilk is served in thick frozen glasses.

Mansura

Victorian House

L'Eglise Street
P.O. Box 387
Mansura, LA 71350
318-964-2073 or 318-964-2889

| A B&B offering southern hospitality in a historic town

Innkeeper: Isma R. Escude. **Accommodations:** 5 rooms (all with private baths). **Rates:** $65. **Included:** Full breakfast, beverages, snacks. **Payment:** Visa. **Children:** 12 and older welcome. **Pets:** Not allowed. **Smoking:** Allowed in kitchen and on porches. **Open:** Year-round.

➤ **In the modern kitchen, Isma Escude whips up the French Avoyelles dishes for which she is famous — boudin (sausage) and beignets (light doughnuts) — as well as some more contemporary dishes such as breakfast pizza.**

This bed-and-breakfast inn on the National Register of Historic Homes is one of the finest homes in Mansura, a French-Acadian town several miles east of Alexandria. The Victorian structure with its wide verandah was built in 1901 by Dr. Thomas Roy, the grandfather of Isma Escude, the innkeeper.

In order to preserve the house, Mrs. Escude, with her daughter Stacy Bordelon and her daughter-in-law Pam Escude, formed a corporation, restored the house, and opened it as a B&B in 1993. They have retained as much of the original aspects of the house as possible, including chandeliers, door fittings, and wainscoting. The central staircase, with its Gothic design, and the elaborate mantels catch the eye. Many of the furnishings are family pieces that are original to the house, and all of the draperies were made by Pam. Arthur Escude, Isma's husband who handles most of the yard work and maintenance, is an important member of the team as well.

The Escudes' favorite room is the kitchen, with its cypress cabinets and large, cypress/red gum table, where a full breakfast is served. Early wake-up coffee is available every morning at six.

Monroe

Boscobel Cottage Bed & Breakfast

185 Cordel Lane
Monroe, LA 71202
318-325-1550, 318-325-7503,
or 318-649-2138
Fax: 318-325-7505 or 318-649-0758

A cotton plantation is now a quiet reprieve for guests

Innkeepers: Cliff and Kay LaFrance. **Accommodations:** 4 rooms (all with private baths). **Rates:** $85–$110; discount rates after first night. **Included:** Full plantation breakfast. **Payment:** Major credit cards. **Children:** Welcome with advance reservations. **Pets:** Welcome with advance reservations. **Smoking:** Allowed. **Open:** Year-round.

➤   Guests love the peace and quiet of Boscobel's country setting, once part of a vast cotton plantation. They also enjoy the LaFrances' cats, dogs, and cockatoo.

Boscobel Cottage, built around 1820, is in northeast Louisiana's cotton country overlooking the Ouachita River. On the National Register of Historic places, the West Indies-style house has many original features — hewn timbers in the foundations, cypress and blue poplar framing, sassafras wood in the walls and ceilings, and Federal mantels. The cottage served as the residence for Judge Henry Bry; later, it was used as an overseer's house.

In 1989, Cliff and Kay LaFrance opened a bed-and-breakfast inn on the property; they and their teenage daughter Adrienne have filled it with antique furnishings. Guests have their choice of three cottages — the Chapel (dating to the 1820s), the garconniere (built as a dependency in 1976), and the dog-trot house (an 1894 structure that has been moved to the site). The latter, renovated in 1993, offers two guest rooms. The inn is rated by AAA and Mobil.

With their Louisiana heritage (Cliff hails from New Orleans), the LaFrances know what entertaining guests is all about. The guest book is filled with comments from visitors who have found Boscobel to be the respite they needed. The LaFrances are avid promoters of tourism, and politicians often find their way to Boscobel. Kay, a former television anchor, is manager of the Main Street program in nearby Columbia, and Cliff has been a pharmacist for more than twenty-five years.

Sometimes the LaFrances will share a potluck supper, but guests usually don't mind the drive to restaurants in Monroe, about 15 miles away. The full plantation breakfast always includes the ever-popular Jalapeno/cheese garlic grits. Honeymooners can order a "champagne dinner" in advance.

Natchitoches

Levy-East House Bed & Breakfast Inn

358 Jefferson Street
Natchitoches, LA 71457
318-352-0662, 800-840-0662

| **An elegant new B&B in the state's oldest town** |

Innkeepers: Judy and Avery East. **Accommodations:** 4 rooms (all with private baths). **Rates:** $105–$150. **Included:** Full gourmet breakfast, complimentary beverages, turndown service. **Payment:** MasterCard, Visa. **Children:** Not appropriate. **Pets:** Not allowed. **Smoking:** Not allowed. **Open:** Year-round except Christmas week.

➤ **Local playwright Bobby Harling wrote the play *Steel Magnolias* in ten days, using his family's personal tragedy as the theme. The hit movie was filmed in Natchitoches.**

The elegant Levy-East House, located in the heart of the Natchitoches National Historic District, overlooks the Cane River and is listed on the National Register of Historic Places. The Greek Revival home, with its wrought iron lace trim, was built in 1838 for Dr. Nicholas Michal Friedelezy, a French Canadian, and was sold at auction in 1854 to John A. DeBussy. Leopold and Justine Levy purchased the house in 1891, and the family lived in it for a hundred years. Avery and Judy East, owners of the East Pharmacy, decided to purchase it and restore it as a bed-and-breakfast inn. They worked on the house for over two years, putting in new wire, refinishing the heart pine floors, and repainting it inside and out. Many of the antiques used in the inn have been a part of the house for well over a century. Future plans call for creating a garden with walkways, sitting areas, fountains, and gazebo in the side yard.

Each of the luxurious guest rooms (two are named for the Easts' daughters) features a queen-sized bed, lavish draperies, television, telephone, piped-in music, and whirlpool bath. Amenities such as fresh ice water and sherry are provided. A videotape of the movie *Steel Magnolias* is available in each room. Guest may relax in the sitting rooms on the second and third floors or on front verandah overlooking the historic Cane River, which meanders through Louisiana's oldest town. There is a private entrance to the second floor. The Easts provide hot coffee in the morning on the second and third floors and serve a full gourmet breakfast, sometimes featuring eggs baked in heart-shaped dishes, in the formal dining room.

Fairfield Place

2221 Fairfield Avenue
Shreveport, LA 71104
318-222-0048
Fax: 318-226-0631

| A luxurious B&B that caters to business travelers |

Innkeeper: Janie Lipscomb. **Accommodations:** 7 rooms and 2 suites (all with private baths). **Rates:** $98–$250. **Included:** Full breakfast. **Payment:** American Express, MasterCard, Visa. **Children:** Well-behaved children welcome. **Pets:** Not allowed. **Smoking:** Allowed on verandahs. **Open:** Year-round.

➤ **Janie provides a lot of extras for her guests. Terrycloth robes, makeup remover, lotion, mouthwash, and dental floss are but a few of the unusual amenities. She also places fresh cut flowers in each room.**

Everything is done to perfection in this luxurious Victorian house — from the coordinated decor of each room to the strawberry butter on the breakfast buffet. In her travels for the Louisiana Board of Dentistry, Janie Lipscomb, formerly a dental hygienist, became fascinated with bed-and-breakfast inns and decided to open her own. She bought the classic Victorian house, located in Shreveport's Highland Historic District, in 1982 and renovated it from top to bottom.

Janie's knack for decorating is evident in every room bearing her special signature. Throughout the house she has used turn-of-the-century Bradbury and Bradbury wallpaper designs, characterized by their unusual color combinations and geometric shapes.

The ceiling of the sitting room in the Parlor Suite is wallpapered in a geometric design; the ceiling in the adjoining bedroom, with gold stars on a teal background. The bed underneath the starred ceiling and the ceiling fan is outfitted with a feather mattress and a goose down comforter by Osborne and Little. The bedding is heaped into a mound in the center so that the bed resembles the one in the fairy tale about the princess who slept on heaps of mattresses. The clawfoot tub in the bathroom is covered on the underside with matching wallpaper. Though the bathroom is small, Janie has made it appear larger by using mirrors on the walls.

In late 1995, Janie acquired the Boldridge home at 948 Boulevard, and two years later finished a complete restoration and made it a part of Fairfield Place. It features two luxurious suites, with a total of three bedrooms, plus a large parlor, dining room, a well-stocked library, and garden room. Much of the garden is a nurtured wildflower meadow, but it has a brick courtyard and a flagstone retreat where guests may seek quiet seclusion.

Guests may have breakfast in the formal dining room of the Boldridge home, on the porches overlooking the gardens, or the courtyard in the garden. (The formal dining room is also used for private dining, small weddings, and corporate meetings.) The menu features fresh juice, rich Cajun coffee, fresh entrees, French pastries, and Janie's own strawberry butter.

The Fairfield is ideal for the business traveler. It is convenient to downtown, but its extensive Victorian setting gardens covering a block are perfect for rejuvenation following a hard day's work. Many guests say upon leaving that The Fairfield offers "the best night's sleep they can remember."

Southern Louisiana

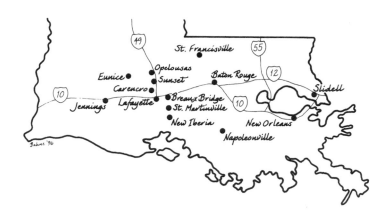

Best Bed-and-Breakfasts

Best City Stops

Best Country Inns

Best Eclectic Find

Best Guest Farm

St. Francisville
Green Springs B&B, 268

Best Historic Inns

Eunice
Portier's Prairie Cajun Inn and GiftBoutique, 243
Lafayette
Bois des Chênes Inn, 245
St. Martinville
The Old Castillo Hotel Bed and Breakfast and La Place
  d'Evangeline Restaurant, 269

Best Plantations

Breaux Bridge
Country Oaks Guesthouse, 241
Napoleonville
Madewood Plantation House, 248
St. Francisville
Butler Greenwood B&B, 267
Sunset
Chrétien Point Plantation, 272

Southern Louisiana is a land of its own. Visitors are fascinated by its language, music, food, and architecture — a blend of the various ethnic cultures that have prevailed here for hundreds of years. New Orleans, the largest city in the region and the state, is the most European-like city in America and one of its most sophisticated. Baton Rouge, the capital, is always lively with its mix of state government and Louisiana State University functions. The real heart of the region, however, is Lafayette, the capital of the Cajun culture. Here and in the surrounding villages and towns people thrive on Cajun food, music, and friendship.

Highlights of your ramblings in New Orleans' French Quarter will include Jackson Square — dominated by St. Louis Cathedral and the eight buildings of the impressive Louisiana State Museum complex. Several other historic Quarter structures welcome visitors, and museum buffs won't want to miss the priceless displays of the Historic New Orleans Collection, housed in four buildings and three courtyards on Royal Street.

Also not to be missed are world-renowned Preservation Hall, where pure and simple classical jazz is performed nightly by old-time masters, and the Café du Monde at the famed French Market, where you can sample hot, strong café au lait and melt-in-the-mouth beignets (little doughnuts dusted with powdered sugar). Nearby, another New Orleans landmark, the 1890s era Jackson Brewery, has been restored and transformed into an elaborate multilevel shopping-dining-entertainment complex.

More stores, restaurants, and specialty shops flourish at the Rouse Company's Riverwalk, on the site of the 1984 World's Fair international pavilion. Adding new vitality to the area is the Woldenberg Riverfront Park, stretching from Canal Street to the Moonwalk (which runs between the Jackson Brewery and Café du Monde). It's a lively gathering place with trees, blooming shrubs, and a brick promenade often displaying works of local artists. Anchoring the park at the foot of Canal Street is the new state-of-the-art Aquarium of the Americas, home to more than four thousand marine species from as far away as the Antarctic and Bering Sea. It showcases aquatic life of the Gulf of Mexico, Caribbean Reef, Amazon rain forest, and the Mississippi River. The cultural and commercial developments along the revitalized riverfront are linked by the "Ladies in Red," vintage streetcars that run frequently throughout the day.

In the central business district, the Louisiana Superdome, one of the nation's largest indoor stadiums, is open for tours except when events are going on. The National Football League's Saints play home games in the stadium, which also hosts the New Year's Day Sugar Bowl.

The St. Charles Avenue Trolley, New Orleans' only remaining streetcar, offers a delightful way to see the handsome mid-city Garden District of fine homes, campuses of Loyola and Tulane universities, and Audubon Park with its excellent zoo and aquarium. You can also reach the park by boarding the *Cotton Blossom* steamboat for a delightful "zoo cruise" from Canal Street dock, returning from Audubon Landing. Several other river and bayou cruises are available, including Mississippi excursions lasting several days.

Storied River Road plantations cluster on both sides of the Mississippi between New Orleans and Baton Rouge. Almost every turn reveals another famous mansion: Greek Revival Italianate Nottoway Plantation; Houmas House, another Greek Revival beauty; Tezcuco, a charming raised cottage-style structure; renowned Oak

Alley, glowing the faintest, softest pink; San Francisco Plantation House, a superb example of steamboat Gothic architecture; and D'Estrehan, the oldest plantation manor house in Louisiana. Many of the plantations offer tours and overnight lodgings, but often they're over-commercialized and short on the southern hospitality you expect in this region. (Your best bet is to stay at a plantation where the owner still resides and assumes the role of host.)

One of Louisiana's oldest towns, St. Francisville, is an ideal base for exploring several of the English-style plantation homes. Just to the east, Rosedown Plantation and Gardens has been called the South's loveliest antebellum restoration. At Oakley Plantation House, now part of Audubon Memorial State Park, naturalist-artist John James Audubon lived for a time, basing more than thirty of his famed *Birds of America* paintings on species discovered in the area. The house displays Audubon memorabilia, and a surrounding 100-acre tract has been set aside as a wildlife sanctuary. Also in the area is the Myrtles, reputed to be America's most haunted mansion.

Baton Rouge, Louisiana's handsome capital, with a population of about 220,000, is among the nation's largest and busiest ports. The state capitol, with its 34-story tower, dominates the skyline. The ornate structure was completed in 1932 by the governor Huey P. Long, whose statue and grave are in formal gardens fronting the building. A plaque marks the spot where he was assassinated in 1935. Across a small lake from the capitol stands the Governor's Mansion, an imposing structure inspired by Oak Alley Plantation. The former Governor's Mansion is now a museum of the Louisiana Arts and Science Center and includes displays about past governors.

Downtown, overlooking the Mississippi River in the restored 1925 Illinois Central train station, the Louisiana Arts and Science Center Riverside displays sculpture, a fine Egyptian collection, and paintings spanning the last three centuries.

In the spirited city of Lafayette, gateway to Cajun country, the superb Acadian Village and Gardens graphically portrays the early settlers' lifestyles. Thoroughbred racing takes place at nearby Evangeline Downs, and there is good fishing in the bayous, lakes, and Atchafayala Basin.

Just south on Bayou Teche, you'll come to the heart of the storied "Evangeline Country," St. Martinville. The charming little town was the locale for segments of Henry Wadsworth Longfellow's poem; in the rear of St. Martin de Tours Catholic Church lies the grave of Emmelijne Lebiche, reputed to be the ill-fated Evangeline. Just north of town, the Longfellow-Evangeline Memorial State Park houses the Acadian House Museum, said to have belonged to Louis Arceneaux, the real-life Gabriel. The structure, held together with wood-en pegs, displays relics of Acadian life and culture.

More remnants of the Acadian heritage linger at New Iberia, jointly settled by French Canadians and Spanish col-onists. Its lovely Shadows-on-the-Teche, one of the South's finest historic homes, is a unique Louisiana adaptation of antebellum architecture.

Baton Rouge

Chateau Louisianne Suite Hotel

710 North Lobdell Avenue
Baton Rouge, LA 70806
504-927-6700, 800-256-6263
Fax: 504-927-6709

**An all-suite city hotel
loaded with amenities**

Innkeepers: Jon and Margaret Fels. **Accommodations:** 50 suites (all with private baths). **Rates:** $69–$125. **Included:** Continental breakfast, morning newspaper. **Payment:** Major credit cards. **Children:** Welcome. **Pets:** Not allowed. **Smoking:** Allowed. **Open:** Year-round.

➤ **The all-suite hotel is an ideal base for exploring the capital. Directly across the street from the Bon Marché Mall, Chateau Louisianne is minutes from downtown Baton Rouge, the airport, and area attractions. There are twenty antebellum homes, as well as numerous Civil War battlefields, within a twenty-mile radius.**

Chateau Louisianne, a contemporary all-suite boutique hotel, offers many luxuries. But it also reflects the influences of southern Louisiana. Works by Louisiana artists are displayed throughout the hotel. The hospitality is welcoming and the service personalized.

The Atrium Suites overlook the three-story atrium lobby; the Garden Suites offer a garden view; and the Honeymoon Suites are made for romance. All feature a bedroom and bath, living room with a sleeper sofa, cable TV, and breakfast area with a coffee-maker. All suites have refrigerators, microwaves, and cable television. Other luxuries include VCR/movie rentals, massage showers, and hair dryers.

For recreation, guests take advantage of the indoor whirlpool and steam room, relax in the outdoor pool, or work out in the exercise room. There is also space for a small meeting. A complimentary Continental breakfast and morning newspaper come with the room.

Breaux Bridge

Country Oaks Guesthouse

1138-A Lawless Tauzin Rd.
Breaux Bridge, LA 70517
318-332-3093, 800-318-2423

> **A place in the country that welcomes children**

Innkeepers: Jim and Judy Allen. **Accommodations:** 2 rooms in main house (with private baths) and 4 cottages (with shared baths). **Rates:** $85, plus $15 for each additional person in cottages. **Included:** Full breakfast, refreshments, use of boats and fishing equipment. **Payment:** Cash or checks. **Children:** Welcome. **Pets:** Not allowed. **Open:** Year-round.

➤ **According to an old legend, the plantation owners buried their valuables in the middle of a triangle of oak trees when the Union soldiers came to the area and then killed their slaves and buried them on top of the gold so the soldiers would not disturb their treasures. The gold has never been found.**

Located in the heart of Cajun country, this B&B sits on 13 acres, characterized by its 3-acre lake, huge live oaks, and walking trails that were once a part of what was the 6,000-acre Magenta Plantation. Owners Jim and Judy Allen moved the main house, at one time a Cajun store, from Lafayette to the site in 1979. (Prior to becoming innkeepers, both were employed at the CBS TV station in Lafayette, where he did a weekly show, *The Jim Allen Fishing Team*, for twenty-five years.)

The farmhouse, which has a beautiful landscaped garden in the front, is lovingly decorated with fine antiques, accented with country crafts, Civil War relics, and Judy's teddy bear collection and Precious Moment figurines. The house has several wood-burning stoves. In addition to the main house, there are four guest cottages. Each one sleeps five and comes with swings, picnic tables, fishing boats and equipment, a television set, and a fully equipped kitchen. The Florence Cottage is a favorite with honeymooners because of its romantic decor. The Farmhouse Cottage is decorated with farm animals and equipment.

Country Oaks offers a multitude of relaxation possibilities, and guests are encouraged to bring their children along. (Judy even provides high chairs.) You can take a walk, cast your line for a fish, go boating, watch the birds, or sign up for a swamp tour. In the evening you can enjoy authentic Cajun food at nearby restaurants, listen to real Cajun music and even join in the dance. The Allens serve a full country breakfast in the dining room of the main house.

Carencro

La Maison de Campagne, Lafayette Bed & Breakfast

825 Kidder Place
Carencro, LA 70520
318-896-6529, 800-895-0235
Fax: 318-896-1494

A Victorian bed-and-breakfast known for its Acadian hospitality

Innkeepers: Fred and Joeann McLemore. **Accommodations:** 4 rooms (all with private baths). **Rates:** $95 and up. **Included:** Full Cajun gourmet breakfast. **Payment:** Major credit cards. **Children:** Check with innkeepers. **Pets:** Not allowed. **Smoking:** Allowed on porches. **Open:** Year-round.

➤ **The two-story turn-of-the-century home sits on eight acres that are covered with live oak and pecan trees. About seven miles north of downtown Lafayette, this quiet setting is conducive to rest and repose. There's a pool on the property that guests may use and relax by.**

You will step back in time at this lovely bed-and-breakfast inn in the country. Don't be surprised if innkeepers Fred and Joeann McLemore meet you at the door in Victorian costume; it's something they often do. Having traveled all over the world while Fred pursued his career with the U.S. Army, the couple is happy to be on home turf again, practicing the southern hospitality they both grew up on.

Once inside La Maison de Campagne, you find yourself amid velvet and lace and other things Victorian. On arrival, you may be treated to some cold lemonade or other nonalcoholic beverage and then shown to your room in the main house — the Country Room, the French Room, or the Magnolia Room, with a Louisiana armoire and a bed from old St. Francisville — or the quaint Sharecropper's cottage, which has a fully equipped kitchen.

The McLemores serve a full Cajun-style breakfast in the formal dining room. Specialties include Cajun eggs, grits, and sausage gravy or crawfish cream, plus homemade breads, pastries, jams, and jellies. Many of these dishes are included in Joeann's cookbook *Lache Pas la Patate* ("Don't Drop the Potato"). They do not serve other meals but will gladly direct guests to their favorite restaurants. La Maison, which has a three-diamond AAA rating, accepts guests by reservation only, so be sure to call ahead.

Eunice

Portiers Prairie Cajun Inn and Gift Boutique

110 West Park
Eunice, LA 70535
318-457-5698

An inn offering a true Cajun experience

Innkeepers: Gaul and Gayle Benoit. **Accommodations:** 8 suites (all with private baths). **Rates:** $60. **Included:** Breakfast basket, turndown service. **Payment:** Major credit cards. **Children:** Welcome. **Pets:** Small pets allowed. **Open:** Year-round.

➤ **The inn is within walking distance of several attractions, including the Liberty Theatre and the Jean Lafitte Cultural Center.**

"Laissez le bon temps roulez!" is second nature in the prairie Cajun town of Eunice, and this inn is something of an attraction in itself. Gaul and Gayle Benoit, natives of the area who are active in tourism, purchased the town's 1920s hospital, renovated it throughout, and furnished it in rustic Acadian decor. Rooms feature iron beds covered with patchwork quilts, chamber pots, and furniture handcrafted from recycled wood from now defunct grocery stores in the area. Each suite has a living room, kitchen, bedroom, and private bath and comes with a breakfast basket filled with gourmet coffee, juice, pastries, yogurt, milk, cereal, fruit, and popcorn.

The Benoits have a forty-passenger Bessenger bus, a '41 Ford, and a carriage, which are available for large parties. The most interesting feature of the courtyard is an original Cajun outhouse, moved to the site by local workmen. The Souvenir Shop on the premises sells authentic Cajun crafts.

Jennings

Creole Rose Manor

214 Plaquemine Street
Jennings, LA 70546
318-824-4936, 800-264-5521
Fax: 318-821-5536

A Victorian B&B in a Main Street U.S.A. city

Innkeepers: Ms. Jay Domingue and Earl Domingue. **Accommodations:** 3 rooms (with private baths). **Rates:** $65. **Included:** Full breakfast. **Payment:** Major credit cards. **Children:** Welcome. **Pets:** Not allowed. **Smoking:** Allowed in designated areas. **Open:** Year-round.

➤ **The original owners brought up their three children in this house and often provided lodging for train travelers who were passing through Jennings. Rates were $1 to $1.50 per night.**

There was a time when, traveling from New Orleans to Houston along Interstate 10, there was no reason to stop in Jennings, Louisiana. But since the Main Street U.S.A. program was implemented, travelers are coming here to see what is happening in Jefferson Davis Parish.

What they find is a thriving turn-of-the-century town with gas lamps, spruced-up storefronts (behind which are antiques shops), the W. H. Tupper General Merchandise Store museum, the Zigler Art Museum, and the Creole Rose Manor, a bed-and-breakfast inn.

The inn, which opened in 1990, was the first home in town to be placed on the National Register of Historic Places. It was built in 1898 by Delino Derouen, a Civil War veteran, and his wife. The two-story Gothic Queen Anne Victorian home features many windows for cross ventilation and galleries where one can catch the breezes. The Flamingo Room has glass in one window that dates to Civil War times, and Confederate money was found in the house during the renovation.

Jay and Earl Domingue have decorated the house in furnishings of the late 1800s. The parlor, wallpapered in a large floral print, features a pair of benches covered in dusty rose velvet. Of special interest to guests is the collection of hand-painted plates by Horitz, Manley, and Currier & Ives.

The Domingues serve a full breakfast, afternoon beverages, and evening desserts, and they will gladly direct guests to local dining establishments. A tour of Creole Rose Manor is included in the room rate.

Lafayette

Bois des Chênes Inn

338 North Sterling Street
Lafayette, LA 70501
Tel. & Fax: 318-233-7816
boisdchene@aol.com
http://members.aol.com/boisdchene/bois.htm

> **An Acadian B&B known for its hospitality**

Innkeepers: Coerte and Marjorie Voorhies. **Accommodations:** 5 suites (all with private baths). **Rates:** $95–$125, plus $30 for each additional person. **Included:** Full breakfast, afternoon wine. **Payment:** American Express, MasterCard, Visa. **Children:** Welcome. **Pets:** Small, well-behaved pets welcome. **Smoking:** Allowed outside. **Open:** Year-round.

➤ **Coerte Voorhies often takes guests on half-day boat tours of the swamps and marshes as well as hunting and fishing trips for an extra fee. Don't worry about getting lost; he formerly worked as a petroleum geolo-**

gist. His swamp tours have been featured on the Discovery Channel, and on international programs.

You're sure to love this historic inn, located in a lush, shaded garden in the heart of Lafayette, the Cajun capital. Hosts Coerte and Marjorie Voorhies have perfected the art of innkeeping and hospitality. They go out of their way to please, making sure their efforts never get in the way of the privacy they have created for their guests.

Guests stay in a restored 1890s carriage house at the rear of the plantation house, and in the main house. Each of the inn rooms bears Marjorie's sense of good taste in decorating — never overstated, never overdone, so that the antique furnishings are the primary focus. Rooms are furnished with tester beds, desks, comfortable chairs, and armories that conceal the cable televisions. A refrigerator, umbrella, radio, flashlight, and plenty of reading materials are provided, but telephones have been deliberately omitted. All the rooms have ceiling fans and individually controlled heating/air conditioning units.

Following the full plantation breakfast, which usually includes boudin (Cajun-style sausage), fresh fruit and juice, French toast and cane syrup, or some other specialty, Coerte conducts a tour of the 1820 Mouton Plantation House. The house, one of the few surviving structures of its type, was restored by the Voorhieses; they have furnished it with family antiques and heirlooms of the period, many of them Acadian. (The French Acadians originally settled in Nova Scotia in 1604 but were exiled by the British 150 years later, and many of them found a new life in the swamps of Louisiana. One of the rooms in the carriage house is also furnished in Acadian pieces.)

The main house was built by Charles Mouton, a first-generation Acadian who was the brother of the first elected governor of Louisiana. (Coerte is a direct descendent.) Following the Civil War, the house came into the possession of the Mudd family of Virginia. A lieutenant governor of Louisiana and two mayors of Lafayette also resided here for a time.

The Voorhieses gladly share information with their guests about visitor attractions and local restaurants that serve real Cajun food. They can also tell you where to hear a good Cajun band.

T'Frere's House & Garconniere

1905 Verot School Road
Highway 339
Lafayette, LA 70508
Tel & Fax: 318-984-9347
http://www.ultranet.comm/inns/data/tfreres.html

A B&B with entertaining hosts

Innkeepers: Pat and Maugie Pastor. **Accommodations:** 6 rooms (all with private baths). **Rates:** $95. **Included:** Oh! La! La! breakfast, Ti-juleps. Cajun canapes. **Payment:** Major credit cards. **Children:** Welcome. **Pets:** Check with innkeeper. **Smoking:** Allowed on galleries or in gazebo. **Open:** Year-round.

➤ **Natives of the Attakapas area, the Pastors know all the places where Cajun culture thrives. Ask them about local restaurants, dance halls, swamp tours, and attractions. Both speak French fluently, and their melodic speech is laced with Cajun history, stories, and humor. After spending a few days with them, you'll understand a little more about Cajun mystique.**

A visit to T'Frere's begins with a complimentary Ti-juleps — always served, as it should be, in a silver Jefferson cup. (The recipe includes Crystal Lite tea, schnapps, and Canadian whiskey.) While you're enjoying this very southern, classic cocktail, you can get acquainted with Pat and Maugie Pastor, who purchased the inn from Peggy Moseley in 1993. Drinks, along with special hors d'oeuvres, are usually served in the glass-enclosed gallery after which the Pastors often give a promenade tour of the house.

The two-story cottage, with a porch across the front and a center dormer balcony, was built in 1880 of native cypress and handmade bricks by Onezophore Comeaux, a sugar planter, as a wedding gift to his wife. There are four guest rooms. One room has a large tester bed, a working fireplace, and a Jacuzzi tub. Scattered through the house are the Pastors' collection of River Road paintings and stained glass pieces. Each guest is provided with terrycloth robes. Morning coffee is served in the room. The Pastors recently added an old-style Garconniere, giving them two more guest rooms, beautifully furnished in primitive antiques.

Breakfast at T'Frere's is memorable, especially the Oh! La! La! Breakfast, for Pat and Maugie were in the restaurant business for many years. They often serve French toast with bread pudding sauce, topped with bananas foster and "Pastor sauce," and boudin (a Cajun-style sausage). The four-course meal is served with china, linens, and silver. Guests may take breakfast on the glassed-in porch or in the cozy kitchen, which has a fireplace, cypress mantel, and a table from Normandy.

Napoleonville

Madewood Plantation House

4250 Highway 308
Napoleonville, LA 70390
504-369-7151, 800-375-7151
Fax: 504-369-9848

The "Queen of the Bayou" offers the ultimate in southern hospitality

Innkeepers: Keith and Millie Marshall. **Accommodations:** 8 rooms (all with private baths). **Rates:** $185. **Included:** Full breakfast, wine and cheese, dinner with wine, brandy. **Payment:** Major credit cards. **Children:** Well-behaved children welcome. **Pets:** Not allowed. **Smoking:** Not allowed. **Open:** Year-round.

➤ Keith and Millie were married in a ceremony at Madewood a few years ago. The celebration afterward featured jambalaya and other local delicacies and entertainment by gospel singers and a full orchestra that played 1940s music. "It was without a doubt a grand wedding, and when the groom hugged the bride after the ceremony, the guests burst into applause," Millie reported in a New Orleans newspaper article.

Madewood may seem grand and imposing, but guests feel right at home here, thanks to owners Keith and Millie Marshall, who practice the "art of innkeeping" with perfection. Though they both have demanding careers in New Orleans (she's a journalist and he runs an art gallery), they usually come home to Madewood on weekends in order to be with guests. And when they're not around, their well-trained staff knows exactly what to do.

"Madewood is different from most of the plantation houses in the area in that it has a very homey atmosphere," says Millie. "Most guests feel as if they've been to a house party in the country. Our guests gather for a glass of chardonnay and a bit of brie at 6 P.M. and then eat together around a huge dining room table. Typically we serve gumbo, shrimp or chicken pie. One of the guests rings a dinner bell between courses. After dinner we invite the guests to have coffee and brandy in the parlor."

In the morning wake-up coffee is provided for guests prior to sitting down to a scrumptious Southern breakfast of ham, sausage, eggs, grits, biscuits, and fruit. It, too, is a memorable experience.

The Marshalls got into innkeeping quite by accident when they received a telephone call one evening in 1985. The people on the other end of the line were inquiring about the availability of rooms in the mansion. Keith did some quick math in his head and answered that they could indeed accommodate three couples for $150 per couple, which would cover an overcharge on the month's utility bill.

In 1964, Keith's mother purchased Madewood without his father's knowledge, and then poured her heart, soul, and money into the restoration. Money from tours provided for the upkeep of the house for a number of years. Keith, who inherited the mansion from his parents, has combined family heirlooms with English antiques throughout the house. (He has a Ph.D. in art history and was a Rhodes Scholar at Oxford with President Clinton.) Unlike most tour homes, which cordon off rooms with ropes, Madewood is completely open to guests. It is especially beautiful at Christmastime. The mansion has hosted arts events, served as the setting for several films and been featured in publications such as *Country Inns, National Geographic Traveler,* and *Travel Holiday.*

The grand 24-room mansion, a National Historic Landmark, was built between 1838 and 1846 by Colonel Thomas Pugh, a sugar cane planter. The lumber used in the house came from the plantation, and bricks were made on the spot (hence the name "Madewood"). The largest plantation home in Louisiana (next to Nottoway), the Greek Revival home is located on Bayou Lafourche in Napoleonville between New Orleans and Baton Rouge. It is distin-

guished by six towering Ionic columns and wide wrap-around verandahs. A broad hallway extends from the front to the rear of the
house, revealing a suspended walnut staircase leading to the guest
rooms. The luxuriously furnished rooms feature Persian carpets,
early South artwork, bookcases lined with books, and special beds
(four posters, half testers, and twin beds from the old Ursuline
Convent in New Orleans) covered with plush bedding. In addition
to the rooms in the mansion, the three-bedroom Charlet House on
the property also accommodates guests. The authentic slave cabin
is rented only on request.

New Iberia

The Inn at leRosier

314 East Main Street
New Iberia, LA 70560
318-367-5306, 888-804-ROSE
Fax: 318-365-1216
http://www.leRosier.com

**A Cajun inn with a
celebrated chef**

Innkeepers: Hallman and Mary Beth Woods. **Accommodations:** 6 rooms (all
with private baths). **Rates:** $95. **Included:** Full country breakfast. **Payment:**
American Express, MasterCard, Visa. **Children:** 12 and older welcome. **Pets:**
Not allowed. **Smoking:** Not allowed. **Open:** Year-round.

➤   **Novelist James Lee Burke often writes about New Iberia in his Dave
Robicheaux novels.**

This is one inn where food and lodging are equally important.
Hallman Woods III, son of the owners Hallman and Mary Beth
Woods, is one of Louisiana's most celebrated chefs. In fact, he rep-
resented Louisiana at the 1996 Washington Rice Celebration in the
nation's capital. The previous year, *Food & Wine* magazine named
him one of America's best new chefs. Woods is known for the Creole flair in his food, prepared with fresh ingredients and herbs. A
self-taught chef, he learned a great deal about food from his lawyer
father, an excellent cook in his own right, and from on-the-job
training at Gautreau's in New Orleans. Breakfast is included in the

room rate at the inn, of course, but dinner is an extra $20 to $30 per person.

The Woods established the inn a few years ago, restoring the 1870 house, located across the street from Shadows-on-the-Teche, a National Trust tour home. They offer six elegant guest rooms, each furnished with antiques and reproductions. Each room has a private bath, telephone, and television. One parlor in the house is for the exclusive use of overnight guests, though all the public rooms in the house are available. A rear deck and patio, as well as a front verandah overlooking the lush, manicured gardens, are popular gathering places.

New Orleans

Bienville House

320 Decatur Street
New Orleans, LA 70130
504-529-2345, 800-535-7836
Fax: 504-525-6079

A small service-oriented luxury hotel in the French Quarter

General Manager: Steve Caputo. **Accommodations:** 83 rooms (all with private baths). **Rates:** $89–$220, plus parking. **Payment:** Major credit cards. **Children:** 18 and under stay free with parents. **Pets:** Not allowed. **Smoking:** Allowed. **Open:** Year-round.

➤ **Many famous restaurants and nightspots are within walking distance of the hotel, located in the French Quarter's trendiest neighborhood.**

Convenience and spaciousness are two advantages of this unique French Quarter hotel. Its rooms occupy three former warehouses, and the hotel recently completed a multi-million dollar restoration. Across the street is one of New Orleans' main attractions, the Aquarium of the Americas, and the hotel is within walking distance of Canal Place, Jackson Square, Royal Street, and Bourbon Street. The owners, the Monteleone family, also own the famous Monteleone Hotel.

Central to the hotel is a lush tropical courtyard with its fountain and swimming pool — a favorite gathering spot for guests. Many of the rooms in the four-story hotel have balconies that overlook this beautiful scene. All of the guest rooms are extra large, and they are furnished with period furnishings, including four-poster beds and armoires. There are three suites in the hotel, each with one or two bedrooms.

As is the case at the Monteleone, service is most important at Bienville House. Valet parking and room service are offered. The hotel can accommodate small groups in the meeting space.

The Delta Queen

1380 Port of New Orleans Place
Robin Street Wharf
New Orleans, LA 70130-1890
504-586-0631, 800-543-1949
Fax: 504-585-0630

| A floating hotel on the Mississippi River |

Owner: Delta Queen Steamboat Company. **Accommodations:** 85 staterooms and 6 suites (all with private baths). **Rates:** $620–$1,990 per person for three nights; $2,350–$8,720 per person for 14 nights. **Included:** Four meals a day, entertainment, and port charges. **Payment:** Major credit cards. **Children:** Welcome. **Pets:** Not allowed. **Smoking:** Not allowed in guest rooms. **Open:** February–December.

➤ **The *Delta Queen* and her sisters, the *Mississippi Queen* and the *American Queen* (the newest member of the fleet), offer overnight accommodations on several major rivers, including the Mississippi, in the Eastern United States. The *Delta Queen,* which dates to 1926, is the only authentic, fully restored overnight steamboat in the world.**

Everyone departing on the *Delta Queen* gets a big sendoff from the dock in New Orleans, complete with calliope music, Dixieland jazz, food, and drinks. It's all a preview of the good times to be had during the three-night, seven-night, or twelve-night journeys up the mighty Mississippi, river trips that have been enjoyed since 1890, the year the line was founded by Captain Gordon C. Greene and his wife, Mary. (The journey to Vicksburg takes a week.) The company also travels the Ohio, Cumberland, and Tennessee rivers.

On board are nightly entertainment, sometimes heralded under a particular theme, and riverboat gambling when the vessel pulls into a port where there is a gambling boat — just as in the good old days. Mark Twain would feel right at home. (Gambling has been made legal recently in a number of states through which the boat passes.) The wheel house is always open for tours. There are plenty of places for unwinding, a favorite being the Texas Bar, a paneled room overlooking the water.

Guest quarters are small but luxurious. Owned by the Delta Queen Steamboat Company, the boat features polished brass, hand-rubbed oak paneling, Tiffany stained glass, velvet upholstery, and polished hardwood floors. The boat was designated a National Historic Landmark in 1989.

The *Delta Queen* began its career as a shuttle between Sacramento and San Francisco. After World War II it was towed more than five thousand miles along the Pacific Coast, through the Panama Canal, up the Gulf of Mexico to New Orleans, and then on to Cincinnati, where it was disassembled for restoration. It has been traveling the inland waterways since 1948. Four meals a day are served aboard the boat.

You can sleep in rooms once occupied by world-famous figures. Room 340, noted for its oak paneling, is where President Jimmy Carter slept in 1979, while his daughter Amy occupied the adjoining room, Number 338. The actress Helen Hayes slept in Room 103, and Princess Margaret occupied the Robert E. Lee Room, Number 119, which features a large bed, a clawfoot tub, and three windows (definitely a luxury).

Hotel Maison de Ville and the Audubon Cottages

727 Rue Toulouse
New Orleans, LA 70130
504-561-5858, 800-634-1600
Fax: 504-528-9939

A historical hotel that emphasizes service

Managing Director: Jean-Luc Maumus. **Accommodations:** 23 rooms, 2 suites, and 7 cottages (all with private baths). **Rates:** $175–$525. **Included:** Continental breakfast, afternoon beverages, evening port and sherry, shoeshine. **Payment:** Major credit cards. **Children:** 12 and older welcome. **Pets:** Not allowed. **Smoking:** Allowed in courtyard. **Open:** Year-round.

➤ **Great attention is given to service at Maison de Ville. If you leave your shoes outside your door in the evening, you'll find them polished the next morning. A Continental breakfast is delivered on a silver tray to your room along with a newspaper, and later in the day the hotel provides complimentary tea, port, and sherry. The concierge will even arrange carriage rides and breakfast from Brennan's delivered to your door.**

The playwright Tennessee Williams wrote a number of plays while staying in Room 9 at the Hotel Maison de Ville. Dick Cavett, Sissy Spacek, and Jason Robards also slept here. Another claim to fame is the hotel's Bistro, voted the "Top Haute New Orleans Restaurant" by *Zagat Survey* in 1993 and duly noted in *Food & Wine, Esquire,* and *Time.*

Parisian in style, with dark red interior and white tablecloths, it offers a variety of reasonably priced delicacies such as Louisiana crawfish with spicy aioli and seared pompano with an Asian-style orzo pasta and lemon grass curry beuvre blanc. (The menu changes daily.) Another distinction is the hotel's membership in Small Luxury Hotels of the World and Historic Hotels of America.

Guests have a choice of accommodations — rooms in the main house, suites, and the Audubon Cottages, named for the American artist who occupied Cottage One while working on *Birds of America.* The rooms in the main house, which was built in 1743 by pharmacist Antoine Peychaud (inventor of the cocktail), are furnished with antiques, four-poster beds, and period paintings. The garçonnière rooms in the former slave quarters are less formal. Rooms on Rue Toulouse tend to be a little noisy, but that's considered part of the atmosphere. A quieter choice is the Audubon Cottages, which date to 1788 and are located a block and a half away on Rue Dauphine. Each contains a living room, bedroom, bath, and private courtyard.

The House on Bayou Road

2275 Bayou Road
New Orleans, LA 70119
504-945-0992 or 504-949-7711
Fax: 504-945-0993

| A petite Creole plantation in the city |

Innkeeper: Cynthia L. Reeves. **Accommodations:** 8 rooms (6 with private baths, 2 with shared bath). **Rates:** $115–$245. **Included:** Full plantation breakfast. **Payment:** American Express, MasterCard, Visa. **Children:** 12 and older welcome. **Pets:** Not allowed. **Smoking:** Allowed outside only. **Open:** Year-round.

➤ **On the National Register of Historic Places, the house was built in 1798 for a Spanish Colonial diplomat. In 1992, owner Cynthia Reeves opened her home to guests after living here for twenty years.**

Guests can hardly believe it when they drive into Cynthia Reeves's driveway: here in the middle of bustling New Orleans, just a few blocks from the French Quarter, is a two-acre West Indies-style Creole plantation.

The House on Bayou Road offers eight guest rooms, four in the main house, three in one cottage, and an entire cottage featuring a whirlpool tub, wet bar, and its own private porch with rocking chairs. All are furnished with queen- or king-sized beds (except one which has a double), and six have private baths. Several of the rooms can be combined with others and sold as suites. The house is furnished in antiques and collectibles. Guests especially enjoy the many places to get lost — on the porches, the patio, the swimming pool, or the gazebo, which has a hot tub. Cynthia provides all kinds of luxuries for her guests, such as complimentary sherry, freshly cut flowers, logo-embroidered robes, a basket of toiletries, and pralines or chocolates on the pillow at night.

Breakfast at the House on Bayou Road, always an auspicious occasion, is served around the pool or in the dining room. The Honduran chef creates all kinds of delicious dishes — eggs Benedict, Honduran corn pancakes, omelets with traditional Louisiana fillings, enchiladas wrapped in banana leaves from the grounds, and other delectables. On weekends there is a champagne brunch.

Cynthia loves spending time with guests and sharing her favorite city with them. A polo player, she raises and trains polo ponies. She has also worked in retailing, public relations, and hotel sales. Cynthia keeps a supply of New Orleans maps and restaurant reviews on hand, and she'll make reservations for guests. Sometimes she gives visitors an orientation tour of the French Quarter, takes them to the bayou country for Cajun dancing and swamp touring, arranges golf games, boat cruises, canoe trips, and deep sea fishing on shrimp trawlers.

Maison Dupuy

1001 Rue Toulouse
New Orleans, LA 70112
504-586-8000
800-535-9177 (outside Louisiana)
Fax: 504-525-5334

> A European-style hotel with lots of extras

General Manager: Heather Strauss. **Accommodations:** 200 rooms (all with private baths, some with private balconies, kitchens, parlors, and wet bars). **Rates:** $185–$245, plus $12 for parking. **Payment:** Major credit cards. **Children:** Welcome; under 17 free in some rooms. **Pets:** Not allowed. **Smoking:** Smoking and nonsmoking rooms. **Open:** Year-round.

➤ **The elegant VIP Suites in the hotel are named for famous writers who incorporated the city into their pages — Tennessee Williams, William Faulkner, Frances Parkinson-Keyes, Anne Rice, Mark Twain, and Truman Capote. The hotel's other claim to fame is Chef Paul Prudhomme, who began his cooking career in the hotel's kitchen.**

This hotel has it all — history, service, a connection to one of the city's most famous musicians, and an appreciation for the literary heritage of the area. Though the hotel was the last to be built in the French Quarter before a building moratorium was declared in 1975, it has a long history. James Pitot built the first cotton press in the country here in 1802. Legend has it that Louis Armstrong played his jazz trumpet on the block where the hotel stands.

The historic site had many uses before it became a hotel. The buildings housed apartments, stores, a blacksmith shop, a glassware company, stone and tile works, and metal works. In 1955, Gloria Anselmo Dubuc saved the site from demolition when she purchased it, in hopes that it would someday become a hotel. In 1973, Milton and Clarence Dupuy incorporated the old buildings into a luxury hotel offering 198 guest rooms and named their inn Maison, French for home. In 1986, the Delta Queen Steamboat Company purchased the hotel and two years ago sold it to Thayer Lodging Group of Annapolis, Maryland. The owner recently spent $4.6 million renovating all the public areas and the guest rooms.

No attention to detail has been overlooked at Maison Dupuy. Guests are welcomed to the hotel by the friendly doorman and are often greeted by name by the staff.

Rooms at Maison Dupuy are luxurious and come in a range of sizes — from standard rooms with a king-size or two double beds to the VIP suites and a private two-bedroom cottage. Many of the rooms and suites, including the Honeymoon Suite, overlook the courtyard, one of the most beautiful in New Orleans.

Dining is offered throughout the day in Dominiques Restaurant, and a relaxed atmosphere prevails in the Cabaret Lautrec Lounge and the Courtyard Bar. The hotel offers room service, meeting space for small groups, an outdoor swimming pool that is heated year-round, a health club, maid service twice a day, nightly turn-down, valet laundry, and guest voice mail.

Melrose Mansion

937 Esplanade Avenue
New Orleans, LA 70116
504-944-2255
Fax: 504-945-1794

**The city's most elegant
B&B**

Innkeepers: Melvin and Rosemary Jones. **Accommodations:** 4 rooms (all with private baths) and 4 suites (all with whirlpool baths). **Rates:** $225–$425. **Included:** Full breakfast. **Payment:** Major credit cards. **Children:** Limited. **Pets:** Not allowed. **Smoking:** Limited. **Open:** Year-round.

➤ **Guests who fly into the city will be met by the chauffeur-driven black limousine, distinguished by its license plate, which reads "Melrose." Others will not feel any less welcome, because the butler greets everyone at the front door and then offers a complimentary drink (a ritual practically any time of the day in New Orleans).**

It looks like something out of a movie — proudly standing on the corner of Esplanade and Burgundy, its three-story Gothic tower and side verandahs all gleaming with white paint, accented with dark green shutters, all brightly lit, ready and waiting to receive guests.

Owners Mel and Rosemary Jones bought the house not knowing what they would do with it. But it wasn't long before they knew that the house had a special destiny — to be a bed-and-breakfast inn. They had always enjoyed entertaining at their home in northern Alabama, so innkeeping seemed the right thing to do in their retirement. It was their first experience with an old house, but Mel's many years spent working on new construction paid off.

Built in 1884 by the Lanaux family, the Gothic Victorian mansion had good design with unusual angles, 14-foot ceilings, bay windows, and heart pine flooring. The restoration took several years. In 1995, the Melrose was named one of the "Top Ten Undiscovered Hotels in America" by Zagat.

The Joneses have left no details to the imagination. Every room has been carefully designed to give it the optimum appearance and usage, and the result is nothing short of breathtaking. All the fabrics and furnishings were carefully chosen and coordinated by Rosemary, who bought all the antiques in the New Orleans area. Though there's not a bad room in the house, the one most often suggested for honeymooners and dignitaries is the Donecio Suite. (Mrs. Lyndon Johnson was the inn's first guest and the first person to stay in the elegant room. Other notable guests have included Major Ronald Ferguson, John Walsh, and Carrie Fisher.) The suite features five windows draped in lacy curtains, which open out onto the balcony overlooking Esplanade. It also has a Jacuzzi. Special amenities in each room include fresh flowers, a decanter of Courvoisier, scented toiletries, and a wet bar.

Guests are served a full Creole breakfast in the formal dining room; they may also have room service or eat outside. Featured items include fresh fruit, home-baked bread, bread pudding, and various hot entrées, including eggs Benedict. The house coffee is hazelnut cream. Guests have use of the entire house, the tropical patio, swimming pool, and the exercise room. The bar is always open, and drinks are complimentary during cocktail hour. The inn is within easy walking distance to New Orleans' many fine restaurants and shops, and the Joneses are always happy to make suggestions.

Royal Sonesta Hotel

200 Bourbon Street
New Orleans, LA 70140
504-586-0300, 800-SONESTA
Fax: 504-586-0335

| A city hotel with lots of European flair |

President/General Manager: Hans U. Wandfluh. **Accommodations:** 468 rooms and 32 suites (all with private baths). **Rates:** $185–$1,100. **Included:** Tower Level residents get morning coffee and croissants, daily newspaper, afternoon sherry, port, and sweets. **Payment:** Major credit cards. **Children:** Under 18 free in room with parents. **Pets:** Boarding arrangements available. **Smoking:** Smoking and nonsmoking rooms. **Open:** Year-round.

➤ **Sonesta has opened another 243-room hotel called the Chateau Sonesta one block away. It is located in the former D. H. Holmes Canal Street Department Store, built in 1849 and recently renovated and restored.**

Take your pick of fun-filled Bourbon Street or the inside courtyard at this New Orleans establishment in the heart of the French Quarter. Whichever side you choose, you'll be entertained, for you are in the midst of all the action. (You should catch lots of beads and doubloons during Mardi Gras.) The hotel isn't centuries old, having been built in 1969, but it's made to look that way.

Guests enter the gleaming marble lobby, with its 19th-century fountain centerpiece, polished brass fixtures, and splashes of pink shell and seafoam green. The guest rooms vary in decor but are consistent in the quality of wallcovers, carpeting, and furniture. Renovated recently, all feature minibars, phone systems with voice mail and dataport, and hairdryers. Several rooms can accommodate the disabled. In addition to the regular rooms are several types of suites — petite suites, split levels, a honeymoon suite, a presidential suite, and others.

There are several choices of dining experiences within the hotel. Begue's features New Orleans–style dishes made from Louisiana products with innovative Creole cuisine and contemporary flair. Other options are the Desire Oyster Bar and Bistro, a casual setting on Bourbon Street offering fresh seafood and poboys, a local specialty. (Of course, hundreds of wonderful restaurants are just a few steps away from the Royal Sonesta.) There are several places of entertainment in the hotel — Can Can Jazz Cafe, Le Booze, Daiquiris Delite, Mystick Den Lounge, and Quarter Deck Bar at the pool — in addition to all the Bourbon Street establishments.

The Royal Sonesta offers just about every kind of amenity you can imagine — especially on the Tower Level, reached via key-accessed elevator. Here personal concierge, a daily newspaper, bottled water, bathrobes, personalized matches, a Continental breakfast, beverages, and sweets are the norm. A fitness room, covered parking garage, valet service, room service, executive business center, and on-site travel agent are but a few of the other services available. The hotel is also an ideal place for meetings because of its location and amenities.

Soniat House

1133 Chartres Street
New Orleans, LA 70116
504-522-0570, 800-544-8808
Fax: 504-522-7708

An elegant family-owned guest house

Innkeepers: Rodney R. and Frances Smith. **Accommodations:** 18 rooms and 6 suites (all with private baths, 7 with Jacuzzis). **Rates:** $170–$550, plus $7.50 per person for breakfast and $14 for parking. **Payment:** American Express, MasterCard, Visa. **Children:** Welcome. **Pets:** Not allowed. **Smoking:** Allowed in designated areas. **Open:** Year-round.

➤ **The staff-to-guest ratio is one to one, so you'll never have to wait for anything. And Soniat House isn't the type of place that gets street traffic (it's open only to guests and their friends), so you'll feel perfectly safe.**

If you're looking for a small European-style hotel in the French Quarter that takes pride in offering service, you won't go wrong at Soniat House. It's historic, elegant, charming, convenient, personal, and service-oriented. In fact, you'll even forget it is a hotel because it is so much like a home.

Owners Rodney and Frances Smith, who formerly worked in fashion and retailing, want it that way. They've combined an 1830 Creole house and a turn-of-the-century boarding house into one of the city's finest hotels. You enter the older building through the shuttered doors on Chartres Street into the brick paved carriage way, which leads to the lush courtyard in the center. The Smiths won an award in 1983 for the restoration; the inn is a member of Historic Hotels of America.

To the left of the carriage way is the reception area, where you are greeted by the staff and offered a drink before being escorted to your room. Guests are welcome to use the well-stocked honor bar at any time as well as partake of the complimentary hors d'oeuvres in the evening. Though the hotel doesn't operate a restaurant, it offers room service, as well as concierge service, 24 hours a day. Valet parking, cleaning and laundry, safe-deposit boxes, umbrellas, and evening turndown service are available. The hotel is only four blocks from Jackson Square, making it easy to walk to restaurants, shops, the river, and attractions.

The rooms at Soniat House are delightful (ask Paul Newman, who has stayed here). Some have balconies, and several open onto the courtyard. Three have fireplaces, and seven feature Jacuzzis. All are furnished in fine Louisiana, French, and English antiques, collected by the Smiths during their travels all over the world. The drapery and upholstery fabrics were custom-made in France, and the bed linens are of the finest quality. Original artwork by contemporary New Orleans artists complements the furnishings. All the guest rooms are equipped with telephones, radios, and televisions plus extras such as goose down pillows and Crabtree and Evelyn amenities.

A Continental breakfast consisting of fresh orange juice, hot biscuits with homemade strawberry preserves, and café au lait is served on a silver tray. It can be delivered to your room, your balcony, or the courtyard.

Windsor Court Hotel New Orleans

300 Gravier Street
New Orleans, LA 70130-1035
504-523-6000, 800-262-2662
Fax: 504-596-4513
Telex: 784060

> An English hotel in every way

Owner: Orient Express Hotels. **Accommodations:** 56 rooms and 268 suites (all with private baths). **Rates:** $235–$990 (summer and Christmas discounts available). **Payment:** American Express, MasterCard, Visa. **Children:** Welcome. **Pets:** Not allowed. **Smoking:** Smoking and nonsmoking floors. **Open:** Year-round.

➤ *Condé Nast Traveler* **has twice rated Windsor Court the number one hotel in America, and for three consecutive years it was highly rated by the Lifestyles of the Rich and Famous television program. In 1993,** *Zagat Survey* **named it the best hotel in the United States.**

One of the "in" things to do in New Orleans these days is to have tea at Windsor Court — British, of course, as the hotel name suggests. It's offered every afternoon in Le Salon, along with live chamber music, and you need an advance reservation.

Afternoon tea isn't the only English experience offered in the European-style hotel; everything about it is English-inspired. The Gallery, which actually is meeting space on the fourth floor, has a fine display of English seascapes, and works by seventeenth-, eighteenth-, and nineteenth-century masters — Reynolds, Gainsborough, Huysman, and others — are featured throughout the hotel. There's also a portrait of Edward VIII, Prince of Wales, in a foyer near the Polo Lounge. Two members of the royal family — Princesses Margaret and Anne — have called on the hotel.

Guest rooms (most are suites) are decorated in English sporting and floral themes. All the suites feature a separate living room, a small kitchen or wet bar, a European mini-bar, a bidet, and a dressing room adjoining the bedroom and bathroom. Each evening guests receive turndown service with imported chocolates. All guests are provided with terrycloth robes and designer toiletries.

The hotel was built in 1984 by James Coleman, Sr., a New Orleans developer, at the suggestion of his son, who spent two years studying in England. Something of a contemporary castle surrounding a lush courtyard, the 23-story hexagonal hotel, in the heart of the New Orleans business district near the French Quarter, is built of rose-colored granite and bronze-tinted glass. It was renovated in 1990–1991. The hotel has a fitness center and a 75-foot swimming pool, valet parking, massage service, 24-hour room service, valet, and concierge. With its multilingual staff, the hotel caters to groups with meeting space and secretarial and fax services.

A member of Preferred Hotels Worldwide and Leading Hotels of the World, Windsor Court was purchased by Orient Express Hotels in the fall of 1991. In its short history, it has accumulated a mountain of awards from more than ten magazines and travel associations.

Opelousas

Maison de Saizan

412 South Court Street
Opelousas, LA 70560
318-948-9898

A restored Victorian home reborn as a B&B

Innkeepers: Louis and Dona Doucet. **Accommodations:** 3 rooms (all with private baths). **Rates:** $75–$130. **Included:** Breakfast, complimentary beverages. **Payment:** Cash or checks. **Children:** Well-behaved children welcome. **Pets:** Not allowed. **Smoking:** Not allowed. **Open:** Year-round.

➤   **Outgoing hosts, the Doucets have the inside track on things to see and do in Opelousas, located in the heart of Cajun country.**

If you happen to be at this unique establishment at the right time, you may be able to swing to the music of a Cajun band on the patio. If not, owners Louis and Dona Doucet can direct you to the places the locals go for entertainment. Louis, the son of the famous "Cat" Doucet (who was appointed sheriff of St. Landry Parish by Governor Huey Long), also offers a boat tour of Two O'Clock Bayou, a virgin swamp area with wonderful wildlife and undisturbed vegetation.

The Doucets, the second family to own Maison des Saizon, have restored this house to its original grandeur, doing much of the work themselves. The Victorian beauty was built by a millionaire doctor for his daughter as a wedding gift in 1889. The house's three guest rooms are furnished in antiques, but have all the modern conveniences — private baths, cable television sets, and telephones. Located in downtown Opelousas, the property boasts some large magnolia trees and beautiful gardens, which guests may enjoy. Future plans call for the addition of a gazebo, an outdoor swimming pool, and a hot tub.

Guests are treated to complimentary wine or soft drinks upon arrival. A full southern breakfast is included in the tariff.

St. Francisville

Barrow House

9779 Royal Street
P.O. Box 1461
St. Francisville, LA 70775
504-635-4791
Fax: 504-635-4769
staff@topteninn.com
http://www.topteninn.com

A highly recommended inn in a historic town

Innkeepers: Shirley Dittloff and Chris Dennis. **Accommodations:** 5 rooms and 3 suites (all with private baths). **Rates:** $85–$150, plus $5 each for full New Orleans–style breakfast and $25–$30 each for dinner. **Included:** Continental breakfast, wine and beer. **Payment:** MasterCard, Visa. **Children:** Well-behaved children welcome. **Pets:** Not allowed. **Smoking:** Allowed. **Open:** Year-round except one week during Christmas season.

➤   **The original house, a New England saltbox with cast-iron railing, columns, and a screened front porch, was constructed in 1809 to serve as a store/dwelling and an addition was built in 1855. The house is named for Dr. A. Feltus Barrow, who cared for the community in horse-and-buggy days. The six-foot-long clawfoot bathtub he used is still in the house.**

No one knows whether it brings good luck, but honeymooners sleep on a mattress made of Spanish moss on a Mallard bed at the Barrow House in St. Francisville, the second-oldest town in Louisiana. Guests have not complained about not sleeping yet, and they have high praises for the food and hospitality.

Though the establishment bills itself as a bed-and-breakfast inn, it is a little different from the norm in that innkeeper Shirley Dittloff and her son Chris Dennis serve not only breakfast but dinner as well (for overnight guests only and if given twenty-four hours advance notice). A Continental breakfast is included in the tariff at Barrow House, but a full gourmet breakfast — featuring eggs Benedict, eggs Creole, or eggs Basin Street — is available for a small extra charge. The innkeepers also enjoy filling guests in on St. Francisville history and take pride in sharing their own 45-minute cassette walking tour of the town.

Shirley Dittloff fell in love with St. Francisville several years ago while vacationing in Louisiana. A few months later, she sold her house in Houston and bought the Barrow House. It needed a great deal of attention, but after a year and a half of intensive restoration work, she opened it to guests in 1986. The inn is furnished in period antiques, complemented with lace bedspreads, curtains, and other accent pieces. Lace collars that belonged to a previous owner are displayed on the walls of several rooms.

The renovated Printer's Cottage across the street is also available to guests. Built in the 1700s for the monks for whom St. Francisville was named, the cottage offers two deluxe suites furnished in a style similar to Barrow House and two rustic rooms upstairs that have a Southwest theme. Guests may use the full kitchen, sunroom, and gazebo and have the option of a Continental breakfast there or the full breakfast at Barrow House.

Butler Greenwood B&B

8345 U.S. 61
St. Francisville, LA 70775
504-635-6312

> A plantation dating to 1796
> that's still in the same
> family

Innkeeper: Anne Butler. **Accommodations:** 4 cottages (all with private baths and full or partial kitchens). **Rates:** $80–$100. **Included:** Continental breakfast, house tour, tour book. **Payment:** Cash or checks. **Children:** Welcome. **Pets:** Check with innkeeper. **Smoking:** Allowed. **Open:** Year-round.

➤ **There are few places in the South where you can meet the direct descendants of the original plantation owners — Anne Butler provides this opportunity. The Butler Greenwood B&B offers an occasion to appreciate authenticity.**

Bed-and-breakfast guests from around the world reach one common conclusion after at night at Butler Greenwood: The B&B is tranquil and authentic. As one Oregon guest summed it up: "There are certain places on this planet that are healing places, both for the body and the spirit, and this is one of them."

Owner Anne Butler, a direct descendent of the original owners who settled here in 1796, has perfected the art of innkeeping. She makes sure that guests have the privacy and quiet they need to enjoy the spacious grounds, which feature gardens and hundreds of moss-draped live oaks, while providing comfortable accommodations, a taste of history, and true southern hospitality. Every guest gets a tour of the main house and a tour book outlining the area's history and plantations. Anne, who usually conducts the tours, is a writer, historian, and owner of the Greenwood Press. She can arrange bicycle rentals, guided nature walks, and bird watching with a local artist (an extra fee is charged).

Guests are housed in four cottages, each one very private with porches and decks overlooking the water. The kitchen, which dates to 1796, is made of bricks and features skylights and exposed beams. The gazebo is a six-sided structure with nine-foot stained glass church windows (very romantic). There are also two Victorian cottages. The plantation is listed on the National Register of Historic Places.

Green Springs B&B

7463 Tunica Trace
St. Francisville, LA 70775
504-635-4232, 800-457-4978
Fax: 504-635-0300
madeline@bsf.net
http://www.lillytr.com/greensprings/

> A B&B on an old plantation

Innkeeper: Madeline Nevill. **Accommodations:** 3 rooms (all with private baths) and 4 cottages (all with private baths, including some with Jacuzzis, plus fireplaces and kitchenettes). **Rates:** $95–$150. **Included:** Full breakfast. **Payment:** MasterCard, Visa. **Children:** Welcome. **Pets:** Not allowed. **Smoking:** Allowed in galleries. **Open:** Year-round.

➤ **One of the most requested dishes at Green Springs is Spinach Madeleine. (Madeline added the extra "e" to the name.) The famous dish consists of creamed spinach and jalapeño cheese.**

Opened in 1992, this bed-and-breakfast inn is housed in a new structure on a 150-acre cattle plantation that has been in the family for more than two centuries. Green Springs, on the historic Tunica Trace, is a natural spring on property that also has a 2,000-year-old Indian burial mound.

Following retirement, Madeline Nevill and her late husband built the 5,000-square-foot inn. They designed their home in the style of an early Feliciana Cottage, with wide porches to catch the breezes, and furnished it with a mixture of antiques and contemporary furniture. Last year Madeline added four cottages to the estate, giving guests more options. She serves a full breakfast and offers tour information on all the interesting sites in St. Francisville, settled by the English and the second-oldest town in Louisiana.

St. Martinville

The Old Castillo Hotel Bed and Breakfast and La Place d'Evangeline Restaurant

220 Evangeline Boulevard
St. Martinville, LA 70582
318-394-4010

An old historic inn in the center of Acadiana

Innkeeper: Peggy Hulin. **Accommodations:** 7 rooms (all with private baths). **Rates:** $50–$80. **Included:** Full breakfast. **Payment:** American Express, Master-Card, Visa. **Children:** Well-behaved children welcome. **Pets:** Not allowed. **Smoking:** Allowed in designated areas. **Open:** Year-round.

➤ **From the inn you can walk to St. Martin Square and Church of the Acadians, which contains a statue of Evangeline and her grave, made famous by poet Henry Wadsworth Longfellow. And at the end of Port Street stands the famed Evangline Oak, "most photographed tree in America," rumored to be the meeting spot of Evangeline and her Gabriel.**

On the banks of the Bayou Tech next to the famed Evangeline oak in St. Martinville, the heart of Cajun country, the Old Castillo Hotel and Restaurant was built as a combination business-residence in 1830 by Pierre Vasseur. Within a decade Madame Edmond Castillo, the widow of a steamboat captain, had taken over the management, and the inn was noted in *Harper's Monthly* as a center of hospitality and gala balls. When she died, it became a Catholic girls' school, and remained so until 1986, when the Sisters of Mercy left the community. Peggy Hulin returned the building to its original use when she bought and restored it in 1987.

The downstairs of the Greek Revival three-story building is devoted primarily to dining. The restaurant serves gumbo, shrimp, crab, and fish, plus such items as alligator boulettes, broiled frogs' legs, and crawfish pie . For breakfast, you can get beignets (Creole doughnuts) and French toast. The restaurant also caters to groups and bus tours.

Guest rooms are furnished in rice poster beds, armoires, and other antiques. They are comfortable, not overdecorated, and they're reasonably priced. There's a balcony on the second floor where guests can catch the breezes.

Slidell

Salmen-Fritchie House Bed & Breakfast

127 Cleveland Avenue
Slidell, LA 70458
504-643-1405, 800-235-4168
Fax: 504-641-7631
sfritbb@communique.net

> **A beloved family home is now open to B&B guests**

Innkeepers: Homer and Sharon Fritchie. **Accommodations:** 5 rooms in main house (all with private baths) and cottage (with bath and fully equipped kitchen). **Rates:** $75–$125; $150 for cottage, plus $25 for each additional person. **Included:** Full southern breakfast, wakeup coffee, refreshment center, and home tour. **Payment:** Major credit cards. **Children:** 10 and older welcome. **Pets:** Not allowed. **Smoking:** Allowed on porches. **Open:** Year-round.

➤ **Slidell has spruced up its Olde Towne to entice visitors. In recent years nearly fifty business owners have made the town more attractive. One of the main attractions is Antique Row.**

Homer and Sharon Fritchie have a special love for this turn-of-the-century Queen Anne/Colonial Revival home. Homer grew up in the house, which was built by his great-uncle Fritz Salmen, one of the founders of the Salmen Brickworks and Lumber Company in Slidell. Homer and Sharon inherited the house from his mother and spent a considerable sum of money restoring it. Homer's father was mayor of Slidell for thirty-two years. The house has been placed on the National Register of Historic Places.

Once owners of a large antiques shop, the Fritchies used several pieces that are original to the house and carefully selected the remaining antiques for each room. The names of the guest rooms suggest the type of furnishings in each — the Mallard Room, the Poster Room, the Oak Room, and the Twin Room. And there is also a honeymoon suite for the romantically inclined. (Three of the rooms can be made into suites.) The cottage has a living/kitchen area, bedroom, bath with a double whirlpool tub, and a private courtyard and screened-in porch. The Italian marble statue of mother and child in the central hall and the twelve oak chairs in the dining room were owned by Fritz Salmen.

Guests have the full run of the downstairs; the Fritchies occupy the second floor. The wide Great Hall is used as a sitting area for guests and the formal dining room is a favorite congregating area. Breakfast is served in the glass-enclosed breakfast room after which there is a tour.

Homer and Sharon offer refreshments upon arrival and make sure guests are aware of the refreshment center, where they can help themselves to beverages anytime. They assist guests with dinner reservations, provide turndown service, and offer desserts in the evening. (The Romance Package includes champagne and a dozen long-stemmed roses.)

Sunset

Chrétien Point Plantation

Route 1, Box 162
Sunset, LA 70584
Tel. & Fax: 318-662-5876
800-880-7050
http://www.louisianatravel.com
http://www.virtualcities.com

> **A historic plantation home that the owners love to share with guests**

Innkeepers: Louis and Jeanne Cornay. **Accommodations:** 5 rooms (all with private baths). **Rates:** $110–$225. **Included:** Full plantation breakfast, mint juleps, hors d'oeuvres, house tour. **Payment:** MasterCard, Visa. **Children:** Welcome. **Pets:** Not allowed. **Smoking:** Allowed on galleries. **Open:** Year-round.

➤ **Candlelight dinners/ghost tours begin at dusk, and guests are treated to tales of the Chrétiens, the Creole family who built a fortune on cotton and contraband, and stories of the pirate Jean Lafitte and the Union general who spared the mansion during a Civil War battle fought in the yard.**

Located in the middle of the country, about 11 miles north of Lafayette via I-49, this early Louisiana Greek Revival plantation home, with its two-story verandah and columns, dates to 1831. Built by Hypolite Chrétien II, it was for a time the last outpost on the frontier. One story goes that in 1840 the proprietress, Felicité Chrétien, by then a widow who was earning quite a bit of money by gambling, killed a lawless pirate on the stairs. (The blood stains remain to this day.) The same stairs are believed to have been the pattern for the stairs on which Scarlett O'Hara shoots a Yankee soldier in *Gone With the Wind*. Needless to say, the house is believed to be haunted, but sightings and encounters have been friendly.

On October 15, 1863, the Red River Campaign occurred here. The house would have been totally demolished, had not the occupants given the Masonic distress signal. As fate would have it, some of the Union soldiers ransacked the house from the rear, stripping it of its treasures. Reenactments are held every year on the anniversary of the battle.

When the Cornays bought the house in 1974, it was a shambles, having stood vacant and used to store hay for years. But Louis's talents as an interior designer went to work, and the family, including the Cornays' four children, moved in six months later. Now that their children are grown, the Cornays have opened the house to overnight guests. They also offer daily tours of the house and make it available for weddings, receptions, and parties.

Guests at Chrétien Point are made to feel very welcome by the Cornays, who enjoy sharing their love for the house and its antique treasures over a home-cooked breakfast served on the long plantation table. At one end of the table they display some of the artifacts that have been found on the property — cannonballs, pottery shards, and other items. Only a few pieces of furniture are original to the house, but it is filled with many antiques acquired by the Cornays over the years. Guests get a true sense of plantation life while sleeping in heavy four-poster tester beds as the summer breezes blow and the moonlight casts soft shadows on the wall.

Mississippi

Best Bed-and-Breakfasts

Best City Stop

Best Country Inn

Best Historic Inns

Jackson
Fairview Inn, 294
Vicksburg
Cedar Grove Estate, 318
Anchuca, 316

Best Plantations

Chatham
Mt. Holly Plantation Inn, 287
Lorman
Canemount Plantation, 298
Rosswood Plantation, 300
Natchez
Monmouth Plantation, 305
Oakwood Plantation, 306

Best Resort

Philadelphia
Silver Star Resort & Casino, 312

Mississippi, indisputably Deep South, retains an agrarian flavor, combined with impressive recent commercial and industrial growth. The Gulf Coast with its broad, white, sandy beaches is a resort playground quite different in tone and atmosphere from the rest of the state. Northward stretch the flat fertile farmlands of the Delta and the pine-clad central prairies. Gently rolling northeast hills, at one point reaching a height of 806 feet, mark the state's highest elevation.

Even in the midst of New South vitality there is concern about preserving the past and the heritages it nurtured. In many towns and rural regions you'll find a more relaxed lifestyle and hospitable, cordial Mississippians who want to make you linger just a bit longer. New to the state are dockside casinos offering Las Vegas–style gaming on the Gulf Coast and the Mississippi. The casinos never close.

Today's visitors to the Magnolia State have wonderful opportunities to recall historic happenings within the framework of modern times. Among the nation's most significant historic routes, the Natchez Trace Parkway is being developed by the National Park Service to parallel the Old Natchez Trace, a post road and pioneer pathway that stretched from Natchez to Nashville. When completed, it will run nearly 500 miles across segments of Mississippi, Alabama, and Tennessee. Along the route are numerous wayside exhibits, interpretive markers, and self-guiding trails. You can walk on short portions of the old Trace, worn down in deep furrows long ago by boots, hooves, and wheels. Such quiet spots echo with the memories of rugged "Kaintucks," rough-and-ready flatboatmen of the Mississippi River who trekked along the Trace from the saloons and gambling halls of Natchez-Under-the-Hill back to Nashville. There they boarded their cumbersome craft to start their journeys all over again, navigating the Cumberland and Ohio rivers to enter the Mighty Mississippi for their return to Natchez.

Latter-day visitors may enjoy their forays into Mississippi's great outdoors in much more civilized fashion. From spring through early autumn, the Gulf Coast resort communities are popular spots for sailing, sunning, surfing, and other water sports. From May through September, saltwater fishing is usually superb. You can board a charter boat to go for grouper, bonito, lemon fish, red snapper, and king mackerel, frequently found near offshore islands and oil rigs. Farther out, deeper waters of the Gulf of Mexico have yielded record marlin and sailfish catches.

Boating and fishing enthusiasts can also take to a 234-mile stretch of the Tennessee-Tombigbee Waterway, connecting the Gulf of Mexico with the interior. Lakes and pools created during the route's construction are top fishing spots, and the waterway's serene surface assures pleasurable boating and water skiing.

From both Biloxi and Gulfport, you can board ferries to Ship Island, part of the Gulf Islands National Seashore, a 150-mile chain of barrier islands stretching from Fort Walton Beach, Florida, to Pascagoula, Mississippi. When the weather is not too humid, this is a delightful spot for swimming, beachcombing, and birdwatching. Here also you can take a free guided tour of massive Fort Massachusetts, a prison for Confederate soldiers during the Civil War. From here, Union forces staged their attack on New Orleans.

Mississippi's oldest community, the attractive little town of Ocean Springs, is a popular artists' and retirees' colony. It was the home of the eccentric yet brilliant artist, the late Walter Anderson. You can view his stunning murals depicting the arrival of the area's first European settlers on inside walls of the Community Center. Anderson also originated famed Shearwater Pottery, notable for its luminous glazes. Members of his family carry on production today.

In late April, Ocean Springs celebrates its heritage with a festival commemorating the landing of d'Iberville in 1699.

A major shrimping center, neighboring Biloxi stages an elaborate Shrimp Festival the first weekend in June, with parades, carnivals, street dancing, a seafood jamboree, and the crowning of the Shrimp King and Queen. The festival is highlighted by the colorful Blessing of the Shrimp Fleet, when hundreds of festooned boats pass in procession to receive the blessing of the bishop. You can also get glimpses of the area's early shrimping and fishing days at Biloxi's Seafood Industry Museum at the foot of the Ocean Springs Bridge.

About 100 yards north of Biloxi's splendid broad beach stands its landmark 1847 Old Lighthouse. A small band near the top is painted black, a reminder of the time just after the Civil War when the entire structure was painted black, not as legend goes in mourning for President Lincoln, but to protect the structure from rust.

In the mid-1800s, the Mississippi Gulf Coast became an exclusive summer retreat for wealthy Mississippi and Louisiana families escaping the interior's steamy summers. Alas, Hurricane Camille in 1969 hit this beautiful coast with a wrenching blow from which it has never totally recovered. Some historic mansions that do remain include Old Brick House and the Tullis-Toledano Manor in Biloxi and Grass Lawn in Gulf Port.

Historic Beauvoir, west of Biloxi on Beach Boulevard, stands impeccably restored on picturesque garden grounds, its majestic 1853 facade fronting the now serene waters of the Gulf. This was the last home of Jefferson Davis, president of the Confederacy. After Davis died, Beauvoir became a home for Confederate veterans and their families. After the last widows were moved to a nursing home, Beauvoir became a museum. It is furnished with many original family pieces. The displays are a treasure trove of papers, books, uniforms, guns, medical instruments, and personal effects of Confederate soldiers. Many of these priceless artifacts were damaged by the wind and flood ravages of Hurricane Camille; their artful renovation and restoration are a valiant testimony to the work of scores of dedicated historic preservationists. A cemetery on Beauvoir's extensive grounds contains the graves of seven hundred Confederate soldiers and includes the Tomb of the Unknown Soldier of the Confederate States of America.

The exquisite city of Natchez remained virtually an oasis during much of its long history, linked to other places only by the Mississippi River and the Natchez Trace. During the Great Depression, a group of local women decided that the city's antebellum homes should be shared with visitors. Thus originated the concept of pilgrimages to houses and gardens, now widespread in cities and towns throughout the South. Proceeds from the pilgrimages were used to refurbish the splendid mansions, and visitors now see them as they appeared at the height of their grandeur. Annual Natchez pilgrimages are held from mid-March to mid-April, from early to late October, and during the Christmas season in December. During the Spring Pilgrimage, you can attend the Confederate Pageant, a lavish celebration of the Old South, and *Southern Exposure,* a tongue-in-cheek spoof of the Pilgrimage.

Some houses on the pilgrimages are open only during those times, but a significant number of others welcome visitors year-round. Some of these outstanding showplaces include the Briars, the setting for Jefferson Davis's wedding to Varina Howell; Connelly's Tavern, built in the late 1700s; stately d'Evereux and Dunleith mansions; cottagelike Hope Farm, its earliest segments dating from 1775; Linden, circa 1800; octagonal Longwood, under construction during the Civil War and never completed; Monmouth Plantation, home of Mexican War hero General John Quitman; Rosalie, local headquarters for the Union Army during the Civil War; elaborate 1857 Stanton Hall, one of the nation's largest antebellum homes; and 1855 Weymouth Hall, on a bluff overlooking the Mississippi River. A number of Natchez' historic homes have overnight accommodations. And at many of them you'll be treated to lavish plantation breakfasts of eggs, ham, bacon, or sausage, cheese grits, homemade biscuits and preserves, served at tables set with heirloom china, silver, and crystal.

For a glimpse of the "other Natchez," meander down to the riverfront to visit Natchez-Under-the-Hill, where gamblers, boatmen, and various unsavory characters gathered to carouse in questionable structures built under the bluffs. Many of the buildings have slipped away, eroded by the river; others now house popular restaurants and shops. Outside town, the Grand Village of the Natchez Indians has been partially restored. This was the main ceremonial town of a remarkable people who lived here from 1682 until 1729. After battles with the French, the Indians were banished, forced to scatter among other tribes. Remaining mounds on the site were once the bases of ceremonial temples. A museum displays significant artifacts found on the site.

A little over ten miles north of the entrance of the Natchez Trace Parkway is Emerald Mound, an 8-acre earthen ceremonial center dating to about A.D. 1300–1600, built by ancestors of the Creek, Choctaw, and Natchez Indians. This is the third largest Indian ceremonial complex in the United States. Two smaller mounds on the flat top of the larger were apparently temple sites.

Vicksburg, one of the state's most historic cities, lies about 70 miles north of Natchez. More than most communities of the South, this city of about 26,000 lives in the shadow of its Civil War experience. From its high bluffs overlooking the Mississippi River, the "Gibraltar of the Confederacy" withstood a disastrous 47-day siege by Union forces before surrendering on July 4, 1863. The Old Courthouse Museum contains notable Civil War relics, including the chair used by Union General Ulysses S. Grant during the siege.

Some of Vicksburg's fine antebellum homes are open only during the Spring Pilgrimage, late March through early April. Several outstanding structures, though, are open year-round. They include Anchuca, a beautifully restored Greek Revival house; Balfour House, a treasure trove of period furnishings; Cedar Grove, with original furnishings, crystal, and china, along with two cannonballs still embedded in the parlor wall and floor; Grey Oaks, resembling Scarlett O'Hara's Tara; and McRaven House, representing three periods of architecture. Anchuca, Balfour, and Cedar Grove welcome overnight guests. In another historic structure, the Biedenharn Candy Company Museum, is a restored candy store and soda fountain, where Coca-Cola was first bottled in 1894. It has a fascinating Coca-Cola bottle collection.

Vicksburg National Military Park and Cemetery, one of the nation's best-preserved battlegrounds, rims the eastern and northern portions of Vicksburg. Markers and memorials honor troops from both sides of the Civil War and crucial points of action are described along a scenic drive. The visitor center shows an excellent film tracing the battle and its significance. The U.S.S. *Cairo*, a Union ironclad sunk in the Yazoo River by the Confederacy, is also displayed at the park.

Jackson, Mississippi's flourishing capital, with a population of about 210,000, has the atmosphere of a vigorous New South city. Founded in 1821, the city was so systematically burned in 1863 by Union General William T. Sherman's forces that only a veritable forest of chimneys remained standing. Among surviving structures were a few houses, including the now restored 1857 Gothic Revival Manship House, home of Jackson's Civil War mayor. Also remaining were the classical-columned 1842 Governor's Mansion, among the nation's oldest executive residences, and the 1833 Old Capitol, now home of the State Historical Museum.

In recent years, Jackson has come into its own as a southern showcase of performing arts; its Mississippi Symphony Orchestra and Ballet Mississippi have achieved national prominence. The contemporary Mississippi Museum of Art includes works by regional and Mississippi artists, as well as paintings of Renoir,

Picasso, Georgia O'Keeffe, Robert Rauschenberg, and others of national or international acclaim.

At the adjacent Russell C. Davis Planetarium/Ronald McNair Space Theater, state-of-the-art equipment is used for astronomical presentations, laser light shows and Cinema-360 films. A portrait gallery and space displays and artifacts honor McNair, the late space shuttle astronaut who was aboard the ill-fated *Challenger*.

Outside town, the restored Fortenberry Parkman Farm, a farm house and more than a dozen outbuildings, most dating from the 1860s, illustrate rural life on a large working farm in the 1920s. Costumed workers and farm animals help bring the setting to life. Nearby a 1920s crossroads town has been recreated with a service station, general store, church, school, and other buildings moved from throughout the region. The collections are part of the Mississippi Agriculture and Forestry/National Agricultural Aviation Museum. A large contemporary building has impressive displays on the history of the state's agriculture, forestry, and agricultural station.

North of Jackson, off I-55, you can reenter the Natchez Trace Parkway, following it to Tupelo, site of the Natchez Trace Parkway Headquarters/Tupelo Visitor Center. Here a museum chronicles the parkway's history and current development; you can also view an audiovisual program and follow scenic nature trails. For a portion of the drive from Jackson, the stretch skirts the pine-clad shores of the huge Ross Barnett Reservoir, part of the Pearl River water conservancy district. Nature trails lead through a cypress swamp to an area of beaver dams, and side roads provide access to scenic lookouts.

In Tupelo, the Elvis Presley Center contains the humble white frame house that was the birthplace, on January 8, 1935, of one of the world's most famous contemporary entertainers. The site, on a 15-acre park, also includes a memorial chapel.

The prosperous city of Columbus, population about 30,000, lies in the heart of Mississippi's cotton-rich Black Prairie, named for the fertile soils that supported a flourishing agricultural economy. Settled as a trading post in 1817 at the point where de Soto reputedly crossed in his 1541 explorations, the community on the Tombigbee River soon thrived as a commercial and trading center as well. Never attacked by Union forces, Columbus has preserved more than one hundred antebellum homes. Some are open year-round, and numerous others open their doors during Spring Pilgrimage the first two weekends in April. Tours begin at the 1844 Blewett-Harrison-Lee Home, its facade richly adorned with iron grillwork cast in New Orleans. Casualties of the 1862 Battle of

Shiloh, which occurred just over the Tennessee border, are buried in Columbus's Friendship Cemetery. Here the first Memorial Day was reputedly observed on April 25, 1866, when local women gathered to decorate the graves of both Confederate and Union soldiers. Nearby Starkville, the home of Mississippi State University, also hosts annual pilgrimages with a Victorian theme.

Oxford, a pleasant city of about 14,000, also has a number of antebellum homes. Best known is 1844 Rowan Oak, home of the Nobel laureate William Faulkner, who purchased the house in 1930. It's maintained as a public shrine by the University of Mississippi. You'll see furnishings and accessories just as they were at the time of Faulkner's death in 1962; the outline of his novel *A Fable* is scribbled on his study walls. On the grounds of the university, best known as "Ole Miss," you can view exhibits of southern art, literature, and photography at the Center for the Study of Southern Culture. The University Museums display changing exhibits of American paintings, Civil War artifacts, Greek and Roman antiquities, and African and southern folk art. The University of Mississippi Blues Archives, also on campus, contains a vast variety of blues memorabilia and recordings, including the personal collection of B. B. King.

For more information, contact the Mississippi Department of Economic and Community Development, Division of Tourism, P.O. Box 1705, Ocean Springs, Mississippi 39566-1705, 800-WARMEST, http://www.mississippi.org.

Biloxi

The Father Ryan House
Bed & Breakfast Inn

1196 Beach Boulevard
Biloxi, MS 39530
228-435-1189, 800-295-1189
Fax: 228-436-3063
frryan@datasync.com
http://www.frryan.com

The beachside home of a
Confederate poet is now a
lavish B&B

Innkeepers: Rosanne McKenney and Dina Davis. **Accommodations:** 11 rooms
(all with private baths). **Rates:** $85–$150. **Included:** Full gourmet breakfast,
afternoon refreshments, turndown service. **Payment:** Major credit cards. **Children:** Well-behaved children welcome. **Pets:** Not allowed. **Smoking:** Not allowed. **Open:** Year-round.

➤ **Nearby attractions include Beauvoir, the last home occupied by Confederate President Jefferson Davis after the Civil War, and Fort Massachusetts on Ship Island. Local museums, art galleries, and antiques shops also lure visitors.**

Definitely a showstopper, this beachside bed-and-breakfast is one
to watch. Open since 1995, the Father Ryan House Bed & Breakfast
Inn has already been reviewed by *Travel and Leisure Magazine*
(naming it one of the top beach resorts in 1996), *Southern Living,*
Fodors, Star Service, and the Globe Pequot Press. The owners recently added three more guest rooms in separate cottages and built
a large dining hall and commercial kitchen.

Named for Father Abram Ryan, the "Poet Laureate of the Confederacy" who lived here for fourteen years following the Civil
War, the historic home features framed excerpts of his works
throughout, plus an extensive library of literary classics. Guest
rooms, most of which look out over the Mississippi Gulf Coast, are
elegantly furnished in antiques dating to the mid-1800s and feature
amenities such as down comforters and pillows, bathrobes, cable
television, and a telephone with data port. A favorite retreat is Sea
Rest, a third-floor suite that takes its name from one of Father

Ryan's most famous poems. Others are the verandahs and balconies, the swimming pool, and the quiet landscaped gardens.

Rosanne McKenney and Dina Davis serve a full breakfast of different entrees, fresh breads, and fruits, and all the trimmings. During the week guests take their meal in the Lemon Room, a breakfast room, and on weekends in the main dining room, where special dinners are also staged. Dining out is also an option, as the inn is within walking distance of several good seaside restaurants.

Originally known as the Wade House, the historic structure was built between 1840 and 1841 by Judge Wade, who later sold it to the wife of a wealthy cotton merchant from New Orleans. When Father Abram Ray lived here, he wrote many of his famous poems. In the later part of the 1800s, the house was purchased by Thomas Carter, who added the second and third floors, new windows, and an indoor staircase. Between 1900 and 1970, the house was used for several purposes — a place where women delivered their babies, a vacationers' boarding house, and an apartment house. Jefferson and Rosanne McKenney purchased the house in the 1970s, saved it from demolition, and began restoration. Proceeds from the house go directly to a hospital project in Honduras through the nonprofit Cornerstone Foundation.

Chatham

Mt. Holly Plantation Inn

140 Lake Washington Road, East
Chatham, MS 38731
601-827-2652

A restored plantation
offering an authentic
plantation experience

Innkeepers: T. C. and Ann Woods. **Accommodations:** 8 rooms (5 with private baths, 3 with shared bath). **Rates:** $75–$95. **Payment:** MasterCard, Visa. **Children:** 6 and older welcome. **Pets:** Not allowed. **Smoking:** Not allowed. **Open:** Year-round.

➤ **The house's original owners — the Johnsons of Kentucky — were related to Henry Clay. Shelby Foote, the noted Civil War historian, spent a lot of time here visiting his grandparents.**

Located in the flat Mississippi Delta community of Foote, where cotton and other crops are still farmed on a massive scale, this 1853 plantation home offers an overnight experience that takes you back to the antebellum era — a time when more than 150 slaves worked the land of a 1,900-acre spread. Guests sleep in high-ceilinged rooms and in the morning gather in the conservatory overlooking Lake Washington and the cotton fields for a hearty breakfast of eggs, grits, sausage, bacon, biscuits, and all the trimmings. During the rest of the day there's plenty of time for fishing, enjoying the peace and quiet of the country, or visiting local historic sites.

The Italianate house is built of bricks made by slaves on the spot. Very modern in its time, the house featured built-in closets, indoor bathrooms, and a water reservoir from which water could be pumped directly into the kitchen. Mt. Holly has served as a bed-and-breakfast inn since 1986, but the present owners, T. C. and Ann Woods, have lived here for many years. In addition to breakfast, the couple also prepare dinner for guests, provided they are given advance notice. T. C. is headmaster of a local academy; Ann devotes full time to innkeeping. They also enjoy entertaining their children and grandchildren when they come to visit.

Columbus

Amzi Love Bed & Breakfast

305 7th Street South
Columbus, MS 39701
601-328-5413

> A B&B enveloped in history where guests get lost in time

Innkeepers: Sid and Brenda Caradine. **Accommodations:** 3 rooms and 2 suites (all with private baths). **Rates:** $85–$100. **Included:** Full southern breakfast, welcome beverage, and house tour. **Payment:** MasterCard, Visa. **Children:** 6 and older welcome. **Pets:** Not allowed. **Smoking:** Not allowed in guest rooms. **Open:** Year-round.

➤ **The innkeeper's great-great-grandfather was Amzi Love, whose mother and grandmother lived in the house for a time.**

Sid Caradine is a member of the seventh generation to occupy this Greek Revival home, built by Amzi Love for his bride, Edith Wallace, in 1848. He's charming, hospitable, and entertaining. Attuned to culture and the finer things of life, he writes poetry and collects children's art, and his dream is to someday establish a museum or gallery to honor the work of children. His wife Brenda assists Sid in running the inn.

Sid also has a great appreciation for his family, and he knows history so well that you feel that you are talking with someone who just stepped from a book. During the house tour, he may point out a fan that is the same one in an old tintype, or he may show you a watch fob made out of hair that belonged to one of his aunts several generations back. A letter describing an incident during the Civil War is displayed under glass on a desk in the parlor, along with other letters, invitations, and memorabilia belonging to the family.

All the furniture in the house is original. Sid is careful to note that just about everything in the house is in the same place it has been for more than a hundred years, but it looks as if someone just put it there. The house has been loved and cared for by the family for generations. The family moved to the area from Chester County, South Carolina, in 1830. Sid grew up in Memphis, but his family used to spend holidays and vacations in Columbus. Guests stay in two suites.

The home next door, built by Amzi Love's father in 1833, has been lovingly restored by the Carradines and renamed the Carriage House because the lower level was used as a stable during the Civil War. It offers three guestrooms. A Smithsonian representative has called it one of the best restorations he has ever seen. A footbridge and beautiful English gardens connect the two historic homes. The centerpiece of the gardens is a gold fish pond.

Sid, a former stockbroker, and Brenda, a journalist, welcome guests with espresso or wine and do all the food preparation on an old Vulcan stove. They serve eggs, bacon, homemade muffins, orange juice, garlic and cheese grits, and amaretto coffee for breakfast.

Guests of the Amzi Love give the inn high marks for its authenticity. Overnighters have included such celebrities as pianist Elena Klionsky, opera singer Marguerite Piazza, William Styron, Roger Mudd, John Grisham, Doug Marlette, Anthony Herrera, Barbara Rush, Elizabeth Forsythe Haley, and Princess Maria Katharina von Thurn und Taxis-Koster of Germany.

Corinth

Robbins Nest Bed and Breakfast

1523 Shiloh Road
Corinth, MS 38834
601-286-3109

> An old family home, now a
> B&B

Innkeepers: Tony and Anne Whyte. **Accommodations:** 3 rooms (all with private baths). **Rates:** $85. **Included:** Full breakfast, refreshments. **Payment:** MasterCard, Visa. **Children:** 12 and older welcome. **Pets:** Not allowed. **Smoking:** Allowed on verandah. **Open:** Year-round.

➤ **The Robbins Nest is one of many historic homes in Corinth, "the crossroads of the South."**

This lovely southern Colonial home, presently owned by Tony and Anne Whyte, has been in Anne's family for more than half a century. Once part of a large estate, it now occupies two acres and was originally built for the Don Street family in 1870 on the road that Southern troops used to retreat from Shiloh in Tennessee. It was later owned by the Candler family. The Whites have recently completed an extensive remodeling project on the house, which is furnished in family heirlooms and antiques. Among its outstanding features are a walnut staircase, pine floors, and walls constructed of 15-inch planks.

The Whytes now share their home with bed-and-breakfast guests, offering them the best in southern hospitality. There are three guest rooms, each with a private bath and conveniences such as telephones and television sets. Tony, an engineer, is a native of Oxford, England, and a graduate of Oxford University; Anne is a retired schoolteacher.

Hattiesburg

Tally House Historic B&B

401 Rebecca Avenue
Hattiesburg, MS 39401
601-582-3467
http://www@virtualcities.com

> **A B&B that's a show stopper**

Innkeepers: C .E. "Red" and Sydney Bailey. **Accommodations:** 4 rooms (all with private baths). **Rates:** $65–$80. **Included:** Full breakfast, complimentary beverages, turndown service. **Payment:** MasterCard, Visa. **Children:** 12 and older welcome. **Pets:** Not allowed. **Smoking:** Not allowed. **Open:** Year-round.

➤ **Established in the 1880s on the crossroads of two major rail lines, Hattiesburg offers a plethora of things to do — historic sites, antiques shops, museums, golf courses, and parks.**

One of Hattiesburg's grand timber showcase homes, Tally House was built in 1907 by a prominent Mississippi judge whose surname was Tally. The two-and-a-half story, 13,000-square foot Colonial Revival home features wrap-around porches on three sides of two levels. Located in the Historic District and listed on the National Register of Historic Places, the home is a standout with its white paint and red roof.

Tally House has served as the private home of C. E. and Sydney Bailey for the past fifteen years. Since opening their home to guests in 1992, they've entertained people from all over the world. They came to appreciate B&Bs during their own travels, which have taken them to many faraway places. (She's a biology professor at a local college; since retiring he has restored eighteen homes in the Historic District, including Tally House.)

Each of the four guest rooms is individually decorated in period styles ranging from Eastlake Victorian to Art Deco and includes beautiful antiques, collectibles, and fine bed linens. The social area on the second floor was designed with the guests in mind; it offers a fax, television, VCR and tapes, magazines, books. a stocked refrigerator, and microwave. There's also an upstairs verandah with a swing and wicker furnishings. The formal gardens and formal rooms downstairs are also available to guests, as are the meeting rooms for small conferences.

The Baileys serve a full country breakfast of fresh fruit and juice, eggs, meat, muffins, homemade jellies and preserves, coffee, and tea. The meal is an event, and guests often linger for conversation.

Jackson

Fairview Inn

734 Fairview Street
Jackson, MS 39202
601-948-3429, 888-948-1908
Fax: 601-948-1203
fairview@teclink.net
http://www.fairviewinn.com

> A family home that now
> welcomes overnight guests

Innkeepers: Bill and Carol Simmons. **Accommodations:** 3 rooms and 5 suites (all with private baths). **Rates:** $100–$150, plus $15 for each additional person. **Included:** Full breakfast, refreshments, turndown service. **Payment:** Major credit cards. **Children:** Check with innkeepers. **Pets:** Not allowed. **Smoking:** Not allowed. **Open:** Year-round.

➤ **One of Jackson's landmark properties, Fairview is listed on the National Register of Historic Places and is featured in the 1998 National Trust Historic Preservation calendar.**

When Carol Simmons agreed to host a wedding reception for a friend's daughter in 1984, little did she know that she was starting a full-fledged business. But as the word of her talents began to spread, she found herself booking more and more parties and receptions. In 1992, she and Bill decided to do an extensive renovation of their home and open it to overnight guests.

Today they offer eight guest rooms in the Colonial Revival home that has been in the Simmons family since 1930. (Four guest rooms are located in the main house, the Hayloft Honeymoon Suite and others in the Carriage House.) Fairview was built in 1908 by Cyrus G. Warren, a successful lumberman. The elegantly furnished rooms feature antiques and reproductions, collectibles, fine linens and draperies, telephones (including voice mail), televisions, and VCRs. A fax, copier, and modem are available as well. All the rooms have private baths, some whirlpool tubs. The public areas of the house are stunning, especially the foyer which has a gleaming marble floor and a chandelier from the Burn Plantation in Natchez.

Bill and Carol are always on hand to greet guests upon arrival and provide refreshments and turndown service at night. They serve a full breakfast of juices and fresh fruits, bacon or sausage, eggs, cheese grits, warm biscuits and cinnamon rolls, freshly brewed coffee and hot tea. The inn has earned AAA's four diamond rating.

Millsaps Buie House

628 North State Street
Jackson, MS 39202
601-352-0221
800-784-0221
Fax: 601-352-0221

An elegant capital city restoration where you can hang your hat

Innkeeper: Nancy Fleming. **Accommodations:** 11 rooms (all with private baths). **Rates:** $85–$155, plus $15 for each additional person. **Included:** Full southern breakfast. **Payment:** Major credit cards. **Children:** 12 and older welcome. **Pets:** Not allowed. **Smoking:** Allowed on porches. **Open:** Year-round.

➤ **The architect Robert Canizaro of Jackson worked closely with the interior designer Berle Smith to create the High Victorian atmosphere at Millsaps-Buie.**

The Millsaps Buie House has been in the same family for well over a hundred years. The Queen Anne Victorian structure was built in 1888 by Major Reuben Webster Millsaps, who had served in the Confederate army; sixty years later his nephew Webster Millsaps Buie remodeled it, adding a front porch and four classical columns. Today it is owned by Buie's grandchildren, the Love family.

When the sale of the house to an oil company failed to materialize, the family decided to restore it, only to have ninety percent of it subsequently gutted by arson. But with a lot of determination and dedication, the Loves rebuilt the home. In late 1987, it opened as a bed-and-breakfast inn, offering the finest overnight accommodations in Jackson.

Since the house is on the National Register of Historic Places, the restoration was made as authentic as possible and includes some family furnishings (luckily in storage when the fire broke out). The house has 14-foot ceilings, hardwood floors, stained glass, and many windows. Just a block from the capitol in the heart of downtown Jackson, the house is one of the few structures of its type left in the neighborhood. Though the front entrance is still in place, most guests enter from the parking lot via the side entrance into the lobby/reception area. Afternoon cocktails may be purchased here. The library and the elegant parlor, furnished with a grand piano, and other fine antiques, are off to one side. Guests usually eat in the parlor after serving themselves at the breakfast buffet set up in the foyer.

There are two guest rooms on the first floor, five on the second, and four on the third. A room on the third floor includes a seven-sided observatory. A favorite room with guests is the Millsaps Room, papered in a lovely pink and green floral print and boasting several windows, all covered in mint green satin drapes. The centerpiece of the room is a full tester bed, dating to the mid-1800s.

Because of its proximity to downtown, corporate travelers find the inn a great place to stay. Each guest room has its own telephone and television set, and the inn provides fax services and meeting space. Complimentary copies of the *Wall Street Journal,* the *New York Times,* and *USA Today* are available.

Kosciusko

The Redbud Inn

121 North Wells Street
Kosciusko, MS 39090
Tel. & Fax: 601-289-5086,
800-379-5086

> A B&B offering "the best bed and board" for miles around

Innkeeper: Maggie Garrett. **Accommodations:** 5 rooms (4 with private baths, 1 with half bath). **Rates:** $75–$100. **Included:** Full breakfast, afternoon beverages and snacks, turndown service with chocolates. **Payment:** Major credit cards. **Children:** Welcome. **Pets:** Not allowed. **Smoking:** Allowed on verandahs only. **Open:** Year-round.

➤ **Kosciusko is a great place to shop for antiques (don't miss the shop at the inn), as well as arts and crafts. There are many historical homes to see. Oprah Winfrey's birthplace and the historic French Camp are of interest to visitors.**

You can't miss this bed-and-breakfast near the Natchez Trace Parkway. Once you get on North Wells Street in Koscuisko, it's easy to spot the three-story tower — the beige clapboard house has an onion-domed top, rose-colored trim, and a gray roof. Samuel Anderson Jackson built the Queen Anne Victorian structure in 1884 for his new bride Lillie. A decade later, when he was killed in a duel over politics, she had to take in boarders to support herself and her four children. Around the turn of the century, Pattie Lee

Sallis took over ownership and the house became a teacherage, providing room and board for the teachers in the community. Eventually, the home was passed down to Myrtis Niles, Pattie's daughter, who kept it until 1981. It housed an antiques shop until 1990 when Maggie Garrett, a teacher, converted the house into a B&B and a tea room.

The innkeeper runs a house that's known for its true southern hospitality. She offers five guest rooms, furnished with turn-of-the-century pieces, including the original blinds. She delights in pampering guests — services include afternoon beverages and snacks, turndowns at night, chocolates on the pillows, and information on things to see and do in Kosciusko. A full southern breakfast is included in an overnight lodging, of course, but guests pay extra for lunch and dinner. Lunch is offered weekdays and dinner by reservation only. Chicken and seafood dishes are luncheon favorites, while filet mignon or grilled chicken or fish are served in the evening. The homemade desserts are very popular, especially the hot fudge cake. Dinners are always served by candlelight with fine china and silver on white linen, usually with flowers. The inn also offers catering, private parties, and receptions; romance and honeymoon packages are available. In 1996, the innkeeper published the cookbook *A Taste of the Redbud*, which features recipes used at the inn.

The Redbud Inn has been featured in *Southern Living,* the *New York Times,* the *Denver Post,* the *Atlanta Constitution,* and *Mississippi Magazine.*

Lorman

Canemount Plantation

Highway 552 West
Route 2, Box 45
Lorman, MS 39096
601-877-3784, 800-423-0684
Fax: 601-877-2010
http://www.canemount.com

A working plantation offering B&B accommodations and elegant dining, plus a Plantation Pig Roast

Innkeepers: Ray and Rachel Forest. **Accommodations:** 9 rooms and 3 cottages (all with private baths). **Rates:** $145–$185. **Included:** Full plantation breakfast, dinner, complimentary wine and cocktails, home tour, and jeep tour. **Payment:** MasterCard, Visa. **Children:** 12 and older welcome. **Pets:** Not allowed. **Smoking:** Not allowed. **Open:** Year-round.

➤ **Canemount, which dates to 1855, is listed on the National Register of Historic Places. A part of property includes the historic Windsor Plantation, and the ruins of the lavish home that burned in 1890 still stand.**

If you like peace and quiet, you're going to love staying at Canemount Plantation, located eight miles from the Natchez Trace Parkway. Surrounding the private guest cottages are 6,000 acres of forested land and open fields, abundant with wildlife. Here you can have encounters with the free-roaming white-tailed deer, wild turkeys, Russian boar, small game animals, and hundreds of species of birds. Nature photographers and birdwatchers are in heaven at Canemount. You can explore the plantation on your own or take guided tours either on foot or by four-wheel drive vehicle. Fishing is also a popular pastime. There is a heated swimming pool on the property.

Guests stay in antebellum cottages and the Carriage House that have been lovingly restored and furnished with antiques. The Gray Cottage, once a slave cabin, features a king-sized four-poster bed, a wood-burning fireplace, and a Jacuzzi. The Pond House, temporary living quarters for the Murdock family (original owners of the land), also has a similar bed, a wood-burning stove, and a whirlpool tub. Rick's Cottage, formerly the kitchen dependency, offers a double half-tester bed, a wood-burning stove, and a shower in the private bath. All the cottages have stocked refrigerators and coffee-makers. The recent restoration of the 1829 Carriage House provides six more guest rooms featuring king-sized beds, whirlpool baths, and fireplaces. Since the inn is licensed to serve liquor, a chilled bottle of wine in a silver ice bucket awaits guests upon arrival. The Plantation Pig Roast is a big hit with corporate meetings and catered parties.

The main house, where the owners Ray and Rachel Forest live with their son John, is considered the finest form of Italianate Revival architecture in the area. But Canemount is better known for its isolated setting and wildlife. The Forests have been living on the plantation for a decade now. They moved here from Morganza, Louisiana, after visiting Canemount one weekend. They work closely with the Department of Wildlife and Fisheries, Mississippi State University, and the Claborne County Agricultural Department on wild-life studies and management. (Ray is a petroleum engineer, educator, and farmer.)

The Forests serve their guests a full plantation breakfast and a complete dinner featuring cocktails, appetizers, soup or salad, entrées such as pork tenderloin, vegetables, rolls, dessert, and coffee. Everything is included in the price of lodging.

Rosswood Plantation

Highway 552
Route 1, Box 6
Lorman, MS 39096
601-437-4215, 800-533-5889
Fax: 601-437-6888
whylander@aol.com

> An antebellum plantation
> that's a Mississippi
> landmark

Innkeepers: Walt and Jean Hylander. **Accommodations:** 4 rooms (all with private baths). **Rates:** $95–$125. **Included:** Full breakfast and mansion tour. **Payment:** Discover, MasterCard, Visa. **Children:** Welcome. **Pets:** Not allowed. **Smoking:** Allowed in limited areas. **Open:** February–December.

➤ **The Old South experience at Rosswood is about as close to the real thing as you're going to get. If you want to take home a keepsake of your trip, the Hylanders offer souvenirs, as well as Christmas items, in their gift shop.**

Surrounded by big trees draped in Spanish moss, the large manor house proudly sits on a hill at the end of a winding drive not far from the old Natchez Trace — just like Tara and all the other white-columned antebellum homes you read about in books or see in the movies. It's a setting that's perfect for one of those family reunions where the ragged Confederate soldier limps toward the mansion, after walking maybe hundreds of miles following war's end, and a mother and sister run out to greet him with hugs and tears.

Rosswood is not a Hollywood set; it's a real plantation, built in 1857 for Dr. Walter W. Wade, who recorded in his journal that it was to him "a little bit of heaven." (Entries from Dr. Wade's journal have been framed and hung on the walls.) Wade hired architect David Shroder, better known for Windsor (now in ruins), to design the Greek Revival house and placed it on 1,285 acres at a cost of $10,857. About one hundred slaves had been emancipated by his grandfather two decades earlier — an event that had been heavily contested in the Mississippi courts. Many of them returned to their native Africa. During the "War of Northern Aggression," as it is often called in this part of the world, the house was used as a hospital for Confederate and Union soldiers, many of them wounded at the Battle of Coleman's Plantation nearby. The ghost of a Union soldier buried on the place is said to reside here, but he is friendly and sometimes says hello to guests.

Colonel Walt and Jean Hylander purchased the house and 100 acres in 1975 following his retirement from the U.S. Army. After the Mississippi Landmark was completely restored, it was added to the National Register of Historic Places in 1978. The Hylanders filled it with treasures they had acquired during their travels all over the world and then opened it to guests in 1983. They also grow Christmas trees. Their grandchildren visit often.

Guests have their choice of four bedrooms upstairs — all furnished in beautiful antiques (one has Jamaican mahogany furniture) and accessible to the second-floor gallery via the large central hallway. Each room has a private bath, ceiling fan, color TV, VCR, and phone.

The top gallery is a favorite gathering place in the afternoon. Guests are served a full plantation breakfast in the dining room. Each guest room has a notebook detailing information on area attractions and restaurants. Guests are free to roam the 100-acre property, which includes walking trails and an outdoor swimming pool and spa. Bathrobes are provided for those who want to take a swim. Another diversion is the video library.

Natchez

The Briars

31 Irving Lane
Natchez, MS 39120
601-446-9654, 800-634-1818
Fax: 601-445-6037
wcint@bbbank.com
http://www.natchezpilgrimage.com

> One of the most historic
> homes in Natchez

Innkeeper: R. E. Canon and Newton Wilds. **Accommodations:** 12 rooms and 2 suites (all with private baths). **Rates:** $135–$150. **Included:** Five-course plantation breakfast, refreshments, turndown service. **Payment:** American Express, MasterCard, Visa. **Children:** 12 and older welcome. **Pets:** Not allowed. **Smoking:** Allowed on porches. **Open:** Year-round.

➤ **Following the wedding of Jefferson Davis and Varina Howell here in 1845, guests celebrated in the ballroom.**

Located on a bluff overlooking the Mississippi River, The Briars is a famous house quite familiar to historians. Jefferson Davis, later to become president of the Confederate States of America, and Varina Howell were married here on February 23, 1845. Following their wedding in the parlor, there was a celebration in the ballroom upstairs.

Built between 1814 and 1818 for John Perkins, a wealthy landowner, it is listed on the National Register of Historic Places. The interior and exterior walls are plantation-made brick. The property was acquired by Walter Irvine in 1853, and his family lived there until 1927. By that time the estate was in a state of disrepair, and it was purchased by Mrs. Emma Augusta Wall of New Orleans who extensively restored the house and lived there until her death in 1966. Her granddaughter Emily Stubbs Kelly, who inherited the house, sold it to The Charisma Corporation, which opened it as a Pilgrimage Tour home for several years.

Interior designers Robert Canon and Newton Wild purchased The Briars in 1975 and have completed extensive renovations. They have also added the Guest House, Greenhouse, Grounds House, and Dining Pavilion and developed the extensive gardens. A bed-and-breakfast since 1988, it holds both the four-diamond and the four-star rating.

Guests are housed in the main house, guest house, and pavilion in fourteen spacious rooms, each with a private bath and cable television. All the rooms are elegantly furnished in antiques and period pieces. The innkeepers serve a five-course plantation breakfast in the Pavilion dining room. Guests often retreat to the eighty-foot verandah to enjoy the splendid views of the river. Or they may wander into the beautifully landscaped private gardens. With nineteen acres to roam, there are plenty of places to get lost.

The Governor Holmes House

207 South Wall Street
Natchez, MS 39120
601-442-2366, 888-442-0166
Fax: 601-442-0166

> A historic house considered by some connoisseurs to be the best B&B in Mississippi

Innkeeper: Robert Pully. **Accommodations:** 4 suites (all with private baths). **Rates:** $95, $30 for each additional person in certain suites. **Included:** Full plantation breakfast. **Payment:** Major credit cards. **Children:** 14 and older welcome. **Pets:** Not allowed. **Smoking:** Allowed in designated areas. **Open:** Year-round.

➤ **Located in the heart of downtown Natchez, the inn is convenient to shopping, attractions, and restaurants. Under-the-Hill, which recalls the bawdy early days of Natchez, is nearby.**

Sleep with history in one of the oldest Natchez homes, built in 1794 by Spaniards and now a National Historic Landmark and on the National Register of Historic Places. The house is named for Governor David Holmes, who lived here while serving as the last governor of the Mississippi Territory in 1809 and the first governor of the state in 1817. It is believed that Confederate President Jefferson Davis also once owned the house. The oldest rooms in the house feature plaster and half-timbers.

The Governor Holmes House, vacant for five years before it opened as a bed-and-breakfast inn in 1990, offers accommodations that are a bit different from those in other guest houses in Natchez. Small and intimate, tasteful and immaculately kept, it doesn't overwhelm the visitor. The inn is ideal for threesomes because some rooms have three twin beds or an extra bed. Of course, the most elaborate room in the house is the Governor's Suite. Though the public rooms are very elegant, the house overall is reminiscent of a tavern.

Bob Pully, who calls himself the "chief cook and bottle washer," draws on his many years of experience in the hospitality industry, including thirty-two years at the famed Algonquin in New York and at a B&B in the Catskills. A native of Virginia, he is the host of hosts and delights in giving tours of the house and telling stories laced with legend, nostalgia, and gossip. In 1996, Bob was named the Natchez Convention and Visitor Bureau's Tourism Superstar of the Year. He serves a sumptuous plantation breakfast, including such delights as fried apples, a Yorkshire pudding with hot syrup and scrambled eggs, French toast with a honey-orange sauce, and homemade biscuits, in the formal dining room or the breakfast room.

Monmouth Plantation

36 Melrose Avenue
Natchez, MS 39120
601-442-5852, 800-828-4531
Fax: 601-446-7762
luxury@monmouthplantation.com
http://www.monmouthplantation.com

The loveliest and friendliest historic inn in Natchez

Owners: Ron and Lani Riches. **Accommodations:** 13 rooms and 15 suites (all with private baths). **Rates:** $140–$365. **Included:** Plantation breakfast and mansion tour. **Payment:** Major credit cards. **Children:** 14 and older welcome. **Pets:** Not allowed. **Smoking:** Allowed on porches and grounds only. **Open:** Year-round.

➤ **The grounds are lined with brick walkways that lead through the rose garden, past fountains and statuary, to the wisteria-covered trellises, gazebo, and arched bridge over a portion of the lake. In all, there are 26 immaculately landscaped oak-studded acres.**

As the theme from *Gone With the Wind* plays during the five-course dinner in the candlelit formal dining room of Monmouth Plantation, you almost expect Scarlett O'Hara or Rhett Butler to make an appearance. They never show up, of course, but the experience is as close to Tara as you're probably going to get.

Built in 1818, Monmouth Plantation has been restored by Californians Ron and Lani Riches, who fell in love with it during a visit to Natchez. The Riches are nice people who believe in giving their guests the very best, a philosophy that is characteristic of the entire staff.

Tours of the restored Greek Revival home, a National Historic Landmark, are given throughout the day to the public, and overnight guests receive a complimentary tour following a full plantation breakfast. The tour provides insights on Monmouth's residents, including Governor John Anthony Quitman, a hero of the Mexican-American War. The Quitman Room contains his bed and a dresser where he stored his powdered wigs. His famous bandana that he used in rallying the troops is framed, and his gold sword is displayed in the hall of the main house.

Guests are lodged in the main house, the former kitchen, carriage house, and cottages. Rooms in the main house are furnished in tester beds, armoires, and marbletop dressers; rooms in the brick kitchen quarters are more modern in appearance, though they feature some antiques and reproductions. Each room has cable television and a telephone. Guests are invited to a cocktail hour each evening and receive turndown service with Ghirardelli chocolates. Terrycloth robes and towels are monogrammed with the Monmouth crest, along with toiletries. There is an honor bar for guests at Monmouth, and early risers may take advantage of coffee on the terrace. A five-course dinner is served in the formal dining room and parlors.

Monmouth, a four-diamond property, is a member of the prestigious Small Luxury Hotels of the World group and Historic Hotels of America and was recently named One of the Top 50 Inns in America by *Zagat.*

Oakwood Plantation

12 Oakwood Plantation Road
Natchez, MS 39120
Reservations:
Virginia Harrigan
P.O. Box 27
Fulton, Alabama 36446
800-699-4755 or 800-936-4424

An elegant B&B cottage on an old Mississippi farm

Innkeepers: Dot Sojourner and Virginia Harrigan. **Accommodations:** Two-bedroom cottage (with three baths). **Rates:** $125, plus $25 for each additional person. **Included:** Full plantation breakfast. **Payment:** Cash or checks. **Children:** 12 and older welcome. **Pets:** Not allowed. **Smoking:** Allowed. **Open:** Year-round.

➤ **The farm has been in the Sojourner family since 1814 and is recognized by the state of Mississippi as one of the oldest family-owned farms in the state.**

You can get a taste of southern country life as it was meant to be when you stay at Oakwood Plantation, twelve miles outside of Natchez. Left idle on the family farm for many years, the 1836 Greek Revival country cottage was restored by Dot Sojourner and her daughter Virginia Harrigan, who lives in Alabama. It was opened to guests in 1986. The owners rent the entire house to only one party at a time to ensure privacy. All the architectural features of the cottage have been left intact, but air conditioning, ceiling fans, bathrooms, a modern kitchen, and other comforts have been added.

Sunshine seems to hover over the white house with its multitude of windows. A wide front porch across the front invites you in. The ground level has a large living/reception room with a working fireplace, a formal dining room, a bright cheerful kitchen, and a washer and dryer. Stairs from the kitchen ascend to the bedrooms. All the rooms are furnished in family antiques and country cotton curtains and linens of the period. Memorabilia relating to the family and the Natchez area is displayed throughout the cottage.

Guests at Oakwood have the entire house to themselves, including access to the kitchen. The Mississippi plantation breakfast usually includes eggs; cheese grits; ham, bacon, or sausage; biscuits; jams and jellies; fruit and juice; and hot beverages. With Dot being a historian and her husband Boyd a veteran politician, you can get all the information you might ever want to know about the local area.

Depending on the weather and the time of year, you may opt to sit on the porch in the evening and look for the Big Dipper or curl up with a good book in front of a cozy fire. The next day you can walk around the farm and look at the registered Brahman cattle or go fishing. Oakwood is one of the few Natchez homes still owned by the family for whom it was built and contains many of its original furnishings.

Nesbit

Bonne Terre Country Inn

4715 Church Road
Nesbit, MS 38651
601-781-5100
Fax: 601-781-5466

An elegant country inn near Memphis

Innkeeper: Max Bonnin. **Accommodations:** 12 rooms (all with private baths). **Rates:** $155–$175. **Included:** Full breakfast. **Payment:** American Express, MasterCard, Visa. **Children:** 12 and older welcome. **Pets:** Not allowed. **Smoking:** Not allowed. **Open:** Year-round except Christmas Eve, Christmas Day, and New Year's Day.

➤ **The heart of the inn is the Bonne Terre Cafe, run by Michel Leny, owner of Cafe Society in Memphis.**

Since opening to the public in 1996, this newly constructed country inn has received rave reviews. Located on 100 acres about a 35-minute drive south of Memphis, the inn offers overnight lodging, gourmet dining, and conference facilities. The Bonne Terre is housed in three Greek Revival buildings, which are connected by porches and trellised walkways.

Featuring private porches or balconies, gas fireplaces with antique mantels, and Jacuzzi tubs, guest rooms are elegantly furnished in French and English antiques. Guests are treated to complimentary bathrobes, fresh flowers, feather beds, and down comforters.

A full gourmet breakfast, served in the cafe, comes with the room. The dinner menu, which features French country cuisine, changes every three weeks. Menu selections, under the direction of Michel Leny, include wild boar sausage, crawfish bisque, tequila-lime-cured salmon, grilled duck breast, roasted Cornish game hen, sweet-potato-crusted halibut, stuffed flounder, beef filet with anise and coffee crust, and other delectables.

The inn can accommodate small groups and parties.

Ocean Springs

Who's Inn?

623 Washington Avenue
Ocean Springs, MS 39564
601-875-3251
Fax: 601-875-3251

An art gallery and B&B inn

Innkeepers: Trailer and Sharon McQuilkin. **Accommodations:** 2 rooms (with private baths). **Rates:** $85–$95. **Included:** Continental breakfast, use of bicycles, laptop hookup, fax, and copier. **Payment:** American Express, MasterCard, Visa. **Children:** Welcome. **Pets:** Not allowed. **Smoking:** Not allowed. **Open:** Year-round.

➤ **The Walter Anderson Museum is a must-see in Ocean Springs. The artist, who died in 1965, drew inspiration from the natural beauty and wildlife of the area. Members of the Anderson family still operate Shearwater Pottery here.**

You'll be surrounded by art at this unique inn, offering art and hospitality in combination. Long before Trailer and Sharon McQuilkin began accepting overnight guests, they operated an art gallery in Ocean Springs that has served as a showcase for Trailer's art and other Southern artists. He's known for his beautiful three-dimensional lifelike wildflower sculptures, which he meticulously creates using copper wire, sheet copper, and natural materials and a number of different techniques (cutting, soldering, incising, and painting). His work has been exhibited in galleries all over the country and has found a place in the personal collections of art lovers.

The inn and gallery are housed in a building dating to 1915 that has served as a dental office and a restaurant. It is located in the historic district of Ocean Springs, a quaint art community on the Gulf Coast, and is only two blocks from the beach. The McQuilkins opened their gallery about ten years ago and added the B&B in 1995. Each guest room incorporates original paintings, sculpture, photography, carvings, and glass art in the decor. Most of the furnishings and the artwork are available for purchase. The inn has two rooms; one is accessible to the disabled. Each has a private entrance.

Guests have the entire building to themselves, as the McQuilkins do not live on the property. A Continental breakfast is provided across the street at La Croissant French Bakery. The McQuilkins take delight in offering the "extras" that make guests feel welcome — fresh flowers, candy, a well-stocked refrigerator, and a coffeemaker with all the fixings for coffee. Guests often use the complimentary bicycles for getting about the town or riding to the beach. For the business-minded, a fax, copier, and laptop hook-ups are available.

Pass Christian

Inn at the Pass

1215 East Scenic Drive
Pass Christian, MS 39571
601-452-0333, 800-217-2588
Fax: 601-452-0449

A beautiful B&B inn
overlooking the water

Innkeepers: Vernon and Brenda Harrison. **Accommodations:** 5 rooms (all with private baths). **Rates:** $75–$125. **Included:** Breakfast, beverages, evening refreshments, turndown service. **Payment:** Major credit cards. **Children:** 10 and older welcome in house; all ages in cottage. **Pets:** Small dogs allowed in cottage. **Smoking:** Not allowed. **Open:** Year-round.

➤ **This inn keeps alive a tradition of houses and inns operating at the Pass since the 1830s. The Mansion House, the San Souci, the St. Nicholas House, and the Napoleon House, as well as boarding homes and private guest houses could once be found in Pass Christian.**

The Inn at the Pass was established as a bed-and-breakfast inn in early 1995. It was restored by Vernon and Brenda Harrison, who moved here from Houston, where he practiced law and she worked as a psychologist.

Overlooking the Mississippi Sound, within walking distance of the beach and the harbor, the inn offers four guest rooms and a cottage, each decorated in a special way. The Rose Room, with a raised queen-size bed and decorated with antiques, is reminiscent of the Victorian era. The Hunt Room suggests the great outdoors, while the Bluebonnet Room and the Magnolia Room reflect the Old South. The cottage, a turn-of-the-century bungalow, has its own porch, sitting area, kitchenette, and bath. All the rooms have lighted ceiling fans.

The Harrisons serve a full southern breakfast in the breakfast room, on the front porch, or in the outdoor courtyard. They offer hot and cold beverages throughout the day, and they serve evening snacks.

The inn, which dates to 1885, was built by the Butchert family (Catherine, her son John, and her nephew Nicholas), a prominent family in the business community in the late-nineteenth century. It was called the Artesian Cottage because it was one of the first houses in the area to have running water, supplied by an artesian well. The Adams family acquired the house in 1902 and it remained in that family until 1980. (The second-story roof was blown off during Hurricane Camille in 1969.) E. J. Adam was editor of the *Coast Beacon* newspaper, which had its office next door. In 1994 the house was acquired by a Texas corporation under the direction of the Harrisons.

Philadelphia

Silver Star Resort & Casino

Highway 16 West
P.O. Box 6048
Philadelphia, MS 39350
800-557-0711
Fax: 601-650-1351

| Las Vegas–style gaming is the big attraction at this resort |

General Manager: Mike Driggs. **Accommodations:** 508 rooms (with private baths). **Rates:** $64–$325. **Included:** Property amenities. **Payment:** Major credit cards. **Children:** Welcome at resort but not allowed in casino. **Pets:** Not allowed. **Smoking:** Allowed. **Open:** Year-round.

➤ **Philadelphia offers a number of interesting attractions, such as the Choctaw Indian Museum, Nanih Waiya Cave and Mound, Holy Rosary Catholic Church (an Indian mission site), and the Historic District.**

You'll never be bored at this unique Mississippi resort. You can try your hand at slots or poker in the casino, go nightclubbing, shop, play golf, or relax in the spa.

Opened in July of 1994, the property is owned and operated by the Mississippi Band of Choctaw Indians and managed by the Boyd Gaming Corporation of Las Vegas, Nevada. Open 24 hours a day, the casino features more than 2,800 slot machines; 12 poker tables, and 84 table games, including blackjack, craps, roulette, mini-baccarat, and others. The betting range on table games is $5 to $10,000. When you tire of gaming, you can listen to live piano music in the Blue Note Lounge or go dancing in the Starlight Lounge, which hosts top music groups —Percy Sledge and Randy Travis made appearances in 1997. Many guests choose to relax with a cigar from Cigars et al.

The hotel offers 500 luxurious rooms, 78 suites, and a conference center. There are two swimming pools, joined by a running stream, plus two hot tubs to relax in. Another option is the spa, where you can enjoy a relaxing massage, indulge in a rejuvenating steam bath, or fine-tune your body with a personal trainer. New to the property as of 1997 is the Dancing Rabbit Golf Club, an 18-hole championship course designed by Tom Fazio and Jerry Pate. There's also a game room for kids of all ages.

Silver Star has six different dining options, including the Terrace Café, which is open 24 hours a day. A Sunday champagne brunch is offered in the Galaxy Buffet restaurant every week.

Starkville

Statehouse Hotel

Main and Jackson Streets
P.O. Box 2002
Starkville, MS 39759
601-323-2000, 800-722-1903
Fax: 601-323-4948

A small elegant hotel in a university town

General Manager: Terry Antoine. **Accommodations:** 34 rooms and 9 suites (all with private baths). **Rates:** $54–$114. **Payment:** Major credit cards. **Children:** Welcome. **Pets:** Not allowed. **Smoking:** Smoking and nonsmoking floors. **Open:** Year-round.

➤   **A gathering place and social center for Starkville for decades, the hotel hosts many visitors during the spring pilgrimage of homes and serves as headquarters for Mississippi State University students and alumni during football season.**

One doesn't expect to find a beautiful little hotel like this in a small town. Built as the Hotel Chester in 1925, the immaculately kept inn was renovated in 1985. The marble floors are polished to mirror luster, the crystal chandeliers sparkle, and the furniture shines. Hues of dusty rose and Williamsburg blue predominate in the public rooms.

Guests enter the hotel lobby, a small, intimate room with a baby grand piano, on Jackson Street. Next to the lobby is Antoine's Restaurant, which serves lunch and dinner. (Breakfast is Continental.) Menu selections include chicken teriyaki, filet mignon, Alaskan King crab legs and other seafood delicacies, and a variety of Italian dishes. The dining room opens onto a sunroom, formerly the courtyard, now used year-round for receptions and parties. Next to the restaurant is the library, a mahogany-paneled room with soft lighting. The hotel has a small meeting room that can accommodate twenty people.

Guest rooms and suites are furnished with traditional furniture, including four-poster beds. The executive king rooms have marble-top wet bars and a living area. The Presidential Suite, the grandest in the house, has a spacious bedroom, living room, and a wet bar.

The staff at the Statehouse Hotel is attentive and hospitable. The hotel offers laundry pickup and VIP services such as faxing and copying.

Tupelo

The Mockingbird Inn Bed & Breakfast

305 North Gloster
Tupelo, MS 38801
601-841-0286
Fax: 601-840-4158
http://www.bbonline.clm/ms/mockingbird/

Tupelo's first B&B takes you around the world

Innkeepers: Jim and Sandy Gilmer. **Accommodations:** 7 rooms (all with private baths). **Rates:** $65–$125. **Included:** Full breakfast, evening refreshments, newspaper, use of fax machine. **Payment:** Major credit cards. **Children:** 10 and older welcome. **Pets:** Well-behaved pets welcome; $10 donations accepted for Humane Society. **Smoking:** Allowed on outside patio and porches. **Open:** Year-round.

➤   **The inn is located across the street from the junior high school that Elvis Presley attended, and the legendary star's birthplace and museum are nearby.**

The Mockingbird Inn was built as a private residence in 1925 for Douglas and Mary Potter. Surviving the 1936 tornado that devastated the town, it was used as a temporary hospital. (Mr. Potter was a ticket agent at Tupelo's old train depot.) The house remained in the Potter family for three generations and served as an apartment complex, pool and patio store, and clothing boutique before becoming an inn. It combines three architectural styles — Colonial, Prairie, and Arts and Crafts.

You can take a trip around the world during a stay at the Mockingbird Inn—guest rooms transport you to Jim and Sandy Gilmer's favorite places. They carefully researched and sought out colors, fabrics, and decorative objects that would compliment each room. A sleigh bed, lace curtains, antique wooden skis, and a great alpine scene take you to Bavaria. In one room, faux zebra and leopard skins, native art, and mosquito netting over the bed make you feel as though you're in Africa. An 1800s tapestry of Venetian gondolas and the Doge's Palace take you to Venice, the city of canals. Other destinations are Paris, Athens, Mackinac Island, and Sanibel Island. (Each room has its own telephone and television set.)

The innkeepers go out of their way to provide the ultimate bed-and-breakfast experience, whether it be an overnight stay or a romantic weekend, with in-room massage therapy, gift baskets, and carriage rides. They welcome guests at a reception every afternoon at five o'clock, and they treat them to a lavish breakfast the next morning. Favorite entrees include gingerbread waffles; French toast a l'orange; sausage, cheese and egg casserole, and puffed pancakes — served with bacon, ham or sausage, homemade hash browns, and all the trimmings. The Gilmers offer romance packages, gift baskets, floral arrangements, and gift certificates.

The couple established the B&B in 1994, naming it for the state bird. They have entertained guests from all over the United States and many countries abroad. In 1997, they earned AAA's three-diamond rating. Jim Gilmer is president of Gilmer Enterprises, Inc., and he runs Tupelo Recycling and also serves on the Board of Directors for the Tupelo Convention & Visitors Bureau and the Mississippi Restaurant Association. Sandy is vice president of the family business and is a member of the Professional Association of Innkeepers International.

Vicksburg

Anchuca

1010 First East Street
Vicksburg, MS 39180
601-631-6800, 800-469-2597

> **The oldest mansion in Vicksburg, now restored, serves as a B&B**

Innkeeper: May C. Burns. **Accommodations:** 6 rooms (all with private baths). **Rates:** $85–$250. **Included:** Full breakfast and home tour. **Payment:** Major credit cards. **Children:** Welcome. **Pets:** Not allowed. **Smoking:** Allowed in designated areas. **Open:** Year-round.

➤ **The name Anchuca comes from the Choctaw Indian word meaning "happy home." Though quite elegant, the inn is an inviting house where guests feel at home. A player piano is a whimsical touch.**

This historic Vicksburg home dates to 1830. Built as a one-level home by J. W. Mauldin, it was later enlarged to two stories and elaborate columns were added to the front, making its architectural style Greek Revival. Confederate President Jefferson Davis delivered a speech from the second-story balcony, calling for secession. Though unprotected, the house survived forty-three days of shelling by Union troops in 1863.

May Burns, the current owner and innkeeper, is a former schoolteacher who brought up her children in the house and then decided to open it to visitors as a bed-and-breakfast inn. She spent six years carefully selecting the proper furnishings — fine antiques, including tester and half-tester beds, marble-top dressers, and superior china and silver. Guests have a choice of rooms in the main house or in the 1890 guest cottage.

Guests find an assortment of menus from local restaurants in their rooms to help them choose a place for dining. Evening turn-downs with chocolates are offered, and an honors bar is available.

In the morning, a full southern breakfast is served in the formal dining room — scrambled eggs, pancakes, cheese grits, biscuits, and coffee. Afterward, guests may take the house tour, visit other historic homes and sites related to the Civil War, or relax in the swimming pool or hot tub.

The Belle of the Bends

508 Klein Street
Vicksburg, MS 39180
601-634-0737, 800-844-2308

A Victorian B&B and one of the area's best restorations

Innkeepers: Wally and Jo Pratt. **Accommodations:** 4 rooms (all with private baths). **Rates:** $95–$125, plus $20 for each additional person. **Included:** Full breakfast and home tour. **Payment:** Major credit cards. **Children:** 6 and older welcome. **Pets:** Check with innkeepers. **Smoking:** Allowed on verandahs. **Open:** Year-round.

➤ **You learn all about Mississippi River history and activities from inn-keeper Jo Pratt, granddaughter of Tom Morrissey, who was a riverboat captain.**

The name is not only intriguing but fitting: You can see the bend of the Mississippi River as it winds its way through historic Vicksburg, and the house, located on a hill in the Kleins Landing Historic Community, is really named for one of the finest steam-boats that ever plied the Mississippi. Built in 1898, the *Belle of the Bends* ran between Vicksburg and Greenville for a number of years before being put into service as an excursion boat between Vicksburg and New Orleans in 1910.

Jo and her husband, Wally, opened the inn in early 1991 after doing a complete restoration on the classic Victorian Italianate house, one of the best-preserved homes of its type in the area. It was built by Senator Murray F. Smith in 1876, the year the river changed its course. The house sparkles with fresh wallpaper and paint, and each of the four guest rooms is beautifully decorated in Victorian furnishings and colors. Besides heirloom antiques, the home features distinctive woodwork, ornate marble mantels, decorative plaster molding, and lovely medallions encircling the gas-burning chandeliers. Two verandahs, upstairs and downstairs, provide a ringside seat to river activities, the newest being gambling at the Riverboat Casino. Migratory birds that follow the river often make their way to the inn's beautiful garden.

The Pratts welcome guests with afternoon refreshments. The next morning they serve a full plantation breakfast with the house specialty coffee and Flora's melt-in-your-mouth angel biscuits. (Everyone wants her recipe.) As longtime residents of the area, the Pratts are knowledgeable on sights to see and the best restaurants in town. The house is often used for wedding receptions and small meetings.

Cedar Grove Estate

2200 Oak Street
Vicksburg, MS 39180
601-636-1000, 800-862-1300
Fax: 601-634-6126
http://www.cedargroveinn.com

A grand antebellum mansion where you're surrounded by history

Innkeeper: Rhonda Abraham. **Accommodations:** 28 rooms and suites (all with private baths). **Rates:** $85–$160, plus $20 for each additional person. **Included:** Full plantation breakfast, house tour. **Payment:** Major credit cards. **Children:** Welcome. **Pets:** Not allowed. **Smoking:** Not allowed in main house; limited to two designated rooms. **Open:** Year-round.

➤ **The grounds at Cedar Grove, with formal plantings and statuary, are beautiful beyond description, so be sure to take a stroll. Four of the original 66 acres remain.**

You can almost hear taffeta skirts rustling in this elegant Vicksburg home, the epitome of southern opulence at the time of the Civil War. A hole cut in the parlor floor by a cannonball during the Battle of Vicksburg has been covered with Plexiglas, and the missile itself remains lodged in the wall. The damage to the house was slight, however, compared with that done to most other homes in town during the 1863 siege. The story goes that the house was spared because the lady of the house was General Sherman's niece — an association that caused her to be scorned by her neighbors, many of whom had to flee to the caves on the river to escape being killed. When the city fell to the Union, General Ulysses S. Grant took over Cedar Grove as his headquarters. Many people have felt the presence of spirits in the house.

The two-story 36-room Greek Revival home, with its double balconies and white columns, was built between 1840 and 1852 by John Alexander Klein as a wedding gift to his wife, Elizabeth, who was sixteen at the time of the marriage. At age thirty, he had already amassed a fortune in lumber and cotton. She bore him ten children, one of whom was accidentally killed when he was returning from a hunting trip.

All the gas-burning chandeliers, marble mantels, and plaster medallions (made of molasses, sugar, water, horsehair, and marble dust) are original to the house, as are some furnishings, many of which the Kleins purchased in Europe on their honeymoon. Jefferson Davis, who became president of the Confederacy, is said to have danced in the elegant ballroom. The draperies in the formal dining room are copies of the ones featured in the movie *Gone With the Wind* — and are obviously a later addition to the house.

In 1919, the Klein heirs sold the house and all its furnishings for a mere $9,000. The present owners, Ted Mackey and Estelle Mackey, bought the house in 1983 and have spent a great deal of time and money refurbishing it to its present grandeur.

The guest rooms at Cedar Grove are elegantly furnished in tester and half-tester beds, matching armoires (some of them prized pieces by Prudent Mallard of New Orleans), and Oriental rugs. All of the rooms have telephones and televisions. Guests are lodged in the main house, the carriage house, and guest cottages. A full plantation breakfast of sausage, eggs, cheese grits, biscuits, and all the trimmings is served in the formal dining room or the Garden Room, after which there is a house tour, complimentary to guests. (The house is open for public tours all day.) New Orleans cuisine is offered Tuesday through Saturday evenings in the Garden Room Restaurant in the mansion.

An outdoor pool, tennis courts, and croquet lawn are available for guests, and a gift shop is on the premises. If you'd like to venture beyond the iron gates, the Mississippi River and other attractions are only minutes away.

The Corners

601 Klein Street
Vicksburg, MS 39180
601-636-7421, 800-444-7421

A nineteenth-century wedding gift that's now a charming B&B

Innkeepers: The Whitneys. **Accommodations:** 13 rooms, 1 suite, and 1 cottage (all with private baths). **Rates:** $85–$120. **Included:** Full plantation breakfast, afternoon beverages, and mansion tour. **Payment:** Major credit cards. **Children:** Welcome. **Pets:** Check with innkeeper. **Smoking:** Allowed on verandah. **Open:** Year-round.

➤ **The 68-foot-long verandahs, their columns pierced with card symbols, invite guests to sit for a while and read the morning paper or enjoy a cold beverage while watching the sun set over the Mississippi.**

In the 1870s it was often customary for the father of the bride to present his daughter with a new house as a wedding gift. That was the case with the Corners, built in 1872 by John Alexander Klein for his daughter Susan when she married Isaac Bonhan. The Kleins resided at Cedar Grove just across the street.

The two-story, double-balconied Victorian Italianate Greek-Revival mansion sits on a bluff with views of the Mississippi and Yazoo rivers. The former servants' quarters are now a guest house. Within the iron gates surrounding the main house is a Creole garden, profuse with plantings of flowers and shrubs.

Guests are received in the parlor, where ladies and gentlemen of Vicksburg often danced the hours away. A full plantation breakfast is served in the formal dining room on china and silver or in the glassed-in verandah. No other meals are offered at the Corners, but the inn is close to a half dozen restaurants, including one that's just across the street at Cedar Grove.

Guest rooms are furnished in antique beds and armoires. The Eastlake Room has twelve-foot windows that open onto the back verandah and the gardens. The Library Room, which also overlooks the gardens, has a wood-burning fireplace and walls paneled with cypress and lined with books. (Several other fireplaces in the house burn gas logs.) The galleries offer four luxurious bedroom suites.

Cliff and Bettye Whitney, former residents of Dallas, purchased the house in 1986 and opened it as an inn the following year after extensive renovations. The Whitneys attribute their innkeeping status to destiny; the wrong turn they took on one of their trips East changed their lives forever. Their son Cliff and daughter-in-law Kilby recently joined them.

West

The Alexander House Bed and Breakfast

Corner of Green and Anderson Streets
West, MS 39192
601-967-2266, 800-350-8034

A charming Victorian inn located in West's Historic District

Innkeepers: Woody and Ruth Ray Dinstel. **Accommodations:** 5 rooms (3 with private baths, 2 with shared bath). **Rates:** $65. **Included:** Full breakfast, mountain bicycles. **Payment:** Major credit cards. **Children:** 10 and older welcome **Pets:** Not allowed. **Smoking:** Allowed on back porch. **Open:** Year-round.

➤ **There are plenty of attractions in and around the town of Historic West — including Civil War sites, wildlife refuges, the Natchez Trace, Holmes County State Park, Casey Jones Railroad Museum, and the Little Red School House.**

As president of the West Historical Society, Ruth Ray Dinstel will do anything to preserve the history of her town. So, when the old house on the corner of Green and Anderson Streets was about to be sold for scrap lumber, she and her husband Woody bought it. They had already restored their own residence, the Christmas Cottage, located a couple of blocks from their "new project." Needless to say, townspeople were skeptical of their plans to turn the crumbling, rundown house into a bed-and-breakfast inn. But the Dinstels persevered and accomplished what seemed to be an impossible task. Since opening in 1994, the Alexander House Bed and Breakfast has become the most popular spot in town for special celebrations.

The inn offers five guest rooms, all beautifully decorated with furniture and collectibles the Dinstels acquired while Woody worked abroad for Exxon. Of special interest are Ruth Ray's Valentine collection and the couple's extensive library. Two of the rooms can be rented as a suite. The combination of floral wallpaper, quilt patterns, and lace throughout the house creates a Victorian atmosphere. Guests are free to use all the sitting areas in the house, the screened porch, and the flower gardens. The innkeepers serve a full country breakfast in the formal dining room or the kitchen and will also prepare dinner for guests by appointment and for an extra fee. They will also arrange day trips to historic and recreational sites in the area. An icemaker, coffeemaker, and mountain bikes are provided.

Alexander House, built in 1880, was the home of Captain Joseph T. Alexander, a Civil War veteran. A room in the inn that bears his name contains some of the furniture that belonged to him. Other rooms are named for the Captain's sons and daughters — Dr. Joe, Ulrich, Annie, and Miss Bealle. Civil War buffs, Woody and Ruth Ray are always eager to share stories about the captain and point out skirmish sites and historic cemeteries in which soldiers are buried.

North Carolina

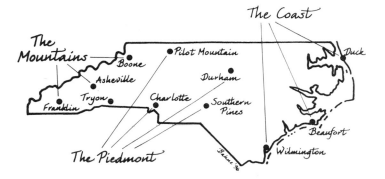

The Coast

The
Mountains

Boone

Pilot Mountain

Asheville

Durham

Tryon

Charlotte

Southern
Pines

Franklin

The Piedmont

Duck

Beaufort

Wilmington

From its Atlantic coast to the soaring Blue Ridge and Great Smoky mountains, North Carolina offers an intriguing variety of places to see and things to do. Barrier islands — the storied, windswept Outer Banks — and wide sounds indent the shoreline, appealing to wilderness lovers, outdoor enthusiasts, and history buffs. Inland, fertile tobacco farms, forests, and heritage-rich towns characterize a quite distinctive region.

This state alone produces more than 70 percent of the nation's bright leaf tobacco, and corn, cotton, fruit, poultry, and livestock are other important crops. Most of North Carolina's industry, commerce, wealth, and population are concentrated in the rich, rolling, centrally located Piedmont region. "Big three" industries — textiles, tobacco products, and furniture manufacturing — have long dominated North Carolina's economy. But its largest city, Charlotte, strong in financial matters since Gold Rush days, has recently emerged as the nation's second largest banking center, and its economy is largely dependent on distribution and wholesaling. In western North Carolina, the Blue Ridge Mountains reach their highest elevations, one summit (Mt. Mitchell) cresting as the highest mountain east of the Rockies.

Today, the Old North State is a land for all seasons. On the coast, the Cape Hatteras and Cape Lookout National Seashores boast 100 miles of broad, open beaches offering camping, swimming, water skiing, and surf fishing. Four national forests and numerous state parks provide more opportunities for camping, fishing, riding, hiking, boating, and swimming. There's challenging whitewater rafting on the Nantahala River and other scenic mountain streams. In the Great Smoky Mountains National Park, hikers can walk 71 miles of the Appalachian Trail, going over the mountain crests for the entire length of the park. You can also boat, water-ski, and fish for bass, crappie, sunfish, and other catches on various natural and manmade lakes, some impounded by hydroelectric dams of the Duke Power Company.

Golf is a popular sport at the posh resorts clustered at Pinehurst and Southern Pines in the Sandhills, and there are some fine mountain and coastal courses as well. The Sandhills also offer major equestrian centers where enthusiasts can ride virtually every day of the year. The Stoneybrook Steeplechase Race at Southern Pines attracts thousands of spectators each year.

Come winter, you can ski the mountain slopes outside Banner Elk, Blowing Rock, Seven Devils, Scaly Mountain, Mars Hill, and Maggie Valley. The quality of skiing varies, as operators must have a base of natural snow before topping it with the manmade variety.

But when the weather is cold enough, even seasoned skiers praise the conditions of the North Carolina slopes.

In this basketball-crazed state, you can cheer for four Atlantic Coast Conference teams: the Blue Devils of Duke University, the Tarheels of the University of North Carolina at Chapel Hill, the Wolfpack of North Carolina State University, and the Demon Deacons of Wake Forest University. And the Charlotte Hornets, a National Basketball Association team, attract fervent fans from both Carolinas. Most games are sellouts, and the team holds the record for attendance in the NBA. Racing is another big spectator sport in North Carolina, with the biggest track being the Charlotte Motor Speedway (actually in Concord), which hosts major races of the National Association of Stock Car Automobile Racing (NASCAR). The Carolina Panthers NFL franchise team play in a state-of-the-art stadium in uptown Charlotte.

Wherever you travel in North Carolina, you'll probably encounter one argument that just won't go away. It's the merits of western versus eastern barbecue. Generally, western barbecue sauce is a combination of vinegar and tomato base; in the east, the sauce usually has no tomato. Purists have been known to drive for hours to get a western barbecue fix in Lexington, about 20 miles south of Winston-Salem.

For more information, contact the North Carolina Division Travel and Tourism Division, Department of Commerce, 430 North Salisbury Street, Raleigh, North Carolina 27603, 919-733-4171 or 800-VISIT-NC.

The Mountains

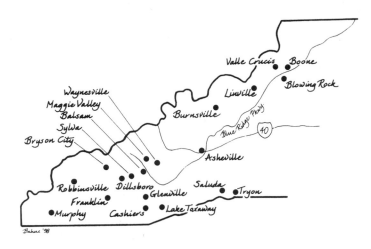

Valle Crucis Boone
Linville Blowing Rock
Waynesville
Maggie Valley
Balsam Burnsville
Sylva Blue Ridge Pkwy 40
Bryson City Asheville
Robbinsville Dillsboro Saluda
Glenville Tryon
Franklin Cashiers Lake Taxaway
Murphy

Bahne '98

Best Bed-and-Breakfasts

Best Country Inns

Best Guest Ranch

Best Resorts

Asheville
Grove Park Inn Resort, 334
Blowing Rock
Hound Ears Resort, 340
Cashiers
High Hampton Inn & Country Club, 346

Best Romantic Hideaways

Glenville
Innisfree Inn —A Victorian Bed & Breakfast, 352
Lake Toxaway
The Greystone Inn, 354
Sylva
Mountain Brook, 364

Best Spa

Burnsville
The Panes, 344

The North Carolina mountains, where the Blue Ridge reaches its highest elevations and the Great Smokies stand astride the border with Tennessee, have such great appeal that many visitors return year after year. The storied Blue Ridge Parkway begins in Virginia where the Skyline Drive ends. Stretching for 469 miles along slopes and crests of the Blue Ridge Mountains, the parkway reaches its terminus near Cherokee, at the southern entrance to the Great Smoky Mountains National Park. Service facilities spaced along the parkway include picnic areas, hiking trails, gas stations, campgrounds, restaurants, gift shops, and a few overnight lodges and cabins. Scenic overlooks provide views of some of the most magnificent scenery in eastern North America.

The Great Smoky Mountains National Park in North Carolina and Tennessee includes the highest concentration of peaks in the Appalachian uplands. U.S. 441, the main route through the park from Cherokee to Gatlinburg, Tennessee, passes over Newfound Gap on the border of the two states. A spur road goes to Clingmans Dome, which offers a magnificent view of the Smokies (on a clear day) from the lookout tower. At Oconaluftee Visitor Center near Cherokee a reconstructed mountain farm of the late 1800s affords glimpses into pioneer mountain life.

Cherokee is the tribal town of the Eastern Band of the Cherokee Nation and home to a brand new casino operated jointly by the tribe and Harrah's. More than eight thousand Native Americans live on the surrounding Qualla Boundary Cherokee Indian Reservation. Customs and history of the tribal nation may be appreciated by visiting the Museum of the Cherokee Indian and by walking through the Oconaluftee Indian Village, where members of the tribe in native dress demonstrate arts and crafts in the setting of an early-18th-century Cherokee town. Summer evenings, performances of Kermit Hunter's splendid outdoor drama *Unto These Hills* trace the history of the Cherokee from the arrival of the first Europeans under De Soto until their tragic removal along the Trail of Tears in 1838.

In North Carolina's High Country, the resort towns of Blowing Rock, Boone, Banner Elk, and Linville lie amid some of the most elevated reaches of the Blue Ridge Mountains, in the northwestern portion of the state. Summer and autumn visitors will enjoy stops at Tweetsie Railroad, between Boone and Blowing Rock, and soaring 5,964-foot-tall Grandfather Mountain. The latter includes a large natural habitat for deer, cougars, black bear, and such endangered species as bald and golden eagles. More fearless visitors may walk across the Mile High Swinging Bridge at the summit. There's more cloud-top expiration on the Linn Cove Viaduct, the final link of the Blue Ridge Parkway. The Grandfather Mountain Highland Games and Gathering of the Scottish Clans, held on the second weekend of July, is among the largest such events in the nation. At Boone, Kermit Hunter's outdoor drama *Horn in the West* depicts tales of Daniel Boone and pioneers in the mountain region. In Ashe County visitors flock to see the Ben Long frescoes in Holy Trinity Church and Saint Mary's Episcopal Church. The area around Spruce Pine is known for its crafts and gem mines.

Asheville, North Carolina's largest mountain city with a population of about 60,000, is noted as the childhood home of the writer Thomas Wolfe. The house — the boarding home Dixieland in *Look Homeward Angel* — is preserved as the Thomas Wolfe Memorial State Historic Site. Biltmore Estate, just outside the city near the Blue Ridge Parkway, preserves the opulent mansion and magnificent gardens of the late George Washington Vanderbilt. On self-guided tours you can explore the upstairs and downstairs portions of the 250-room French Renaissance château, which includes ornate furnishings, antiques, and art objects. The gardens are especially colorful when azaleas, many of them rare hybrid specimens, bloom in early May. In December, the mansion comes alive with vibrant decorations and floral displays during Candlelight Christmas at Biltmore, a lavish Victorian celebration.

Since pioneer days, North Carolina has been noted for its fine folk art and handicrafts: wood carvings, quilts, dulcimers, corn shuck dolls, weavings, ironwork, and other wares produced by mountain artisans. Now, superb contemporary crafts are also produced in the area. You can view many of them, browse and buy as well, at the Folk Art Center, operated by the Southern Highland Handicraft Guild in a handsome, sprawling modern structure at mile 382 of the Blue Ridge Parkway, just outside Asheville. A craft trail extends from the foothills to the Tennessee state line.

In Flat Rock, 25 miles south of Asheville, the Carl Sandburg National Historic Site preserves the famed author's Connemara home and farm much as it was when he and his family lived there. Nearby Brevard hosts the renowned summer Brevard Music Festival, presenting symphonic concerts, chamber music, recitals, and light and grand opera. Another major summer festival, Folkmoot — North Carolina's International Folk Festival, is staged at Waynesville, a popular resort town near the eastern entrance of the Great Smoky Mountains National Park.

Asheville

The Grove Park Inn Resort

290 Macon Avenue
Asheville, NC 28804
828-252-2711, 800-438-5800
Fax: 828-253-7053

> **A legendary hotel dedicated to service**

Vice President and General Manager: James S. France. **Accommodations:** 510 rooms and suites (all with private baths). **Rates:** $109–$230; value season (January–April), $79–$159. **Payment:** Major credit cards. **Children:** Welcome. **Pets:** Not allowed. **Smoking:** Allowed in designated areas. **Open:** Year-round.

➤ **Most visitors take the sayings written on the fireplaces very seriously. One reads, "Take from this hearth its warmth ... Take from this room its charm ... Take from this Inn its amity ... return them not, but return."**

Jack the Giant Killer might be credited with building this monumental inn, an architectural triumph that was completed in 1913. Actually, Dr. Edwin Wiley Grove was the visionary for the Grove Park Inn. Using the Old Faithful Inn in Yellowstone Park as his inspiration, the pharmaceutical giant had the inn built of huge boulders that would have been difficult for even a giant to lift. (They were hauled to the site by Packard engine-powered "trains" and fitted into place by Italian and native stonemasons.) The small Otis elevators tucked away in the massive stone fireplaces, which burn ten-foot logs, still work. The design and early operation of the hotel is credited to Fred Seely, Grove's son-in-law who built the structure without the aid of a contractor or architect.

The inn attracted the beautiful people of the early twentieth century — Henry Ford, Harvey Firestone, Thomas Edison, Woodrow Wilson — who came here to enjoy the serenity of the mountains, good food, and no doubt Dr. Grove's healthful tonics. The Great Hall, with its massive fireplaces, often reverberated in the afternoon with sounds from the Skinner organ and the voices of masters such as Enrico Caruso. During that era children were discouraged, pets were forbidden, and loud talk and slamming doors were not allowed. The U.S. government housed Axis diplomats and returning servicemen here during World War II. In 1955, the hotel was purchased by the late Charles A. Sammons of Dallas, Texas, and is now a subsidiary of Sammons Travel and Resort, Inc. (STAR).

The hotel was once a seasonal property, but it became a year-round destination when it was renovated in the 1980s; two new wings and a sports complex were also added. Now it's popular not only with individuals but with groups of up to 1,000 people. The Grove Park is a destination resort, offering four restaurants and lounges, an 18-hole golf course (formerly the Country Club of Asheville), tennis courts, swimming pool, sauna, Jacuzzi, sports club, and numerous programs and amenities.

All the rooms conform to the arts and crafts style of the original inn, with Roycrofters oak furniture and warm, earthy fabrics in the draperies and bedding. Attentiveness and service continue to be the watchwords for the staff, and guests can make almost any reasonable request and have it granted. Special packages centering on golf, tennis, romance, and the holidays are available throughout the year. From Thanksgiving through New Year's Day, the hotel is decorated with live greenery and brightly lit Christmas trees, and the hotel's famous staff chorus leads Christmas carols weekdays at noon.

Richmond Hill Inn and Conference Center

87 Richmond Hill Drive
Asheville, NC 28806
828-252-7313, 800-545-9238
Fax: 828-252-8726
http://www.RichmondHillInn.com

> **A grand Victorian inn
> where croquet's the game**

Innkeeper: Susan Michel. **Accommodations:** 12 inn rooms, 5 garden rooms, and 9 cottages (all with private baths, 26 with fireplaces). **Rates:** $145–$375 for inn rooms, $175–$375 for garden rooms, $170–$300 for cottages, plus $20 for each additional person (2-night minimum on weekends). **Included:** Full breakfast, afternoon tea. **Payment:** American Express, MasterCard, Visa. **Children:** Welcome. **Pets:** Not allowed. **Smoking:** Not allowed. **Open:** Year-round.

➤ **The new Garden Pavilion offers fifteen guest rooms, and the adjacent Arbor Grille features Southern Nouvelle cuisine.**

Wear your whites and have your mallets ready for croquet, the rage at this three-story Victorian inn overlooking the French Broad River. Guests may stay in the croquet cottages and play on the court, sewn with Pencroft creeping bent grass.

After ten years of restoration, Richmond Hill Inn has become a romantic oasis three miles from downtown Asheville. Guests choose from opulent suites and rooms in the mansion, croquet cottages, and the Gardon Pavilion. The inn was restored and opened to guests in 1989 by Dr. and Mrs. Albert J. Michel of Greensboro. No details were overlooked in the restoration. Built by Richmond Pearson, a former congressional representative and ambassador, and his wife Gabrielle, the imposing house on the hillside was grand for its time — with running water, a communication system, and a pulley-operated elevator.

Guests enter the inn through Oak Hall, a grand foyer with a staircase, all paneled in oak. A parlor, a library, an octagonal ballroom, and Gabrielle's Restaurant are located downstairs. While the formal service at the restaurant mirrors the elegance of a bygone era, the food combines old and new into a totally contemporary culinary experience. An award-winning wine selection and romantic piano music complement dinner.

The newest addition to the inn is the Gardon Pavilion, with fifteen spacious rooms overlooking the Parterre Garden and waterfall. The balcony of the Thomas Pearson Suite offers a picturesque view of the mansion and gardens. Doors from the balcony lead to a cozy sitting room, the bedroom, and a two-person jetted tub in the bath. Each room has a refrigerator stocked with complimentary soft drinks. Also in the Garden Pavilion is a quaint gift shop and the Arbor Grille, a casual restaurant offering both indoor and outdoor dining.

The inn, an ideal place for small meetings, also hosts weddings, receptions, and seminars. The house is listed on the National Register of Historic Places, and both the inn and the restaurant have been awarded four diamonds by AAA.

Balsam

Balsam Mountain Inn

P.O. Box 40
Balsam, NC 28707
828-456-9498, 800-224-9498
Fax: 828-456-9298

A grand dame of the mountains is reborn

Innkeeper: Merrily Teasley and George Austin. **Accommodations:** 50 rooms (all with private baths). **Rates:** $85–$175; additional charge for lunch and dinner, as well as some special events. **Included:** Full country breakfast. **Payment:** Discover, MasterCard, Visa. **Children:** Well-behaved children welcome. **Pets:** Not allowed. **Smoking:** Allowed in designated areas. **Open:** Year-round.

➤ **Located on the highest elevation of any standard gauge railroad in the East (3,314 feet), the hotel offered a chance to escape from the heat of the lowlands. Guests arrived with their steamer trucks by train and spent the entire summer hiking, horseback riding, picnicking, and playing croquet.**

Merrily Teasley first saw the Balsam Mountain Inn on a hiking trip in 1989. The dilapidated structure was boarded up, having been closed by the health department the previous year. And though the Greeneville, Tennessee, native was already running a bed-and-breakfast inn — the Edgeworth Inn in Monteagle, Tennessee — she couldn't get the sad-looking old inn on Balsam Mountain out of her mind. Her attempts to get in touch with the owners for several months after that were unsuccessful. The next summer, when she returned to look at the inn again, she found a For Sale sign posted. She sold her inn in Tennessee and went calling on a number of banks before she found one in nearby Sylva that would back the restoration of the inn.

Restoring the 42,000-square-foot, 100-room hotel was a daunting task, and it took fifty full-time workers several months to complete the job. They installed new wiring, new plumbing, new heating (recycled radiators from a dormitory at Western Carolina University), and a new sprinkler system, water tank, and septic system. The workmen jacked up sagging floors, replaced broken windows and supports that had been removed, and repaired the mansard roof. They removed partitions to enlarge the guest rooms, and installed new bathrooms, giving the inn a total of 50 rooms with private baths. They covered the exterior walls with a pale yellow paint and trimmed the building in white; inside they dressed up the beaded-board walls in pastel colors. In 1996, a sun porch was added to the dining room, providing more light and offering better views of the mountains. Since the inn had been placed on the National Register of Historic Places in 1982, the entire renovation was done according to U.S. Interior Department guidelines.

One of the few remaining turn-of-the-century hotels in western North Carolina, the Balsam Mountain Inn was built between 1905 and 1908 by Joseph Kenney and Walter Christy of Athens, Georgia, to serve passengers on the Murphy branch of the Southern Railroad. Patterned after the Saratoga Inn in New York, the hotel proved to be very popular, attracting the first families of the South for several years until it was sold to E. P. Stillwell of Sylva during the Depression. Couples married and honeymooned at the Balsam Mountain Inn; babies were born; and some guests even passed away (ask about their ghosts).

Merrily worked right alongside the workmen, oftentimes tackling difficult jobs herself. She salvaged as much of the original furniture as she could and added many pieces from the Edgeworth Inn. With her eye for color and knowledge of art, Merrily chose brightly colored chintzes and floral patterns to achieve the comfortable but elegant look the inn now has. As an artist with degrees from Middle Tennessee State University and the University of Tennessee, Merrily viewed each room as an empty canvas that would take on its own special character as she worked on it. Since the hotel dated to the Victorian era, she could take many liberties in decorating. The lobby, with its wicker furnishings and chintz fabrics, the dining room, and the library, with more than two thousand titles, all bear her touches. Much of the artwork in the inn was done by Merrily and her daughters.

Balsam Mountain Inn opened in July of 1991. The inn is near Milepost 443 of the Blue Ridge Parkway in the middle of the Balsam Mountain Range, which includes summits over 6,000 feet. Because of its proximity to the Great Smokies National Park, the Cherokee Indian Reservation, Maggie Valley, and Asheville, the inn serves as headquarters for visitors who are hiking and sightseeing in the area. Others come here simply to relax on the double-decker rocker-lined verandahs or take short walks over the 26 acres of grounds.

Breakfast, lunch, and dinner are served at the inn — simple fresh foods prepared under the direction of a professional chef. Breakfast might feature baked French toast or scrambled eggs, biscuits, gravy, and sliced fresh tomatoes. The rotating dinner menu includes four or more entrées (trout, prime rib, lamb, seafood, and poultry), fresh vegetables, salad, breads, and homemade desserts. The dining room is open to the public every day but Monday. Complimentary tea, coffee, hot chocolate, and cider are available at all times. The inn provides box lunches and free shuttle service to the Blue Ridge Parkway for those who want to hike the Mountains to the Sea trail. Merrily and her staff often stage special events such as wildflower weeks, bluegrass and traditional mountain music concerts, storytelling, theater productions, and hikes.

Balsam Mountain Inn has about twenty-five people on staff, including Lizzie Mae Jones, who has worked at the inn for more than thirty years and is now the official storyteller. The inn's mascot is the family dog, Quintus.

Blowing Rock

Hound Ears Club

P.O. Box 188
Blowing Rock, NC 28605
828-963-4321
Fax: 828-963-8030

| An alpine resort that's known for its golf |

General Manager: Lillian Smith. **Accommodations:** 28 rooms (all with private baths) and 25 private homes on the rental program. **Rates:** Modified American Plan, $220–$540 for lodge rooms, plus an extra charge additional people and a 15 percent gratuity. (European Plan also available.) Inquire about rates for rental homes. **Included:** Breakfast and dinner. **Payment:** Major credit cards. **Children:** 3 and younger free. **Pets:** Not allowed. **Smoking:** Allowed. **Open:** January–February, April–December.

➤ **Hound Ears Club has one of the most unusual swimming pools on the East Coast. Open only during the summer months, it is built in a natural grotto and is surrounded by lush native plants.**

There is beauty at every turn at this 900-acre resort, which takes its unusual name from a rock formation on the property that resembles the ears of a hound. Located on 3,300 to 3,900 feet of the Watauga River in North Carolina High County, the alpine lodge and surrounding hillside homes have a ringside view of rugged Grandfather Mountain.

Built by the Robbins family, who also developed Tweetsie Railroad Theme Park, Hound Ears dates to 1962. Now under different ownership, the resort offers golf, tennis, swimming, hiking, picnicking, an exercise room, and massage service. Horseback riding, carriage rides, trout fishing, whitewater rafting, and canoeing are nearby. A recreational program for children is offered during the summer months. A pro shop, beauty salon, and florist are also on the premises.

Guests may stay in the comfortable 28-room lodge overlooking the golf course or in the lavish private homes and villas on the rental program. The food at Hound Ears is excellent, and jackets and ties are required in the lounge and dining room after 6:30 P.M. Sandwiches are available in the snack bar at the first tee from late May through October.

Boone

Lovill House Inn

404 Old Bristol Road
Boone, NC 28607
828-264-4204, 800-849-9466
(reservations only)
innkeeper@lovillhouseinn.com
http://www.lovillhouseinn.com

A B&B in an old mountain home

Innkeepers: Tim and Lori Shahen. **Accommodations:** 5 rooms (all with private baths). **Rates:** $105–$170. **Included:** Full breakfast, beverages, evening refreshments. **Payment:** MasterCard, Visa. **Children:** Not appropriate for small children. **Pets:** Not allowed. **Smoking:** Not allowed. **Open:** April–February.

➤ **Guests at Lovill House have a wealth of recreational options in the North Carolina High Country — hiking, fishing, canoeing, whitewater rafting, skiing in winter, and shopping for traditional mountain crafts. Nearby Appalachian State University offers a variety of cultural programs.**

Built in 1875 by Captain Edward Francis Lovill, this two-story mountain home was considered grand in its day, with its wide wraparound porches, pine flooring, and arched doorways. And because of its owner, a decorated Confederate officer, state senator, and founding trustee of Appalachian State University, the house is considered one of Boone's most historic homes. The papers for establishing the university were drafted by B. B. Daughtery in the front parlor.

Tim and Lori Shahen, former residents of New Mexico, decided to move east and try their hand at innkeeping. (Tim was formerly involved in commercial banking, and Lori served as a hospital financial services director.) They opened Lovill House Inn in 1993 after completing extensive renovations on the farmhouse and relandscaping eleven acres that surround it. They plan to add seven guest rooms onto the house and turn the weathered barn into their living quarters. The inn, which received the coveted four-diamond rating from AAA in 1997, is furnished in traditional pieces, with a scattering of antiques.

The Shahens serve a full gourmet breakfast of juices, seasonal fruit, homebaked breads and pastries, and a choice of Belgian waffles, garden vegetable stratta, omelets or eggs Benedict with bacon, ham, or sausage. In the evenings they host a social hour, either outside or by the fireplace, depending on the weather.

Bryson City

Hemlock Inn

P.O. Drawer EE
Bryson City, NC 28713
828-488-2885

**A true country inn in the
heart of the Smokies**

Innkeepers: Morris and Elaine White. **Accommodations:** 26 rooms (all with private baths). **Rates:** Modified American Plan $122–$165. **Included:** Breakfast and dinner. **Payment:** Discover, MasterCard, Visa. **Children:** Welcome. **Pets:** Not allowed. **Smoking:** Not allowed in dining room, sun room, and library. **Open:** Mid-April–October.

➤ **The Arthur Stupka Trail begins at the end of the shuffleboard court on the property. Stupka was the Great Smoky Mountains National Park's first naturalist and a frequent guest at the Hemlock Inn.**

Meals are an event at this country inn in the Smokies, where Lazy Susan tables groan with good food. A bell announces the beginning of every meal, served family-style, then everyone stands behind his/her chair until the blessing is said. Country ham, fried chicken, homemade biscuits with mountain honey, yeast rolls, fresh vegetables and fruits from the garden, and made-from-scratch desserts are standard fare. Many of the inn's best recipes were contributed by guests and have made their way into the *Recipes from the Front Porch* cookbook.

The inn serves breakfast at 8:30 A.M. and dinner at 6:30 P.M., but no lunch except on Sunday when the 12:30 meal is substituted for dinner. However, the staff will prepare box lunches with a day's notice for an extra fee, as well as a bag breakfast if you're planning to take an early ride on the Great Smoky Mountains Railroad.

After each meal some guests linger in conversation, while others make their way to the rocking chairs on the front porch. In the printed literature, guests are reminded that the rockers cannot be reserved and are available on a first-come, first-served basis. With all there is to do in the area — from hiking the trails in the nearby Great Smoky Mountains National Park to tubing on Deep Creek — guests usually don't sit too long.

In addition to the guest rooms in the inn, there are four cottages, all with fully equipped kitchens except the Log Cabin (a favorite with honeymooners). The decor at Hemlock Inn is cozy, comfortable, and casual, created with antiques and pieces made by mountain crafts people.

Hemlock Inn began in 1952 with nine rooms, with additions in 1965, 1970, and 1971, resulting in a total of 26 rooms today. All the owners have hailed from Georgia — first the Haynies, followed by the Johnsons in 1964, and then John and Ella Shell, who purchased the inn in 1969. The Shells' daughter and son-in-law, Elaine and Morris White, are now in charge.

Burnsville

The Panes

Route 3, Box 312A
Burnsville, NC 28714
828-682-4157
Fax: 828-456-9298
JMinatra@aol.com.

> A private spa where you are the only guest

Innkeepers: Nena Parkerson-Smith and Jody Mac Smith. **Accommodations:** 1 suite (with private bath, steam room, and Jacuzzi). **Rates:** $125 per person. **Included:** Full breakfast, dinner, spa treatment, and access to all amenities. **Payment:** Cash or checks. **Children:** Not appropriate. **Pets:** Not allowed. **Smoking:** Not allowed. **Open:** Year-round.

➤ **The Panes takes its name from the many salvaged stained glass windows that are used in the house and were collected by Nena for many years.**

This has to be the ultimate private escape — certainly in western North Carolina. Nena and Jody Smith, who built their three-story dream home on a 17-acre tract near Burnsville over a period of several years, accept only one guest or one couple at a time.

Most guests who come here are looking for more than a place to sleep; they want to take advantage of the spa services. Nena, who has spent a lifetime garnering the skills she now shares with guests, offers massage therapy, facials, pedi care, body cleansing, and mud masks. Her healthy cuisine is also a part of the experience. Two meals and a one-hour spa treatment come with the room, but guests may sign up for additional services and packages, such as the Panes Sampler, King or Queen for a Day, and the Royal Treatment.

The huge guest suite features a steam room, indoor Jacuzzi, two porches, and several stained glass windows that Nena found. There is also an outdoor hot tub, complete with deck, gazebo, pergola, and waterfall. Jody gets credit for the exquisite woodwork in the house.

The gourmet dinner is served on china and silver in the beautiful dining room. Morning begins with coffee in your suite or on one of the porches, followed by breakfast on the screened porch.

Nena began her career as a dental hygienist after graduating from the University of North Carolina at Chapel Hill in 1964; she then became interested in massage therapy. She has studied at the Institute for Holistic Studies in Ventura, California, at the Florida School of Massage, and at the Florida School of Massage Therapy and Esthetics.

Cashiers

High Hampton Inn & Country Club

P.O. Box 338
Cashiers, NC 28717
828-743-2411
800-334-2551, Ext.200

> **A mountain resort that has served generations**

Innkeepers: Will and Becky McKee. **Accommodations:** 33 lodge rooms, 19 cottages, and several private homes and villas on the rental program. **Rates:** $78–$103 per person. **Included:** Three meals a day and many recreational options. **Payment:** Major credit cards. **Children:** Welcome. **Pets:** Welcome in the inn's kennels. **Smoking:** Allowed everywhere but the dining room. **Open:** April–November.

➤ **The High Hampton Inn & Country Club has been likened to a family summer camp. Guests enjoy meeting each other and renewing old acquaintances during the many activities that are scheduled each day.**

High Hampton Inn & Country Club is not for everyone, but it is definitely a place that families have loved for generations. The lodge looks very much as it did in the 1920s, with its dormitory-like rooms and rustic lobby. The grounds, framed by Rock and Chimney Top mountains, are among the state's loveliest. Guests like the many scheduled activities — bridge games, nature programs, golf clinics, and holiday parties. But most of all, they enjoy getting together with old friends.

The inn's history dates to antebellum days. Confederate General Wade Hampton of South Carolina, who inherited the estate from his father in 1836, came here to hunt, fish, and relax. His niece Carolina Hampton and her husband landscaped the grounds and established the beautiful Dahlia Gardens. E. L. McKee bought the property in 1922 and established the inn, passing it on to his son

Bill McKee. Will and Becky McKee, his son and daughter-in-law, are continuing many of his traditions, while adding their own special touches.

Guests who like to be in the middle of activities prefer to stay in the main lodge or the surrounding cottages; those who want more privacy and more luxurious accommodations opt for one of the private homes or villas on the rental program.

No one lacks for something to do at High Hampton. Golf, tennis, lawn games, swimming, sailing, boating, fishing, nature walks, hiking, bird watching, classes and workshops keep guests busy. The inn hosts seniors and ladies golf tournaments each year at the 18-hole George Cobb–designed course, famous for its scenic eighth hole in the midst of Lake Hampton. In addition to golf tournaments, there are classes on fly-fishing, wildflowers and native plants, water colors, and other subjects. Events such as the July 4th picnic, Labor Day weekend party, and the Thanksgiving party are popular traditions. The inn also offers programs for children and teens in the summer months. Just about any amenity is available, from massage therapy to fax service.

Meals at High Hampton feature tried-and-true recipes such as cream of peanut soup, cranberry Waldorf salad, sausage bread, and lumpy peach ice cream. Guests enjoy gathering for afternoon tea in the lobby and happy hour in the Rock Mountain Tavern. Since the inn is located in a "dry" county, guests may provide their own alcoholic beverages.

The Millstone Inn

Highway 64 West
P.O. Box 949
Cashiers, NC 28717
828-743-2737, 888-645-5786
Fax: 828-743-0208
millstone@wcu.campus.mci.net
http://www.millstoneinn.com

> A mountain retreat where
> the main agenda is relaxing

Innkeepers: Paul and Patricia Collins. **Accommodations:** 7 rooms and 4 suites (all with private baths, 3 suites with fully equipped kitchens). **Rates:** $99–$150. **Included:** Full breakfast. **Payment:** Discover, MasterCard, Visa. **Children:** Well-behaved teenagers welcome. **Pets:** Not allowed. **Smoking:** Allowed in garden and on patio and balconies. **Open:** March–December.

➤ **The Millstone Inn serves as a living room to the natural beauty of Cashiers, an area that is noted for its mountain vistas, cascading waterfalls, and hiking trails. Silver Slip Falls is a short hike from the inn.**

Nature puts on a continuous show at the Millstone Inn, located in the Chattooga River Valley. Whiteside Mountain, Devil's Courthouse, and the surrounding mountains change according to the season and the time of day. The mountains may be shrouded in mist, illuminated by bright sunlight, or bathed in silvery moonlight.

Guests come to the Millstone primarily to relax, to read, to converse with others, and to enjoy the serenity of the mountains. They're also attracted to the hiking trails and waterfalls in the adjacent Nantahala National Forest.

Paul and Patricia Collins, who purchased the inn in 1994, delight in pleasing guests. They have added a 24-hour "guest kitchen" where complimentary cookies, soda, hot chocolate, coffee, and tea are provided. They serve a gourmet breakfast in the glass-enclosed porch overlooking Whiteside Mountain. Wonderful old favorites, such as baked apple oatmeal, join other tasty and wholesome dishes like ham and asparagus strata and fresh blueberry pancakes.

Built in 1933 as a private home, the U-shaped inn has a shingled exterior. The main building features original knotty pine paneling, rock maple floors, exposed beam ceilings, and a fireplace. Decorated in antiques, period furnishings, and lovely artwork, the inn takes its name from the millstones located on the property, including a large round stone set in the fireplace in the sitting room. The inn has been featured in numerous publications, the most recent being *National Geographic Traveler* and *Southern Living.*

Dillsboro

Squire Watkins Inn

West Haywood Road
P.O. Box 430
Dillsboro, NC 28725
828-586-5244, 800-586-2429

A town squire's home now serves as a B&B

Innkeepers: Tom and Emma Wertenberger. **Accommodations:** 4 rooms (with private baths), 2 efficiencies, 1 cottage (with private baths and kitchens). **Rates:** Rooms: $68–$78; efficiencies and cottage: $64–$85 daily, $325–$375 weekly. **Included:** Full breakfast. **Payment:** Cash or checks. **Children:** 12 and older welcome in inn; younger children welcome in cottages. **Pets:** Not allowed. **Smoking:** Not allowed in the dining room. **Open:** Year-round.

➤ **You can catch a ride of the Great Smoky Mountains Railroad, a scenic train that runs daily excursions through the mountains during the summer months and weekend trips in the spring and fall. Shopping for mountain crafts is another popular pastime in quaint Dillsboro.**

The Tuckasegee River will lull you to sleep at night and the Great Smoky Mountains Railway may awaken you from a late morning slumber at this mountain inn, just steps away from the heart of Dillsboro. Built in 1880 by Squire J. C. Watkins for his bride, Flora Zachery, the Queen Anne structure has served as an inn since 1984. Innkeepers Tom and Emma Wertenberger gave up the fast corporate life in Florida to devote all their time to innkeeping.

The couple have restored and preserved the architectural integrity of the house. The two-story structure features a widow's walk on the roof and boxy bay windows on either side of the double-decker front porch. The windows have been left bare in the parlor and dining room to let in the sunlight and provide views of the grounds, screened with hedges and planted with mountain flowers. The parlor, where guests enjoy playing the piano and chess, has a balustrade staircase to the second floor, where the guest rooms are located. Furnishings used in the inn are a mixture of antiques and family pieces, accented with framed art prints and Emma's needlework. The cottages and efficiencies are less formal and feature working fireplaces.

The inn uses natural air conditioning and ceiling fans for cooling, since the temperatures rarely get very high in the Smokies. Guests are not bothered by phones or television sets. The Wertenbergers serve a full breakfast in the brightly lit formal dining room, which is decorated with fresh flowers in season. They also do turndown service at night. No other meals are served at the inn, but several restaurants, including the Jarrett House, known for its family-style country cuisine served family-style, are nearby.

Franklin

The Franklin Terrace — A Bed and Breakfast

159 Harrison Avenue
Franklin, NC 28734
828-524-7907, 800-633-2431

A charming B&B in the Smokies

Innkeepers: Ed and Helen Henson. **Accommodations:** 9 rooms (all with private baths). **Rates:** $59–$69. **Included:** Full breakfast. **Payment:** Major credit cards. **Children:** 3 and older welcome. **Pets:** Not allowed. **Smoking:** Allowed on verandahs. **Open:** April–mid-November.

➤ **A 49-pound corundum crystal found in the area is on display in the museum operated by the Franklin Gem and Mineral Society.**

Helen Henson became an innkeeper in quite a strange fashion. While attending an auction, she gave the opening bid and soon found herself the owner of a very large two-story house with wraparound porches in Franklin. Since she and her husband Ed already had a beautiful home, she decided to put her culinary and decorating talents to use and convert the new acquisition into a bed-and-breakfast inn, with room for an antiques and gift shop. The Hensons modernized the bathrooms and added central heat and air conditioning, plus a breakfast room. That was several years ago, and the Hensons are still enjoying their role as hosts. Ed, who has a dental practice in Franklin, is also the town's mayor.

The Franklin Terrace offers nine guest rooms, each decorated in a different style and named for a stone found in the Cowee Valley, known for its gemstone mines. The Hensons serve a deluxe Continental breakfast of assorted cereals, home-baked muffins, breads, croissants, quiche, seven different kinds of fruit, and coffee or tea. A specialty of the house is an English muffin topped with sausage, cheese, and a poached egg.

Located in the heart of town, near the gem shops, The Franklin Terrace is listed on the National Register of Historic Places. It was built as a school in 1887 and converted into an inn in 1915 by the Willis family of Florida. Newspaper accounts of those days make reference to "delightful bridge teas at the Terrace" and call the guests "fine, elegant folks from Atlanta." The building was heavily damaged by a fire in 1935 but continued to operate as an inn until the 1960s. It was rescued from demolition by Pat Reed in 1978, and after spending a decade restoring it, she sold the building at the auction attended by Helen Henson.

Innisfree Inn — A Victorian Bed & Breakfast

P.O. Box 469
Glenville, NC 28736
828-743-2946, 800-782-1290

A lakeside inn that's ideal for romance

Innkeeper: Henry Hoche. **Accommodations:** 3 rooms and 5 suites (all with private baths, 4 with fireplaces), 6 cottages (with private baths, fireplaces, and fully equipped kitchens). **Rates:** July–October and holidays: $119–$235. November–June: $109–$225. **Included:** Full breakfast. **Payment:** All major credit cards. **Children:** Welcome in cottages. **Pets:** Not allowed. **Smoking:** Allowed on verandah. **Open:** Year-round.

➤ **Lake Glenville, the highest lake east of the Rockies, offers 26 miles of shoreline, scenic waterfalls, and secluded islands. Innisfree offers a private dock for securing your boat, and rentals are available nearby.**

Any lover of literature will relish a stay at this romantic lakeside inn in the mountains. The name itself is taken from William Butler Yeats' "The Lake Isle of Innisfree," and the words of the poem beckon, "I will arise and go now, and go to Innisfree. . ." Suites in the Garden House are named for famous authors, and there are books galore for reading.

Henry Hoche hadn't planned on opening his imposing Victorian home to guests, but had so many requests to see it that he decided to try his hand at innkeeping. To his amazement, he loved it — so much so that he built the Garden House, giving an additional four suites. Henry, who studied to be an English professor, runs Innisfree Realty in addition to playing host.

What he has created on Lake Glenville is a modern-day Victorian fantasy. Around five in the afternoon Henry pours wine for guests and assists them with dinner reservations, usually at restaurants in nearby Cashiers. Upon returning, guests are invited to relax by the Count Rumford fireplace and enjoy Irish coffee or hot chocolate with peppermint schnapps. Of course, the conversation is always interesting. Special bedside treats are Godiva chocolates.

Breakfast at Innisfree is always elegant. It's served on china in the formal dining room, an octagonal two-story tower with a 25-foot ceiling. Guests staying in the Garden House have breakfast brought to their suites. Before or after breakfast, guests often take walks around the lake or on the grounds, which are especially beautiful when Henry's prizewinning dahlias are in bloom. Or they may relax on the verandah with one of the Henry's prized cats in view — Lover Boy, Mother Theresa, Jello (Michaelango) and Vivian (Van Gogh). On rainy days guests often retreat to the observatory to read a book or work on a puzzle.

Each room at Innisfree is different. The favorite room in the main inn is Victoria's Grand Suite, featuring a queen bed and Jacuzzi tub. Lording over the tub is a gold and silver blackamoor holding the soaps and towels. Comparable suites are offered in the new Garden House, named for famous English writers — Lord Tennyson, Elizabeth Barrett, Emily Brontë, and Charles Dickens. All the suites have two-sided fireplaces (one side opens into the bathroom), garden tubs for two, picture windows, televisions, and balconies overlooking the mountains, lake, and/or gardens. The most elaborate suite in the Garden House is Lord Tennyson's Suite. It comes with a cape and wide-brimmed hat to wear if you wish. In the sleeping chamber, the fireplace faces the sleigh bed. The suite includes a tower room — ideal for having breakfast, writing, or playing games. Innisfree offers a number of special honeymoon and anniversary packages.

Lake Toxaway

The Greystone Inn

Greystone Lane
Lake Toxaway, NC 28747
828-966-4700
800-824-5766 (outside
 North Carolina)
Fax: 828-862-5689
http://www.greystoneinn.com

**A private mansion now
serves as a country inn**

Innkeepers: Tim and Boo Boo Lovelace. **Accommodations:** 33 rooms (all with private baths). **Rates:** $265–$525, discounted rates for seven or more nights; additional charge for airport pick-up. **Included:** Full breakfast and gourmet dinner, afternoon tea, beverages and bar setups, hors d'oeuvres, newspaper, turndown service, party boat cruises, use of recreational facilities. **Payment:** American Express, MasterCard, Visa. **Children:** Welcome. **Pets:** Not allowed. **Smoking:** Allowed in public areas. **Open:** April–November, weekends in December.

➤ **Greystone, which offers a variety of planned activities such as picnics, hikes, fishing excursions, mountain bike treks, and special classes and seminars, has been acclaimed by prestigious travel magazines, including *Conde Nast Traveler,* which named it one of the best places to stay in the world.**

This charming inn is a welcome sight for drivers along the winding North Carolina mountain roads between Hendersonville and Highlands. A private residence until recent times, the inn recalls the past grandeur of Lake Toxaway when Tiffany's operated a mine here and the likes of Thomas Edison, George Vanderbilt, and Harvey Firestone arrived via their private railcars to spend a few days at the now defunct Lake Toxaway Inn.

Mrs. Lucy Armstrong Moltz of Savannah, Georgia, built her six-level Swiss-style mansion that now serves as the Greystone Inn in 1915 after camping on the lakeside spot for several months to be sure she had chosen the best site. Over the years she came to love her mountain retreat so much that she gave up her residence in Georgia and lived out her days here in the peace and tranquillity of the Blue Ridge Mountains. A year after Mrs. Moltz moved in, however, the earthen dam gave way, taking with it the lake and the once faithful following of inn devotees. This left only a handful of residents, including Mrs. Moltz. Eventually, the Toxaway Inn fell into ruin.

Forgotten for many years by most travelers, the area had a resurgence in the 1960s when the dam was restored and new roads were built, priming it for redevelopment. A few years later, Mrs. Moltz sold her home to the Lake Toxaway Country Club for use as a clubhouse. The fate of the dwelling took another turn shortly thereafter when retired financier Tim Lovelace formed a partnership with the Lake Toxaway Company and extensively renovated the mansion and opened it as an inn in the summer of 1985. The following year the inn was placed on the National Register of Historic Places.

Today Tim, his wife, Boo Boo, and their three children cater to guests. A born entertainer, Tim conducts daily historical tours of the area and daily party boat excursions, weather permitting. Boo Boo's talent for decorating is evident throughout the guest rooms. Rich chintz fabrics and textured fabrics that have a homespun look set off the elegant furnishings — four-poster mahogany rice beds that are common to the Low Country of South Carolina and heavy brass beds that might have been your grandparents' pride and joy, complemented with marbletop dressers. Televisions are easily concealed in armoires, and telephones don't detract from the ambiance of the rooms. Their children, Hope, Heather, and Clark, often work at the desk, wait tables, or do odd jobs when they are not away at school.

Since opening the inn, the Lovelaces have added twelve guest rooms in a separate building called the Hillmont, giving a total of 33 rooms. All rooms at the inn are equipped with working fireplaces, whirlpool baths, and private balconies overlooking the lake and the mountains. The ultimate room, however, is the Presidential Suite, the former library. It is a massive room with windows on three sides, 25-foot ceilings with exposed beams, a huge stone fireplace, and a double marble Jacuzzi in the bathroom.

A dining room was also added, providing the perfect backdrop for the inn's award-winning meals that have been acclaimed in publications such as *Bon Appétit* and *Gourmet*. Breakfast and dinner are included in the tariff, but a special picnic lunch for a day's outing can be provided upon request. The most recent addition to the inn is the spa, offering everything from facials to body wraps.

Tea is a social highlight almost every afternoon at Greystone, followed by the sunset cruise on the *Mountain Lily II*. Before dinner, hors d'oeuvres and setups, wine, and beer are offered in the library lounge. The staff pays close attention to detail and service. During the dinner hour the staff straightens rooms, adds fresh towels, and turns down the beds, so that guests always have a sense of their importance at the inn.

Greystone is open year-round, weekends only in January, February, and March. During six months of the best weather in the mountains, guests play golf and tennis at the adjoining Lake Toxaway Country Club, go hiking, ride horses over 3,000 acres of unspoiled forest, and enjoy water activities around the scenic mountain lake. Within a few miles of the hotel are countless trails that lead to natural cascades, quiet mountain streams, lofty majestic peaks, and other wonders of nature. Everything except golf fees and spa treatments are included in the rates. However, during certain months of the year, golf is complimentary; during certain days in May golf carts are also gratis. Other diversions include shopping for crafts in Highlands, taking in a play at Flat Rock, or attending musical concerts in Brevard.

Linville

Eseeola Lodge

175 Linville Avenue
Box 99
Linville, NC 28646
828-733-4311, 800-742-6717
Fax: 828-733-3227

> **A seasonal mountain inn**
> **that's still highly rated**

General Manager: John M. Blackburn. **Accommodations:** 31 rooms (all with private baths). **Rates:** $200–$375. **Included:** Breakfast and dinner. **Payment:** MasterCard, Visa. **Children:** Welcome. **Pets:** Not allowed. **Smoking:** Allowed. **Open:** Mid-May–late October.

➤ **In the early days, local folks entertained city slickers with lathered hog races, ox races, and mountain orations. The author Shepherd M. Dugger described those times in *The Balsam Groves of Grandfather Mountain* and *The War Trails of the Blue Ridge*.**

This mountain classic, located at the base of Grandfather Mountain in the North Carolina High Country, has been the social center of Linville since the summer colony started in the 1890s. Weddings, tea parties, and sporting celebrations have attracted the first families of the South to the inn for decades — families that still escape to the high elevations in the summertime.

When the original inn burned, the current structure, dating to 1926, replaced it. The long, two-story wooden building, with its rustic balconies, is covered on the outside with chestnut bark. The interior, redecorated in recent years, is warm and inviting, with its cheerful fireplaces and wormy-chestnut paneling. Guests often gather in the public rooms for card games, parties, and individual activities such as reading. Guest rooms are decorated in handmade quilts and antiques. The dining room is unique, with a stream flowing underneath. The hearty breakfasts and five-course dinners are included in the tariff; on Thursday evenings there is a seafood buffet. Lunch is offered at the Linville Golf Club.

The 18-hole championship golf, the focus of the resort, was designed in 1924 by Donald Ross, a Scotsman who left his mark on many courses in the Sandhills of North Carolina. Clay tennis courts, a croquet course, playground, and an outdoor heated swimming pool offer other diversions. Guests also enjoy fishing and hiking. The inn operates a day camp for children.

Eseeola Lodge holds a four-star Mobil rating and *Golf Magazine*'s silver medal. Guests are welcomed with fresh flowers and a fruit basket, and in the evening they are given Godiva chocolates with turndown service.

Maggie Valley

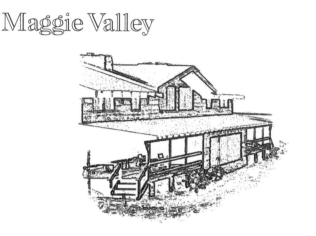

Cataloochee Ranch

Fie Top Road
Route 1, Box 500
Maggie Valley, NC 28751
828-926-1401, 800-868-1401
Fax: 828-926-9249

A dude ranch with lots of history and tradition

Innkeeper: Tim Rice. **Accommodations:** 13 rooms in lodges, 11 cabins (all with private baths). **Rates:** Late April–June, late August–September, November: $120–$210, plus $45–$55 each additional person. July–late August, October, December: $135–$250, plus $50–$60 each additional person. Additional charge for horseback riding. **Included:** Breakfast and dinner, all activities except horseback riding. **Payment:** American Express, MasterCard, Visa. **Children:** 6 and older welcome. **Pets:** Not allowed. **Smoking:** Allowed in designated areas. **Open:** April–October, mid-December–February.

➤ **Situated high in the clouds, the ranch affords spectacular views of the mountains in every direction. The ranch takes its name from the Cherokee word "Cataloochee," meaning "wave upon wave."**

Cataloochee Ranch is one of those places caught in a time warp. Guests who stayed at the ranch fifty years ago might return today and find themselves in familiar surroundings, enjoying the same experiences they had so long ago when Tom Alexander, a young forester from Georgia, and his wife, Miss Judy, started the operation. The couple's children and grandchildren are carrying on the traditions that evolved at the ranch over the past half century — trail rides, pack trips into the Smokies, mountain hoedowns, and pumpkin-carving contests at Halloween.

Guests gather in the main lodge, formerly an old stone barn, for hearty family-style meals. Sometimes local mountain musicians are called in, and guests try to imitate real clogging, a local dance consisting of slaps, shuffles, and toe taps. In the evening they sit around a roaring fire (evening temperatures are always on the chilly side at the mile-high ranch) and swap tales until the wee hours.

A few things at the ranch have changed since the early days — for the better. Guests don't help with pitching hay or grubbing potatoes, as they once did. They are a more pampered lot these days, with lots of free time for riding horses over the 1,000-acre spread, hiking marked trails and hunting for wildflowers in the adjoining Great Smoky Mountains National Park, fishing for trout, or relaxing in the heated pool. All these activities wind down about November, and the ranch gears up for downhill skiing, which lasts through mid-March. Cataloochee opened the first ski slope in North Carolina more than twenty-five years ago. With the emphasis on the outdoors, there's little need here for formal attire; blue jeans and western shirts are acceptable anytime, even for big celebrations such as the annual Fourth of July party.

Accommodations are comfortable but not luxurious (casual elegance). Guests sleep in four-poster antique beds under colorful patchwork quilts made by one of the local women who helps with housekeeping. Rooms in the old lodge and in the log cabins are what you might call rustic. The floors even squeak in certain places. Rooms in Silverbell Lodge, built a couple of years ago, are more contemporary and spacious.

Murphy

Huntington Hall Bed & Breakfast

500 Valley River Avenue
Murphy, NC 28906
828-837-9567, 800-824-6189
Fax: 828-837-2527
hhhallbnb@grove.net

> A delightful B&B in North
> Carolina's westernmost
> region

Innkeepers: Bob and Kate Delong. **Accommodations:** 5 rooms (all with private baths). **Rates:** $85. **Included:** Full breakfast, refreshments, turndown service. **Payment:** Major credit cards. **Children:** Welcome. **Pets:** Not allowed. **Smoking:** Allowed outside. **Open:** Year-round.

➤ **The inn was named for the area's first settlement, located on the confluence of the Valley and Hiwassee Rivers. The town's name, Murphy, was later adopted to honor the founder of the North Carolina Public School System.**

Huntington Hall Bed & Breakfast is known for its murder-mystery weekends and white-water rafting packages. The circumstances surrounding the "crime" and clues that might help participants are laid out at the Friday evening reception, hosted by Bob and Kate Delong. Saturday dinner is a sleuthing session and finale, ending with a solution to the crime. The mystery packages includes two-night's lodging, the reception and dinner, and two breakfasts. River packages include rafting on the Ocoee River, arranged through the Nantahala Outdoor Center.

The Delongs offer five guest rooms, individually decorated to enhance the old wood floors and tall windows of the century-old home that was built for J. H. Dillard and his wife Dixie. Each room, its name borrowed from the English countryside, has a private bath and cable television. Telephones, fax machine, and a copier are available. Guests are treated to refreshments around five o'clock in the afternoon, turndown service with chocolates, and a full breakfast.

The Delongs belong to a number of innkeeping organizations, and Bob is currently serving as president of North Carolina Bed & Breakfasts and Inns.

Robbinsville

Snowbird Mountain Lodge

275 Santeetlah Road
Robbinsville, NC 28771
828-479-3433
Fax: 828-479-3473

A rustic mountain lodge in the Smokies

Innkeepers: Robert and Karen Rankin. **Accommodations:** 20 rooms (all with private baths). **Rates:** $125–$225, plus $42 for each additional person in corner room or cottage. 2-night minimum on weekends; 3-night minimum during all holidays and in October. **Included:** All meals, in-room coffee and tea. **Payment:** MasterCard, Visa. **Children:** 12 and older welcome. **Pets:** Not allowed. **Smoking:** Not allowed. **Open:** April–November.

➤ **The Joyce Kilmer Forest, named for the author of *Trees and Other Poems*, is only a short distance from Snowbird Mountain Lodge.**

Snowbird Mountain Lodge is a study in woods. Opened in 1941, the inn and all its furnishings were crafted from different native hardwoods that grow or used to grow in the surrounding forests. The main inn and cottages are located in the middle of the Nantahala National Forest (3,000 feet in elevation) in the Smokies. The front porch yields panoramic views of the surrounding mountains and Lake Santeetlah, one of several Tennessee Valley Authority dams built during the Roosevelt era.

The lobby — with its cathedral ceilings, solid chestnut beams, butternut paneling, and massive stone fireplaces — serves as the main congregating area for guests. Guests are housed in the main lodge and two cottages. Meals, featuring local specials such as grilled, fresh mountain trout, are served on handcrafted maple tables, dressed in linen, in the cherry-paneled dining room. Breakfast, a picnic lunch, and dinner are included in the tariff.

Karen and her husband Robert purchased the inn in the spring of 1996, calling it a "nine-month odyssey filled with joy, challenge, and nail-biting anticipation." Karen is a professional chef, and Robert has been involved in the outdoor industry for several years. Building on traditions established by previous owners, they have added their own touches — including a 2,500-volume library and ceiling fans and coffeemakers in the rooms.

The Rankins offer a full schedule of special events — canoeing and kayaking classes, dulcimer clinics, wildflower walks, day hikes, photography seminars and fly fishing clinics. Horseback riding, whitewater rafting, canoeing, mountain biking, massage therapy, outings on the Great Smoky Mountain Railway, and many other activities are also available at Snowbird.

Saluda

The Orchard Inn

Highway 176 East
Post Office Box 725
Saluda, NC 28773
828-749-5471, 800-581-3800
Fax: 828-749-9805
orchard@saluda.tds.net
http://www.orchardinn.com

> **A mountaintop inn with a new look**

Innkeepers: Bob and Kathy Thompson. **Accommodations:** 9 rooms and 3 cottages (all with private baths). **Rates:** $105–$175; 2-night minimum on weekends. **Included:** Full country breakfast. **Payment:** Discover, MasterCard, Visa. **Children:** 10 and older welcome. **Pets:** Not allowed. **Smoking:** Allowed on outside porch. **Open:** Year-round except during the Christmas holidays.

➤ **The inn is on the outskirts of Saluda, a mountain hamlet south of Asheville. Built in 1900 as a summer lodge for the International Brotherhood of Railway Clerks and Engineers, it has the architectural style of a country farmhouse with a wide wraparound porch.**

New innkeepers Bob and Kathy Thompson continue the Orchard Inn's tradition of fine dining and gracious hospitality. They encourage guests to relax on the porches, choose a book from the cozy library, take a stroll down the nature trail, or pitch horseshoes. Hiking, golfing, antiquing, and fishing are nearby attractions.

The Orchard Inn is a place of relaxation and enjoyment, with stunning mountain vistas and places to get lost amid its twelve acres. Handmade quilts in the bedrooms and a cozy hearth and Oriental tugs in the living room add to the inn's warmth.

Meals are served on a wraparound, glassed-inn dining porch overlooking the Warrior Mountain Range. Breakfast specials include puffed French toast and cheese grits. Dinner entrees, such as mountain trout, salmon, beef tenderloin, and stuffed quail, are beautifully prepared and presented. Jackets are suggested for gentlemen during dinner. (Dinner, by reservation only, is served Tuesday through Saturday. Because the inn is located in a dry county, guests may bring their own spirits.) Complimentary hors d'oeuvres are offered as a prelude to dinner. Picnics are also available to guests.

Sylva

Mountain Brook

208 Mountain Brook Road, # 34
Route 2, Box 301
Sylva, NC 28779-9659
828-586-4329
vacation@mountainbrook.com
http://www.mountainbrook.com

A romantic mountain hideaway

Innkeepers: Gus and Michele McMahon. **Accommodations:** 14 cottages (all with private baths and fully equipped kitchens). **Rates:** $80–$150; honeymoon packages available. **Included:** Firewood. **Payment:** Cash. **Children:** Under 18 free. **Pets:** Not allowed. **Smoking:** Allowed. **Open:** Year-round.

➤ **From check-in to check-out, couples are reminded of their togetherness. Hearts, flowers, and framed quotes such as "Love is something you learn by heart" or "Happiness is being married to your best friend" add romantic touches to each cabin.**

Cozy fireplaces, bubble tubs for two, and a spa house in the woods guarantee romance at this secluded brookside hideaway in the Smokies, whether you're a newlywed or celebrating your twenty-fifth anniversary. The buildings were constructed of native stone and logs as tourist cabins by Hardy Clark during the Depression. Gus and Michele McMahon renovated the units and transformed them into romantic hideaways for 1990s couples. Mountain Brook has hosted hundreds of couples looking for romance, as evidenced by the growing number of carved love logs displayed on the property.

Names of guests are written on slate blackboards on each cabin, and flowers and champagne welcome those celebrating a special occasion. Whatever guests want, Gus and Michele try to provide. Honeymooners often request the Honeymoon Compliment, which includes matching T-shirts, a special honeymoon picture, chocolates, and fireplace potpourri.

Romance cottages have king-size beds, hot tubs, and a fireplace. With no phones or televisions, guests can concentrate on each other. Firewood is provided, and the kitchens contain everything (except the groceries) to cook a special dinner for two. Guests often go to Franklin or Sylva for dinner. There's an old-time porch swing where you can sit and hold hands. Each cabin has a notebook containing information about the resort, local restaurants, and things to do in the area.

The Spa House, nestled in the laurels and rhododendron, provides a private treat. The resort also features a picnic area, grills, playground, horseshoe pit, game room, nature trail, and a stocked trout pond. In all, there are 200 acres to explore.

The McMahons have been working on the property since 1979, and they keep making improvements. A former policeman, Gus handles the books. Michele, a devoted homemaker, takes care of the decorating, reservations, correspondence, and oversees the housekeeping.

Tryon

Pine Crest Inn

200 Pine Crest Lane
Tryon, NC 28782
828-859-9135, 800-633-3001

An elegant country inn in hunting country

Innkeepers: Jeremy and Jennifer Wainwright. **Accommodations:** 22 rooms, 9 suites, and 6 cottages (all with private baths). **Rates:** $125–$200. **Included:** Full Continental breakfast. **Payment:** Major credit cards. **Children:** Welcome. **Pets:** Not allowed. **Smoking:** Smoking and nonsmoking rooms. **Open:** Year-round.

➤ **One of the most exciting times to be at the Pine Crest Inn is during the annual Block House Steeplechase. Held at the Foothills Equestrian Nature Center (FENCE), it is "the" social event of the year. People wear their finest threads and lay out elegant tailgate picnics.**

Built in 1917 and on the National Register of Historic Places, this mountain inn took on new life under the helm of Jeremy and Jennifer Wainwright. They have totally renovated the inn and added a small conference center. Pine Crest Inn has a four-diamond AAA rating.

The Wainwrights chose an equestrian theme for the inn, located near the Foothills Equestrian Nature Center. The original owner, Carter Brown, was instrumental in establishing Tryon's famous Block House Steeplechase. Many of the rooms have a rich, dark look, with Ralph Lauren linens, equine art, and brass accents. Jennifer's teddy bear collection, assembled in the upstairs hallway of the main inn, adds a warm touch.

The main lobby houses the reception area, the Fox and Hounds Bar, the Colonial tavernlike restaurant, and several guest rooms. In addition to this building, there are several cottages on the nine-acre estate, including a 200-year-old log cabin, a woodcutter cottage, and a stone cottage. Famous guests have included F. Scott Fitzgerald and Ernest Hemingway. The Pine Crest Inn is known far and wide for its excellent cuisine, created by the executive chef. The full Continental breakfast includes homemade granola, scones, wild blueberry muffins, banana bread, Danish, yogurt, cereals, and more. A la carte items are crab hash, eggs Benedict, and omelets. The dinner menu features filet mignon, pork tenderloin cassis, grilled swordfish, potato-crusted salmon, fresh sauteed soft-shell crab, and roasted rack of lamb.

The state-of-the-art conference center is ideal for small corporate meetings. (Having spent many years in banking, Jeremy has thought of every amenity that would enhance a meeting.) The center is spacious, elegant, and equipped with all the modern conveniences.

Hiking, jogging, bicycling, volleyball, and a putting green are offered at the inn. Golf, tennis, and swimming can be arranged.

Valle Crucis

The Inn at the Taylor House

Highway 194, Box 713
Valle Crucis, NC 28691
828-963-5581
Fax: 828-963-5818

A European-style B&B Inn

Innkeepers: Carol "Chip" Schwab. **Accommodations:** 9 rooms (all with private baths). **Rates:** $135–$235. **Included:** Full breakfast. **Payment:** MasterCard, Visa. **Children:** Welcome by prior arrangement. **Pets:** Not allowed. **Smoking:** Allowed on porches. **Open:** Year-round except March.

➤ **The wide wraparound porch, furnished in white wicker, is ideal for catching the summer breezes, enjoying a glass of iced tea, chatting with a newfound friend, or reading a book.**

Located in serene Valle Crucis, a quiet mountain hamlet whose main attractions are the Church of the Holy Cross and the Mast General Store, the Inn at the Taylor House has always been one of the area's finest homes. Built in 1911, it attained a heightened level of elegance when Chip turned it into a bed-and-breakfast inn, filling it with art treasures and antiques from around the world.

Breakfast is the only meal served, but it is a memorable event, with every dish perfect in taste and presentation. Everything is fresh, much of it from her own garden or her neighbor's. Chip, a native of Michigan, has a culinary background. (Several years ago she operated Truffles Cooking School in Atlanta.) Special dishes might include sour cream pancakes with fruit topping, eggs Benedict, breakfast potatoes, and fresh vegetables.

The Inn at the Taylor House operates on the natural air conditioning of the cool mountains. (Guests find the duvets quite appealing even in the summertime.) Television is never a competitor, and telephones are few and far between.

Waynesville

Grandview Lodge

466 Lickstone Road
Waynesville, NC 28786-5300
828-456-5212, 800-255-7826
Fax: 828-452-5432
sarnold@haywood.main.nc.us
Http://www.bbonline.com/nc/grandview/

> **A mountain country inn that gets rave reviews for its food**

Innkeepers: Stan and Linda Arnold. **Accommodations:** 9 rooms in lodge and 2 apartments (all with private baths). **Rates:** $100–$110. **Included:** Breakfast and dinner. **Payment:** Cash or checks. **Children:** Welcome (no charge for infants). **Pets:** Not allowed. **Smoking:** Not allowed. **Open:** Year-round.

➤ **Chocoholics always ask for Linda's chocolate tart for dessert. The primary ingredients are chocolate and chocolate liqueur.**

Stan and Linda Arnold admit that "delicious food served family-style is the added secret ingredient of Grandview Lodge's success."

Guests return year after year for the food and hospitality that has made the mountain inn so famous, and the Arnolds are quite willing to share their recipes. They always include some of the inn's most popular ones in their newsletter and have made most of the recipes available in the ever-popular *Grandview Lodge Cookbook.*

Linda, who holds degrees in home economics and nutrition and also trained at the Culinary Institute of America, serves as the inn's chef. Last year she was featured in the *Atlanta Journal/The Atlanta Constitution* as a "Chef of the South." A native of North Carolina, she uses only the freshest ingredients, utilizing produce that's grown in the area, and everything is made from scratch, including all the dinner breads, breakfast muffins, and biscuits, as well as the jellies, jams, and relishes. Many of her recipes are low in fat, salt, and sugar and high in fiber without sacrificing taste or quality, but favorites such as marinated pork roast, sweet potato casserole, and chocolate tarts defy calories and fat. Her sumptuous breakfasts and dinners are included in the tariff. Given prior notice, Linda will accommodate guests with special dietary requests.

Stan, the other half of the hospitality team at Grandview who acts and host and general manager, was born in Poland and speaks Polish, Russian, German, and English. Educated at the University of Washington and Harvard Business School, he spent 30 years in corporate management before deciding in the mid-1980s that he was ready for a change. That's when he and Linda went shopping for an inn and found Grandview.

After acquiring the inn in 1986, the Arnolds completed extensive renovations on the 100-year-old home, a rambling structure located on two and a half acres of rolling land dotted with apple orchards, a grape arbor, and a rhubarb patch in the heart of the Smoky Mountains. With their own special touches and the warmth they convey, the couple welcome guests as family, and the inn has become a favorite spot for reunions, romantic weekends, and home-away-from-home vacations. (Their own family includes two sons and four grandchildren.) The porch is lined with rockers and the common room has a piano. All the guest rooms have private baths and color televisions; three have gas-burning fireplaces.

Tourism promoters, Stan and Linda are knowledgeable about area attractions, including golf courses, tennis courts, shops, and the attractions of Waynesville and Maggie Valley, Cherokee, and the Great Smoky Mountains National Park. Stan is past president of the Rotary Club and the Haywood County Chamber of Commerce and past chairman of the Haywood County Tourism Development Authority.

The Swag

2300 Swag Road
Waynesville, NC 28786-9624
828-926-0430 or 926-3119,
800-789-7672
Fax: 828-926-2036

A country retreat in the Great Smoky Mountains

Innkeeper: Deener Matthews. **Accommodations:** 16 rooms (all with private baths, 9 with fireplaces or wood stoves). **Rates:** $340–$510, plus 15% gratuity and taxes. **Included:** Three meals a day, afternoon tea, hors d'oeuvres. **Payment:** Major credit cards. **Children:** 7 and older welcome in main lodge; 7 and under welcome in cabins. **Pets:** Not allowed. **Smoking:** Allowed on porch. **Open:** Mid-May–October.

➤ **Though many guests never leave the mile-high retreat until time for departure, the area offers a number of interesting diversions: the Great Smoky Mountains National Park, Ghost Town Theme Park, the Stompin' Ground (clogging center), and the Cherokee Indian Reservation.**

The only North Carolina inn to be included in *The Discerning Traveler*'s romantic hideaways list in 1993, The Swag is a mile-high retreat in the Great Smoky Mountains. To reach the inn, one must drive six miles on a winding, narrow paved road and then two and a half miles on a gravel road. The experience that awaits you, however, is well worth the journey.

At the end of the road you are greeted by the hostess, Deener Matthews. The wife of the Rev. Dan Matthews, the rector of Trinity Episcopal Church in New York City, she is the epitome of southern hospitality, offering fine food and lodging and every comfort imaginable to her guests. (Her husband vacations at the inn.)

While living a few hours' drive from Waynesville, the Matthews had the retreat constructed of old log buildings they found in various parts of the mountains. The main part of the inn used to be the Lonesome Valley Primitive Baptist Church in Hancock County,

Tennessee. Each room includes Deener's special decorating touches, including handmade quilts and mountain crafts. Many of the rooms offer breathtaking views of the surrounding mountains; several have fireplaces or wood stoves. Guests looking for privacy often choose the Woodshed, an authentic pioneer house with a living room, queen bedroom, fireplace, and porch, or the Cabin, a hand-hewn log cabin with two bedrooms, living room, fireplace, wet bar, billiard room, and private deck. All the rooms have hairdryers, coffeemakers, plush bathrooms, and telephones.

Due to the remoteness of the inn, Deener serves three meals a day at the Swag — all of them memorable. Entrées might include baked cider chicken, beef tenderloin with western hot sauce, local trout with citrus concassé, cumin crusted pork with red currant wine sauce, or shrimp with chili-horseradish sauce, served with a soup, salad, vegetables, bread, and dessert. She welcomes guests with hot and cold beverages and hors d'oeuvres just before dinner. Because the inn is located in a dry county, guests may bring their own alcoholic beverages.

Guests never lack for something to do at the Swag — throughout the season Deener has a full schedule of special events and workshops on various subjects such as bird watching, nature, quilting, photography, and hiking. There are also times for self-reflection, and writing classes. Guests are free to roam the 250 acres adjoining the Great Smoky Mountains National Park, play racquetball, badminton, or croquet, lie in the hammock, relax in the whirlpool and sauna or spa (with 50-mile views) or simply enjoy the scenery from the porch.

The Piedmont

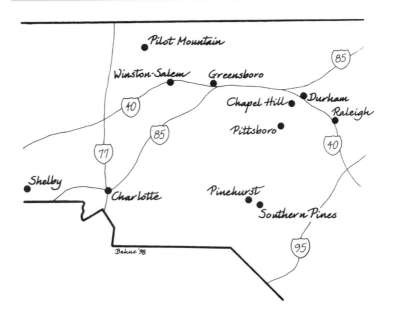

Best Bed-and-Breakfasts

Charlotte
The Homeplace, 381
Shelby
Inn at Webbley, 395
Raleigh
The William Thomas House Bed and Breakfast, 393

Best City Stops

Chapel Hill
The Siena Hotel, 380
Charlotte
The Morehead Inn, 383
The Park Hotel, 384
Durham
Washington Duke Inn & Golf Club, 385
Greensboro
The Biltmore Greensboro Hotel, 387
Winston-Salem
The Brookstown Inn, 398

Best Country Inn

Pittsboro
Fearrington House, 391

Best Golf Resorts

Pinehurst
Pinehurst Resort & Country Club, 389
Southern Pines
Pine Needles Resort, 397

Best Romantic Hideaway

Pilot Mountain
Pilot Knob Inn, 388

The state's major industries are located in the rolling hills of the Piedmont between the coastal plain and the mountains. There are three major population centers — the Triangle region, containing Raleigh, Durham, and Chapel Hill; the Triad made up of Greensboro, High Point, and Winston-Salem; and Charlotte, the largest city in the state. On the fringes of the Piedmont are the Sandhills, a vacation retreat offering more than three dozen golf courses.

In the Sandhills the community of Pinehurst resembles a New England village, with roads and drives meandering past luxurious resorts, inns, and beautiful estates that admittedly may be a bit more pretentious than those in New England or elsewhere. Roadways and parks were laid out by Frederick Law Olmsted, designer of New York's Central Park. Pinehurst's seven championship golf courses include two that are ranked among the nation's most challenging. Nearby Southern Pines, started as a winter resort in 1880, is noted for more golf courses, attractive resort facilities, and equestrian events. Its 425-acre Weymouth Woods Nature Preserve protects specially adapted animal communities and plant life of the Sandhills.

In and around the small nearby community of Seagrove, distinctive handmade ceramics are still produced by traditional methods, notably by Jugtown Pottery and the Owen and Teague families. In recent years, contemporary artisans have also set up studios in the area, considered one of the nation's most distinctive craft communities.

At nearby Asheboro, the North Carolina Zoological Park, under long-range development, will be the world's largest natural habitat zoo when completed. It's home to some eight hundred African animals and birds, and its climate-controlled tropical rain forest, the African Pavilion, contains two hundred rare and unusual creatures. There's also a vast free-flight aviary.

Catalyst for much of the growth in the Triangle has been the impressive Research Triangle Park, a premier center for government and industrial research that's minutes from Raleigh-Durham International Airport. Raleigh, North Carolina's capital, has a population of about 170,000. Its Neoclassic state Capitol, dating from 1840, contrasts with the contemporary Legislative Building. The North Carolina Museum of Art, one of the Southeast's finest, along with the North Carolina Museum of History and North Carolina Museum of Natural History, provides insights into the lore and background of the state.

Chapel Hill, home of the University of North Carolina, is a charming academic community of 32,000. Morehead Planetarium on the campus presents programs and displays on outer space and the solar system throughout the year.

At nearby Durham, population 102,000, the ornately designed Duke University Chapel, on the college's Gothic-style West Campus, offers weekday carillon concerts and special organ concerts. The Duke University Museum of Art, on the Georgian-style East Campus, has impressive collections of Greek and Roman antiquities, along with American and European paintings and sculptures. The North Carolina Museum of Life and Science on Murray Avenue contains exhibits ranging from prehistory to the space age, along with a nature center showcasing North Carolina animals.

In the Triad, Winston-Salem, population about 144,000, is one of the oldest Piedmont cities, dating from 1766 when a colony of Moravians settled there. Today at Old Salem, near the center of the city, the community they established has been largely restored and reconstructed. Sturdy brick, wood, and half-timbered buildings attest to the skills and stolid virtues of those Germanic migrants who came to North Carolina from Pennsylvania. Salem College and the Home Moravian Church adjoin the historic area. The Museum of Early Southern Decorative Arts, with period rooms and furnishings from the 1600s to 1820, is also in the historic area. One day in mid-December Old Salem Christmas is celebrated, with costumed guides interpreting Moravian Christmas traditions.

With a population of about 160,000, Greensboro is the Triad's largest city. An educational, manufacturing, and distribution center, it was named for General Nathanael Greene, patriot hero of the Battle of Guilford Courthouse. Here in March 1781, the Patriots met the army of British Lord Cornwallis but were defeated. The Greensboro Historical Museum has changing exhibits portraying 19th-century Greensboro, regional events, early settlement, transportation, and military history. There's also a special exhibit on O. Henry, famous for his short stories with surprise endings.

High Point, "the world's furniture capital," at last count boasted 125 furniture manufacturing plants. It's home of the International Home Furnishings Market, which attracts buyers from throughout the nation. Its Furniture Discovery Center is the country's only museum illustrating the total procedure of furniture manufacturing.

Burlington, fifteen miles east of Greensboro, is a major textile manufacturing center. Nationally known for its factory outlets, it attracts thousands of shoppers who come to buy clothing, textiles, towels, sheets, carpets, leather goods, and household items.

Charlotte, with a population of about 417,000, is North Carolina's largest city. Its skyline, virtually transformed within the past few years, is dominated by the sixty-story NCNB Corporate Tower, which was designed by renowned architect Cesar Pelli and contains Ben Long's frescoes depicting the history of the city. The Performing Arts Center is part of the complex. Ericsson Stadium is the home of the NFL team, The Carolina Panthers. Charlotte also has an NBA team — The Charlotte Hornets.

The most popular attraction, however, is Discovery Place, a nationally recognized hands-on science and technology museum, where exhibits include a three-story rain forest, Aquarium Tidal Touch Pool, and Life Center, detailing human physiology. The Michael J. Smith Wing features the Charlotte Observer Omnimax Theatre and Kelly Spitz Space Voyager Planetarium. The planetarium dome is said to be the largest in the United States.

In an upscale residential area, the Mint Museum of Art is located in a handsome contemporary structure that encompasses a jewel-like 1837 building that served as a branch of the United States Mint. It includes important pre-Columbian and African collections, European and American art, period costumes, and gold coins and currency pertaining to North Carolina's gold rush. The museum's collection of historic displays and varieties of Wedgwood is considered among the nation's three best of this type.

Family vacationers will want to visit Paramount's Carowinds Theme Park, located on the South Carolina/North Carolina border. Attractions include movies and moviemaking, thrill rides, and live entertainment, which are geared to visitors of all ages. Well-known entertainers perform some evening weekends and holidays at the 8,200-seat Paladium Amphitheatre (there is a separate admission charge). A similar experience is offered at the Blockbuster Pavilion near the University of North Carolina at Charlotte.

Chapel Hill

The Siena Hotel

1501 East Franklin Street
Chapel Hill, NC 27514
919-929-4000, 800-223-7379
Fax: 919-968-8527

A luxury hotel that's affiliated with Summit Hotels International

General Manager: Anita Vaughan. **Accommodations:** 80 rooms (all with private baths). **Rates:** $130–$200. **Included:** Full buffet breakfast, newspaper, turndown service, 24-hour concierge, free local calls. **Payment:** Major credit cards. **Children:** Welcome. **Pets:** Not allowed. **Smoking:** Smoking and nonsmoking rooms. **Open:** Year-round.

➤ **Chapel Hill, often called "the southern side of heaven," has been romanticized so much that some people think of it as a state of mind.**

A touch of Italy came to this university town in 1987 when Sam and Susan Longiotti opened the Siena Hotel. Named for the city of Siena, Italy, whose motto is "she opens her heart as wide as her doors," the luxury hotel embodies the spirit and personality of the Italian city located in the northern hills of Tuscany.

"We've always loved Siena because of its warm people and beautiful Tuscan landscape," says Susan, who, with Sam, makes an annual pilgrimage to Siena for the Palio horse race.

In keeping with the hotel's Italian theme and connection, rooms are filled with imported furnishings and art work. Each room has a marble bath, three telephones, and remote-control television, plus amenities and services such as plush towels, fine soaps, complimentary shoe shines, and newspapers delivered to the door.

Il Palio Ristorante, the elegant four-diamond restaurant and several-time winner of *Wine Spectator's* Award of Excellence, gets rave reviews for its Northern Italian cuisine. The Continental breakfast buffet — featuring hot entrees, freshly baked breads, seasonal fruits, yogurts, juices, teas, and Libano coffee — is included in the room rate. All meals are available through room service as well.

Guests have access to the Spa Health Club, within easy walking distance of the hotel. This modern facility offers aerobics classes, a pool, sauna, eucalyptus steam room, free weights, LifeCycles, stair climbers, and Nautilus machines. Complimentary airport transportation is provided by reservation to and from the Raleigh-Durham International Airport.

Charlotte

The Homeplace

5901 Sardis Road
Charlotte, NC 28270
704-365-1936

> **A Victorian inn filled with period pieces**

Innkeepers: Frank and Peggy Dearien. **Accommodations:** 2 rooms and 1 suite (all with private baths). **Rates:** $98–$135. **Included:** Full breakfast, hot and cold beverages. **Payment:** American Express, MasterCard, Visa. **Children:** Not appropriate for small children. **Pets:** Not allowed. **Smoking:** Allowed on porches. **Open:** Year-round.

➤ **The Deariens have used original art throughout the house, the most prized pieces being paintings of bygone days by the late John Gentry, Peggy's father. Most of his works were painted during his octogenarian years.**

This suburban B&B, once in the country, is everything its name implies, thanks to the love and care that owners Frank and Peggy Dearien have put into it. The appearance, the ambiance, the friendliness, even the aromas from Peggy's kitchen, suggest home.

Built in 1902, the structure, with its wraparound porches and widow's walk on the tin roof, was the home of the Rev. R. G. Miller, a minister who preached at the nearby Sardis Presbyterian Church. The Deariens bought the property in 1984 and turned it into an inn. Frank retired from his accounting job to devote all of his time to innkeeping, and Peggy keeps the house at perfection — you will never see any dust or an item out of place.

In keeping with the Victorian era, the Deariens have filled the house with period furnishings. The three guest rooms are located upstairs, each with its own character. The Victorian Lady Room focuses on a cross-stitch picture made by the Deariens' daughter.

The innkeepers serve a full breakfast of eggs, homemade breads, pastries, jellies, and fresh fruit in the dining room. Hot and cold beverages are available to guests throughout their stay.

The Morehead Inn

1122 East Morehead Street
Charlotte, NC 28204
704-376-3357
Fax: 704-335-1110

One of Charlotte's showplaces

General Manager: Billy Maddalon. **Accommodations:** 13 rooms (all with private baths). **Rates:** $110–$230, plus $10 for each additional person. **Included:** Continental breakfast. **Payment:** Major credit cards. **Children:** Welcome. **Pets:** Not allowed. **Smoking:** Allowed in courtyard and on patio. **Open:** Year-round.

➤ **The story goes that original owner Charles Coddington was the first to drive a Buick south of the Mason-Dixon line. He became the exclusive distributor of Buick automobiles in the Carolinas.**

Built as a private home for entertaining in 1917, the Morehead Inn has always been a showplace. Since becoming an inn in 1984, it has welcomed overnight guests and hosted special celebrations and parties, executive meetings and corporate retreats, luncheons, teas, and other events. With its spacious public areas and pleasing architectural features, including a sweeping grand staircase and intimate fireplaces, the 14,000-square-foot inn provides the perfect backdrop for such occasions.

Nancy Bergmann converted the house into an inn and then sold it; the inn was sold again a later date. In the fall of 1995, it was purchased by a group of local investors, including Billy Maddalon, who now serves as the general manager. After extensive renovations, the inn reopened in early 1996. Antiques, valued at over $275,000, have been added and are available for purchase. Billy grew up just down the street and had always admired the house; he was delighted when he was given the opportunity to live and work at the inn.

The inn offers thirteen guest rooms and suites (including two rooms in the Carriage House), named for streets in Dilworth. The largest and most elaborate suite is The Solarium. It features a wall of mullion windows and a large sunken bathroom with a whirlpool tub.

Located in Historic Dilworth, a National Historic Trust District close to uptown Charlotte, the inn was originally the home of Charles and Marjorie Coddington. The successful Buick dealer hired British-born architect William Peeps to create a house for entertaining which contained all the modern conveniences, including electricity, gas, and air conditioning. For years their home was a social center of Charlotte. Both died tragically in separate drowning accidents in 1925 and 1928. In 1976, the house was Charlotte's Showcase House for the local chapter of the American Society of Interior Designers and subsequently was featured in the Dilworth Home Tour in 1984, 1985, and 1992. It became a Charlotte Historic Landmark in 1985.

The Park Hotel

2200 Rexford Road
Charlotte, NC 28211
704-364-8220
Fax: 704-365-4712

| Charlotte's premier hotel |

General Manager: Wayne Shusko. **Accommodations:** 194 rooms (all with private baths). **Rates:** $170–$220. **Included:** Morning coffee, newspaper, turndown service, health club. **Payment:** Major credit cards. **Children:** 17 and under free in room with parents. **Pets:** Not allowed. **Smoking:** Smoking and nonsmoking rooms. **Open:** Year-round.

➤ **Morrocrofts is the "place to be and be seen" in Charlotte. Some say there are more business deals conducted and closed over breakfast in this restaurant than in any other eating establishment in the city.**

Charlotte's premier hotel, the Park Hotel has hosted some of the city's most important visitors — industry leaders, movie and television stars, and heads of state, including President Ronald Reagan. Zagats named the Park Charlotte's best hotel in 1995–1996. The Park is the only hotel between Washington, D.C., and Jacksonville, Florida, that is a member of the prestigious Preferred Hotels & Resorts Worldwide and one of only two hotels in North Carolina to receive AAA's four-diamond award and Mobil's four-star award.

Built in 1984, the property is located in the heart of SouthPark, a thriving community of shops office buildings, apartments and private homes, shops, and restaurants south of the city. Guests enter the hotel through the quiet lobby, decorated with period furnishings, fresh flowers, and original art by world-renowned artists, including the French master Yoland Antissone. The hotel offers 194 elegant guest rooms that featuring 30 different decors and 8,500 square feet of meeting space. The hotel has a Jacuzzi, fitness area, and outdoor pool.

Fine dining is offered in Morrocrofts, and in-room dining is available 24 hours a day. The restaurant — with its rich leather seats and mahogany furniture, its extensive menu and wine list, plus piano entertainment. enjoys an impeccable reputation. Menu favorites are pasta Acadian (chicken strips, artichoke hearts and spring onions in a tomato cream sauce over angel hair pasta), Low Country French onion soup, and crab soup. The country brunch, served from 10:30 A.M. until 2 P.M., features traditional breakfast items as well as seafood, poultry, and vegetables.

Durham

Washington Duke Inn & Golf Club

3001 Cameron Boulevard
Durham, NC 27706
919-490-0999, 800-443-3853
Fax: 919-688-0105
wd.@netmar.com
http://www.washingtondukeinn.com

| **An elegant hotel with connections to a premier university** |

General Manager: Don DeFeo. **Accommodations:** 171 rooms (all with private baths). **Rates:** $145–$245. **Included:** Turndown service, newspaper, valet parking, and voice mail. **Payment:** Major credit cards. **Children:** 17 and under stay free with parents. **Pets:** Not allowed. **Smoking:** Smoking and nonsmoking rooms. **Open:** Year-round.

➤   **If you want to learn more about the Duke family, the Duke Homestead, including the museum devoted to tobacco production, is a short drive from**

the hotel. The Gothic Duke Chapel and Duke Memorial Gardens are within walking distance.

This posh hotel on the campus of Duke University is a far cry from the simple homestead where Washington Duke began his tobacco business that grew to become the American Tobacco Company. Visitors can trace the rise to prominence of the Duke family, which eventually became the university's primary benefactor, through the memorabilia displayed in the glass cases scattered around the grand lobby. Here you see christening dresses, ball gowns, photographs, awards and honors, and the family crest (also the inn's symbol). Guests can take advantage of the many cultural activities and sporting events on the campus. (The Duke Blue Devils won the NCAA basketball championship in 1991 and 1992.)

The five-story structure overlooks Duke's 18-hole golf club, designed by Robert Trent Jones and open to guests of the inn. The hotel also has an outdoor swimming pool and jogging paths through the Duke Forest, and tennis courts are nearby.

Rooms are furnished in traditional walnut furniture that includes armoires and writing desks. The rooms also include alarm clocks, extended luggage racks, irons and ironing boards, Internet access, and telephones equipped with modems and voice mail. Turndown service and a morning newspaper are complimentary.

Fine dining is offered in the Fairview Restaurant, with entrées such as Carolina crab cakes, grilled lamb chops, and roasted duck. On Sunday there is a fabulous brunch. A pianist performs several nights a week. The Terrace-on-the-Green is used for outdoor dining and receptions, and the Bull Durham Bar offers a clublike setting for cocktails.

Greensboro

The Biltmore Greensboro Hotel

111 Washington Street
Greensboro, NC 27401
336-272-3474, 800-332-0303
Fax: 336-275-2523
thebiltmore@juno.com
http://web-am.com/1/bghotel

The finest hotel in Greensboro

General Manager: Larissa Cannon. **Accommodations:** 25 rooms and suites (all with private baths). **Rates:** $75–$110. **Included:** Full European breakfast, evening reception. **Payment:** Major credit cards. **Children:** Welcome. **Pets:** Not allowed. **Smoking:** Allowed. **Open:** Year-round.

➤ **This small luxury hotel is committed to the "Any Guest Request Is Granted" promise, and the staff places great emphasis on personal attention. Full services include a complimentary Lincoln Town Car and company van, room service, laundry, and 24-hour concierge.**

Located in the former Cone Mills headquarters in the heart of old Greensborough, this small European-style luxury hotel is perfect for business travelers and individuals who want to be convenient to the city. The building dates to 1895 and contains the original elevator and flooring; in 1983 it was renovated and turned into the Greenwich Inn Bed & Breakfast. The hotel became affiliated with Grande Hotels and Resorts International in 1992, and after extensive renovations in 1993, reopened as the Biltmore Greensboro Hotel.

Guests arrive through the elegant walnut-paneled parlor containing an oil portrait of an anonymous English gentleman who was dubbed "Lord Greenwich" by the previous owners. The Biltmore serves complimentary hors d'oeuvres, wines, and beers each evening and a full European breakfast featuring juice, fresh fruit, pastries, muffins, croissants, cereal, and Columbian coffees and teas. The concierge service is also available around the clock, and limousine service is offered. Guests have access to computers, printers, copiers, and a fax machine in the hotel's business center.

The rooms are furnished in a traditional style, with four-posters, canopy beds, and hardwood floors. Each room has a writing desk, mini-refrigerator, television, and phone. Numbers 16 and 23 are favorites, as is number 30, the Executive Suite, which features Palladian windows. All the bathrooms sparkle with brass and marble.

Pilot Mountain

Pilot Knob Inn

Box 1280
Pilot Mountain, NC 27041
336-325-2502
jrouse850@aol.com
Http://members.aol.com/jrouse850/pkbnb.html

A wonderful spot for romance

Innkeeper: Jim Rouse. **Accommodations:** 6 cabins (all with private baths). **Rates:** $110–$130. **Included:** Full breakfast. **Payment:** MasterCard, Visa. **Children:** Not appropriate. **Pets:** Not allowed. **Smoking:** Not allowed in library or dining room. **Open:** Year-round.

➤ **Often when couples check into the rustic but elegant cabins (old tobacco barns that were moved to the 50-acre site) they are not seen again until they check out. In fact, innkeeper Jim Rouse knows of seven proposals and five Pilot Knob babies.**

Romance is guaranteed at this secluded spot in the shadow of Pilot Mountain, which rises 1,500 feet and is topped by a distinctive knob, in the foothills of the Blue Ridge Mountains. The cabins have whirlpool tubs and fireplaces with amenities such as bathrobes, hair dryers, fresh fruit, and flowers. They are furnished with handcrafted and antique beds and eighteenth-century-style sofas.

Those who do venture forth from the cabins usually find their way to the barn, where Jim's mother, Pat, serves chocolate chip sour cream coffee cake, sausage, waffles, biscuits, and various other specialties plus fresh fruit in season and beverages. (Jim's father, Don, also works at the inn.) After breakfast, guests may take off for a hike in the adjoining state park, go fishing in the six-acre lake, swim in the outdoor pool (weather permitting), enjoy the sauna, or listen to classical music or read in the common room, also in the barn. The common room has a 300-year-old Italian marble fireplace, flooring from the Versailles, and Oriental carpets, plus a six-thousand-record library that belongs to Jim's silent business partner, Norman Ross of Chicago. The inn has a conference room to accommodate a small meeting of 15 to 20 people.

Since the inn does not serve any meal but breakfast and cabins are not equipped with kitchens, guests dine at local restaurants in Pilot Mountain, but greater selection is offered in Winston-Salem and Mount Airy, a short drive away.

So popular is this inn that there is a waiting list for rooms, especially on weekends.

Pinehurst

Pinehurst Resort & Country Club

Carolina Vista, Box 4000
Village of Pinehurst, NC 28374
910-295-6811
800-487-4653 (reservations only)
Fax: 910-295-8503
pinehurst-info@PinehurstResort.com
http://www.Pinehurst.com

A full-service resort that gets better with age

President: Patrick Corso. **Accommodations:** 310 rooms, suites, and villas; 135 condos (all with private baths). **Rates:** $110–$382, spring and fall; $110–$312, summer; $65–$268, winter. **Included:** Breakfast and dinner. **Payment:** Major credit cards. **Children:** Welcome. **Pets:** Not allowed. **Smoking:** Allowed. **Open:** Year-round.

➤ **Tufts offered his clientele every conceivable recreational activity — croquet, tennis, horseback riding, trap and skeet shooting, and, almost by accident, golf, the very sport that put Pinehurst on the map. Annie Oakley gave shooting lessons at the gun club from 1916 until 1922.**

Pinehurst Resort & Country Club was a dream come true for James Walker Tufts, a wealthy Bostonian seeking escape from the harsh winters of the North, who envisioned a haven for himself and his friends. He took what was deemed worthless land in the pine barrens and turned it into a golf oasis. The wooden hotel was built as the Carolina in 1901 to accommodate northern tourists who arrived by railcar in nearby Southern Pines to vacation for the winter in the Sandhills. Its most distinguishing feature is its copper-clad cupola, visible from just about anywhere in the New England–style village that was designed by Frederick Law Olmsted. Pinehurst was awarded National Historic Landmark status in 1996.

Owned by Club Corporation of America today and a member of Historic Hotels of America, the resort continues to offer many of the same activities. Guests have their choice of eight different golf courses, including the famous Pinehurst No. 2, site of the 1999 U.S. Open Championship and ranked number 2 in the top U.S resort courses. The resort offers computerized tee times, golf instruction via video, and an expanded pro shop. Tennis is also very popular, as indicated by *Tennis* magazine's choice of Pinehurst as one of the top fifty U.S. tennis resorts. Croquet is making a comeback.

There are afternoon teas, cocktail parties, Sunday brunches, dinner dances, and all sorts of social events for guests, including many centered on various holidays. Horse-drawn carriage rides through the village are popular with honeymooners and anniversary couples. The resort also offers a program for children and teens. A conference center can accommodate over one thousand people. When guests want to slow down, rocking chairs await them on the wide verandahs. The resort offers a number of attractive packages designed around sports and special holidays.

Guests have their choice of rooms in the main hotel, condominiums, or the Manor Inn, a 46-room property that is within walking distance. Service continues to be an important element of the total vacation experience at Pinehurst. Dining is offered in the Carolina Dining Room, Donald Ross Grill, Ryder Cup Lounge, and Mulligan's Sports Bar & Grill.

Winner of AAA's Four Diamond Award for twelve consecutive years, Pinehurst has been noted in numerous golf and meetings magazines.

Pittsboro

Fearrington House
Restaurant & Country Inn

200 Fearrington Village Center
Pittsboro, NC 27312
919-542-2121
Fax: 919-542-4202
fhouse@fearrington.com
http://www.fearrington.com

> **An award-winning country inn**

Owner: R.B. Fitch. **General Manager:** Richard Delany. **Accommodations:** 28 rooms (all with private baths). **Rates:** $165–$275. **Included:** Continental breakfast, afternoon tea, beverages. **Payment:** American Express, MasterCard, Visa. **Children:** 12 and older welcome. **Pets:** Not allowed. **Smoking:** Not allowed in guest rooms. **Open:** Year-round.

➤ **Fearrington is the only five-diamond inn and restaurant in North Carolina, and the restaurant is the only one in the state to be named a Distinguished Restaurant of North America.**

One of 350 inns and restaurants around the world to be associated with Relais et Châteaux, this country inn continues to garner awards, including Uncle Ben's Best Inn of the Year several years in succession, plus continued exposure in prestigious national magazines.

Everything at the Fearrington is impeccable, down to the smallest detail — from the decor to the food to the service. Based on a master plan drawn up by developer R.B. Fitch, the village is patterned after those found in Provence and the Cotswolds. Started in 1974, development of the 1,100-acre community will take about thirty years to complete and currently includes not only the inn, restaurant, and shops, but more than eight hundred homes. Fearrington is located on a two-hundred-year-old dairy farm once owned by the Fearrington family. Today Galloway cows graze in the pasture.

The village complex is just off Highway 15-501 between Chapel Hill and Pittsboro. The restaurant is housed in the old farmhouse, a two-story colonial affair that has been transformed into something you might see in *Home and Garden.* Various shades of salmon are used throughout and hidden surprises are found everywhere in the form of wall and floor stenciling. Artwork by North Carolina artists is showcased throughout the inn.

Chef Cory Mattson, a graduate of the Culinary Institute of America, is known for his five-course dinners featuring such delectables as sautéed scallops with lemon garlic butter and toasted almonds, lemon sorbet, Carolina crabcakes with mustard mayonnaise or beef tenderloin with a Merlot and peppercorn sauce, followed by chocolate soufflé with warm chocolate sauce and whipped cream (which made the cover of *Gourmet*). More casual fare is offered in the Market Café, housed in the old granary, also the space for the Market and Deli.

There is beautiful landscaping around the complex. Herbs grown in the gardens are used in cooking, and flowers that explode with color are used extensively in the decorating. Some rooms look out over the garden, an arrangement of roses, trellises, gazebos, and sculpture. There's also an English knot garden near the restaurant.

Guest rooms at Fearrington House are very private, with views of the gardens and the pasture. Some are clustered around a courtyard with a flowing fountain in the middle, while others overlook the twelve-acre Camden Park. All rooms are furnished in English pine and beautiful chintz fabrics. In some of the rooms are ecclesiastical doors used as headboards, canopy beds, and flooring from an English workhouse. The luxurious bathrooms include towel warmers. Number 11, overlooking the garden, is a favorite with honeymooners.

Two public areas — the Garden House and the Sun Room — serve as congregating centers for guests. A full breakfast and afternoon tea are included in the room rate. Guests often use the complimentary bicycles to travel to the swim and croquet club, a short distance from the village. Shops in the village include A Stone's Throw jewelry store, McIntyre's: Fine Books and Bookends, and Dovecote: A Home and Garden Shop.

Raleigh

The William Thomas House
Bed and Breakfast

530 North Blount Street
Raleigh, NC 27604
919-755-9400, 800-653-3466
Fax: 919-755-3966
http://www.bbonline.com/nc/wmthomas

> **An inn that's close to
> downtown Raleigh**

Innkeepers: Jim and Sarah Lofton. **Accommodations:** 4 rooms (all with private baths). **Rates:** $98–$135. **Included:** Full breakfast, snacks and beverages, wine and cheese reception, turndown service, local calls. **Payment:** American Express, MasterCard, Visa. **Children:** Infants and children 7 and older welcome. **Pets:** Not allowed. **Smoking:** Allowed on porches and deck. **Open:** Year-round.

➤ **The William Thomas House is associated with several prominent Raleigh families. Frances Gray, the daughter of the editorial writer Robert L. Gray, was the author of *Good Morning, Miss Dove*. Margaret (Mug) Richardson was Miss North Carolina of 1934 and Arthur Godfrey's "Girl Friday."**

This bed-and-breakfast inn captures the warmth and spirit of the Victorian era, when it was built as a private home for a Raleigh attorney. Owners Jim and Sarah Lofton occupy a part of the second floor, but share their home with guests. Located in downtown Raleigh, it's within easy walking distance of the Governor's Mansion, the state capitol, museums, shops, and restaurants.

Guests enjoy gathering in the public rooms of the house — around the 1863 Steinway Grand piano in the parlor, the gracious dining room where breakfast is served, and in the library, which features a collection of North Carolina bird carvings and bird-hunting trophies. Each guest room, named for the Loftons' three children and other family members, offers a quiet reprieve — the James Room has acorn finial beds; the Clarinda Room is decorated in lavender and rose; the Clara-Helen Room is named for Jim's mother, with its matelasse bed coverings; and the Melissa Room is a cozy retreat with white bed linens and a queen four-poster bed. All have private baths, a private telephone line, and cable television. The inn has a three-diamond rating from AAA.

A complimentary wine and cheese reception is held for guests in the late afternoon, and soft drinks and snacks are available any time of day. Guests have a choice of a full or Continental breakfast. The hosts have had plenty of entertaining experience. Sarah was the executive assistant to First Lady Dottie Martin, and Jim, now president of a commercial contracting firm, was secretary of administration under Governor Jim Martin.

The Loftons purchased the home in 1993 and spent six months renovating it prior to opening the inn. Known in its previous life as the Gray-Fish-Richardson House, the two-and-a-half-story frame house reflects the original character of Blount Street.

Shelby

The Inn at Webbley

403 South Washington Street
Shelby, NC 28150
Mailing Address:
P.O. Box 1000
Shelby, NC 28150
704-481-1403, 800-852-2346
Fax: 704-487-0619
omgiii@ bellsouth.net
http://www.bbonline.com/ nc/nccbbi/
http://www.innbook.com

> **An elegant B&B in Shelby's Historic District**

Innkeepers: O. Max and Victoria Gardner. **Accommodations:** 10 rooms (all with private baths). **Rates:** $165–$195. **Included:** Full breakfast, turndown service. **Payment:** Discover, MasterCard, Visa. **Children:** 12 and older welcome. **Pets:** Kennels available in area. **Smoking:** Allowed on porches and in courtyard. **Open:** Year-round.

➤ **Luminaries who have visited the Gardner home include President Harry S. Truman, President and Mrs. Franklin D. Roosevelt, Lady Bird Johnson, Jack Benny, Ava Gardner, Andy Griffith, Floyd Patterson, and others. The United States Department of the Interior cited Webbley as one of the most distinguished residences in North Carolina.**

The doors of the Inn at Webbley have been open to governors, presidents, and movie stars throughout its history, and today Shelby's most famous private dwelling welcomes bed-and-breakfast guests. O. Max Gardner III, a semi-retired attorney, and his wife

Victoria, a former court reporter, purchased the 11,000-square-foot Greek Revival mansion in 1989 from his uncle's heirs and spent a considerable sum on renovations before opening it to the public. As the grandson and namesake of a North Carolina Governor, O. Max Gardner III spent his early years at Webbley.

The Gardners received several awards for their efforts, including the prestigious Gertrude S. Carraway Award. The inn, which dates to 1852, has been featured in several publications and was awarded a four-diamond rating AAA and invited to join the Independent Innkeepers' Association last year. It has also been noted by Mobil, the North Carolina Bed and Breakfast Association, and the American Bed and Breakfast Association. In 1994, the inn was named one of the ten outstanding new inns in America by Inn Marketing.

Currently a social center for Shelby, the inn not only welcomes overnight guests but hosts weddings, receptions, parties, executive retreats, and other events. A professional chef prepares the complimentary breakfast, as well as gourmet multi-course dinners by reservation 24 hours in advance. The Inn Bar is open from 5 until 11 P.M. each evening, offering fine wines, spirits, and imported and domestic beers. Cocktails are served at 5 P.M.

Rooms at Webbley are lavishly furnished with French and English antiques, Oriental carpets, and canopied beds. Rich fabrics enhance the decor and every luxury is provided, including goose down duvets, fluffy robes, fresh flowers, elegant toiletries, and turndown service with a card, mint, or fresh rose. Rooms are named for the famous people in history who have slept here, including Governor Gardner, of course. Guests are also drawn to the courtyard garden's roses, perennials, statuary, and Italian market umbrellas. And with the inn's location in the historic district, there are interesting walks to take.

Elected to the state's highest office in 1928 and known as the New Deal Governor, Max Gardner's grandfather was a key figure in the state's famous "Shelby dynasty," a group of Cleveland County Democrats who dominated North Carolina politics during the first half of this century. He later served as chairman of the Advisory Board of the Office of War Mobilization and Reconversion under President Roosevelt and then undersecretary of the Treasury under President Truman. Just before his death of a heart attack in 1947, O. Max Gardner was appointed ambassador to the Court of St. James but never served. During Gardner's political years he often entertained dignitaries in Shelby. His wife, Fay Webb Gardner, who inherited Webbley from her parents, was equally vibrant and was at ease whether entertaining at home, in Raleigh, or in Washington. Gardner-Webb University was named for the famous couple.

Southern Pines

Pine Needles Lodge and Golf Club

P.O. Box 88
Southern Pines, NC 28388
910-692-7111, 800-747-7272
Fax: 910-692-5349

A resort known for its golf instruction

Innkeeper: Peggy Kirk Bell. **Accommodations:** 71 rooms (all with private baths). **Rates:** Bed & Breakfast package: $55–$80. Full American package: $80–$155. **Payment:** American Express, MasterCard, Visa. **Children:** Welcome. **Pets:** Not allowed. **Smoking:** Allowed. **Open:** Year-round.

➤ **A player on the Curtis Cup team in the 1950s, Mrs. Bell is a member of the Ladies' Professional Golf Association Hall of Fame. (In her younger days she also flew airplanes.) Pat McGowan, the teaching professional, was on the PGA tour for fifteen years.**

Chosen to host the 1996 U.S. Women's Open, Pine Needles is owned and operated by professional golfer Peggy Kirk Bell and her family. Centered around a Donald Ross course, the resort dates to 1953, but it has become better known for its Golfarias and Learning Centers that Mrs. Bell and her son-in-law, Pat McGowan, operate.

The Learning Centers operate year-round. Ladies' Golfaris are usually held in February, May, and September. In addition, there are adult camps, junior camps for children, the annual Golf Jamboree for couples, and private lessons. Instruction is available to anyone who wants to learn to play golf or improve his/her game, regardless of gender, ability or commitment to golf.

Mrs. Bell and her late husband, Warren "Bullet" Bell, bought the property in 1953 and built several contemporary-style lodges and a clubhouse over a sixteen-year period. Today, Mrs. Bell, her three children, and their spouses run the resort — a family operation for families. The resort is devoted to making each guest's stay a quality experience, and for that reason has never sold local memberships.

Pine Needles, though modern in appearance, has an interesting history. James Walker Tufts, the founder of Pinehurst, commissioned golf architect Donald Ross to build the golf course in 1927.

The Dunlop family bought the property in the 1930s, but it was used by the U.S. Army during World War II. After the war the Dunlops sold it to the Catholic Church. The hotel was converted into a hospital, and the golf course was leased. The Bell family has since made the resort what it is today.

In addition to golf, the resort offers tennis, an outdoor swimming pool, and a recreation room with pool tables, Ping-Pong, table games, and shuffleboard. Massages are available by appointment. Meals are served in the main lodge, a rustic but comfortable wood and stone building. Elaborate buffets are offered for breakfast and lunch, but evening meals are served off the menu.

Winston-Salem

The Brookstown Inn

200 Brookstown Avenue
Winston-Salem, NC 27101
336-725-1120, 800-845-4262
Fax: 336-773-0147

An old mill near Old Salem now offers overnight lodgings

General Manager: Carol Hogan. **Accommodations:** 40 rooms and 31 suites (all with private baths, some with garden tubs and wet bars). **Rates:** $90–$125, plus $10 for each additional person. **Included:** European breakfast, afternoon wine and cheese, homemade cookies with milk, turndown with chocolates, newspaper, parking. **Payment:** Major credit cards. **Children:** 12 and under free. **Pets:** Not allowed. **Smoking:** Allowed. **Open:** Year-round.

➤ **Quilts from Meadows of Dan, Virginia, handcrafted baskets, and wood carvings from New England are used throughout. The public rooms contain antiques from the British Isles and carpets woven in Romania.**

If you fall in love with the handmade quilt you sleep under in this one-of-a-kind inn, you can buy it and take it home. But you won't have the same option when it comes to furniture and the hand-crafted Beddingfield chandeliers and sconces.

Built in 1837, this brick structure near the heart of Old Salem, a restored Moravian village dating to the 1700s, was used as a cotton mill, flour mill, and warehouse until its restoration and conversion into an inn in 1984. Originally, the mill was called the Salem Cotton Company and was operated by the Moravians, but by 1856 it had been sold and turned into a flour mill. Graffiti written by female mill workers in the 1840s is preserved under Plexiglas on the fourth floor. Wrote Carolina Lumly, who died of measles in 1843: "When I am [gone] from this place and numbered with the dead Remember Carolina Lumly that you seen my face when these fine lines are read."

So well received was the inn that more rooms were created in adjoining buildings in 1986 and 1990. Today the inn is owned by Winthrop Hotels and Resorts. Great care has been taken to leave the distinguishing features intact — brick walls, open 20-foot ceilings, exposed pipes, and pine and brick flooring. At the same time no modern convenience or luxury has been omitted. Recently redecorated guest rooms feature custom-made four-poster beds with matching armoires, and some even have garden tubs and wet bars. Room 401 is great for families. The inn has a conference room for small meetings.

Breakfast is served in the dining room and wine and cheese are served in the afternoon in the parlor, also called the library. While guests enjoy dinner at a nearby restaurant such as Leon's Cafe or the Salem Tavern, they receive turndown service and Brookstown fudge. The inn can arrange horse-drawn carriage rides through Old Salem as well as tickets to the village.

The Coastal Plain

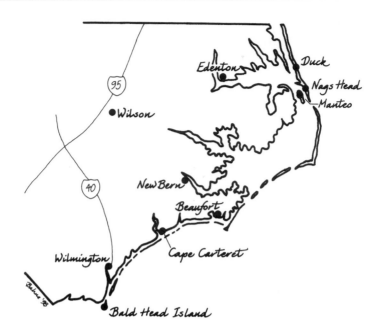

Best Bed-and-Breakfasts

Best City Stop

Best Country Inn

Best Resorts

Best Seaside Inns

The Outer Banks, narrow, sandy barrier islands separating the Atlantic Ocean and the Currituck, Albemarle, and Pamlico sounds, are rich in natural lore and history. Fort Raleigh National Historic Site, on Roanoke Island, includes what is thought to be the earthen remains of a fortress built by an unsuccessful colonizing expedition. During summer evenings, Paul Green's outdoor drama *The Lost Colony,* is presented in the Waterside Theatre, recounting a fictional version of 1587 colonists who attempted permanent settlement but disappeared without a trace. Nearby, the Elizabethan Gardens memorialize the lost colonists and display plantings that would have existed had the colony survived.

Across from the Manteo waterfront, the Elizabeth II State Historic Site includes a replica sailing vessel of the type employed in Sir Walter Raleigh's expeditions. Interpreters decked out in Elizabethan costumes welcome visitors on board and explain the lifestyles of early colonists. The North Carolina Aquarium displays fish, turtles, and sea creatures native to the state's coastal waters.

At the Outer Banks resort community of Kill Devil Hills, the Wright Brothers National Memorial commemorates the site of the first successful use of a flying machine in December 1903. A memorial shaft marks the spot; a museum includes a replica of the Wrights' plane.

Cape Hatteras National Seashore, reached via Route 12 from Roanoke Island, extends for about 70 miles along Bodie, Hatteras, and Ocracoke islands. Wide sandy beaches, dunes, wildlife refuges, Coast Guard stations, lighthouses (including Cape Hatteras, the tallest in the United States), and small fishing villages characterize the seashore.

At Hatteras Village, a major deep-sea fishing base, you can board a charter boat for Gulf Stream fishing. The highway ends at the small village of Ocracoke, accessible only by ferries from Hatteras Island to the north and Cedar Island to the south. Serene little Ocracoke is notable for its sandy streets, picturesque harbor, beautiful white lighthouse, and quiet isolation.

Cape Lookout National Seashore, relatively undeveloped, includes 28,500 acres of barrier islands. It's reached by ferries from Harkers Island, Atlantic, and Davis; service usually shuts down in winter. On Portsmouth Island an abandoned village is being restored, and an 1859 lighthouse is still in operation.

The Lower Cape Fear Country offers fascinating glimpses into vestiges of colonial and antebellum life. In the flourishing port city of Wilmington (population about 45,000) a wide-ranging waterfront restoration and refurbishment of downtown historic structures have brought about a literal transformation. The beautifully restored Burgwin-Wright House and Gardens, Revolutionary War headquarters of the British general Lord Cornwallis, includes 18th-century furnishings. In recent times the refurbished Thalian Hall has become the cultural center of the city once again, with an ongoing schedule of plays, concerts, and art exhibits. Movie production has become big business in Wilmington, and it is often referred to as the "Hollywood of the East."

Permanently moored beside the Cape Fear River stands one of the North Carolina's most beloved landmarks, the U.S.S. *North Carolina* memorial. You may tour the venerable World War II "battlewagon" and see gun emplacements, crew and officer quarters, galley, and communications rooms. On summer evenings, "The Immortal Showboat," a sound-and-light presentation, traces the dramatic history of the famed vessel.

Farther inland, the coastal plain is dotted with large farms that grow hundreds of acres of tobacco, soybeans, corn, cotton, and other crops. In the town centers tobacco warehouses and auctions represent a passing culture. Here, too, are historic towns, preserving the past for generations to come.

Bald Head Island

Bald Head Island

P.O. Box 3069
Bald Head Island, NC 28461
910-457-5000, 800-234-1666
Fax: 910-457-9232
Ferry reservations: 910-457-5003

A resort island accessible
only by ferry

Property Manager: Patricia Howarth. **Accommodations:** 150 condos, cottages, villas (all with private baths and fully equipped kitchens). **Rates:** Weekly summer rates $800–$3,950; inquire about lower daily rates in spring, fall and winter (2-night minimum required). **Included:** Electric golf cart, use of resort facilities and activities. **Payment:** Major credit cards. **Children:** Welcome. **Pets:** Not allowed. **Smoking:** Allowed. **Open:** Year-round.

➤ **Discovered in 1524 by the Italian explorer Giovanni da Verrazano, the island was a hideout for pirates in the 18th century. During the Civil War, blockade runners used the island to get goods through. From the 1880s**

through the mid-1930s, its lifesaving station and lighthouse were an important part of Coast Guard operations.

A stay on Bald Head Island, located on North Carolina's southernmost coastal point, begins with a short ferry ride from Southport. You should have a reservation, arrive early, park and lock the car, and take clothes, sports equipment, and special food supplies that you'll need. (The island does have a grocery store and shops that carry clothes.)

As you approach the island, look for Old Baldy, built in 1817 and the oldest lighthouse on the North Carolina coast. Adjacent to the historic structure is a beautiful wooden chapel that's a popular spot for weddings. One side of the island is a maritime forest; the other is primarily beach and dunes.

From the marina an escort will take you to the registration center and then to the place where you'll be staying. If your destination is a bed-and-breakfast inn, a host will meet you. While on the island, you'll have access to a golf cart, as no cars are allowed. A temporary club pass will get you into the swimming pool, tennis courts, and golf course at a reduced rate. Fees are also charged for bicycles, canoes, and the Adventure Club day camp for children aged five to twelve.

You may stay in a bed-and-breakfast inn, a condo near the marshes, a golf villa, or a cottage in the dunes. All the units are completely furnished and equipped with everything you'll need, except groceries. Firewood is even provided. The resort has several restaurants, but hours may be limited during the winter. The Bald Head Island Club serves the best food on the island and is recommended upscale dining. Make sure you confirm your return ferry reservation.

People come to Bald Head Island for various reasons — to play golf, tennis, or croquet; to walk or hike; to go bicycling or canoeing; to be alone; to take pictures; to watch birds; to commune with nature. Some come to observe the annual hatching of the baby loggerhead turtles on the east side of the island during August, September, and October. This exciting event is sponsored by the Bald Head Island Conservancy, and members who become Hatching Helpers may adopt and monitor the hatching process. (Membership is open to anyone and costs a nominal fee.) When there's a full moon in June, "turtle walks" are conducted by a naturalist. Hundreds of nests have been recorded over a period of years. The island also has a large bird and alligator population. Visitors are strongly advised to keep their distance from the alligators.

There are about one hundred permanent residents on the island, and more are moving here as housing becomes available. Bald Head is especially attractive to retirees.

Theodosia's: A Bed & Breakfast

P.O. Box 3130
Bald Head Island, NC 28461
910-457-6563, 800-656-1812
Fax: 910-457-6055
http://www.southport.net

> The island's first B&B is
> named for a ghost

Innkeepers: Steve and Lydia Love. **Accommodations:** 10 rooms (all with private baths, one room handicapped accessible). **Rates:** $115–$195. **Included:** Full breakfast, afternoon refreshments, evening desserts, golf carts, golf equipment storage, island bicycles. **Payment:** Major credit cards. **Children:** Not appropriate. **Pets:** Not allowed. **Smoking:** Not allowed. **Open:** Year-round.

➤ **Theodosia's body was never found, and many stories of her fate continue to be told. Some people believed she survived the ordeal at sea, but lost her sanity and spent the rest of her days wandering up and down the North Carolina coast.**

Steve and Lydia Love were the first to open a bed-and-breakfast inn on Bald Head Island in 1995. They named the three-story structure in memory of Theodosia Burr Alston (the daughter of Aaron Burr), who was captured at sea by pirates and forced to walk the plank in 1812. They included a room for her in the inn, but she hasn't moved in yet, although there have been several sightings of her in recent years. The Loves do have a resident cat, Spice, a stray that now welcomes guests and bids them adieu.

Former residents of Kinston, the Loves started coming to Bald Head for vacations in 1981 and finally sold their wood manufacturing business to build the inn and devote full-time to innkeeping. Lydia, Lithuanian by birth, met Steve in Germany while he was serving in the Army; they subsequently lived in Australia.

The innkeepers have filled the B&B with their own personal furniture and collectibles, creating a friendly, eclectic mix that reflects their personalities and lifestyle. They make every effort to attend to the needs of guests, including requests for celebrating special occasions such as anniversaries and honeymoons. The Honeymoon Suite is lavishly furnished and includes a whirlpool tub and great views of the harbor. All rooms come with cable television, and telephones are available.

Beaufort

Langdon House Bed & Breakfast

135 Craven Street
Beaufort, NC 28516
252-728-5499

| A B&B with a master host |

Innkeeper: Jimm Prest. **Accommodations:** 4 rooms (all with private baths). **Rates:** $60–$128. **Included:** Continental or full breakfast. **Payment:** Cash or checks. **Children:** 12 and older welcome. **Pets:** Not allowed. **Smoking:** Allowed on verandah. **Open:** Year-round.

➤ **A fascinating attraction, the Old Burying Ground, is located across from Langdon House. The cemetery dates to 1731 and includes some bizarre graves — that of a young girl preserved in a keg of rum; a British soldier buried standing up, facing his homeland; and Captain Otway Burns, a naval hero.**

If walls could talk, this historic house dating to 1733 in the old seaport town of Beaufort could tell many tales. And since the structure was restored and turned into a bed-and-breakfast inn several years ago, its walls have heard many more stories — stories shared by guests who come from near and far to sample owner Jimm Prest's hospitality.

A former investigator for a beverage company, Prest bends over backward to please his guests. He packs picnic lunches, fills ice chests, arranges sailboat rides, hands out suntan lotion, and fulfills just about any reasonable request. He even provides bicycles and fishing rods. His breakfasts are legendary, and guests often sit around the table for several hours savoring his food. Favorite recipes include orange pecan waffles with orange butter, banana nut waffles with blueberry/lemon butter, and French toast stuffed with herbs, cheeses, and fruit preserves. Jimm also accommodates guests with special needs — from vegetarian to low cholesterol to no-fat diets. Full breakfasts are served on weekends, and guests may choose a Continental or full breakfast on weekdays.

Rooms in Langdon House are furnished in period antiques, many of them on loan from Beaufort residents who want to be a part of preserving the area's history. The front corner bedroom to the right of the central hall is a favorite with guests. An Estes pump organ in the parlor is always a temptation.

Guests are on their own for lunch and dinner. Jimm can always suggest a good restaurant in Beaufort. After dinner, it is relaxing to sit in the parlor or on the front porches, depending on the weather and the time of year.

Cape Carteret

Harborlight Guest House Bed and Breakfast

332 Live Oak Drive
Cape Carteret, NC 28584
252-393-6868, 800-624-VIEW

This romantic seaside inn was originally a restaurant

Innkeepers: Bobby and Anita Gill. **Accommodations:** 9 suites (all with private baths, handicapped accessible). **Rates:** $75–$200. **Included:** Gourmet breakfast, newspaper. **Payment:** Major credit cards. **Children:** Not appropriate. **Pets:** Not allowed. **Smoking:** Not allowed. **Open:** Year-round.

➤ **The surrounding coastal area of Carteret County is a vacation paradise, offering uncrowded beaches, museum and historic sites, wildlife refuges, excellent fishing and boating, and wonderful seafood restaurants.**

Bobby and Anita Gill, former residents of Raleigh, searched from Cape May to Key West before finding the building that they miraculously converted into their "dream B&B" in 1993. Located near the old ferry landing on Bogue Sound, the Harborlight sits on a peninsula commanding panoramic views of the water.

Constructed in the early sixties to house the popular Harborlight Restaurant for a number of years, the 8,000-square-foot building was converted to apartment use when the bridge to Emerald Isle replaced the ferry. It was in terrible shape when the Gills launched their massive project. Renovation of the first and second floors was completed in a record 105 days, with Bobby and two construction crews doing all the work The inn started out with seven spacious rooms and suites, each with its own private entrance, plus a reception area, dining room, kitchen, and the innkeepers' living quarters. The third floor was renovated after the inn opened, yielding a total of nine suites. All the rooms have ceiling fans, a refrigerator, and coffee maker; the luxury suites also feature fireplaces and/or Jacuzzi tubs, and wet bars. None of the rooms has phones, but a portable one is available. The Gills used light colors in their decorating scheme, adding seascapes and nautical scenes for the finishing touches. Bobby used his professional expertise as a landscape architect in putting the grounds into shape, and Anita's experience as an emergency room nurse prepared her for the unexpected.

Harborlight guests have many different reasons for escaping to this seaside retreat. Many are looking for romance or a special place to renew old ties. Others just want a quiet place to unwind. Whatever their reasons, guests are seldom disappointed. The Gills go out of their way to accommodate their guests, and just about everyone who spends a night here leaves as a friend. It's not uncommon for the Gills to receive thank you letters, Christmas cards, and pictures from former guests. Breakfast, featuring Anita's favorite recipes, is served in the rooms or in the dining room. The Gills assist guests with dinner reservations and island excursions, offer sightseeing tips, and provide all the little extras.

Duck

The Sanderling Inn Resort

1461 Duck Road	
Duck, NC 27949	**An ocean resort that's been called Greenbrier by the Sea**
252-261-4111, 800-701-4111	
Fax: 252-261-1638	

General Manager: Christine Berger. **Accommodations:** 77 rooms, 11 suites, and villas (all with private baths). **Rates:** Summer: $194–$432; off season: $121–$325 (3-night minimum on holidays). **Included:** Continental breakfast, afternoon tea, health club, welcome gift. **Payment:** Major credit cards **Children:** Well-behaved children welcome ($25 extra person charge). **Pets:** Not allowed. **Smoking:** Allowed. **Open:** Year-round.

➤   **The inn sits on twelve secluded acres, most of it in its natural state, with boardwalks leading through the shrub-covered dunes to the ocean and five miles of open beach. Immediately due south is Sanderling, an upscale residential community; to the north is the Pine Island Audubon Sanctuary and Pine Island Club, an exclusive hunting club.**

If you aren't looking for the sign to the Sanderling Inn on State Route 12 five miles north of Duck, you might not notice the weathered gray shingled buildings in the hilly dunes between the Currituck Sound and the Atlantic.

The inn restaurant is actually the 1899 Caffey's Inlet lifesaving station, one of many that once lined the treacherous coast, and the architecture is typical of early buildings and beach cottages of Old Nags Head, several miles south. Designed to look weathered and old, the Main Inn was built in 1985, the North Inn and Conference Center in 1989, the Health Club in 1990, and the South Inn in 1994.

The lobby interior and guest rooms in the inn — decorated in natural Carolina pine, brass lanterns, Audubon prints, carved birds, designer fabrics, and wicker and contemporary furniture — exude casual elegance. The North Inn lobby looks out over a manmade waterfall, and the rocker-lined verandahs of the Main Inn offer ringside seating for nature's continuous show. More contemporary in style, the South Inn offers oceanside rooms with microwaves and refrigerators. It also features six suites with Jacuzzis and sound systems for relaxing.

Room 215, a typical suite in the Main Inn, features a sitting area, kitchenette, dining area, and half bath downstairs with an outside deck facing the water. The ceiling extends two stories to the open loft, with its bedroom and full bath. The Conference Center houses the 1,500-square-foot Presidential Suite, the most luxurious suite in the inn. All the buildings at the Sanderling are connected by decks, ramps, gardens, and gazebos.

Guests receive a welcome gift upon arrival, luxurious terrycloth robes and beach towels, and Gilbert and Soames toiletries. Each room has a clock radio and flashlight, and safety deposit boxes are available. The inn offers dry cleaning and laundry services.

Sanderling guests are active. In the Health Club you can work on the exercise equipment and then enjoy the whirlpool, sauna, and indoor pool. The club has a pro shop with bike and tennis rentals, clothing, and health products. There are two outdoor Jacuzzis (one a swim-spa) and two Omni surface tennis courts. An outdoor pool is located beside the Health Club, and a five-mile walking trail along the Sound meanders through the Audubon Sanctuary. Indoor tennis, racquetball, and squash are available at the nearby Pine Island Indoor Racquet Club. A new Eco-center — offering kayaking, canoeing, paddleboating, and guided kayak tours through the Audubon Preserve — was added in 1997. Bicycle rentals are available year-round, weather permitting.

Guests have the most options during the summertime when the weather is at its best, but the resort may be enjoyed any time of the year. It is ideal for romantic retreats and holiday gatherings.

The restaurant, decorated in nautical antique brass lanterns and hand-carved birds, is known for its excellent cuisine, especially fresh fish and hickory-grilled dishes. Each day starts with the breakfast buffet. Soups, salads, and sandwiches are the featured luncheon items. Dinner is special, with a variety of entrées, including fresh fish, prime rib and steaks, lamb, and chicken dishes. From the Swan Bar on the upper level you get a great view of the surrounding area and its wildlife. The restaurant offers an extensive selection of imported wines and beers.

The Sanderling Inn Resort is truly another world, a place to unwind and luxuriate in style and comfort, a place to rejuvenate the soul.

Edenton

The Lords Proprietors' Inn

300 North Broad Street
Edenton, NC 27932
252-482-3641
Fax: 252-482-2432

A country inn in a Colonial town

Innkeepers: Arch and Jane Edwards. **Accommodations:** 20 rooms (all with private baths). **Rates:** $185–$235 per couple. **Included:** Full breakfast and dinner. **Payment:** Cash or checks. **Children:** Welcome. **Pets:** Not allowed. **Smoking:** Allowed in parlors. **Open:** Year-round.

➤ **This highly successful Edenton inn is a member of Historic Hotels of America.**

A stay at the Lords Proprietors' Inn may begin with a tour of Mount Auburn, the owner's river plantation home outside of town that dates to around 1800. But your stay really revolves around the historic inn.

The Edwards, originally from Oklahoma, visited Edenton in 1979 and decided to develop the inn, a complex of four buildings, including a Queen Anne Victorian, an 1800s Federal home, and a tobacco pack house that was moved to the site. The rooms are decorated in a traditional style with antiques, handcrafted beds by Benjamin Hobbs, hand-sewn braided rugs, and colonial accessories. All have telephones, cable TVs, and VCRs.

Breakfast and dinner are served in the Whedbee House, a separate building behind the main inn, and the menu, under the direction of Chef Kevin Yokley, changes daily. After dinner, homemade cookies, port and sherry are served in the parlors. There is a gift shop in the reception area.

Manteo

Tranquil House Inn

405 Queen Elizabeth Avenue
Manteo, NC 27954
252-473-1404
Fax: 252-473-1536
DJust1587@aol.com
http://www.TranquilInn.com

A waterside inn overlooking the Manteo harbor

Innkeepers: Don and Laurie Just. **Accommodations:** 25 rooms (all with private baths). **Rates:** $79–$159, plus $10 for each additional adult. **Included:** Continental breakfast, wine and cheese reception, use of bicycles. **Payment:** Major credit cards. **Children:** Up to two children under 16 stay free with parents. **Pets:** Not allowed. **Smoking:** Not allowed. **Open:** Year-round.

➤ **The *Elizabeth II*, a reconstruction of a sailing vessel used by the first colonists to cross the Atlantic, sits across the harbor from the inn.**

Located on the waterfront, the Tranquil House Inn was constructed in 1988 near the site of the original house, which was built around 1885 and burned in the 1950s. Built in the style of Outer Banks inns of the past century, it offers twentieth-century conveniences.

The inn features cedar shingle siding, gables, and open breeze-ways on its exterior, while interior features include custom cypress woodwork, beveled glass doors, and stained glass.

Each of the 25 guest rooms has hardwood floors and is uniquely decorated with designer wallpapers, custom comforters, Oriental rugs, Berber carpets, and dried floral arrangements. Choose from a variety of rooms with canopied or four-poster beds, queens or kings, or a suite with a kitchenette.

Guests are treated to a wine reception in the evening and wake up to hot coffee and tea in the morning. The Continental breakfast fare includes pastries, bagels, croissants, fruits, juices, and cereals. Iced tea and lemonade are available throughout the day. 1587, the inn's restaurant overlooking Shallowbag Bay, commemorates the year that English colonists first arrived in North Carolina. It has been featured in *Gourmet Magazine* and on CNN's *On the Menu*. Entrees include penne pasta with shrimp, arugula, and roasted shallots; pan-seared snapper with roasted jalepeno beurre blanc and sweet corn flan; and curried duck with spicy crawfish dumplings.

Nags Head

First Colony Inn

6720 South Virginia Dare Trail
Milepost 16
Nags Head, NC 27959
252-441-2343, 800-368-9390
Fax: 252-441-9234
first.colony.inn@worldnet.att.net

An old seaside inn that thrives

Innkeepers: The Lawrence family. **Accommodations:** 26 rooms (all with private baths, 2 with Jacuzzis, one accessible to the disabled). **Rates:** $145–$250 in summer, $115–$200 in spring and fall, $80–$175 in winter, plus an extra charge for additional people. **Included:** Breakfast, beach towels, chairs, umbrellas, local calls. Turndown service on request. **Payment:** Major credit cards. **Children:** Welcome. **Pets:** Not allowed. **Smoking:** Not allowed. **Open:** Year-round.

➤ **Located near Roanoke Island, the site of the first attempt at colonization in North America, First Colony is named for the first settlers who came here in 1587. It is convenient to all area attractions — the National Seashore, Nags Head Woods Preserve, Jockeys Ridge, the Elizabethan Gardens, the Wright Brothers Memorial, Elizabeth II, and the Lost Colony outdoor drama.**

Nine Lawrences operate this lovely seaside inn on the Outer Banks, with Alan serving as the manager and Richard and Camille doing all the other jobs associated with innkeeping. Among them are enough professionals to boggle the mind: engineers, professors, architects, designers, and accountants. Needless to say, a stay at the First Colony Inn can be quite entertaining. It was the Lawrence family who stepped forward and saved this historic structure when it appeared that it was about to be lost forever. Because the tides threatened the inn in its original location, they had the building cut into three sections, moved several miles to the west side of the beach road, and put back together. Then, at great expense, the family restored the "Grand Old Lady of the Sea" to its original beach-style condition — plus adding all the modern conveniences and filling it with antiques and period furniture.

Now on the National Register of Historic Places, First Colony is the lone survivor of the golden days when hotels of its kind lined the beach. In 1994, it received the Gertrude S. Caraway Award of Merit for historic preservation.

First Colony was built in 1932 when families spent their days sunbathing, fishing, boating, and sightseeing and their nights dancing to big bands in Nags Head. Today it is welcoming guests once again, and some of the same old-fashioned pastimes are still popular — the beach, board games and puzzles, croquet, afternoon tea, and area attractions.

Guests may partake of the Continental breakfast buffet or have breakfast delivered to the room on a silver tray, curl up with a good book by the fire in the library take a walk on the beach, enjoy such luxuries as heated towels and whirlpool tubs or television and VCRs, relax in a rocking chair on one of the verandahs, and meet new friends at afternoon tea. A romance package is available.

New Bern

Harmony House Inn

215 Pollock Street
New Bern, NC 28560
252-636-3810, 800-636-3113
harmony@nternet.net
http://www.harmonyhouseinn.com

A historic inn in a historic
town

Innkeepers: Ed and Sooki Kirkpatrick. **Accommodations:** 8 rooms and 2 suites (all with private baths). **Rates:** $89–$140. **Included:** Full breakfast, homemade cookies, beverages. **Payment:** Discover, MasterCard, Visa. **Children:** Children welcome. **Pets:** Not allowed. **Smoking:** Not allowed. **Open:** Year-round.

➤ **Harmony House is steps away from Tryon Palace. The palace, reconstructed on the original site from early blueprints, was the home of the Royal Governor William Tryon and a meeting place for the Colonial assembly during the 18th century.**

This historic home, now a bed-and-breakfast inn, served as headquarters for the Union Army's Company K, 45th Regiment of the Massachusetts Volunteer Militia. After taking New Bern on March 14, 1862, the Union Army maintained a base of operations here for the duration of the Civil War. In a letter to his family, Private Henry Clapp described white homes in the area as "shabby genteel"; black homes as "low and dark."

Memorabilia from that time, including a photograph of Company K and illustrations from *Harper's Weekly*, are displayed at Harmony House. When the picture was taken, the Greek Revival home was just a few years old; it was built in 1853 by Benjamin Ellis, a successful businessman. As his family grew, he enlarged his home, sawing it in half once and moving the west side of it over nine feet to allow for a new hallway and stairs. The suite named for Ellis occupies two rooms and is ideal for families. The Eliza Ellis Suite, added in 1997, has a king-sized bed and two-person, heart-shaped Jacuzzi.

The inn is filled with Sooki's handmade crafts and furniture made in the area. The full breakfast features different entrées each day — stuffed pancakes, cheese strata or apple-bacon quiche, and baked French toast with orange-honey butter, plus fruit, juice, and coffee. Homemade cookies and beverages are always available. The inn has earned a three-star rating from AAA.

Wilmington

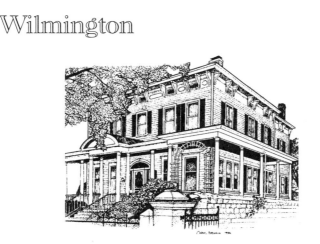

Catherine's Inn

410 South Front Street
Wilmington, NC 28401
910-251-0863
http://www.bbonline.com/nc/Catherine's/

A historic inn overlooking the Cape Fear River

Innkeepers: Catherine and Walter Ackiss. **Accommodations:** 5 rooms (all with private baths). **Rates:** $95–$105. **Included:** Full breakfast, early morning coffee, refreshments, fresh flowers. **Payment:** Major credit cards. **Children:** 12 and older welcome with prior arrangement. **Pets:** Not allowed. **Smoking:** Allowed outside. **Open:** Year-round.

➤ **Catherine's Inn was originally located on Orange Street but moved to this address in order to be near the Wilmington's waterfront. The owners completed beautiful restorations on both properties.**

After working in education and retail for several years, Catherine Ackiss found her niche in innkeeping. She and her husband, Walter, who owns his own business and represents a French company, opened their first Wilmington inn in 1988 and moved the business two blocks away to South Front Street in 1994. Owning a B&B was a lifelong dream for Catherine.

The inn now occupies the 1888 Forshee-Sprunt home, an Italianate structure with a wraparound front porch overlooking the Cape Fear River. It has proven to be an ideal location because of its easy access to downtown, waterfront attractions, restaurants, and shops. Other diversions are horseshoes, croquet, and bicycling. The Ackisses offer five elegant guest rooms, each with a king or double bed and a private bath and decorated in antiques and local artwork, as is the entire house. The focus of the Blue Room is a queen sleigh bed, complimented by an antique washstand, chest, and small couch. The Magnolia Room has a king-size canopied bed that's decked out in lace. The Wicker Room features floral prints. The Purple Room is, as the name suggests, purple, with violets on the nightstand. The Garden Room features floral wallpaper and dark antique furniture. The focus of the dark green living room is an antique grand piano, which guests may play; the second parlor, with its sitting space and books, is a great place to relax and unwind. Guests may enjoy river views from the screened-in porch and city views from the wraparound porch.

Morning begins at Catherine's Inn with coffee delivered to the door of each guest room, followed by a hearty full breakfast in the dining room. Complimentary beer, wine, and soda are always available, plus cake and coffee in the evenings and liqueur at bedtime.

The Inn at St. Thomas Court

101 South Second Street
Wilmington, NC 28401
910-343-1800, 800-525-0909
Fax: 910-251-1149

> **A small luxury hotel near the Cape Fear River and downtown Wilmington**

Innkeeper: Paul Wasserman. **Accommodations:** 34 suites (all with private baths). **Rates:** $135–$210. **Included:** Deluxe Continental breakfast, newspaper, local calls, and off-street parking. **Payment:** Major credit cards. **Children:** Not appropriate. **Pets:** Not allowed. **Smoking:** Allowed outside. **Open:** Year-round.

➤ **While in town you might see a play at Thalian Hall, a restored performing arts center, take a cruise on the Henrietta II paddlewheeler, or tour the U.S.S. *North Carolina* Battleship Memorial.**

The owners' worldwide travels have resulted in the creation of a luxury hotel that offers every imaginable amenity. Because of its location in downtown Wilmington, within walking distance of the Riverwalk and the business district, the inn is ideal for vacationers who want to spend a few days seeing the sights and business travelers looking for convenience and service. Fax, copy, office, and secretarial services, as well as a small conference room, are available to guests.

Combining four commercial buildings, the owners have created spacious guest suites, all elegantly decorated and furnished in traditional furnishings. Two of the suites have two bedrooms and two bathrooms. Some feature fully equipped kitchenettes and washer/dryers, while others have wet bars and microwaves. Breakfast, along with a newspaper, is delivered to the suites at times selected by the guests. The caring staff will make dinner reservations at nearby restaurants or deRosset, the inn's sister facility located next door. Seven luxury suites will open to guests in deRosset in the spring of 1998.

The hosts can arrange golf, tennis, or sailing on the ocean. Theater tickets are available for many fine productions in the area. Parties, events, or private dining can be arranged at deRosset.

Wilson

Miss Betty's Bed & Breakfast Inn

600 West Nash Street
Wilson, NC 27893-3045
252-243-4447, 800-258-2058

| A B&B with an antiques shop |

Innkeepers: Fred and Betty Spitz. **Accommodations:** 14 rooms (all with private baths). **Rates:** $60–$80. **Included:** Full breakfast. **Payment:** Major credit cards. **Children:** Not appropriate. **Pets:** Not allowed. **Smoking:** Limited. **Open:** Year-round.

➤ **Wilson is considered by many to be the antique capital of the state because of its many shops. It's also well known for its eastern North Carolina barbecue.**

You can browse for antiques in the shop on the grounds and then surround yourself with them at this in-town bed-and-breakfast inn. Guests have their choice of rooms in four different buildings — an 1858 two-story structure that was built on the site, turn-of-the-century houses that were moved here from other locations, and a

1940s building. The inn sits on a spacious corner lot in the historic district of Wilson.

The oldest home on the property was built by James Davis, a merchant, who moved to the area in 1853 and married into the prominent Rountree family. Howell Gray Whitehead, who bought the house in 1872, is credited with adding the Italianate features. Fred and Betty Spitz (she's Miss Betty, of course) opened the inn in the spring of 1990. They completely renovated the buildings, adding modern-day conveniences and amenities to make them comfortable. (The Spitzes recently opened four executive suites for long-term business travelers; they are run separately from the inn.) The main parlor, with its Victorian furniture and elegant decor, is very striking, and the bright yellow kitchen is the most cheerful room in the house. Miss Betty serves a full breakfast in the formal dining room.

South Carolina

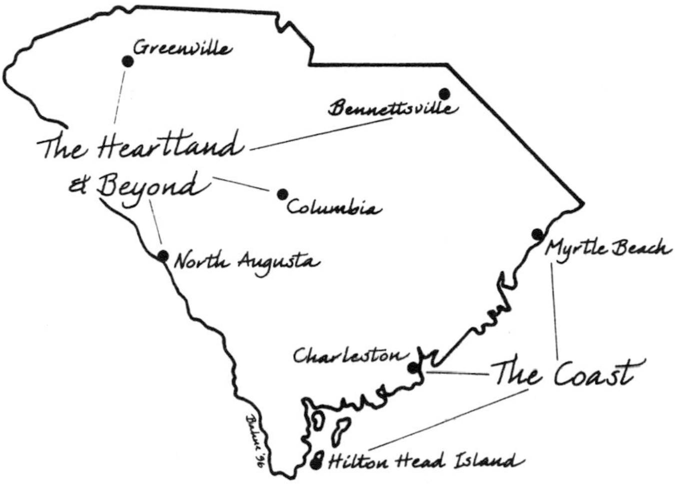

Greenville

Bennettsville

The Heartland
& Beyond

Columbia

North Augusta

Myrtle Beach

Charleston

The Coast

Hilton Head Island

South Carolina, with 31,055 square miles, is the smallest of the southern states — and vibrant proof that good things come in petite packages. Southward from Myrtle Beach and the adjacent resort communities of the Grand Strand, the coastline meanders along the Atlantic Ocean to the Georgia border. Several of the state's offshore barrier islands have been developed to include some of the finest resort communities on the eastern seaboard.

On a slender peninsula bordered by the Ashley and Cooper rivers stands the serene old city of Charleston. Its low-profile skyline dotted by church spires and steeples, it fronts a broad harbor, resembling an 18th-century etching come to life. Often called the "Mother City of the South" because of its influence on the mores, manners, and lifestyles of the region, Charleston is among the nation's most beautifully preserved cities. Today it's also a vital commercial, industrial, and cultural center, with a population of 80,414 (506,875 in the metro area).

This coastline is usually a gentle land, where broad white sandy beaches sparkle in the sun and green-gold marsh grasses sway gently in the breeze. Inland, in the adjacent Lowcountry, giant live oaks fringed with Spanish moss line roadsides and shade centuries-old communities. Once in a while, though, this placid environment is threatened. Hurricane Hugo took a tremendous toll in 1989, mowing down houses and cutting wide swaths through the forests. The Low Country folk, the most sincerely hospitable and welcoming hosts you'll ever meet, bravely weathered the storm and with an indomitable spirit faced the future. Countless numbers had to rebuild their homes and replace all their furnishings.

The landscape changes as you journey inland, but the welcome remains just as friendly and sincere. In the Piedmont heartland, with its prosperous rolling farmland and burgeoning industrial growth, the tempo of daily living quickens in such urban centers as vibrant Columbia, the state's capital and largest city with a population of almost 100,000. In the state's northwestern corner, the upcountry, where the Blue Ridge Mountains edge just over the border from North Carolina, are some of the state's most scenic lakes and parks. Greenville, the region's largest city, boasts a population of 58,282.

Southward the hills give way to pasturelands and fenced-in farms, and in the area around Aiken thoroughbreds spend their days training to be champions.

For more information, contact the South Carolina Division of Tourism, P.O. Box 71, Columbia, South Carolina 29202, 803-734-0235.

The Heartland
and Beyond

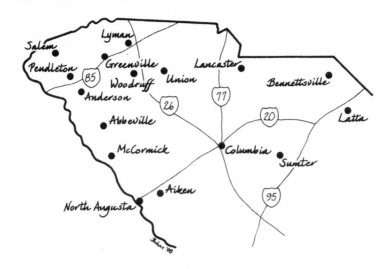

Best Bed-and-Breakfast Inns

Best City Stops

Best Farm and Guest Ranch

Best Historic Inns

Best Parks

In the state's heartland the capital, Columbia, reduced to rubble by General Sherman's troops during the Civil War, flourishes as a governmental, cultural, commercial, and educational center. In the beautifully restored Capitol, bronze stars cover scars imposed by Sherman's army. A trio of historic homes reveals important facets of South Carolina life: Hampton-Preston Mansion, seventeenth-century home of statesman-planner Wade Hampton; Robert Mills Historic House and Park, home of the designer of the Washington Monument; and Woodrow Wilson's boyhood home.

Adding vibrancy to the downtown area are the Koger Performing Arts Center, among the South's most widely acclaimed, and the South Carolina State Museum, where the state's history, science, technology, and natural history are showcased in the former 1894 Columbia Mills Building. Near downtown, the splendid Riverbanks Zoological Park and Gardens, one of the nation's most modern zoos, is notable for habitat areas where wild creatures roam freely. It also includes an outstanding Aquarium Reptile Complex and a new botanical garden with woodland paths.

Fascinating traces of the past linger throughout interior South Carolina. In 1860, the first secession document was presented at Abbeville, and in 1865 Confederate President Jefferson Davis held his last cabinet meeting at the Burt-Stark House, which is now open to visitors. Hence the town claims to be the "Birthplace and the Deathbed of the Confederacy." In the Abbeville Historic District the jewellike restored Opera House, where Fanny Brice and Jimmy Durante are said to have performed, now stages a popular annual series of dramas and musicals.

In Aiken, in the midst of thoroughbred country, racing memorabilia are preserved at the Thoroughbred Hall of Fame at Hopeland Gardens. Nearly one thousand racing, trotting, steeplechase, and polo horses winter here each year. Three weekends of steeplechase and harness racing are held at Aiken each March. Camden, founded in 1732, is South Carolina's oldest inland city and another major equestrian center. Springdale Course hosts the Carolina Cup in the spring and the Colonial Cup in the fall. At Historic Camden, a 92-acre site that is affiliated with the National Park Service, early Federal and pioneer structures have been restored and reconstructed. Also in the same area that is known as the Olde English District is Cheraw, a quaint town with a town green dating to 1768, buildings dating to the early 1800s, and beautiful homes (a few offer rooms and breakfast). Automobile racing fans can see their favorite NASCAR drivers hurtle flat out at Darlington in the late March or early April Trans South 400, followed by the "granddaddy of them all," the Mountain Dew 500, on Labor Day weekend.

In South Carolina's scenic upcountry, you can follow the Cherokee Foothills Scenic Highway (S.C. 11), which winds through foothills and serene mountain terrain from the Georgia line to near the North Carolina border. A few miles off the highway are some of the state's finest state parks. On Lake Jocassee, near the northern border at Salem is Devils Fork State Park. A 7,500-acre lake yields rainbow and brown trout, bass, and other finny specimens. Near Clemson, Duke Power Company's World of Energy Museum has exhibits depicting uses and production of energy, and hands-on computer games tell the story of electricity.

Clemson, home of Clemson University ("tiger paw country"), also is the site of Fort Hill, the beautifully restored home of antebellum statesman John C. Calhoun. Nearby Pendleton is headquarters of the Pendleton Historical, Recreational, and Tourism District, which preserves historic and scenic attractions in Anderson, Oconee, and Pickens counties.

Greenville, in the Piedmont Plateau, is site of the annual Freedom Weekend Aloft in late May, one of the South's major balloon races. Any time of year, you may visit the Gallery of Sacred Art and Bible Lands Museum on the campus of Bob Jones University; the Greenville County Museum of Art, with notable collections of American and Southern art; and the Peace Center for the Performing Arts. In nearby Spartanburg, historic sites include Walnut Grove, a 1765 manor house; the 1795 Price House; and the 1790 Seay House.

Eastward on I-85 at Gaffney, you will spot the "Peach-oid," a huge, realistic, glowing pink peach atop the town's water tower — a landmark and symbol for this peach-producing region. Just south of the North Carolina state line, Kings Mountain National Military Park preserves the site of a crucial Revolutionary War battle fought between Loyalist backwoodsmen and Tory forces in September 1780. Nearby Cowpens National Battlefield was the scene of a brilliant tactical engagement in 1781 when the Loyalist forces decisively defeated the British.

In the scenic hilly Waxhaw district, Andrew Jackson was born in 1767 of Irish pioneer parents. The exact site is not known — and both Carolinas claim it! At the Andrew Jackson State Historical Park, seven miles north of Lancaster, frontier relics are exhibited in a museum, and a fine equestrian statue by Anna Hyatt Huntington shows the young Jackson leaving the area to seek his fortune. The Museum of York County and Historic Brattonsoille lie to the west. A few miles north is Paramount's Carowinds Theme Park.

Abbeville

Abbewood Bed & Breakfast

605 North Main Street
Abbeville, SC 29620
Tel. & Fax: 864-459-4822

A historic B&B that's loaded with charm

Innkeepers: Charles and Ruth Freeman. **Accommodations:** 3 rooms (1 with private bath, 2 with shared bath). **Rates:** $65–$75. **Included:** Continental breakfast, refreshments, turndown service. **Payment:** MasterCard, Visa; cash or checks preferred. **Children:** Check with innkeepers. **Pets:** Not allowed. **Smoking:** Allowed on verandahs. **Open:** Year-round.

➤ **Abbeville has the distinction of being both the birthplace and the death place of the Confederacy. A monument in the square honors native sons who fought in the War Between the States.**

Built around 1860 just before Abbeville residents led the first call to secede from the Union, this home has had a succession of owners. Early in this century Sarah Norwood Calhoun, the wife of John A. Calhoun who was a nephew of John C. Calhoun, purchased it at auction and then resold it. The McMurray family occupied it for the longest period (1916–1964). By the time Charles and Ruth Freeman bought the house in 1989, it was in a sad state of repair.

But thanks to the couple's hard work and perseverance, Abbewood never looked better and now welcomes overnight guests. The house has many outstanding features, including wraparound verandahs, beautifully restored woodwork, tiled fireplaces, and two original mahogany mantels. The leaded glass front door leads into a stunning central hall with a formal ladies' parlor and a dining room on either side and a stairway to the upper floor. A private stairway, which had been closed off, was discovered and reopened during the three-year restoration.

The Freemans serve a Continental breakfast of homemade muffins and breads, fruit, juice, and coffee. Their Theatre Package includes tickets to the Opera House, where there's a full schedule of productions year-round. Ruth often acts in the plays and the theatre is often a topic of conversation at breakfast. Built around 1906, the theatre was once a stopover for actors and actresses between Richmond, Virginia, and Atlanta, Georgia. Legend goes that Jimmy Durante, Fanny Brice, Groucho Marx, and Sarah Bernhardt performed at the Opera House.

Before retiring to Abbeville from the Washington, D.C., area, Charlie spent his career with the General Services Administration, and Ruth worked for the U.S. Chamber of Commerce. (Charlie is native of Alabama and Ruth has roots in Pennsylvania.) Both are very active in community affairs and love to promote Abbeville as a tourist destination. They are charter members of the South Carolina Bed and Breakfast Association. Ruth has served as president of the Chamber of Commerce.

Aiken

The Willcox Inn

100 Colleton Avenue
Aiken, SC 29801
803-649-1377, 800-368-1047
Fax: 803-643-0971

A historic inn in the middle of horse country

General Manager: Fran B. Cuthbertson. **Accommodations:** 24 rooms and 6 suites (all with private baths). **Rates:** $95–$35, plus $15 for rollaway bed. **Included:** Continental breakfast. **Payment:** Major credit cards. **Children:** Welcome. **Pets:** Not allowed. **Smoking:** Allowed. **Open:** Year-round.

➤ **The same families have been coming to the inn for decades — an old familiar place where high standards are still maintained. Newcomers are drawn here, too.**

Set amid the multimillion dollar horse farms and homes in the middle of historic Aiken, a winter colony for the equestrian set, this classic inn continues to please. It was built in 1898 by Frederick Sugden Willcox, an Englishman, and his Swedish-born wife Elise. The family managed the inn until 1957, and during their tenure they hosted dignitaries such as Winston Churchill (the writer, not the statesman), Elizabeth Arden, and Averill Harriman. After a succession of owners, the hotel was acquired and refurbished by James Barggren, a historic preservationist who owns several other properties. Under his direction the inn has earned the Golden Fork Award and AAA's four diamonds. The Willcox Inn is on the National Register of Historic Places.

The lobby, paneled in rosewood, is a favorite congregating area, as is the Polo Pub, which has an equestrian theme. Gourmet cuisine is offered in the Pheasant Dining Room — meals on weekdays, lunch and dinner on Saturdays, and brunch on Sundays. The bright, cheerful guest rooms feature traditional furnishings. The most popular and most elaborate room is the Winston Churchill Suite. The exterior of the inn is a blend of Second Empire and Colonial Revival, with a front porch that is supported by Doric columns.

Golf, historic tours, and carriage rides through the village can be arranged. Because of its central location in Aiken, guests may walk to the local attractions and restaurants. The town is usually quiet except during major equestrian events such as the Aiken Triple Crown. Weekend, golf, and honeymoon packages are available.

Anderson

Anderson's River Inn B&B

612 East River Street
Anderson, SC 29624
864-226-1431
Fax: 864-226-1431

> **A former doctor's home
> turned B&B**

Innkeepers: Pat Clark and Wayne Hollingsworth. **Accommodations:** 3 rooms (all with private baths). **Rates:** $85. **Included:** Full breakfast, snacks, use of hot tub. **Payment:** Major credit cards. **Children:** 12 and older welcome. **Pets:** Not allowed. **Smoking:** Allowed on verandahs. **Open:** Year-round except Christmas week.

> ➤ **There's no question that Pat Clark loves raccoons. She has hundreds of them, and images of the furry creatures are on the B&B sign.**

The River Inn is as fine a bed-and-breakfast as you'll find anywhere, but its uniqueness lies not in the house itself but in the innkeepers. Pat Clark and Wayne Hollingsworth, who moved into the house in 1974 and brought up their six children here, are interesting folks who enjoy sharing their lives with guests.

You won't be inside the doors of the inn very long before you notice that hundreds of pairs of eyes are staring at you. Pat's lovable raccoon collection — made of wax, sand, ground pecan shells, rocks, and other materials — is everywhere. The largest groups are displayed in the entrance hall and on the fireplace mantel in the dining room. Wayne has a passion for lanterns, and his collection can be seen in the butler's pantry. The couple are also into bluegrass music and jazz and gladly share their CD collection, as well as an extensive library of books, with guests. (Pat is a great niece of the famous banjo picker Earl Scruggs.)

Pat and Wayne opened their home to guests in 1990. Both are tourism promoters and members of the state B&B association. The house was built in 1914 by Dr. Archer LeRoy Smethers, who used it for his medical practice and private residence. Located in the city on the original carriage route to Columbia, it features dark woods and several working fireplaces.

River Inn offers three guest rooms — two are named for members of the Smethers family and one for Alice Humphries, an author and schoolteacher. Each room has a fireplace and television.

A full breakfast is included in the rate, and is always served with grits on a huge round table in the dining room. Morning coffee is delivered to each guest room prior to breakfast. The Hollingsworths will prepare dinner, picnic baskets, and fruit-and-cheese trays by advance reservation.

Bennettsville

The Breeden House Inn and Carriage House

404 East Main Street
Bennettsville, SC 29512
843-479-3665

An old southern mansion,
now a three-diamond inn,
welcomes guests

Innkeepers: Wesley and Bonnie Park. **Accommodations:** 6 rooms (all with private baths). **Rates:** $65–$95. **Included:** Full breakfast, welcome beverages, bedtime treats. **Payment:** Discover, MasterCard, Visa. **Children:** Welcome. **Pets:** Not allowed. **Smoking:** Allowed on verandah. **Open:** Year-round.

➤   **The Parks had been shopping for an old house to renovate and saw this one advertised in a magazine while vacationing in North Carolina.**

Built in 1886 by Thomas Bouchier as a wedding gift for his bride, Shadie Townsend, this beaux-arts mansion has served as a bed-and-breakfast inn since 1981. The front porch and balcony, including twenty-fine columns, were added in 1907.

Restored by the Grulick family who gave it its current name, the inn was purchased by Floridians Wesley and Bonnie Park in 1988. At the same time they purchased another home nearby, the Carriage House (formerly the Betty Drake home), and renovated it to be used as a part of the inn. Since Bonnie had been in the antiques business for a number of years they had most of the furnishings they needed for the house. Wesley, a CPA, simply moved his practice to Bennettsville, where he serves as director of finance for the city. In addition to falling in love with the house, they also like the small-town atmosphere for their two school-age children, Asher and Jenny.

The innkeepers serve beverages to guests upon arrival and assist them with dinner reservations. They provide a "What to Do While You're Here" directional guide. In the evening, the Parks offer a bedtime sweet treat. Breakfast, featuring a variety of dishes, is served in the formal dining room.

For entertainment, guests may relax by the swimming pool or on the verandah with a good book, go birdwatching, or take walks. Cable TV is also available in every guest room.

Columbia

Claussen's Inn at Five Points

2003 Greene Street
Columbia, SC 29205
803-765-0440, 800-622-3382
Fax: 803-765-0440

> A city B&B, once a bakery, that caters to business travelers

Owner: Charming Inns of Charleston, Inc. **Accommodations:** 21 rooms and 8 loft suites (all with private baths, 2 with refrigerators). **Rates:** $79–$130. **Included:** Continental breakfast, newspaper, parking, wine and sherry, turndown service with brandy and chocolates. **Payment:** American Express, MasterCard, Visa. **Children:** Welcome. **Pets:** Not allowed. **Smoking:** Smoking and nonsmoking rooms. **Open:** Year-round.

➤ **Claussen's is owned by Charming Inns of Charleston, Inc., which also owns three inns in Charleston.**

More than sixty years ago you would not have been able to sleep in this building. It functioned as Claussen's Bakery then, but since 1987 it has served as a bed-and-breakfast inn. Claussen's Inn is especially popular with business travelers because of its convenience to downtown and the amenities it offers.

On arrival, guests are welcomed with wine or sherry in the two-story, tiled atrium lobby. The inn doesn't serve dinner, but the staff will gladly suggest nearby places to eat as well as make reservations. Turndown each night is accompanied by chocolates and brandy, and mornings begin with a complimentary Continental breakfast and a newspaper.

All the rooms are furnished in four-poster or brass beds and complementary reproductions. Some rooms are carpeted; others have original hardwood floors. The loft suites feature a living room downstairs with a sleeper sofa, wet bar, and television; a bedroom upstairs; and a bath and a half. Ten rooms in the inn open onto a courtyard, where the outdoor Jacuzzi is located.

Richland Street Bed & Breakfast

1425 Richland Street
Columbia, SC 29201
803-779-7001
Fax: 803-765-0370

> **A Victorian B&B offering luxurious lodgings**

Innkeepers: Jim and Naomi Perryman. **Accommodations:** 7 rooms (all with private baths). **Rates:** $79–$120. **Included:** Continental breakfast, afternoon beverages, desserts, turndown service, chocolates. **Payment:** American Express, MasterCard, Visa. **Children:** 12 and older welcome. **Pets:** Not allowed. **Smoking:** Not allowed. **Open:** Year-round.

➤ **In the gathering room guests often find their way to the melodeon, a unique instrument that's a cross between a piano and an organ.**

Jim and Naomi Perryman decided to build this Victorian inn in the heart of Columbia's historic district when they couldn't find a house that they felt would offer the number of rooms they wanted for a bed-and-breakfast. In the new structure they incorporated ideas from inns they had visited all over the country. In the fall of 1992 the Perrymans opened the Richland Street Bed and Breakfast, and they've been entertaining guests ever since.

The house covers most of the property, which is surrounded by a wrought-iron fence. The front porch has a gazebo on one end, and a small upstairs balcony overlooks the street. The foyer leads into a large gathering room, decorated in rich, dark colors; this is where guests have meals and relax. Upstairs, there are seven guest rooms. All are furnished in reproductions and have private baths, television sets, and telephones. They are named for South Carolina governors. The Bridal Suite is the most elaborate, with its whirlpool bath and access to the balcony.

The Perrymans serve complimentary afternoon refreshments, desserts, and a Continental breakfast featuring hot casseroles and freshly baked bread. They also do turndown service and assist guests with dinner reservations.

Greenville

Embassy Suites Hotel

670 Verdae Boulevard
Greenville, SC 29607
864-676-9090, 800-EMBASSY

A hotel and conference center in the upcountry

General Manager: Patrick Wilson. **Accommodations:** 268 suites (all with private baths). **Rates:** $119–$139. **Included:** Breakfast buffet, manager's reception. **Payment:** Major credit cards. **Children:** Welcome. **Pets:** Not allowed. **Smoking:** Smoking and nonsmoking rooms. **Open:** Year-round.

➤ **The par 72, 6,757-yard golf course features Bermuda fairways and Penncross Bentgrass greens. It includes a driving range and practice green.**

Open since 1993, the Embassy Suites hotel complex is noted for its conference center and Willard C. Byrd golf course, where hotel guests may request preferred tee times. Everything necessary for conducting business has been thought of, from meeting rooms featuring the latest technology to leisure spaces to comfortable guest rooms. The complex was developed by John Q. Hammons Hotels, Inc., though the hotel operates under the Embassy Suites name.

The two-room luxury suites (268 in all) open onto a dramatic eleven-story atrium that has fountains, waterfalls, and tropical plants. The hotel's design is similar to that seen in other Embassy Suites hotels. In the atrium lobby there is a reception each evening; in the morning a breakfast buffet is offered here. One can also request a cooked-to-order breakfast. All the hotel suites have wet bars, refrigerators, coffeemakers, and microwave ovens.

Lancaster

Wade-Beckham House

3385 Great Falls Highway
Lancaster, SC 29720
803-285-1105

> A historic plantation house
> that welcomes guests

Innkeeper: Jan Duke. **Accommodations:** 3 rooms (all with private baths). **Rates:** $75. **Included:** Breakfast, fresh fruit, snacks, beverages. **Payment:** Cash or checks. **Children:** 16 and older welcome. **Pets:** Not allowed. **Smoking:** Allowed on grounds. **Open:** January–November.

➤   The house is filled with interesting family artifacts and memorabilia such as early Edgefield pottery, Confederate bonds, an original *Gone With the Wind* program, family wills and papers, and a small South Carolina state flag that was carried to the moon on Apollo 16 by astronaut Charles Duke, William's twin brother.

Only two families have occupied the Wade-Beckham House since it was built between 1802 and 1811 — the Wades until the 1880s and then the Beckhams. (Sons of the Wade family served in the Lancaster Militia during the Civil War.) Jan Beckham Duke, a registered nurse who occupies the house with her physician husband Dr. William Duke, is the fourth generation Beckham to live here.

Listed on the National Register of Historic Places, the house is one of about a dozen surviving plantation houses in Lancaster County. Additions and alterations were made to suit the changing needs of its occupants. The oldest part of the house has heart pine flooring, hand-carved mantels, wide board ceilings, and original window panes and doors.

The Greek Revival front was added about 1832. Located a little over six miles from town, it sits amid 450 acres, with ample space for horses, cows, cats, dogs, and a crowing rooster.

The Dukes, who have four grown children and five granddaughters, purchased the house from Jan's aunts in the late 1980s. After extensive renovations and the addition of modern conveniences, they opened it to guests. Jan also runs The Old Store, an antiques/consignment shop that's located in a turn-of-the-century wooden building on the property.

The inn's three guest rooms are located on the second floor. The Wade Hampton Room is furnished with family pieces and features historic military artifacts, including a signed portrait of the famous South Carolina statesman and Confederate general. The Rose Room honors the house's collection of art and china centering around the theme of the rose. A hand-painted rose plate on the mantel was spared when General William T. Sherman burned one of the family farms on his March to the Sea. The Summer House Room is decorated in lacy antique fans, a fan-patterned quilt, and a pine armoire from Ireland.

Only one reservation is accepted at a time at the Wade-Beckham House, so the guests may have the entire second floor to themselves. The Dukes serve a full gourmet breakfast and evening desserts. First-time guests receive a wooden replica of the house as a memento.

Latta

Abingdon Manor

307 Church Street
Latta, SC 29565
803-752-5090, 888-752-5090

| A former state senator's home now welcomes guests |

Innkeepers: Michael and Patty Griffey. **Accommodations:** 4 rooms and 1 suite (all with private baths). **Rates:** $95–$120. **Included:** Gourmet breakfast, afternoon refreshments and hors d'oeuvres, complimentary sherry, use of bicycles and exercise room. **Payment:** MasterCard, Visa. **Children:** 12 and older welcome. **Pets:** Not allowed. **Smoking:** Allowed on verandahs. **Open:** Year-round except during Christmas.

➤ **The town of Latta boasts several art galleries, where the work of local artists is exhibited and sold. The annual Springfest includes a juried art show, local crafts, and entertainment.**

Abingdon Manor is a large house, with more than 8,000 feet of interior space and 2,000 feet of verandahs and porches made of lumber cut from the property. The Greek Revival home, located in the Historic District, was built between 1902 and 1905 by James and Florence Manning, who had twelve children. A prosperous cotton planter, he served as a state senator for a number of years.

Former residents of Miami, Michael and Patty Griffey have created a luxurious inn that is getting rave reviews from bed-and-breakfast connoisseurs. With their extensive travels and their knowledge of fine food, they couple want to provide the ultimate experience for their guests. They serve a full gourmet breakfast and treat guests to all kinds of special amenities, including hors d'oeuvres, homemade cookies, fresh flowers, wine, and sherry. They offer a guest telephone, fax machine, and a workout room with a stationary bike, rowing machine, and hot tub. Big promoters of Latta and area attractions, the Griffeys will gladly share information on things to do while staying at the inn. They will also recommend restaurants. Their inn received a four-diamond rating from AAA in 1997.

Abingdon Manor is quite luxurious, with an elaborate formal parlor, library, and dining room. The two-room suite is named for Senator Manning; the others, for their unique color. They are beautifully decorated to enhance the unusual features of the house are fireplaces, wooden mantels, and hand-blown windows.

Lyman

Walnut Lane Bed & Breakfast

110 Ridge Road
Lyman, SC 29365
864-949-7230
Fax: 864-949-1633

> **A new B&B on an old cotton plantation**

Innkeepers: Park and Marie Urquhart. **Accommodations:** 6 rooms (all with private baths). **Rates:** $85–$105. **Included:** Full gourmet breakfast, appetizers and refreshments, turndown service. **Payment:** Major credit cards. **Children:** Well-supervised children welcome. **Pets:** Not allowed. **Smoking:** Allowed on porches. **Open:** Year-round.

➤ **The Urquharts sometimes wear kilts and bring in bagpipers for special occasions in order to share their Scottish heritage. Park's brother is an accomplished bagpiper.**

Park and Marie Urquhart opened their inn in the spring of 1996. Before that, they operated the Fifth Street Mansion B&B in Hannibal, Missouri, for about five years before Park's company transferred him to the Upstate/Asheville region. (He is now semiretired.) After seeing the house and grounds, they decided to buy the property and open it to the public. The twenty-five-room house was built in 1902 by A. B. Groce, a planter who grew cotton on the surrounding acreage until the early 1940s.

Park and Marie named the property "Walnut Lane" for the canopy of black walnut trees lining the front lane. Eventually, they plan to add a tennis court, swimming pool, and horse shoe courts. The Urquharts welcome both leisure and business travelers, as well as small, corporate meetings. They host many weddings and parties at Walnut Lane. They can arrange tee times at nearby golf clubs.

McCormick

Hickory Knob State Resort Park

Route 1, Box 199-B
McCormick, SC 29835
864-391-2450, 800-491-1764
Fax: 864-391-5390

A state resort park with a variety of accommodations

Owner: State of South Carolina. **Accommodations:** 77 lodge rooms, 3 suites, 18 duplex cabins, 1 guest house (all with private baths). **Rates:** $40–$80. **Payment:** Discover, MasterCard, Visa. **Children:** Welcome. **Pets:** Allowed on leash in campground. **Smoking:** Allowed in designated buildings. **Open:** Year-round.

➤ **Formerly called the Clarks Hill Reservoir, Strom Thurmond Lake has more than 1,200 miles of shoreline. The Visitor's Center at Thurmond Dam includes an aquarium and exhibits.**

Take your pick of accommodations at this lakeside retreat on the South Carolina–Georgia border. You can stay in motel rooms, private cabins (available only by the week during summer months), or a restored French Huguenot home dating to the 1700s, but the latter is the most unusual. The quaint cottage has a fireplace, a fully equipped kitchen, two full baths, and two bedrooms — all furnished in beautiful antiques. The cabins come with fully equipped kitchens. The motel rooms are standard variety. Because of the park's popularity, reservations are required.

Meals are available at the restaurant on the premises, and unlike most state park facilities, it has a beer and wine license. (Liquor by the drink is available in the golf pro shop.) Meals at the restaurant are served both buffet-style and from the menu.

Fishing for bass, catfish, crappie, and a variety of panfish is one of the primary activities at Hickory Knob, because of the resort park's location on Strom Thurmond Lake. The lake is ideal for sailing, water skiing, and boating. The park rents john boats and has a number of boat slips and a launching ramp. You can purchase a state fishing license and supplies at the bait and tackle shop.

The park also offers an eighteen-hole golf course with a pro shop, a swimming pool, tennis courts, a skeet range, and two short walking trails. Guests also enjoy pool, television, and the piano in the lodge room. A recreation specialist plans and schedules activities during the summer months.

Because of the many activities available and the variety of accommodations, Hickory Knob is the perfect place for meetings, seminars, conferences, and other gatherings. The staff can assist groups in planning meetings. The meeting building has a kitchenette and audiovisual equipment. The main hall can accommodate up to a hundred people, and two additional lakeview rooms can handle sixty people each.

North Augusta

Rosemary Hall & Lookaway Hall

804 Carolina Avenue
North Augusta, SC 29841
803-278-6222, 800-531-5578
Fax: 803-278-4877

A historic property offering luxurious accommodations

Owner: New Wind. **Accommodations:** 23 rooms (all with private baths). **Rates:** $75–$195. **Included:** Full gourmet breakfast, afternoon tea, evening hors d'oeuvres, off-street parking. **Payment:** Major credit cards. **Children:** Welcome. **Pets:** Not allowed. **Smoking:** Allowed on verandahs. **Open:** Year-round.

➤ **The Victorian homes, both on the National Register of Historic Places, have been restored to their original splendor and now serve as a luxury inn.**

Two historic homes near the Augusta National Golf Club in legendary thoroughbred country have been combined to form one grand estate offering overnight accommodations. Both homes were built around the turn of the century by two brothers using the same blueprints. Rosemary Hall was the home of hotelier James U. Jackson, owner of the famed Hampton Terrace Hotel. It was named for the rosemary bush, signifying "sweet remembrances." Walter Jackson named his home Lookaway Hall because its imposing verandah overlooked the Savannah River. It contains a great deal of the original furnishings. A new wing was added on during the renovation a few years ago.

The primary goal of the inn is to offer guests an experience they won't find anywhere else. Upon arrival in the afternoon, guests are served English tea in the parlor. The full gourmet breakfast, prepared by the chef, is a formal affair as well. The innkeeper always assists guests with dinner reservations and offers tour information.

Pendleton

Liberty Hall Inn

621 South Mechanic Street
Pendleton, SC 29670
864-646-7500, 800-643-7944
Fax: 864-646-7500
libertyhall@carol.net

> An old summer home in
> historic Pendleton now
> welcomes visitors year-
> round

Innkeepers: Tom and Susan Jonas. **Accommodations:** 10 rooms (all with private baths). **Rates:** $64–$74. **Included:** Continental breakfast, wine. **Payment:** Major credit cards. **Children:** Well-behaved children welcome. **Pets:** Not allowed. **Smoking:** Not allowed. **Open:** Year-round.

➤ **The two-story wooden building sits on four acres in the middle of Pendleton, a historic town in the upcountry near Clemson University. Guests may enjoy sitting on the piazzas and walking to historic attractions within the town. Lake Hartwell is only five miles away.**

Originally a summer residence for wealthy planters of the Low Country, Liberty Hall Inn was built by Thomas and Nancy Sloan of Charleston in 1840. The original structure had five large rooms, plus a detached kitchen. It passed to the W. B. Hall family and then to Mr. and Mrs. Bonneau Harris, who enlarged and operated it as a boarding house and a dairy farm. During the 1970s, the building was used as a rooming house for students. Now fully restored, it has served as a country inn since 1985. The present owners are Tom Jonas, a former St. Louis advertising executive, and his wife

Susan, a native of Kentucky. The two-story wooden frame structure has wraparound piazzas on both levels.

The Jonases run a busy operation and cater to business clientele,
those with ties to the university, and individual travelers. They
aim to please guests without hovering over them.

Though an old building with lots of charm, the inn has all the
modern conveniences, including telephones and television sets.
The Continental breakfast buffet and wine are included in the
room tariff, but dinner, available by reservation in the dining room
Thursday, Friday, and Saturday evenings, is extra. A popular eating
spot in Pendleton, Liberty Hall Inn features entrées such as beef
tenderloin, breast of chicken, and seafood, served with fresh vegetables and homemade desserts. Rooms in the inn are painted in
pastels and furnished in antiques, some of which came with the
inn; other antiques were added by the Jonases.

Salem

Devils Fork State Park

161 Holcombe Circle
Salem, SC 29676
864-944-1459

**A lakeside state resort park
in the Foothills**

Park Superintendents: Pete Davis. **Accommodations:** 20 villas (all with private
baths, fireplaces, and fully equipped kitchens). **Rates:** $90–$120 (2-night minimum). **Payment:** MasterCard, Visa. **Children:** Welcome. **Pets:** Not allowed.
Smoking: Allowed. **Open:** Year-round.

➤ **The 7,500-acre lake is something of a challenge because of its deep
waters, populated by rainbow and brown trout, several types of bass,
threadfin shad, bluegill, and black crappie.**

This park in the South Carolina upcountry, located between the
Cherokee Foothills Parkway and the North Carolina state line,
receives record numbers of visitors. When Devils Fork opened in
the fall of 1991, people practically lined up at the gate to rent its
contemporary villas overlooking scenic Lake Jocassee, which is
formed by the Toxaway and Whitewater rivers flowing out of the
Blue Ridge Mountains.

Each villa has central heating and air conditioning, as well as a fireplace and screened porch, and comes completely furnished with contemporary pieces, linens, cooking utensils, and dishes. (The villas sleep four to eight persons and are available only by the week during summer months.) The park also has boat ramps, a tackle shop, picnic areas, and nature and hiking trails.

Fishing is one of the popular pastimes in the park. Duke Power Company, co-developer of the park with the state of South Carolina, is constructing an underwater dam, or weir, to protect the brown trout from damages that occur with changes in temperature and water flow in its coldest habitats.

In developing the 500-acre park, Duke Power has taken great care in designing it so that it harmonizes with nature and has minimal impact on the environment.

Sunrise Farm

325 Sunrise Drive
Mailing Address:
P.O. Box 164
Salem, SC 29676
864-944-0121, 888-991-0121
Fax: 864-944-6195
sfbb@bellsouth.net
http://www.bbonline.com/sc/sunrisefarm

This upcountry farm, now a B&B, brings back memories of the past

Innkeepers: Ron and Barbara Laughter. **Accommodations:** 4 rooms, 1 suite, and 2 cottages (all with private baths). **Rates:** $80–$100. **Included:** Full breakfast, beverages. cookies. **Payment:** Major credit cards. **Children:** Welcome. **Pets:** Not allowed. **Smoking:** Allowed outside. **Open:** Year-round.

➤ **Though the farm may seem like it's in the middle of nowhere, it's not very far from many of South Carolina's wonderful parks, hiking trails, lakes, and rivers (ask about whitewater rafting). Restaurants are limited in the area, but Cashiers and Highlands, just over the North Carolina line, have some outstanding places to eat.**

Owning a bed-and-breakfast inn is a lifelong dream for Ron and Barbara Laughter who moved from Wisconsin to the Upcountry of South Carolina when they purchased the Sunrise Farm Bed & Breakfast Inn, established by Jim and Jean Webb in 1989. Now consisting of ten acres, the farm was once part of a thousand-acre cattle ranch.

The Laughters have redecorated the 1890 Victorian farmhouse and continue to serve guests just as the Webbs did, but they have given the inn a new focus. They are hosting parties, luncheons, and weddings, and they plan to make the farm a vacation destination for families with children. Already, they have a small petting barnyard with three pygmy goats, two rabbits, and Hamlet the pot-bellied pig. There is also a children's play area with swings, slide, and a sandbox. Cribs, playpens, and high chairs are provided at no extra charge.

New to the inn are "Adventure" and "Celebration" packages that combine a variety of activities and amenities and the price of the room. The "Procrastinators Special" allows a guest to reserve a room for any weekday night for $50, including a full breakfast, if they call after 12 noon of that day.

Guests may choose from two cozy cottages or four farmhouse rooms with private baths. Each room is decorated with family antiques, handmade quilts, and all the comforts of a country home. The Laughters provide a welcome basket to guests and unlimited cookies and serve a delicious home-cooked breakfast. Picnic baskets are available.

Sumter

Magnolia House Bed & Breakfast

230 Church Street
Sumter, SC 29150
803-775-6694, 888-666-0296
magnoliahouse@sumter.net

> **The epitome of a southern home & B&B**

Innkeepers: Buck and Carol Rogers. **Accommodations:** 5 rooms (3 with private baths, 2 with shared bath). **Rates:** $65–$125. **Included:** Full breakfast, afternoon refreshments. **Payment:** Major credit cards; cash or checks preferred. **Children:** Welcome. **Pets:** Check with innkeepers. **Smoking:** Allowed outside. **Open:** Year-round.

➤   **Swan Lake and Iris Gardens are home to eight different types of swans from around the world. The Iris Festival is held the last week of May, when the gardens are at their peak bloom.**

Magnolia House, located in Sumter's historic district, is the epitome of the Old South, with its towering Corinthian columns, wraparound porches with overstuffed chairs and cypress swings, and a walled garden resplendent with statuary and flowers of every hue. Furnished in lovely antiques, the house features inlaid oak floors, stained-glass windows, and several fireplaces. Built by C. A. Lemmon, it has been home to four families over the years.

Buck and Carol Rogers, the current owners, purchased the home when Buck retired from the U.S. Air Force after a long career as a fighter pilot. They spent months restoring the house before opening it as a bed-and-breakfast inn. Each of the five guest rooms is decorated in antiques from a different era. (Carol ran an antiques store in Sumter for ten years.) Lata's Salle, outfitted in white Battenburg with accents of dark blue, has a three-sided mirrored wardrobe and a private bath with a clawfoot tub. The British Safari room, with chamois leather painted walls, is known for its kangaroo pelts and safari tea set. Victoria's Retreat, as its name suggests, reflects that era. The Sunflower Suite, offering two adjoining bedrooms with a shared bath, is a turn-of-the-century in decor.

The Rogers serve a full southern breakfast in the dining room. Entrees include shrimp and grits, quail eggs in hollandaise sauce, and other delights.

Union

The Inn at Merridun

100 Merridun Place
Union, SC 29379
864-427-7052
Fax: 864-429-0373
http://www.bbonline.com/sc/merridun/

This grand southern home is an elegant country inn

Innkeepers: Jim and Peggy Waller. **Accommodations:** 5 rooms (all with private baths). **Rates:** $85–$105. **Included:** Full breakfast, evening desserts, and beverages. **Payment:** Major credit cards; cash or checks preferred. **Children:** 12 and older welcome. **Pets:** Not allowed. **Smoking:** Allowed outside. **Open:** Year-round.

➤ **The Wallers often invite interesting people in the community to have dinner with guests at Merridun. Nancy Basket, a Cherokee artist who is**

known for her kudzu paper art and note cards, is a frequent visitor. J.D., the resident cat, often entertains guests.

Little did Jim and Peggy Waller know they would end up in a small southern town when they went searching for property to convert into a bed-and-breakfast inn. As careerists with the U.S. Navy medical department, they had considered buying a place near their home in Chula Vista, California. They had even taken courses on innkeeping and served weekend apprenticeships to learn the business. Their roots were in the East, however. When Jim spotted a Sotheby's ad in 1990 listing a large Union, South Carolina, home, he had to check it out.

"Magnificent 1855 Greek Revival Mansion on the National Register. 7,900 square feet includes seven bedrooms, five baths. Portico with marble floor and Corinthian columns," read the ad. A telephone call to his brother-in-law Mark Hayes in Myrtle Beach and a trip to South Carolina resulted in their buying a house called Merridun.

Because the house had not been occupied for twenty years, the Wallers had their work cut out for them. While Peggy finished up her last year in the navy, Jim came East to begin the restoration of the house — scraping, painting, wallpapering, replacing and restoring walls, floors, ceilings, windows, and doors. One of the most tedious projects — cleaning the frescoed ceilings in the dining room and the music room — required the work of professionals. They also installed new plumbing, new wiring, and a commercial kitchen. The Wallers worked a year and a half on the restoration, finally opening their inn to the public in 1992.

This was not the first time the house had received a major facelift. Originally built as a Georgian-style plantation house for the Keenan family, the house was "remodeled" in the 1890s. Corinthian columns replaced Doric columns, and side marble porticos were added, resulting in 2,400 square feet of porch space. It was T. C. Duncan, owner of cotton mills in Union and Buffalo, who gave the house the name Merridun, a combination of the names of the three families associated with the house — Merriman, Rice, and Duncan.

Merridun offers five guest rooms, all with private baths, phones, and televisions. Each room has a distinctive decor, reflective of South Carolina history, and is furnished with antiques and reproductions. The Senator's Chamber is masculine in appearance, while Lucy's Garden Retreat is feminine. Since opening, the inn has become a haven for corporate travelers.

Jim and Peggy are both good cooks, having more than 800 cookbooks between them, so dining at Merridun is an enjoyable treat. They serve a full gourmet breakfast, desserts in the evening, and dinner by advance reservation. The inn is also available for luncheons, teas, suppers, weddings, cooking classes, and special events, including murder mystery weekends, wine tastings, chocoholic weekends, and cooking seminars. A computer, telephone, fax, and copier are available to guests.

Woodruff

Nicholls-Crook Plantation House B&B

120 Plantation Drive
Woodruff, SC 29388
Tel. & Fax: 864-476-8820

The oldest brick house in Spartanburg County serves B&B guests

Innkeepers: Jim and Suzanne Brown. **Accommodations:** 3 rooms (2 with private baths and 1 suite with shared bath). **Rates:** $75–$150. **Included:** Full breakfast, refreshments, turndown service. **Payment:** American Express. **Children:** 6 and older welcome. **Pets:** Check with innkeepers. **Smoking:** Allowed on grounds. **Open:** Year-round.

➤ **Located near Cowpens National Battlefield, the inn was once the home of Katie Barry, the daughter of Revolutionary War heroine Kate Barry.**

More than two hundred years of history await you at this plantation in the Upstate region, with innkeepers Jim and Suzanne, who live and breathe history, as your attentive hosts. (Jim is a history professor at the University of South Carolina at Spartanburg and the president of the Spartanburg Historical Society; Suzanne is a former language teacher and caterer.)

Constructed of local clay bricks in 1793, the house was built by Thomas Williamson who moved it from its original site in Spartanburg to its present location when he began to feel "crowded." The second owners, Jessie and Katie Crook brought up their large family in the house and grew huge cotton crops on the plantation, which by the 1830s had increased to over a thousand acres. When they died, their daughter Catherine, who married Major George Nicholls, inherited the house. Her husband and her son both served as the county sheriff during the 1800s. The Bryson family, owners in the first half of this century, grew cotton and raised cattle on the property. Bob and Bedie Overman saved the house from deterioration and modernized it. The Browns purchased the house from Mrs. Overman in 1987 after stumbling on it during a sightseeing tour. When they acquired the house, they believed it dated to around 1815, but Jim's meticulous research in the state archives verified that it was actually twenty-two years older. He's also discovered that many state governors were guests at the house.

Listed on the National Register of Historic Places, the house's outstanding architectural features are the original Adam-style fireplace in the living room and the large fireplace on the south side of the house. Local antiques and furnishings, collected by the Browns over a period of years, harmonize perfectly with the house. They've been careful to use simple furnishings that reflect the times when the house was built. The dining room has been decorated to resemble a Colonial tavern.

In addition to the full breakfast, which comes with the room, the Browns offer an open hearth dinner for an extra fee, by advance reservation. Special dishes include venison stew, chicken-on-a-string, and apple pie baked over coals. Cooking a meal on the open hearth takes about three and a half hours.

The Browns offer three guest rooms and lots of amenities, including stocked refrigerators in the rooms. They often pick up guests at the airport, and Suzanne conducts local tours. Telephones and fax service are provided for business travelers. The inn can accommodate small meetings.

The Coast

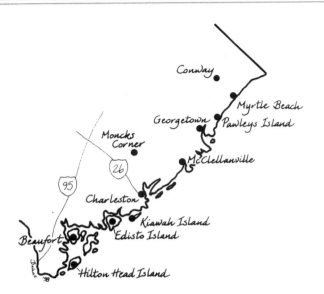

Best Bed and Breakfasts

Beaufort
TwoSuns Inn Bed & Breakfast, 470
Charleston
Brasington House Bed & Breakfast, 472
The Cannonboro Inn Bed & Breakfast, 473
Two Meeting Street Inn, 478
Conway
The Cypress Inn, 481

Best City Stop

Charleston
Charleston Place, 477

Best Country Inn

Pawleys Island
Litchfield Plantation Country Inn, 498

Best Historic Inns

Beaufort
The Rhett House Inn, 468
Charleston
John Rutledge House Inn, 474
Villa de la Fontaine Bed & Breakfast, 480
Georgetown
1790 House, 484

Best Plantations

Charleston
Middleton Inn at Middleton Place, 476
Edisto Island
Cassina Point Plantation, 482
McClellanville
Laurel Hill Plantation Bed & Breakfast Inn, 493

Moncks Corner
Rice Hope Plantation Inn, 495

Best Resorts

Hilton Head
Crowne Plaza Resort, Hilton Head Island, 486
Disney's Hilton Head Island Resort, 487
Hyatt Regency Hilton Head Resort, 488
The Westin Resort, Hilton Head Island, 490
Kiawah Island
Kiawah Island Resort, 492
Myrtle Beach
Kingston Plantation, 496

South Carolina's coast, from the Grand Strand southward to the resort islands — Hilton Head, Isle of Palms, Seabrook, Kiawah, Fripp, and Edisto — offers incomparable opportunities for beach basking, swimming, sailing, boating, water skiing, windsurfing, and fishing from piers, in the surf, or offshore. Saltwater catches may include amberjack, barracuda, bonito, grouper, and mackerel. Inland on Lake Marion is Santee State Park, a sporting paradise offering fishing, tennis, nature trails, and a swimming lake, cabins, and campsites.

The coast is also known for its impressive number of championship golf courses. The Grand Strand offers nearly 100 courses, and Myrtle Beach is also the official "miniature golf capital of the world." One of its offerings, the Hawaiian Rumble, erupts fire every twenty minutes and rumbles, and emits steam constantly.

Although water sports and golfing rank high on the list of Grand Strand activities, this is also one of the eastern seaboard's top family fun spots. It is home to several theaters, including Dolly Parton's Dixie Stampede; the Alabama Theatre; The Palace at Broadway at the Beach; The Gatlin Brothers Theatre, Medieval Times, and the All American Music Theatre at Fantasy Harbor; Calvin Gilmore's Carolina Opry. Myrtle Waves Water Park offers drenching rides and a giant wave pool. Other attractions are Alligator Adventure and Ripley's Aquarium.

Another popular pastime on the Grand Strand is shopping, and bargain hunters flock to the Outlet Park at Waccamaw Mall, Waccamaw Pottery, Broadway at the Beach, and the Barefoot Landing Waterfront Shopping and Dining Festival.

Southward at Murrells Inlet is Brookgreen Gardens. Here the nation's largest outdoor collection of classic American sculpture is dramatically displayed in a beautiful setting of moss-strewn oaks, blooming plants, and reflecting pools. The sculpture includes many works of the late Anna Hyatt Huntington who, with her husband, established the gardens. At nearby Huntington Beach State Park, which includes Atalaya, Huntington's studio, you can follow boardwalk nature trails, camp, and picnic.

The delights of historic Charleston are best savored by leisurely strolls, pausing at will to visit impeccably preserved homes, churches, and public buildings. Notable house museums open year-round include the Nathaniel Russell House, a fine example of Adam architecture; the Edmonston-Alston House, another Adam-style mansion; and the Heyward Washington House, with most of the distinctive furnishings made in Charleston. The Charleston Museum is distinguished for the arts, crafts, and furnishings of colonial and antebellum South Carolina; and in the Gibbes Art Gallery, paintings and sculptures are highlighted by a valuable collection of miniatures. The 1736 Dock Street Theatre, still in use for performances, is among the nation's oldest playhouses.

At the well-preserved 1841 City Market, you can browse for souvenirs and such collectible crafts as locally made sweetgrass and palmetto palm baskets at adjacent open air stalls. Nearby there are more shopping opportunities in the specialty stores of Rainbow Market, Market Square, and State Street Market. Charleston is a major antiques center, and you'll discover fine galleries and shops scattered throughout the city.

Dining ranks among Charleston's most distinctive delights. There's great emphasis on the use of local fresh seafoods, although Continental specialties appear on menus of many upscale restaurants. She-crab soup is a not-to-be-missed Charleston and Low-country concoction — it's made with the roe of the female crab and is liberally seasoned with sherry.

Outlying area points of interest include Fort Sumter National Monument, where the first shots of the Civil War were fired; Charles Towne Landing, a park preserving the site of the first British settlement in 1670; and Patriots Point Naval and Maritime Museum, where the *U.S.S. Yorktown* aircraft carrier, the "Fighting Lady" of World War II, is berthed.

North of the city, Charleston's trio of famed public gardens — Middleton Place, Magnolia, and Cypress — welcome visitors year-round, but they're especially beautiful during the spring blooming season. For a month each spring, the Historic Charleston Foundation's Festival of Houses showcases private homes and gardens not usually open to visitors. It's followed in late May to early June by the renowned Spoleto Festival USA, an internationally acclaimed celebration of performing and visual arts, established by composer Gian-Carlo Menotti.

South of Charleston via U.S. 17 and 21 lies the lovely old town of Beaufort, delightful to browse and explore in a leisurely fashion. Eastward about 16 miles, a magnificent span of palm-lined beach has been preserved at Hunting Island State Park. Paths lead through plant and wildlife refuges; an iron-sheathed lighthouse guards the shore. There are camping and picnic sites, along with furnished beach cabins and a fishing pier.

The resort islands are also home to some challenging golf links and outstanding tennis centers. Harbour Town, at Sea Pines Resort on Hilton Head Island, is the site of the annual spring MCI Heritage Classic, a top PGA Tour event. The stunning Pete Dye–designed Ocean Course on Kiawah Island, site of the 1997 World Cup matches, is considered one of the nation's most formidable layouts. Hilton Head Island annually hosts the Family Circle Magazine Cup Tennis Tournament.

Beaufort

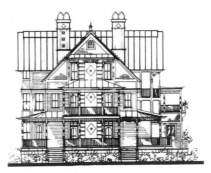

The Beaufort Inn

809 Port Republic Street
Beaufort, SC 29902
803-521-9000
Fax: 803-521-9500

> **One of the most talked-about inns on the East Coast**

Innkeepers: Russell and Debbie Fielden. **Accommodations:** 13 rooms (all with private baths). **Rates:** $125–$195. **Included:** Gourmet breakfast, high tea, turndown service. **Payment:** Major credit cards. **Children:** 8 years and older welcome. **Pets:** Not allowed. **Smoking:** Allowed on porches. **Open:** Year-round except December 24 and 25.

➤ **Be sure to inquire about winemaster dinners, special holiday celebrations, and Chef Peter de Jong's Saturday cooking classes at the inn.**

Russell and Debbie Fielden opened the Beaufort Inn in 1994 after completely renovating the turn-of-the-century structure. They've hosted a long list of celebrities as overnight guests or patrons at their award-winning restaurant — including Julia Roberts, Paula Zahn, Robert Duvall, Lyle Lovett, and Sharon Stone. And the Beaufort Inn has been featured on several television shows and in a number of prestigious magazines, including *Southern Living, Country Inns,* and *American Historic Inns,* which placed the inn among the top ten in the country. Both the inn and the restaurant have been awarded four diamonds by AAA.

The Fieldens, who spent several years working on Hilton Head Island, returned to Debbie's hometown in order to be closer to family and to go into business for themselves. They are the parents of two daughters. "We wanted an inn that would be tastefully elegant, peaceful, comfortable, and would have the feel of what Beaufort is all about — a friendly, small town offering southern hospitality in a beautiful landscape," they said.

Debbie, who wears a number of different hats, usually greets guests at the front door. Rusty, also an outgoing person, works behind the scenes in administration and marketing.

Executive chef Peter de Jong is a native of Amsterdam, Holland. He was trained in his native country and worked for seven years in New York before joining the Fieldens. Using local produce and fresh local fish, he conjures up dishes which are called "works of art" — grilled crabmeat stuffed pork chops with a corn and tasso sauce, Thai-style roasted chicken with a green curry sauce, grilled grouper over Mexican-style red lentils topped with a fresh mango salsa, and other unique recipes. Breakfast entrees, included in the room rate, vary from eggs Benedict made with Daufuskie crabcakes to whole-grain French toast stuffed with Brie and sun-dried peaches served with warm maple syrup. On certain nights the restaurant features ethnic dinners. The Fieldens also cater parties in the restaurant and provide room service to the inn during breakfast and dinner hours.

Located in Historic Beaufort, a block from Beaufort River Waterfront Park, the house has an interesting past. It was built in 1907 by William Sidney Smith, a prominent attorney, as a summer retreat for his wife and seven children. During the 1920s, it was used as a boarding house. From the early 1930s until the 1960s, it was called the Beaufort Inn and served as a teacherage.

In terms of its appearance, the inn probably looks better than it has ever looked. The Fieldens completely gutted the house, added a third floor and a foyer, and bared no expense in its restoration and decoration. The house features mahogany trim created by local craftsmen. Rooms bear the names of Low Country plantations and feature photographs detailing their history. Several of the bathrooms have whirlpool tubs, and all have in-room refrigerators with wet bar. For the business traveler, there are in-room data ports, telephones, voice mail, and fax and copy service. The inn has meeting space for up to forty. The Fieldens plan to add a large garden courtyard directly behind the inn for weddings and receptions.

The Rhett House Inn

1009 Craven Street
Beaufort, SC 29902
803-524-9030
Fax: 803-524-1310
rhettse@hargray.com
http://www.innbook.com/rhett.html

> **A small town luxury inn that hosts movie stars**

Innkeepers: Steve and Marianne Harrison. **Accommodations:** 17 rooms (all with private baths, many with Jacuzzis and fireplaces). **Rates:** $125–$225. **Included:** Full breakfast. **Payment:** American Express, MasterCard, Visa. **Children:** 5 and older welcome. **Pets:** Not allowed. **Smoking:** Allowed on verandahs and in garden. **Open:** Year-round.

➤ *Gone With the Wind* **fans are usually happy to find this inn because it epitomizes the Old South in every way. It's also a perfect place for romance — southern-style.**

This Greek Revival antebellum mansion, located in the historic district near the Intracoastal Waterway, dates to 1820 and was fully renovated to serve as a bed-and-breakfast inn in 1986. (New wiring, plumbing, air conditioning, and full baths were added.) The house is named for Thomas Rhett, a southern aristocrat who lived here with his wife, Caroline Barnwell, prior to the War Between the States. It has several wood-burning fireplaces and Adam-style mantels.

Owners Marianne and Steve Harrison fell in love with the house on their first trip to the South and decided to purchase it and turn it into an inn. They have decorated the inn in fine antiques, which when combined with the chintz fabrics used throughout the house, give it a very elegant, formal look. (The owners confess they aspire for their four-star property to be the Ritz-Carlton of small inns.) Several paintings by Nancy Rhett, a local artist who has a gallery in town and is married to a descendent of the house's namesake, are displayed throughout the house.

The Harrisons seem to have thought of everything a guest might need; each room has a full-length mirror, extra-long bathroom vanities, satin-covered hangers, four pillows, a comforter, telephones, and cable television, compact disc player, in addition to the regular amenities. The honeymoon suite features a whirlpool tub. A newly renovated historic cottage is perfect for romantic getaways.

The innkeepers go out of their way to please guests. They will fix picnic lunches and pick up boaters traveling the Intracoastal Waterway. Concierge service is available 24 hours a day. The full "healthy" breakfast consists of pancakes, French toast, or eggs, fresh fruit, southern grits, home-baked muffins, and freshly rewed coffee.

During the filming of *The Prince of Tides* in Beaufort, Barbra Streisand and Nick Nolte were guests at the inn, and Robert Zemeckis, director of *Forrest Gump*, and Rick Carter of *Jurassic Park* fame have also stayed here.

TwoSuns Inn Bed & Breakfast

1705 Bay Street
Beaufort, SC 29902
Tel. & Fax: 803-522-1122
843-532-4244 (reservations only)
twosuns@islc.net
http://www.twosunsinn.com

> **A waterfront B&B with two talented hosts**

Innkeepers: Ron and Carrol Kay. **Accommodations:** 6 rooms (all with private baths). **Rates:** $105 and up, discounts and low-season rates available. **Included:** Full breakfast, afternoon "tea and toddy" hour, bicycles. **Payment:** Major credit cards. **Children:** 12 and older welcome. **Pets:** Not allowed. **Smoking:** Allowed on verandah and screened porch. **Open:** Year-round.

➤ **A champagne mimosa private breakfast and a picnic basket filled with goodies are available. Guests may make other special requests, such as cut flowers, cheese and fruit trays, birthday or anniversary cakes, and souvenirs.**

Known for their holiday decorations, impromptu gatherings, and Halloween celebrations, Carrol and Ron Kay took the name of their bed-and-breakfast inn from the movie *2010*. A former high school music teacher and administrator at the University of Miami, Ron is a creative business and B&B consultant. Carrol, an office manager in her former life, is a weaver and can be found most days working at her loom in the parlor. She is also a juried artist at the South Carolina Artisans Center in nearby Walterboro.

Combining their multiple talents, the couple bought the 1917 Neoclassic Revival structure overlooking Beaufort Bay in the spring of 1990, filled it with Victorian furnishings, and decorated it in time for Historic Beaufort Foundation's Fall Tour of Homes in October. The restoration was awarded U.S. Department of the Interior Historic Structure Certification in 1996.

Designed by Morton Levy of Savannah for the Keyserling family, the house featured the latest in modern conveniences when it was built, including indoor plumbing (the first in Beaufort), steam radiator heating and skylight ventilation system (now restored), a Roman heat distribution system, a servants' call-box system, kerosene water heaters, closets, and a bathroom with a brass body shower (now restored and fully operational and called "the giggle shower"). In addition to the main house, the property at one time included a servants' home, a two-car garage with step-down grease pit, and a clay tennis court. The house served as the county teacherage for a number of years and then stood vacant for twelve years before some restorations were attempted prior to the Kays' efforts.

Carrol has created almost all the window and bed treatments, including some that are hand-woven. TwoSuns is filled with antiques and collectibles. The Kays' mini-banana museum adds a whimsical touch. A full breakfast is served in the dining room each day and features a variety of dishes. In the afternoon the Kays host their now-famous Tea and Toddy Hour, and guests are welcome to help themselves to nonalcoholic beverages any time of the day.

For entertainment, guests may choose croquet or bicycles or take a tour of the historic Low Country town, dating to 1711.

Charleston

Brasington House Bed & Breakfast

328 East Bay Street
Charleston, SC 29401
803-722-1274

A B&B with interesting inn-keepers who give personal service

Innkeepers: Dalton and Judy Brasington. **Accommodations:** 4 rooms (all with private baths). **Rates:** $98–$124. **Included:** Full breakfast, wine and liqueur, offstreet parking. **Payment:** MasterCard, Visa. **Children:** Not appropriate. **Pets:** Not allowed. **Smoking:** Not allowed. **Open:** Year-round.

➤ **Having lived in the area for several years (Dalton is the third genera-tion of his family to live in the city), the Brasingtons are most knowledge-able about anything to do with Charleston, from attractions to festivals to the best restaurants.**

You'll never go away wondering who the innkeepers are at this Charleston B&B. The Brasingtons are always available — checking guests into the inn, serving wine and cheese in the afternoon, as-sisting with dinner reservations and touring plans, and hosting breakfast, an elaborate meal that's served in the formal dining room. They take innkeeping very seriously, and they believe in giving their guests personal service.

Dalton and Judy have been running the Brasington House since 1989. A former geography teacher, he devotes all of his time to the inn, while Judy still maintains a "real job" as an instructional tele-vision consultant with the South Carolina Department of Education. They have stayed in many inns around the world, and Brasington House reflects their global interests. The Brasingtons spent over fifteen months in 1987 and 1988 restoring the antebellum Greek Revival home, which had been badly abused as an apartment building. It is a three-story single Charleston house, with its double verandahs turned to the side to catch the breezes. Central heating and air conditioning were installed during the renovation and private baths added. The rooms are furnished in antiques, but each has a telephone, cable television, and service for making coffee, tea, and hot chocolate in the room.

The Cannonboro Inn Bed & Breakfast

184 Ashley Avenue
Charleston, SC 29403
803-723-8572
Fax: 803-768-1230
http://www.cannonatcchat.com

A Charleston B&B that's as pretty as a picture

Innkeepers: Bud and Sally Allen. **Accommodations:** 6 rooms (all with private baths). **Rates:** $79–$165. **Included:** Full breakfast, afternoon sherry, evening beverages, homemade cookies, touring bicycles. **Payment:** Major credit cards. **Children:** 10 and older welcome. **Pets:** Not allowed. **Smoking:** Allowed on porch. **Open:** Year-round.

➤ **Building on their success with the Cannonboro Inn, the Allens operate a similar inn — Ashley Inn Bed & Breakfast across the street.**

Combining their talents and personal interests, Bud, a builder and developer, and Sally, a travel consultant and decorator, run a professional operation. The inn is spotless, the decor flawless, and the staff very service-oriented.

The Allens took an old Victorian home and turned it into a bed-and-breakfast inn in 1990. The two-story house has bay windows on the front, and its double piazzas, turned sideways, overlook the garden. Sally's flair for decorating is evident in the perfectly color-coordinated guest rooms. All of the beds in the inn are either four-posters or rice beds with canopies, and every room has a color television.

Guests at Cannonboro Inn are served a full hearty breakfast, plus afternoon sherry, evening beverages, and home-baked treats. Complimentary bicycles are available.

John Rutledge House Inn

116 Broad Street
Charleston, SC 29401
803-723-7999, 800-476-9741
Fax: 803-720-2615

| A historic B&B in the city offering elegant lodgings |

Owner: Richard Widman. **Innkeeper:** Linda Bishop. **Accommodations:** 16 rooms and 3 suites (all with private baths, 2 with Jacuzzis). **Rates:** $215–$325 in high season; $155–$325 in low season; $20 for each additional person. **Included:** Continental breakfast, morning newspaper, full breakfast available for an extra charge. **Payment:** Major credit cards. **Children:** Under 12 free; cribs available. **Pets:** Not allowed. **Smoking:** Allowed in designated rooms only. **Open:** Year-round.

➤ **John Rutledge owned a stable full of horses and a wine cellar, where he kept a fine collection of wines and spirits.**

History was made in the rooms of this three-story house, one of fifteen surviving homes belonging to the signers of the Constitution and the only one that offers lodging. As a young man in 1763, John Rutledge built the Federal-style National Historic Landmark house. Throughout his illustrious career as a lawyer, assemblyman, president of the republic of South Carolina, commander in chief of the state militia, delegate to the First and Second Continental Congresses, U.S. congressman, state supreme court justice, and U.S. Supreme Court Justice, he entertained some of the country's most powerful political leaders, including President Washington.

Significant changes were made to the house in the 1850s when Thomas Gadsden bought it and added the Christopher Werner wrought-iron railings with the palmetto and eagle motifs, Italian marble mantels, and parquet floors from Germany, thus changing the architectural style to early Victorian. During his residence he entertained President William Howard Taft. However, the house's conversion into apartments, schoolrooms, and offices took its toll, and when Richard Widman of Charleston bought it in 1985, it was in disrepair.

After extensive renovation, Widman opened the inn to guests in 1989 and has since earned high marks from the traveling public and travel clubs. Each of the guest rooms has been decorated with painstaking care, using antiques and reproductions of the 18th and 19th centuries. There are eleven rooms on all four levels of the original house, including the wine cellar, and eight rooms in two adjoining carriage houses to the rear of the courtyard. A favorite is the Thomas Heyward Room with its rice four-poster canopy bed and dark green walls that set off the Decorloom print fabric. Suites such as the one named for Colonel William Moultrie feature a formal parlor and bedroom separated by 12-foot pocket doors. All rooms have luxurious baths, color televisions, mini-refrigerators, and telephones.

A Continental breakfast is delivered on a silver tray to the room, along with a morning newspaper, or guests may request a full breakfast for an additional charge. Afternoon tea featuring light refreshments is served on a silver tea service in the ballroom, as are wine and sherry in the evenings. Brandy and chocolates come with the nightly turndown service. The concierge can direct guests to neighborhood restaurants and historic attractions, all within walking distance. Parking is provided for guests at the rear of the inn — a real advantage in Charleston.

Mr. Widman also owns four other fine inns in Charleston — King's Courtyard Inn, Victoria House Inn, Fulton Lane Inn, and Wentworth Mansion, scheduled to open in the spring of 1998. All operate under the umbrella of Charming Inns of Charleston, Inc.

Middleton Inn at Middleton Place

Ashley River Road
Charleston, SC 29414
Tel. & Fax: 803-556-0500
800-543-4774

| A modern-day lodge on an old river plantation |

General Manager: Doyle Gray. **Accommodations:** 50 rooms (all with private baths and fireplaces). **Rates:** $99–$147, (off-season rates available). **Included:** Continental breakfast, morning newspaper, and admission to Middleton Place. **Payment:** American Express, MasterCard, Visa. **Children:** Welcome. **Pets:** Allowed. **Smoking:** Allowed. **Open:** Year-round.

➤ **Middleton Gardens, laid out in 1741, are the oldest landscaped gardens in America and now one of the area's biggest attractions, especially in the springtime.**

Don't expect to sleep in the manor house when you arrive at this Ashley River plantation outside of Charleston. You will certainly be welcome to tour the House Museum and the lavish gardens, but your accommodations will be ultramodern rooms with contemporary furnishings.

Built in 1986 adjacent to the grounds of Middleton Plantation, a National Historic Landmark, the concrete and glass inn features 50 rooms with ceiling-to-floor river views, fireplaces with tools hand-forged by the plantation blacksmith, imported oversize tubs with Italian tile, and mini-refrigerators.

Guests have breakfast in the Café at the Inn and other meals at the Restaurant at Middleton Place, or they may choose to eat in Charleston, about fifteen miles away. The inn offers horseback riding lessons at Middleton Stables, hiking and jogging trails, swimming, and tennis. Golf is available nearby. Tours of other plantations in the area can be arranged. The inn can accommodate small groups for meetings.

Middleton Place was the original home of Henry Middleton, president of the First Continental Congress, and the house, built around 1755, contains priceless silver, china, and furniture belonging to the Middleton family.

Charleston Place —
An Orient Express Hotel

130 Market Street
Charleston, SC 29401
803-722-4900
800-611-5545
Fax: 803-722-6952
http://www.orient-expresshotels.com

**The premier hotel in
historic Charleston**

Managing Director: Dean P. Andrews. **Accommodations:** 440 rooms, including 42 suites, and 80 private concierge-level rooms (all with private baths). **Rates:** $245–$315 (off-season rates and packages available). **Included:** Continental breakfast, hors d'oeuvres, afternoon tea, and open bar on concierge level. **Payment:** Major credit cards. **Children:** Summer daycare program and baby-sitting services available. **Pets:** Not allowed. **Smoking:** Smoking and non-smoking rooms. **Open:** Year-round.

➤   *Conde Nast Traveler* **has recognized Charleston Place as one of the top ten hotels in the United States.**

Built in 1986, Charleston Place—An Orient Express Hotel incorporates the classic traditional look in its decor, using period reproduction furniture, armoires, Botticino marble, and brass fixtures. The lobby — with its sweeping grand staircase, marble floors, and crystal chandeliers — dissolves into the corridors leading to shops and restaurants (twenty-six in all). Charleston Place has three restaurants and lounges — Charleston Grill, under the direction of Chef Robert Waggoner, a *Food & Wine Magazine* chef of the year; the Palmetto Café, a plantation-style restaurant with an open courtyard; and the Lobby Lounge, where afternoon tea and hors d'oeuvres are served.

Guests staying on the club levels receive special services, including a Continental breakfast, hors d'oeuvres, and honor bar, plus same-day and overnight valet, laundry, and shoeshines. Those who choose the Executive Service Plan get even more perks — room upgrades, turndown service, complimentary newspaper, express check-in and check-out, and other services. The hotel offers a fitness center, a twenty-person Jacuzzi, and an indoor pool. Maps of jogging trails in the historic district are provided. Though individuals are an important segment of the clientele, Charleston Place is ideal for business travelers and groups. Several different types of meeting rooms are available.

Throughout the year the hotel offers several packages — starting at $149 per couple — that appeal to individual travelers. Packages such as the Romance Package, Christmas in Charleston, and the Priceless Package are especially popular.

Two Meeting Street Inn

2 Meeting Street
Charleston, SC 29401
803-723-7322

> The belle of Charleston's
> B&Bs, a Victorian delight

Innkeeper: Karen M. Spell. **Accommodations:** 9 rooms (all with private baths, 2 with showers only and 3 with Victorian tubs). **Rates:** $135–$225. **Included:** Continental breakfast and afternoon tea. **Payment:** Cash or checks. **Children:** 12 and older welcome. **Pets:** Not allowed. **Smoking:** Not allowed. **Open:** Year-round except Christmas.

➤ **As pretty as any picture postcard you'll ever see, Two Meeting Street overlooks White Point Gardens, the Battery, and Charleston Harbor.**

The Queen Anne Victorian mansion looks like a wedding cake, with its curved double-decker verandahs, accented with arched columns on the first level and round columns on the second. The house sits on a corner lot, bordered with wrought-iron fencing — all shrouded in green and surrounded by centuries-old live oaks draped in Spanish moss. Inside, Two Meeting Street sparkles — the silver and brass are polished to a gleaming luster. Rich carved English oak dominates the downstairs entry hall and parlors as well as the central stairway.

The house was built in 1892 by Waring and Martha Carrington, who used a wedding gift of $75,000 in order to do so. It has nine stained glass windows; two in the parlor were made by Louis Comfort Tiffany and given by Mr. Carrington to his wife for their fifth wedding anniversary. The chandelier in the foyer is Czechoslovakian cut crystal, made by the same company that cut the beveled glass in the entry hall.

Mrs. Minnie Carr bought the house in 1946 from the Carringtons and operated it as an inn until the early 1980s. The house then passed to the Spells, who did extensive renovations. (Karen Spell, the innkeeper, is Mrs. Carr's great-niece.) Recently, new sofas and rocking chairs were added on the second-floor verandah.

Romancers may want to choose one of two honeymoon suites. One has a private balcony, while the other opens onto the upstairs piazza through French doors. Both have working fireplaces. All the spacious rooms feature family antiques, heirlooms, and Oriental carpets. Honeymooners will find plenty of privacy here, as well as the right atmosphere for romance.

In the afternoon complimentary sherry is served, and the Continental breakfast can be taken to the room or eaten in the formal dining room. Afternoon tea, served from 4:30 to 6:00, features a variety of home-baked goodies and tea, of course. Guests are free to come and go and may walk to all the historic sites and restaurants. The staff gladly arranges dinner reservations, city tours, and horse-drawn carriage rides.

Villa de la Fontaine Bed & Breakfast

138 Wentworth Street
Charleston, SC 29401
803-577-7709
http://www.charleston.cityinformation.com/villa

> **A stately home that's filled with priceless antiques**

Innkeepers: William Fontaine and Aubrey Hancock. **Accommodations:** 4 rooms (all with private baths). **Rates:** $100–$125. **Included:** Full breakfast. **Payment:** Cash or checks. **Children:** Check with innkeepers. **Pets:** Not allowed. **Smoking:** Not allowed anywhere on property. **Open:** Year-round.

➤ **An 1842 advertisement for the house on Wentworth Street noted its "handsomely laid out gardens ... accommodations for servants, store house, carriage house and stable, bathing house, a cistern and well."**

This bed-and-breakfast inn, the first to be licensed in the city, is a stand-out among the dozens of inns for which Charleston is famous. William Fontaine and Aubrey Hancock, who have designed interiors for some of America's first families, spent several years renovating and furnishing their neoclassic home on Wentworth Street which they now share with overnight guests.

Designed by Russell Warren, the house was built for dry goods merchant Edwin L. Kerrison in 1839. Many different people have owned the house throughout its history. The Protestant Episcopal Diocese of South Carolina occupied it for a number of years before selling it to Hancock and Fontaine in 1970.

The inn is furnished in eighteenth century American antiques, some of which even rival those found in the nation's most outstanding museums. They are indeed the finest in Charleston.

Among the house's treasures are a verdi-marble table by William Kent, designer of Hampton Court; Meissen china and Wedgewood porcelain; 1810 ice cream urns; and other priceless pieces. Bedrooms feature four-poster beds, huge wardrobes, and gilded mirrors.

Upon arrival, guests are given a tour of the house. The full breakfast consists of waffles, sausage, eggs Benedict, hash browns, spiced fruit, marmalade, and coffee and is served in the solarium, a bright room with fan windows and a hand-painted mural. The inn has a lovely garden and terraces for the enjoyment of guests.

Conway

The Cypress Inn

16 Elm Street
P.O. Box 495
Conway, SC 29528
803-248-8199, 800-575-5309
Fax: 803-248-0329
http://www.bbonline.com/sc/cypress/

A new B&B on the Waccamaw River

Innkeepers: Jim and Carol Ruddick. **Accommodations:** 12 rooms (all with full baths, some with Jacuzzis and fireplaces). **Rates:** $95–$145. **Included:** Full breakfast, snacks and beverages, newspaper. **Payment:** Major credit cards. **Children:** Check with innkeepers. **Pets:** Not allowed. **Smoking:** Not allowed. **Open:** Year-round.

➤ **The front porch, lined with Carolina rockers, is an ideal place to relax with a glass of lemonade and a good book.**

Jim and Carol Ruddick, resident owners and innkeepers, dreamed and planned and then watched their new inn develop from the ground up. After failing to find an established bed-and-breakfast that suited their needs, they decided to build their own, responding to an invitation from the city of Conway to place the inn in the Riverfront district. The Ruddicks also worked with David Caples, an industry consultant, and attended B&B seminars.

Opening their inn in May of 1997, the Ruddicks earned AAA's three-diamond rating almost immediately. A 15-minute drive from Atlantic beaches, the inn is a three-story wooden structure with bay windows and porches that overlook the marina and the Waccamaw River. There are twelve interesting guest rooms, each with its own theme, a gentle mix of old and new, with alluring names like the Crystal Chamber, Quinlin's Quarters, Celeste's Salon, and Miss Marple. Three rooms suggest the romance of the Old South — Magnolia, Carolina, and Kingston. All the rooms have individual climate controls, cable television, and telephones. Many feature Jacuzzis and fireplaces.

The Ruddicks serve a full breakfast in the sunny breakfast room and offer lemonade, iced tea, coffee, and cookies around the clock.

Guests may choose to rent a boat from the marina or take a sightseeing trip on *The Kinston Lady*. The sports-minded can take advantage of tennis, golf, deep sea fishing, bicycling, and nature walks. Shopping, restaurants, and entertainment are minutes away. Jim and Carol can also arrange visits to a local fitness club.

Edisto Island

Cassina Point Plantation

1642 Clark Road
P.O. Box 535
Edisto Island, SC 29438
Tel & Fax: 803-869-2535

| A beautifully restored island plantation where southern hospitality is practiced with reverence |

Innkeepers: Bruce and Tecla Earnshaw. **Accommodations:** 4 rooms (all with half baths; 2 full baths in hall). **Rates:** $115. **Included:** Full breakfast, afternoon beverages and fruit bowl; canoe and kayak rentals extra. **Payment:** Cash or checks. **Children:** 10 and older welcome. **Pets:** Not allowed. **Smoking:** Allowed on porches only. **Open:** Year-round.

➤ **Former president of the South Carolina Bed & Breakfast Association, Bruce Earnshaw lists and sells B&Bs and country inns throughout South Carolina; Tecla is an accountant.**

Evidence of the Union soldiers' occupation of this island plantation can be seen in the basement, where their signatures and graffiti have been preserved for posterity. Upstairs the mansion has been meticulously restored by Bruce and Tecla Earnshaw as a bed-and-breakfast inn. They purchased the 145-acre property in 1987 and opened the inn three years later after working tirelessly on the restoration.

The mansion, a four-story wooden Lowcountry home, sits 100 feet from Westbank Creek, an inlet of the North Edisto River. To reach it, you must drive along an unpaved country lane through acres and acres of open fields and woodlands. Be sure to get directions, or you may get lost. Downstairs are the formal parlor and dining room, a library, and the kitchen. Up the curved mahogany stairs are four spacious bedrooms, each with a half bath and great views of the plantation. (Two full baths on the floor are also for the use of guests.) The rooms are comfortable and inviting, with Tecla's touches everywhere — balloon shades, lace accents, coverlets, and soft colors on the walls.

Cassina Point has quite a history. It was built for newlyweds James Hopkinson and Carolina Lafayette Seabrook in 1847 on Edisto Island land owned by her father William Seabrook, whose family had been among the first English settlers to come to the island. Prior to the Civil War, the plantation enjoyed many years of prosperity, as it yielded an abundance of fine Sea Island cotton. In 1861, however, all the Sea Islands, including Edisto, were evacuated, and Federal troops moved onto the plantation.

According to the late Ella Seabrook, the Seabrooks buried many of their valuables, including china, crystal, and silver, before the soldiers arrived. When the family returned to the island after the war, they found their home stripped of its fine furnishings. The story goes that the boat containing the furnishings sank on its way to the sea.

Upon arrival at Cassina Point, guests are escorted to their rooms, where a bowl of fresh fruit and ice water await them. The Earnshaws serve wine and hors d'oeuvres in the library or on the back porch and offer suggestions on where to dine and what to see in the area. In the morning the innkeepers serve a full breakfast featuring eggs, pancakes, or French toast, with sausage-stuffed mushrooms or some other special dish — often fresh seafood from the creek — plus juice and coffee.

If you don't want to go anywhere, you can find plenty of diversions on the plantation. You can take a walk; go fishing, crabbing, or shrimping; watch birds; play croquet; look for dolphins in the creek; rent a canoe or kayak; or enjoy the hammock. You can also moor your own boat or board your horse. (Tecla has four of her own in the barn, plus two cats and a labrador retriever named Molly.) Of course, there are many places to explore on Edisto. Though development is slowly creeping in, the island hasn't lost its allure or charm.

Georgetown

1790 House

630 Highmarket Street
Georgetown, SC 29440
803-546-4821, 800-890-7432

A Colonial home in old Georgetown now welcomes B&B guests

Innkeepers: John and Patricia Wiley. **Accommodations:** 5 rooms and 1 suite (all with private baths). **Rates:** $75–$125. **Included:** Full breakfast, afternoon refreshments. **Payment:** Major credit cards. **Children:** 12 and older welcome. **Pets:** Not allowed. **Smoking:** Allowed on outside verandahs and patio. **Open:** Year-round.

➤ **1790 House is within walking distance of all the historic sites in Georgetown, including historic homes and churches and the Rice Museum, which chronicles the history of rice production in the area. At least two old plantations are open to the public at all times and are within driving distance of the inn.**

Here on Highmarket Street in old Georgetown, once the rice capital of the United States, life is celebrated in grand style in the former homes of rice barons. Some are open only at certain times of the year, but the 1790 House can be enjoyed anytime. The inn is operated by John and Patricia Wiley, who moved here from southern California.

The Wileys first spotted the inn in an advertisement and became the owners and proprietors in 1992. John had been in the advertising and printing business for years; Patricia had worked as a legal secretary. They had never tried innkeeping before, but had stayed in many inns and studied the business thoroughly. For a while Patricia remained on the West Coast until their house sold, and John managed the inn on his own.

The 1790 House is believed to have been built around the year of its name, but the first written record of its existence is 1812, when it served as the residence of the Pyatts. The Pyatts owned 750 slaves and grew rice on the vast acreages outside of town. (Many members of the family are buried nearby in the churchyard of Prince George Winyah Episcopal Church.) First renovated in the late 1950s and then again in the 1980s, the house became a bed-and-breakfast inn in 1985.

The architectural style is an adaptation of a plantation-style house of the West Indies. The arches that support the front piazza were built out of coral stone from Bermuda, brought over on ships as ballast. The house contains the original wooden cornices, wainscoting, chair rails, and base molding. All the public rooms, including the formal living room, dining room, keeping room, kitchen, and two guest rooms are located on the main floor. Other rooms are on the second and third floors; the basement, formerly the slave quarters, serves as office space and the innkeepers' living area.

The carriage house, offering complete privacy with easy access to the formal gardens, is a special place. It has a Jacuzzi, full shower, refrigerator, sitting area, and private patio. Some rooms are decorated in the Colonial style, with antique furnishings and reproductions of the period, while a couple of rooms have Victorian touches. The innkeepers leave special treats of candy in all the rooms.

The Wileys serve a full breakfast in the formal dining room, one of the grandest rooms in the house. Menu selections include egg dishes, pancakes, French toast, grit cakes, and homemade muffins and breads, which are always served with juice and coffee. The Wileys serve an English high tea for guests and locals every afternoon in the inn's Angel's Touch Tearoom. No other meals are served, but there are several good restaurants within walking distance on Georgetown's restored waterfront. The Wileys usually assist guests with dinner reservations during the afternoon reception in the common room.

Hilton Head

Crowne Plaza Resort, Hilton Head Island

130 Shipyard Drive
Hilton Head Island, SC 29928
803-842-2400
800-334-1881 or 800-HOLIDAY
Fax: 803-785-8463
Alvinb@crowneplazaresort.com
http://www.crowneplazaresort.com

> **The number-one Crowne Plaza resort for customer satisfaction**

Owner: Holiday Inn Hospitality, Inc. **Accommodations:** 313 guest rooms and 25 suites (all with private baths). **Rates:** $189–$239 (off-season rates available). **Payment:** Major credit cards. **Children:** Welcome. **Pets:** Not allowed. **Smoking:** Smoking and nonsmoking rooms. **Open:** Year-round.

➤ **The first Crowne Plaza Resort in the continental United States, this luxury property opened in Shipyard Plantation in 1993.**

Guests at Crowne Plaza Resort Hilton Head Island are received in the nautical lobby and then proceed to the "living room," a homey setting featuring a parlor, billiards, and board games. Leisure activities coordinators and conference concierges are on hand to assist guests with recreational plans and business needs.

Recreational options include a full-service health club, indoor and outdoor whirlpools, indoor lap pool, and outdoor activity pool. Golf and tennis are available at Shipyard Plantation, with transportation provided. Horseback riding and sailing are other options. The resort offers meeting space and a business services center. Activities for children and adults are scheduled regularly.

The oceanside resort sits on eleven acres of tropically landscaped grounds, formerly occupied by the Marriott Resort. It has 313 guest rooms and 25 suites, each with an in-room safe, coffeemaker, and private balcony. There are two restaurants; one is a full-service restaurant for fine dining featuring a mixture of European and Low Country cuisine and the other is casual dining. In addition, the resort has a nightclub.

Disney's Hilton Head Island Resort

22 Harbourside Lane
Hilton Head Island, SC 29928
803-341-4100, 800-453-4911
Fax: 803-341-4035

Hilton Head Island's newest resort

General Manager: Bill Ernest. **Accommodations:** 102 vacation homes. **Rates:** $135–$450 plus recreational fees (off-season rates available). **Included:** Board games, billiards, fishing pier, swimming pools, spa, fitness center, beach shuttle, beach club. **Payment:** Major credit cards. **Children:** Welcome. **Pets:** Kennels available off property. **Smoking:** Allowed. **Open:** Year-round.

➤ **"Hilton Head Island has a proven track record as a premiere destination spot in America. We see this trend continuing, and this is the reason we have chosen to build our resort here." — Bill Ernest, General Manager**

Mickey and Minnie Mouse joined Disney officials and the Hallelulah Singers, along with a host of South Carolina dignitaries, including the governor, for the grand opening of the first Disney resort outside of Florida and California in the spring of 1996. With a wave of his magic wand, Mickey left a trace of pixie dust scattered around the resort.

Mickey and Minnie are not a part of the permanent scene here, but you may meet some interesting characters when you're walking along the boardwalk or going for a swim. They're here to add a little fun to your overall vacation. You'll also see some whimsical Disney touches around the resort. For instance, carpeting in the vacation homes includes the head of Mickey in the design, and the initials W. D. are carved into benches in the mud rooms. A fictional dog named Shadow who belongs to the make-believe Edmunds family appears in pictures on the wall, and his pawprints are imprinted in the floor tiles.

The Disney resort doesn't look anything like the Spanish-style architecture that prevails in most modern-day Hilton Head Island structures. Located on a fifteen-acre private island within Shelter Cove Harbour, the buildings resemble vacation lodges of the 1940s and 1950s — two-story structures with tin roofs and open balconies and porches that blend in with the landscape. Disney's accommodations range from studios to one- and two-bedroom homes and villas. The larger units include a sitting room that opens onto the balcony or porch, fully equipped kitchen, two bedrooms with private baths (the one in the master bedroom being a whirlpool tub), foyer, and mud room with a washer and dryer. The units can accommodate four, eight, or twelve persons.

The Beach House on the Atlantic Ocean, a short hop via the shuttle, is a "living room for resort guests," with a large den and snack bar next to the swimming pool. The house models the "life safety" houses that dotted the eastern seaboard during the mid-twentieth century. Signal flags are a dominant feature of the interior design.

Special programming for guests is unique to the Disney property. Guests may sign up for shrimping and crabbing, ecology programs (including bird walks), fishing, arts and crafts, movies, bicycle riding, dolphin watching, and more. You won't be disappointed in any of the activities at the resort — on a dolphin excursion the lovable creatures swim right up to the boats. In addition, the resort has access to ten championship golf courses and tennis facilities. You can also rent bicycles, play arcade games and billiards, or have a picnic. The recreational opportunities are unlimited.

Food is available in the resort dining room and Signal's Snackbar at the Beach House, and good restaurants and shops are within walking distance. The Broad Creek Mercantile sells drinks, snacks, beach items, and souvenirs.

Hyatt Regency Hilton Head Resort

One Hyatt Circle
Palmetto Dunes
P.O. Box 6167
Hilton Head Island, SC 29938-6167
803-785-1234, 800-55 HYATT
Fax: 803-842-4695
hyatthiltonhead@msn.com
http://www.hyatthiltonhead.com

> **The largest oceanfront resort for hundreds of miles**

General Manager: Steve Dewire. **Accommodations:** 474 rooms and 31 suites (all with private baths). **Rates:** $115–$285. **Included:** All amenities and admission to Club Indigo. **Payment:** Major credit cards. **Children:** Under 18 free with parents; Camp Hyatt offered for ages 3–12 during the summer and holidays. **Pets:** Not allowed. **Smoking:** Allowed. **Open:** Year-round.

➤ **Hilton Head gets most of its visitors between March and late November, but the weather is moderate year-round, with temperatures averaging**

between the mid-50s and mid-80s. The island is situated off the southernmost tip of South Carolina, about 35 miles north of Savannah, Georgia.

Three continuous miles of private beach are yours at this 2,000-acre island resort. Located within Palmetto Dunes, the Hyatt Regency Hilton Head is the largest oceanfront resort between Atlantic City and Palm Beach, and it offers practically every recreational amenity known.

You can play golf on five different eighteen-hole championship courses or tennis on one of twenty-five hard, grass, or clay courts, located in the Palmetto Dunes Tennis Center. The George Fazio course was rated as one of "America's 100 Best" by *Golf Digest*, and the resort's tennis center as one of the top fifty in the country by *Tennis* magazine. You can work out in the glass pyramid that houses the Hyattspa. You can swim in a twenty-five-meter lap pool on the beach, go water skiing and windsurfing, or take a canoe around the lagoons that stretch for miles and miles. Shelter Cove Harbour, the largest marina on the island, offers 200 slips and can accommodate boats up to 140 feet long. Or you can explore the 12-mile-long barrier island on horseback or by bicycle. Hilton Head Island, which teems with wildlife, has four nature preserves and rookeries.

All the luxurious rooms come with a private balcony overlooking the Atlantic or the Palmetto Dunes resort. Guests have the option of the Regency Club level offering concierge service for a nominal fee. Rooms are furnished in contemporary furniture and soft contemporary colors. The suites feature a living room, bedroom(s), dining area, and luxurious baths. (Luxurious villas and single-family vacation homes may be rented through Palmetto Dunes Resort. For those who want a more permanent hold, real estate is always available.) With more than 30,000 square feet of meeting space, the Hyatt Regency can accommodate large groups.

Guests have several dining options — Possum Point, a casual poolside eatery, which doubles as J. J. Pepperonio's at night; Point Comfort, an oceanfront snack bar; the Café, which offers three meals a day; and Hemingway's, which serves fresh seafood in a Key West atmosphere. Live entertainment is offered nightly in Hemingway's Lounge and Club Indigo. The Hyatt Regency's public areas exude contemporary elegance and serve as a showcase for its art collection.

The Westin Resort, Hilton Head Island

Two Grasslawn Avenue
Hilton Head Island, SC 29928
803-681-4000, 800-WESTIN-1
Telex: 62893418
Fax: 803-681-1087

> An island resort
> reminiscent of Hawaii

General Manager: Ken Pilgrim. **Accommodations:** 372 rooms and 30 suites (all with private baths). **Rates:** $135-$355. Additional: $6 daily fee for morning coffee, use of health club, shuttle service, and telephone service; children's program available seasonally and during holidays at an additional cost. **Payment:** Major credit cards. **Children:** 18 and under free with parents; Camp Wackatoo program for ages 4–12, Memorial Day–Labor Day. **Pets:** Not allowed. **Smoking:** Smoking and nonsmoking rooms. **Open:** Year-round.

➤ **The resort is located within Port Royal Plantation, where the largest amphibious landing was made prior to World War II. Approximately 13,000 federal troops stormed the island in 1861, crushing the 2,000 Confederates.**

Except for the absence of mountains, you might think you're in Hawaii when you stay at the Westin Resort, Hilton Head Island. The sounds of Gullah (a combination of English and African that is spoken by islanders), Civil War history, and Low Country cuisine are a dead giveaway, however, that this is an Atlantic paradise.

Every comfort and facet of southern hospitality has been considered at this highly rated resort — marble Jacuzzis, built-in hair dryers, terrycloth robes, and twice-a-day maid service.

The 24-acre oceanfront resort offers a smorgasbord of recreational activities, including many that are geared to children and families, such as Camp Wackatoo, and a golf program where children play free. Guests may choose from 54 holes of award-winning golf, 16 tennis courts (with Grand Slam playing surfaces), 3 swimming pools, a croquet lawn, a health club, and miles and miles of broad Atlantic beaches. They also have access to boat rentals, riding stables, and nature and bicycle paths. Guests enjoy Daufuskie Island Seafaris, dolphin watches, sunset sails, and other special activities.

The Westin is configured in two long wings that join in a V-shape, with outdoor pools and gardens in the center. A variety of room arrangements is available to guests, but mini-refrigerators, wall safes, and marble and mirrored bathrooms are common to all rooms. The suites offer just a little bit more. Guests in a Carolina Suite get a double balcony with an island or ocean view; VIP Suites feature a large living room; Director Suites, a Jacuzzi and sauna. The ultimate is the Port Royal Suite with a gazebo deck overlooking the ocean. The Royal Beach Club level offers extras such as a private lounge, daily Continental breakfast, cocktails and hors d'oeuvres, concierge and valet service. Guests may also choose to stay in private two- and three-bedroom villas.

Since the hotel was designed to be a meeting center, the public rooms are spacious and beautifully decorated with Oriental rugs and artwork. The hotel has a separate conference wing with 16 meeting rooms.

Dining is as important at the Westin as the rooms and recreational options. Guests celebrate special occasions at the Barony, which offers classic cuisine with Low Country touches; families delight in Sunday brunches and nightly seafood buffet extravaganzas in the Carolina Café. The Gazebo Lounge is the setting for afternoon teas and cocktail hours during the cooler months, while the Playful Pelican and Pelican Poolside offer light fare and beverages when the weather is mild.

Kiawah Island

Kiawah Island Resort

Mailing address:
12 Kiawah Beach Drive
Charleston, SC 29455-2357
803-768-2121, 800-654-2924
Fax: 803-768-9339

> A resort island with lots of
> recreational choices

Managing Director: Preni Duadas. **Accommodations:** 150 rooms and 450 villas (1–5 bedrooms). **Rates:** Inn rooms: $115–$180 March; $150–$230 April–October; $115–$180 November. Villas: $120–$330 daily, $581–$1,631 weekly, March; $160–$455 daily, $777–$2,352 weekly, April–October; $120–$330 daily, $581–$1,631 weekly, November. **Payment:** Major credit cards. **Children:** Welcome (children's program and babysitting services available). **Pets:** Not allowed. **Smoking:** Allowed in designated rooms. **Open:** Year-round.

➤ **Ten miles long, one and a half miles wide, and covering 10,000 acres, Kiawah Island is one of the premier vacation spots in the Palmetto State. In 1993 it was named one of America's 30 Favorite Family Resorts by** *Better Homes and Gardens.*

Pronounced "kee-a-wah," the barrier island off the coast of South Carolina originally belonged to the Kiawah Indians and was occupied by the British during the Revolutionary War. It has changed hands only a few times during the past centuries, however — from the Lords Proprietors to the Raynors, then to the Vanderhorsts and the Royals before being developed as a resort in the mid-1970s.

Shrimping, oystering, crabbing, and shopping for sweetgrass baskets are but a few of the activities you can enjoy on the island. Of course, golf and tennis are big around here, with four golf courses and twenty-eight tennis courts to choose from. Ocean Course was the site of the Ryder Cup Matches in 1991 and the World Cup in 1997.

The island resort is really two separate villages. West Beach includes the inn, villas, tennis club, Gary Player's Cougar Point Golf Course, and the straw market. East Beach is made up of villas, Jack Nicklaus's Turtle Point, Tom Fazio's Osprey Point, and Peter Dye's Ocean Course, plus tennis facilities, a recreation and pool complex, conference center, shops, and Indigo House Restaurant. Everything is within walking or biking distance, and cars are discouraged.

Rooms and villas are designed with the vacationer in mind — they are light and spacious and reflect island life in their decor. Each room has a private balcony overlooking the ocean, dunes, or forest. The inn has four separate lodges, with the Jasmine Porch Restaurant and the Topsider Lounge centrally located within. The privately owned villas are completely furnished and come with fully equipped kitchens, washers and dryers, a living/dining area, and one to four bedrooms.

McClellanville

Laurel Hill Plantation Bed & Breakfast Inn

8913 Highway 17 North
McClellanville, SC 29458
803-887-3708, 888-887-3708

> An authentic reconstruction of a plantation home where you can kick off your shoes

Innkeepers: Dr. Lee and Jackie Morrison. **Accommodations:** 4 rooms (all with private baths). **Rates:** $85–$95. **Included:** Full breakfast, afternoon beverages. **Payment:** American Express, MasterCard, Visa. **Children:** Check with innkeepers. **Pets:** Not allowed. **Smoking:** Allowed on porches only. **Open:** Year-round.

➤ **The Morrisons scoured the country for two years while furnishing the house. One of their finds was the door to Lee's room at the Citadel in Charleston, now incorporated into the house.**

Completely destroyed by Hurricane Hugo on September 21, 1989, this plantation home was rebuilt on Cape Romain, incorporating bits and pieces of the original house that were salvaged after the storm. Anyone who looks through the photograph albums that record the devastation and the rebuilding are simply amazed that the owners would have the courage to rebuild in the exact same spot, much less the same area, after Hugo. But determination and persistence won out, and Dr. Lee and Jackie Morrison moved back into their new home, a replica of the original, in 1991.

The original house, listed on the National Register of Historic Places, had been built by the Legare family in the 1850s. It too was swept away in a storm, but another house was built away from the water by the second owner, Richard Tilla Morrison, Lee Morrison's great-great-grandfather and a founder of McClellanville. After the plantation, which at one time encompassed 26,000 acres, passed out of the family, it stood empty for many years before Lee and Jackie bought it. They moved it to the present site in 1983, not far from where the first building stood.

The Low Country plantation house is a two-story cottage with dormer windows and a wraparound porch that overlooks the marsh and the creek. It is filled with primitive antiques, as well as sweet-grass baskets made in the area, handmade pottery, and nostalgic memorabilia. Old quilts and vintage linens are used on the beds.

Jackie admits that she's not overly fond of cooking, but enjoys rustling up a good breakfast for guests and serving afternoon refreshments. Breakfast is guaranteed to "deliciously disregard calories, fat, and cholesterol and tantalize your taste buds."

Life at Laurel Hill is laid-back. Guests are free to do as they please — go fishing or crabbing, look for birds in the marshes, lie in the hammock with a good book, go boating, or browse for antiques in Jackie's shop. The Morrisons warn everyone to be on the lookout for fire ants, alligators, and snakes, as they thrive in the creeks and marshes. Other diversions can be found in McClellanville, Georgetown, and Charleston, the latter two destinations being about 25 miles away.

The inn was recently one of twenty-five recipients of the first annual America's Favorite Inn Awards by the editors and readers of *America's Favorite Inns, B&Bs, and Small Hotels.*

Moncks Corner

Rice Hope Plantation Inn

206 Rice Hope Drive
Moncks Corner, SC 29461
803-761-4832

An old rice plantation now hosts B&B guests

Innkeepers: Richard and Doris Kasprak. **Aooommodations:** 5 rooms (3 with private baths, 2 with shared bath). **Rates:** $60–$80. **Included:** Continental breakfast, Monday–Saturday; full breakfast, Sunday; afternoon beverages and snacks. **Payment:** American Express, MasterCard, Visa. **Children:** Welcome. **Pets:** Not allowed. **Smoking:** Allowed on porches only. **Open:** Year-round.

➤   **The Kaspraks are bringing up their children at Rice Hope, so they welcome guests with children and make them a part of the family.**

The tranquil setting of this bed-and-breakfast inn on the Cooper River is sure to slow your pace. There are gardens to enjoy, paths to explore, and terraces where you can sit and contemplate the beauty around you.

Early settlers discovered the scenic spot in the late 1700s. Colonel John Harleston, the first owner, gave the property (then a part of the Comingtee Plantation) to his daughter Sarah in 1790. Her husband, Dr. William Read, who was prominent in the Revolutionary War, cleared the land and built a home here in 1795. He also cultivated rice and established the gardens (a 200-year-old camellia from that era still thrives). By the mid-1800s, the estate had over 1,700 acres of timber and 370 acres of rice fields. The original house either burned or fell into ruin, and a second structure on the site suffered the same fate.

In the 1920s Senator Frelinghuysen of New Jersey built the sprawling 9,000-square-foot, 31-room mansion, with its cypress siding and slate roof, as a winter home and hunting lodge. It was a tour home for a while and then a boys' school. Rice Hope Inn went through a succession of owners before Gene and Sue Lanier bought it and turned it into a bed-and-breakfast inn. The Kaspraks purchased the property in 1992 and, after some redecorating, reopened the inn. (Doris devotes all of her time to the inn; Richard works as a stockbroker.) Guests are free to enjoy the public rooms, roam the grounds, go fishing, or have cookouts on the lawn. Bicycles may be rented for $5 a day.

The inn has five guest rooms, all furnished with antiques and reproductions, including rice beds. The Kaspraks serve a Continental breakfast of fruit, muffins, and coffee every day but Sunday, when everyone indulges in a full breakfast of eggs or waffles with all the trimmings. Afternoon refreshments, including snacks, are always available. Dinner, which features an appetizer, main course, and dessert, is available for $16–$20 per person; reservations should be made in advance. (The inn is fairly isolated, being about 10 miles from Moncks Corner.)

Myrtle Beach

Kingston Plantation

9800 Lake Drive
Myrtle Beach, SC 29572
803-449-0006, 800-333-3333
Fax: 803-497-1110

An oceanside resort offering a variety of accommodations

General Manager: Rich Knutson. **Accommodations:** 740 suites (all with private baths). **Rates:** Hotel: $209–$299. Oceanfront towers: $169–$359. Villas: $159–$359 (lower rates in off-season). **Payment:** Major credit cards. **Children:** Welcome. **Pets:** Not allowed. **Smoking:** Allowed. **Open:** Year-round.

➤ **The resort does not have its own golf course, but guests may play at most of the one hundred courses in the Grand Strand area. Several inclusive packages are available to guests.**

Definitely Myrtle Beach's premier resort, this 145-acre oceanfront all-suite resort includes the only Embassy Suites on the ocean, plus plantation condominiums and lakeside townhouses and villas that offer a home-like setting.

The one-level villas offer views of the lake, tennis courts, pool, and surrounding woods. The two-story townhomes feature sundecks, sunrooms, and enclosed courtyards. The lodges offer one and two bedrooms, while the exclusive condominium towers provide unobstructed views of the ocean. The oceanfront Embassy Suite Hotel has 255 spacious suites.

Guests enjoy a variety of amenities and services, including a concierge staff that will make reservations for theater shows and arrange tours to local area attractions. On-site dining is offered at Azalea's Oceanfront Cafe and the SPLASH! Beach Club, while nightlife can be found in Nightwatch, an oceanfront lounge. Guests of Embassy Suites are treated to a complimentary breakfast buffet and two drink coupons daily.

The Sport & Health Club is the center of recreational activities and programs. There are indoor and outdoor pools, nine lighted tennis courts, squash and racquetball courts, a fitness room, tanning booth, whirlpool, and sauna. A certified trainer can recommend an exercise program to suit each guest. A full-time golf director and staff can arrange tee times, lessons, and transportation to and from ninety of the finest golf courses in the area. (In 1996 and 1997, Kingston was designated a Golden Links Certified Course by *Corporate Meetings & Incentives Magazine* because of the resort's affiliation with these courses.)

Owned by Texas-based FelCor Suite Hotels and managed by Promos Hotel Corporation, Kingston Plantation is also known for its meeting and conference facilities. There are more than 50,000 square feet of meeting space. In early 1998, Kingston Plantation hosted the annual South Carolina Governor's Conference on Tourism & Travel.

Pawleys Island

Litchfield Plantation Country Inn

P.O. Box 290, King's River Road
Pawleys Island, SC 29585
803-237-9121, 800-869-1410

| An old plantation that's now a country inn noted in the 1997 *Zagat Survey* |

General Manager: Sally Gomex. **Accommodations:** 2 rooms and 2 suite in main inn (all with private baths) and 26 cottages (all with private baths and fully-equipped kitchens). **Rates:** $150–$195 for inn rooms, $115-$175 for cottages. **Included:** Continental breakfast, daily maid service, concierge, and resort amenities. **Payment:** Major credit cards. **Children:** Welcome in cottages. **Pets:** Not allowed. **Smoking:** Allowed in designated units. **Open:** Year-round.

➤ **Pawleys Island's most famous ghost is Alice Flagg. Her father wanted her to marry a rice planter, but she fell in love with a young man from New England who did not meet her family's approval. Her suitor pledged his undying love for her with the gift of a ring. Alice's brother later took the ring from her, and she died of a fever within a few days. Alice has been sighted many times looking for her lost ring on the island.**

Litchfield was a working rice plantation during the 1700s and 1800s, and its lands extended from the Waccamaw River to the Atlantic Ocean. It survives today as a luxurious country inn set amid a small, premier residential community.

"The moment you come into Litchfield Plantation from the ordinary world is as dramatic as Alice going through the looking glass. . . . You are enveloped in wonder. Here, there is nothing else," wrote the late James Dickey, long-time resident, poet laureate of South Carolina, and the author of *Deliverance*.

Guests have the option of staying in the restored Plantation House or the guest cottages. The house was built around 1750 when the rice crop made its owner rich and powerful. It is approached via the Avenue of Live Oaks extending for a quarter of a mile. The historic house has two guest rooms and two suites, all beautifully decorated to reflect the golden plantation era. Each room and suite has cable television and phones with voice mail. The largest room is the 1,200 square foot Ball Room Suite featuring a living room, bedroom, and bath with an oversize whirlpool tub. Located on the second story, it commands a wonderful view of the grounds and the Intracoastal Waterway. The Gun Room on the first floor has a full canopy bed, private entrance, and sitting room with an additional half bath. It is said that the ghost of Dr. Tucker, the old plantation doctor who used to visit all the surrounding plantations, causes a bell to ring alerting the gate attendant to open the gates following his return from a house call. (The bell is no longer there, however.) The old rice fields can be seen from the Blue Room and the Red Room.

The cottages are scattered throughout the 600-acre estate. Offering two and three bedrooms, they are ideal for families. Cottage guests are treated to the same amenities and services as Plantation House guests. A Continental breakfast of fresh fruit, juices, cereals, pastries, muffins, coffee, and tea is laid out in the kitchen area of each accommodation. The Carriage House Club featuring Low Country dishes and international cuisine is open to guests for dinner by reservation.

Litchfield Plantation offers a number of amenities not available in many country inns — use of the Beach Club House on Pawleys Island, tennis courts, heated swimming pool with cabana, and small marina. The concierge desk can arrange everything from golf tee times to fishing expeditions to theater tickets to live stage productions in Myrtle Beach. Litchfield Plantation is also ideal for small corporate retreats.

Tennessee

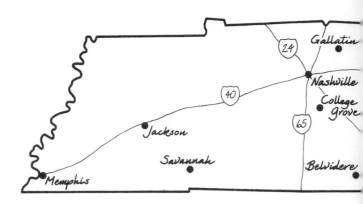

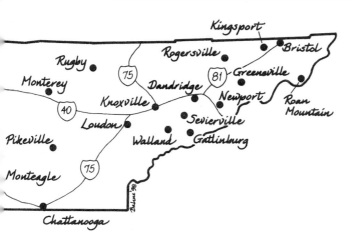

Best Bed-and-Breakfasts

Best City Stops

Best Country Inns

College Grove
Peacock Hill Country Inn, 521
Gatlinburg
The Buckhorn Inn, 526
Monteagle
Adams-Edgeworth Inn, 540
Monterey
The Garden Inn, 543
Newport
Christopher Place —An Intimate Resort, 548
Walland
The Inn at Blackberry Farm, 566

Best Farm and Guest Ranch

Dandridge
Mill Dale Farm, 523

Best Historic Inns

Gallatin
The Hancock House, 524
Rogersville
Hale Springs Inn, 554
Rugby
Newbury House at Historic Rugby, 558

Best Parks

Pikeville
Fall Creek Falls State Resort Park, 550
Roan Mountain
Roan Mountain State Resort Park, 553

Best Resort

Nashville
Opryland Hotel, 544

Best Romantic Getaways

Gatlinburg
Hippensteal's Mountain View Inn, 528
Sevierville
Blue Mountain Mist Country Inn — Shagonage, 562

Tennessee is so varied that it might be three states. In its western region, the flat rich flood plain bordering the Mississippi River lends itself to the cultivation of cotton, corn, and soybeans on large plantations. Here, too, the state's largest city, Memphis, with a population of 652,000 (one million in the metro area) overlooks the Great River from atop high bluffs.

Between the downward slopes of the Cumberland Plateau and the western prong of the Tennessee River, the state's heartland is a scenic region of bluegrass pastures and prosperous cities and towns offering a delightful welcome for visitors who enjoy musical entertainment, history, and lake-studded rolling countryside. This is also the site of Tennessee's capital and second largest city, Nashville, with a population of 462,500, (850,500 in the metro area). From the gently undulating Cumberlands to the heights of the Great Smokies, East Tennessee is a variety vacation area, laced with valleys, ridges, rivers, and lakes. Its two major cities are Chattanooga, with a population of 165,000, and Knoxville, population 174,000.

Throughout this 42,244-square-mile state, you can enjoy the great outdoors at every turn. The Great Smoky Mountains National Park, the United States' most visited, is shared by Tennessee and North Carolina. You can escape the crowds by hiking the park's trails, which range from moderate to challenging. You can also rent saddle horses, go fishing, enjoy camping, or shoot the rapids in the area's largest rivers. Tennessee's extensive state park system, with more than fifty units, is among the nation's best. It includes several resort parks with luxurious lodges. You can enjoy fishing, swimming, and water sports in the park lakes, as well as in the vast lake network of the Tennessee Valley Authority.

Because of its strategic location in the Lower Mississippi valley, Memphis emerged as a center for inland shipping, transportation, and cotton marketing and as a business, cultural, and social center for northern Mississippi, eastern Arkansas, and western Tennessee. After World War II the city hit its stride as an inland port for manufactured products, cotton spot marketing, furniture making, transportation, brewing, and the hospitality industry.

The city has many attractions of interest to visitors. On Mud Island the River Center features exhibits such as the Grand Salon of an 1870 steamboat, the River Walk for a miniaturized view of the Lower Valley, and World War II bomber *Memphis Belle.* The Great American Pyramid near the I-40 Hernando De Soto Bridge, inspired by the Great Pyramid of Cheops north of ancient Memphis, serves as a sports arena, music exhibition area, and display space for Egyptian lore. The *Memphis Queen* sternwheeler boat offers sightseeing excursions on the Mississippi River. Also downtown is the Beale Street Historic District with such highlights as B. B. King's Blues Club and A. Schwab's Dry Goods Store dating from 1876. The National Civil Rights Museum, on the site of the Lorraine Motel where Dr. Martin Luther King, Jr., was assassinated, traces the civil rights movement with powerful interactive exhibits, memoranda of famous leaders, and an interpretive educational center. Visitors enjoy the IMAX theater at the Memphis Pink Palace Museum. Hunt Phelan Home, considered by Smithsonian to be the "most exciting discovery in fifty years," is open for tours.

Elvis Presley's Graceland reputedly attracts more visitors than any other mansion in the United States except the White House. Tours include Elvis's den, formal living room and dining room, a collection of his many awards and trophies, and the Hall of Gold, devoted to his gold records. Also on view are Elvis's personal tour bus, private jet, valuable automobiles displayed in a separate museum, and the Meditation Garden where he lies buried with family members. Nashville, astride the Cumberland River in a broad bluegrass basin, has earned dual identity as the Athens of the South and the world's country music capital. In midtown Centennial Park stands the world's only full-scale reproduction of the fifth-century B.C. Athenian Parthenon. Inside is a 42-foot-tall replica of the ivory and gold statue of Athena Parthenon, goddess of wisdom and patron deity of the ancient Greek city-state.

The Nashville "sound" permeates the city. Yet if only one evening can be devoted to its pursuit, it should be at the Grand Ole Opry, which has been broadcast continuously on WSM radio since 1925. It provides an opportunity for up-and-coming singers and seasoned stars alike to perform. Shows are staged weekend evenings throughout the year, with summer matinees in the posh Grand Ole Opry House. Advance reservations are a must.

Adjacent Opryland USA, a 120-acre musical entertainment theme park, celebrated its twenty-fifth season in 1996. Here visitors have a choice among a dozen or so live shows, restaurants, specialty shops, craft demonstrations, and sidewalk artists. A variety of tummy-tingling thrill rides includes such breath-takers as the Old Mill Scream, the double loops of Wabash Cannonball, a twisting, turning Screamin' Delta Demon, and Chaos, the world's first laser-video-audio roller coaster, which manages to attack all the senses. Opryland's musical showboat, the *General Jackson*, cruises the Cumberland River during daytime and evening. Onboard dining ranges from southern-style breakfasts and luncheon buffets to a special evening cruise with a three-course prime rib dinner and a sprightly musical show in the Victorian Theatre.

Nashville's Country Music Hall of Fame and Museum has exhibits of stars, past and present, along with a replica of RCA's renowned Studio B, where many luminaries recorded some all-time favorites. Country music fans can also tour the 1891 Ryman Auditorium, former home of the Grand Ole Opry; it contains original backstage props and dressing rooms. Recently renovated, the historic music hall is hosting concerts again. Several new attractions — including the Hard Rock Cafe, Planet Hollywood, and The Wild Horse Saloon — have been built in the Second Avenue district.

A dozen miles east of Nashville is the Hermitage, Tennessee's premier historic attraction, the eloquently restored home of the nation's seventh president, Andrew Jackson. Its Andrew Jackson Center commemorates Old Hickory's life and times. Tennessee's 1859 state Capitol stands on a hill in the center of downtown. Just a few blocks away, on the banks of the Cumberland River, a blockade and stockade replica of Fort Nashborough commemorates the founding of the city on Christmas Day 1779.

West of Nashville, the Natchez Trace Parkway begins at Highway 100. Developed by the National Park Service, it commemorates the early nineteenth-century pathway that extended 500 miles through Tennessee, Alabama, and Mississippi to Natchez, linking the lower Mississippi River valley with the rest of the country. At the Meriwether Lewis Site, the explorer, famed for his role in the Lewis and Clark expedition, lies buried.

Jack Daniel founded his distillery in 1866 at Cave Spring, noted for its pure limestone water, in the small town of Lynchburg. As the oldest registered distillery in the United States it is on the National Register of Historic Places. Free guided walking tours show

visitors the various stages of the art of sour mash whiskey manufacturing, including the charcoal-mellowing process for which Jack
Daniel's is internationally esteemed.

In Lynchburg visitors can stroll around the square, which is
dominated by the 1884 Moore County Courthouse. Afterward,
drop in at the Lynchburg Hardware and General Store, where the
motto is "All goods worth price charged." In nearby Shelbyville in
late August and early September, equestrians from all over the
world gather for the Tennessee Walking Horse National Celebration.

Chattanooga and Knoxville, eastern Tennessee's major cities, lie
astride the Tennessee River and derive much sustenance from their
favorable locations. Chattanooga is among the state's most storied
cities. Here a contingent of the Cherokee Indian Nation began a
journey along the tragic Trail of Tears in 1838; later, crucial battles
of the Civil War were fought near the city. After the war, Chattanooga came into its own as a leading railroad, shipping, commercial, and industrial center. Given a big boost by the Tennessee Valley Authority and an international image engendered by the
popular "Chattanooga Choo Choo" song, the city has been unusu-
ally attractive for visitors. It offers an extraordinary range of things
to see and do in a beautiful region of mountains and lakes.

The Chattanooga Choo Choo Terminal and Station helps bring
alive earlier times. The focal point is the 1905-vintage Southern
Railroad Terminal, noted for its fine architectural details and central dome. Here are restaurants, shops, and a model railroad exhibit. A car and engine from the original Chattanooga Choo Choo,
which began service in 1880, are on display. Also at the complex,
the 360-unit Chattanooga Choo Choo—Holiday Inn has several
Pullman car accommodations for those who enjoy overnighting in
Victorian-style luxury.

Lookout Mountain Incline Railway, among the world's steepest,
leads to the vicinity of Point Park, overlooking the city and the
Mocassin Bend of the Tennessee River. Chickamauga and Chattanooga National Military Park, located in both Tennessee and Georgia, is the nation's oldest and largest Civil War commemorative
battle site. Also on Lookout Mountain are Rock City Gardens,
Ruby Falls, and posh neighborhoods. With ambitious plans to turn
a sprightly new face to the river, Chattanooga is literally trans-
forming much of its downtown core. Warehouse Row, a multi-use
complex, contains a designer outlet mall and office space. At Ross'
Landing, where the city was established as a trading post in 1815,
the $45 million Tennessee Aquarium traces the Tennessee River
system from a mountain stream to the Gulf of Mexico. A recent

addition is the creative Discovery Museum for children. Visitors can also board the *Southern Belle* for riverboat excursions. Two miles of concrete walking and hiking trails, woodlands recreation areas, and a fishing center with piers have been completed on the planned twenty-mile Tennessee River Park and the Market Street Bridge is now a pedestrian walkway across the Tennessee River. A new area attraction is the Bessie Smith Performance Hall.

Although Knoxville is the oldest major city in Tennessee, its ideas and attitudes are refreshingly upbeat and forward-looking. Home of the University of Tennessee (where football fever runs rampant during the fall), it has been the recipient of vital intellectual and cultural influences. During the Great Depression, Knoxville was chosen as the headquarters for the vast Tennessee Valley Authority, which now supervises fifty dams and about forty thousand employees. Then, in 1982, the upstart little regional city hosted a World's Fair. Though the event received few kudos, some innovative adaptive-use projects have developed at the site, now a park. The Convention and Visitors Bureau has offices in the base of the Sunsphere, the towering symbol of the fair. In the spring of 1990, the splendid Knoxville Museum of Art opened. It has a 4,400-square-foot Great Hall overlooking World's Fair Park. The handsome structure, faced in Tennessee pink marble, was designed by the museum architectural firm of Edward Larrabee Barnes and Associates in New York.

Knoxville's past comes to life at the Governor William Blount Mansion. Built in 1792, it was the first wooden frame home west of the Alleghenies. While territorial governor, Blount named the small fortress settlement after his friend Major Henry Knox, secretary of war in President George Washington's cabinet. Many of the negotiations leading to Tennessee's admission to statehood in 1796 took place in Blount's office at the home, sometimes called the "birthplace of Tennessee." The Knoxville Zoological Gardens are especially noted for a rare red panda on view only in summer and one of the nation's largest big cat collections, including the white tiger. New to the zoo is a gorilla habitat. Tennessee River cruises aboard the *Robert E. Lee* include one-hour daily excursions along with dinner, Sunday brunch, and special entertainment programs.

Jonesborough, Tennessee's oldest town, showcases vivid remnants of its passage through time. Architectural styles range from the two-story hewn log Christopher Taylor house to lavish wooden Victorian fretwork on the porch of the Chester Inn and the Neoclassical lines of the imposing Washington County Courthouse. Shops in the vintage buildings on Main Street border brick sidewalks where an impetuous young lawyer named Andrew Jackson once walked.

During the first weekend in October, Jonesborough attracts thousands of visitors to its National Storytelling Festival, which originated here in 1973. Participants now come from across the United States and abroad to participate in this event, which has been largely responsible for reviving the telling of tall tales, Jack tales, folkloric myths, and legends from around the world. Now under construction is a new $3 million National Storytelling Center. The History Museum at the contemporary Jonesborough Visitors Center displays many pioneer artifacts from days of early settlement; exhibits about the spirited but short-lived late-18th-century Lost State of Franklin; and copies of *The Emancipator*, the nation's first abolitionist periodical, which started here in 1832.

Founded in 1783, Greeneville was named in honor of Revolutionary War patriot hero General Nathanael Greene. Greeneville's most significant resident was Andrew Johnson, seventeenth president of the United States. Born in North Carolina and trained as a tailor, he and members of his family crossed the southern Appalachian Mountains in a two-wheel ox cart. He opened a modest shop in Greeneville and married a local schoolteacher, who taught him writing and mathematics. Subsequently entering state politics, he became governor and U.S. senator, representing a Civil War–era district predominantly antislavery and pro-Republican. Appointed Lincoln's vice president in 1864, he succeeded to the presidency after the Great Emancipator's assassination.

At the Andrew Johnson National Historic Site, the visitor center museum displays his original tailor shop and notes he took during his impeachment trial. His homestead, where he lived from 1852 to 1875, was acquired by the National Park Service with virtually all family furnishings and accessories intact. His grave site on a high hill is marked by a monument in honor of his democratic ideals and concerns for everyday people.

Not too many decades ago only a handful of venturesome vacationers found their way to Gatlinburg, an obscure village beside the Little Pigeon River in the deep shadow of Mount Le Conte. Today, though, to Gatlinburg and neighboring Pigeon Forge about five miles away, visitors come in ever-increasing numbers to savor the singular delights of cool green mountains, native crafts, and delectable foods reminiscent of yesteryear. Both towns boast a wide array of accommodations, restaurants, and shops.

Popular family attractions in Gatlinburg include Christus Gardens, where full-scale dioramas depict the life of Christ, the American Historical Wax Museum, Sky Lift to Crockett Mountain, and Aerial Tramway to Ober Gatlinburg amusement park and ski resort. In Pigeon Forge, families find enjoyment at the 1830-era Old Mill, where authentic stone-ground cornmeal can be purchased, and in Dollywood theme park, handiwork of country music super-star Dolly Parton, where musical shows, thrill rides, crafts demon-strations, and restaurants keep everyone happily entertained. Both Gatlinburg and Pigeon Forge have trolley systems to help visitors get around.

In Gatlinburg, one of the South's major handicraft centers, spe-cialty shops stock unique arts and crafts, one-of-a-kind creations that may well become tomorrow's treasured family heirlooms. Visitors can also follow a scenic eight-mile drive to see shops and studios in the Great Smoky Mountains Arts and Crafts Commu-nity. Skilled artisans produce splendid items ranging from hand-tied brooms, wood carvings, and fabrics colored with natural dyes to ceramics, sturdy home furnishings, corncob dolls, and musical instruments.

A journey into the Great Smoky Mountains National Park from Gatlinburg begins at Sugarlands Visitor Center two miles south of town. Audiovisual programs, exhibits, bro-chures, films, and park rangers provided detailed information about this most-visited na-tional park. Newfound Gap Road (U.S. 441), a scenic 40-mile highway, is the major visitor route through the park, linking Gat-linburg and Cherokee, North Carolina. At Newfound Gap, the bor-der of the two states, the road bisects the Appalachian Trail at an elevation of 5,048 feet. A seven-mile paved spur road leads to 6,643-foot Clingmans Dome, where a lookout tower provides views in all directions. More than 900 miles of trails lead through the park. Hiking options range from easy strolls to vigorous back-packing. Hordes of wildflowers come to peak bloom in the spring, and autumn brings forth vivid panoramas of red and russet, yellow and gold foliage.

Off Laurel Creek Road, about twenty miles west of Sugarlands Visitor Center, you can drive along a loop through Cades Cove, an idyllic mountain-girded valley of farms and pastures, pioneer houses, barns, churches, and wildlife. Fox, deer, wild turkey, and black bear often wander through the valley, still arcane in the midst of creeping civilization.

For more information, contact the Tennessee Department of Tourist Information, 320 6th Avenue North, 5th floor, Nashville, Tennessee 37243, 615-741-2158, 800-836-6200.

Belvidere

Falls Mill Bed and Breakfast Log Cabin

134 Falls Mill Road
Belvidere, TN 37306
615-469-7161

> **A log cabin at which you can escape to a simple time**

Innkeepers: John and Janie Lovett. **Accommodations:** One cabin (with a private bath). **Rates:** $65, plus $5 for each additional person. **Included:** Continental breakfast, tour of mill and grounds. **Payment:** MasterCard, Visa. **Children:** Welcome. **Pets:** Not allowed. **Smoking:** Allowed on porches. **Open:** Year-round except Wednesdays and major holidays.

➤ **No visit to Falls Mill is complete without a stop at the old country store, housed on the second floor of the mill. Here you may purchase mill products, books, and souvenirs. Children enjoy feeding the fish, ducks, and peacocks by the mill.**

This is one place where you can leave the hustle and bustle behind, where you have to shift to slow motion. That's exactly what John and Janie Lovett want to happen. They have worked tirelessly to re-create this living museum, documenting the authenticity and history of every building and piece of equipment associated with the land. The site includes an operating grist and flour mill, a country store, power and industry museum, and bed-and-breakfast inn. Currently under way is the reconstruction of the 1836 Rocky Springs Stagecoach Inn, which will provide more guest rooms and space for a small restaurant, and also will allow the Lovetts to host workshops in crafts such as weaving and blacksmithing.

Falls Mill and Country Store and the Museum of Power and Industry, one of the area's most popular attractions, draw more than 20,000 visitors a year. The Lovetts acquired Falls Mill in 1984 after negotiating for three and a half years; they operate the site from sales, admission fees, and donations. John, an engineer with a Ph.D. in industrial engineering, has always had a fascination for early technology; Jane, with a bachelor's degree in sociology and anthropology, has worked as a travel consultant for several years. They decided to establish the Museum of Power and Industry while living in Chattanooga.

The mill, which dates to 1873, has been used to process cotton and wool, as a cotton gin, as a woodworking shop, and as a grist and flour mill. As early as 1815 this site, located in Franklin County west of Chattanooga on the Alabama border, was designated for milling because of its stream and natural waterfall. The Lovetts are developing exhibits that will chronicle the interesting history of milling at Falls Mill. Much of the equipment in the museum, which includes a wool picker from the Civil War era and a large collection of nineteenth-century textile machinery from a woolen mill in Kentucky, has been donated.

The Lovetts' bed-and-breakfast inn has been in operation since 1989. The cabin was moved to the site from a mountain near Huntland, Tennessee. It features hand-hewn, dovetail-notched logs, a working fireplace, balcony and front porch, and tin roof. The kitchen is fully stocked with everything you need for a Continental breakfast — homemade breads and pastries, fresh fruit, cereal, juices, tea, and coffee.

There is no restaurant at the B&B, but the Lovetts provide a list of some that are within a twenty- to thirty-minute drive of the mill.

Bristol

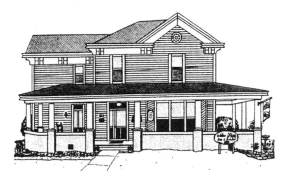

New Hope Bed & Breakfast

822 Georgia Avenue
Bristol, Tennessee 37620
423-989-3343, 888-989-3343

> A Victorian home
> away from home

Innkeepers: Tom and Tonda Fluke. **Accommodations:** 4 rooms (all with private baths). **Rates:** $75–$105. **Included:** Full breakfast, fruit, desserts, beverages, bathrobes, use of bicycles. **Payment:** MasterCard, Visa. **Children:** Welcome. **Pets:** Not allowed. **Smoking:** Allowed on porch. **Open:** Year-round.

➤ **In the hallway at the top of the stairs, there's a mini-country music museum featuring photographs and newspaper stories of Tennessee Ernie Ford and the Carter family.**

Guests feel as if they've stepped back into their grandmother's home when they enter the doors of New Hope Bed & Breakfast, a turn-of-the-century Victorian home.

Hosts Tom and Tonda Fluke learned to appreciate B&Bs and antiques while living in England and decided to open their own inn when he retired from the Air Force. They found the perfect house for their new business venture in Bristol, creating four bedrooms and baths and private living quarters for themselves. The house's first owners were M.D. and Eudora Andes, who purchased it in 1891 from developer Abram D. Reynolds, reputed to have been the youngest major in the Confederate Army and the brother of R. J. Reynolds, who started the famous tobacco company. Tonda, an interior decorator, used dark colors and Victorian furnishings in her decorating scheme, including clawfoot bathtubs and pedestal sinks in each of the private bathrooms. (Future plans call for the garage to be converted into a recreation room.)

Rooms in the inn are named for previous owners. The Andes Room on the first floor features oak furnishings and a fireplace with gas logs. Upstairs are the Reynolds Room, a favorite with honeymooners; the Allen Room, furnished in wicker; and the Arnold Room, a cozy, comfortable retreat. Bathrobes and bath amenities are provided for guests.

Guests are free to use all the public areas of the house and the grounds, with refreshments and board games provided. The wrap-around verandah, with its swing and dining tables, is very popular, as are the complimentary bicycles. The Flukes serve a full breakfast of casseroles, breads, fruits, and beverages in the formal dining room, on the verandah, or, by special request, in the guest rooms.

Chattanooga

Adams Hilborne

801 Vine Street
Chattanooga, TN 37403
423-265-5000
Fax: 423-265-5555

| A small European-style hotel that exemplifies opulence |

Innkeepers: David and Wendy Adams. **Accommodations:** 6 rooms and 4 suites (all with private baths, one accessible to the disabled). **Rates:** $100–$275 (corporate and off-season rates available). **Included:** European Continental breakfast, complimentary parking. **Payment:** American Express, MasterCard,

Visa. **Children:** Check with innkeepers. **Pets:** Kennels located nearby. **Smoking:** Allowed on porches. **Open:** Year-round.

➤ **Wendy Adams, a professional chef, studied at the Culinary Institute of America. She has been featured on *Inn Country USA*.**

While staying at this luxurious small hotel, you might forget that you're really in Chattanooga, not a European city. Offering ten rooms, small meeting and reception rooms and areas, a grand ballroom, and upscale dining, the Adams Hilborne is an exciting new addition to Chattanooga. Leisure and business travelers alike will not be disappointed, as it's a perfect setting for every occasion — from romantic getaways to corporate meetings.

Built for the Mayor Edmond G. Watkins in the Fort Wood District in 1889, the castle-like Victorian Romanesque stone mansion has been used as a private residence, offices, apartments, and a funeral home, and in 1995 was the Designer's Show House. Among its outstanding features are sixteen-foot coffered ceilings, original cherry paneling and curved staircase, hand-carved moldings, and Tiffany windows.

Using photographs and descriptions of a "Twin House" built in New Orleans the same year, owners David and Wendy Adams (who also run the Adams-Edgeworth Inn in Monteagle) tried to make their renovation as authentic as possible while adding all the modern conveniences. They also gave it their own personal touches, naming the rooms for family members and using furnishings that have a story or meaning. A desk that Wendy's father, Benjamin Hilborne Oehlert, used while serving as ambassador to Pakistan under President Johnson, is located in the foyer, and her mother's bridge table and chairs have a place in the music room

The house is filled with fine antiques, original artwork, and expensive fabrics and bedding. Approximately 175 yards of fabric were used in decorating the Honeymoon Suite, which also features a 300-gallon soaking tub. With windows on three sides, the Anniversary Suite, decorated in a Ralph Lauren blue-and-white print, offers the best views of the surrounding mountains. The Lookout Suite has a private balcony that overlooks Lookout Mountain and is decorated in an outdoor theme. The Presidential Suite is the epitome of elegance, with its leather card tables and chairs, floor-to-ceiling mirrors, and 600-gallon marble soaking tub for two.

A Continental breakfast is included in the tariff, and in the evening Chef Lee Towery serves a five-course, prix fixe dinner, plus a Sunday brunch. (Dinners run $37.50 each; brunch is $19.50.) Two choices are usually offered with each course. For example, evening entrees might be seared marinated Florida swordfish with lobster-papaya quesadilla, avocado salsa, and lime garlic butter or herb-crusted lamb chops with tabouleh, sauteed vegetables, and red wine mint sauce.

The Chattanooga Choo Choo — Holiday Inn

1400 Market Street
Chattanooga, TN 37402
423-266-5000, 800-TRACK 29
Fax: 423-265-4635
http:www.choochoo.com

> A hotel with a railroad theme offers unique lodgings

General Manager: Bob Doak. **Accommodations:** 305 rooms and suites, 45 rail cars (all with private baths). **Rates:** $85–$105. **Payment:** Major credit cards. **Children:** Welcome. **Pets:** Not allowed. **Smoking:** Smoking and nonsmoking rooms. **Open:** Year-round.

➤ **The actual Chattanooga Choo Choo ran from Cincinnati to Chattanooga, and the engine that began the service in 1880 is displayed on the grounds.**

The cars don't go anywhere, but your slumber can be like a journey in this one-of-a-kind hotel — a complex of passenger coach cars turned guest rooms, restaurants, and a train station (now used as a lobby). And if the name has a ring to it, there's a reason: it was made famous by Glenn Miller's hit song "Chattanooga Choo Choo" in the 1940s.

The parlor cars are permanently parked in the arrival/departure area of the station, which has been beautifully landscaped with blooming flowers and shrubs. Deep, rich burgundies and golds, reminiscent of the Victorian era, are used in the railcar rooms, furnished with traditional reproductions. You don't have to sleep in a rail car, however; more rooms are located in other buildings that were added to the complex when it was restored in 1973. There is a large convention hall for meetings and conventions.

The original station has an interesting history. The plans, drawn by Don Barber of New York City, won the Beaux Arts Design Prize in Paris in 1900. Nine years later it was built in Chattanooga, after Barber made some modifications, adapting architectural features from the National Park Bank of New York City. The building's distinguishing feature is its massive dome, covering an area of 68 by 82 feet. Today the grand hall is used as the central reception area, offices, small meeting rooms, and the Gardens Restaurant, which has a Tivoli atmosphere. Other dining facilities on the property include Dinner in the Diner, a formal dining experience in a posh dining car; the Station House featuring singing waiters and waitresses; and the Silver Diner, an informal eatery offering pizzas and subs. Guests also enjoy the Choo Choo Espresso, featuring gourmet coffees, pastries, desserts, and sandwiches.

In addition to one indoor and two outdoor swimming pools, the Chattanooga Choo Choo has some diversions you won't find anywhere else. You can ride on the authentic New Orleans trolley around the complex or take a trip to the Tennessee Valley Railroad Museum on the Downtown Arrow (trains run seasonally). You can also visit the world's largest HO-gauge model railroad on site or shop for train memorabilia, pottery, glassware, and souvenirs in the retail shops. Or hope aboard the city's free shuttle and go to the unforgettable Tennessee Aquarium and other points of interest in downtown Chattanooga.

Radisson Read House Hotel and Suites

M. L. King Blvd. and Broad St.
Chattanooga, TN 37402
423-266-4121, 800-333-3333
Fax: 423-267-6447

| A restored city hotel where tradition still thrives |

General Manager: Steve Coe. **Accommodations:** 102 rooms and 135 suites (all with private baths). **Rates:** $59–$118, plus $6 a day for valet parking. **Payment:** Major credit cards. **Children:** Welcome. **Pets:** Not allowed. **Smoking:** Smoking and nonsmoking rooms. **Open:** Year-round.

➤ **A hotel has been located downtown since 1847 — first the Crutchfield House, which burned in 1867, and then the Read House, built in 1872. Through the years it has welcomed such dignitaries as Winston Churchill, Charles Laughton, Tallulah Bankhead, Gary Cooper, and Al Capone.**

Cinderella could certainly meet her Prince Charming here, and if she left her slipper behind, it would blend into the room. The setting for Chattanooga's most important socials for years, the Radisson Read House's Silver Ballroom has to be the most ornate ballroom within hundreds of miles. Its off-white walls are adorned with decorative silver scrollwork, which is complemented by Waterford silver and crystal chandeliers.

Certainly, the ballroom is grand and elegant, but other public rooms are also charming. The lobby is paneled in rich quarter-sawed black walnut and adorned with decorative gilded woodwork and the family crests of the Reads and Crutchfields, associated with the hotel in its early days.

The Green Room is the setting for elegant dining, and Madelyne's Tavern offers casual dining in an contemporary setting that brings the street action into full view. Furnishings in the enlarged guest rooms are by Drexel Heritage. The hotel is listed on the National Register of Historic Places and is a member of Historic Hotels of America.

College Grove

Peacock Hill Country Inn

6994 Giles Hill Road
College Grove, TN 37046
615-368-7727,
800-327-6663 (reservations only)
http://www.bbonline.com/tn/peacock/

| A luxurious country inn |

Innkeepers: Walter and Anita Ogilvie. **Accommodations:** 10 rooms and suites (all with private baths). **Rates:** $110–$225. **Included:** Full or Continental breakfast, snacks, refreshments, turndown service. **Payment:** Major credit cards. **Children:** Welcome in cabin. **Pets:** Free boarding in barn; horses welcome. **Smoking:** Not allowed. **Open:** Year-round.

➤ **Peacock Hill is close to a number of area attractions, including Historic Franklin, the Henry Horton State Resort Park, Opryland, and the Grand Ole Opry. Many guests attend the annual Tennessee Walking Horse National Celebration in nearby Shelbyville.**

Get ready for a real farm experience when you come to this country inn, located in Middle Tennessee near Nashville and all its attractions. "Farm One" is a 640-acre working cattle and horse farm, with a winding creek and miles of trails for walking, hiking, and horseback riding. Don't be surprised if you see one of the owner's 35 peacocks strutting around the farm. You can even bring your horse along, because Peacock Hill offers overnight boarding. At night you can sit on the porch and listen to the cows and the cicadas.

Guests are housed in a pre–Civil War farmhouse which includes five guest rooms in a new wing that was added on during the restoration, each with a whirlpool bath and shower, or in the reconstructed two-story Log Cabin Suite, a favorite with honeymooners. The Grainery Suite, available for extended visits, features a Cottage Toile bedroom with a fireplace, European limestone bath with a double whirlpool tub and shower, and a fully-equipped kitchen. The McColl House, which opened in late 1997, offers three luxury suites.

The rooms, named for the children of the owners, Walter and Anita Ogilvie, are quite a cut above what you'd normally expect in a farmhouse, with handsome quilts and coverlets, comfortable beds, an eye-pleasing decor, and all the amenities found in the most luxurious hotels — ice buckets, fluffy towels, signature soaps, fresh flowers, and piped-in music that can be controlled with a button. A limited number of TV/VCRs are available for use in the rooms, along with videotapes, and the log cabin has its own TV/VCR and coffeemaker.

The public rooms, featuring exposed cedar beams and sandstone fireplaces, are also inviting. Guests often gather around the open fire in the den, living room, or dining room. On cloudy days the bright sun room is popular.

Guests have the option of a full or Continental breakfast, served in the dining room. The inn's specialty is "Lob Scouse," a dish of scrambled eggs with bacon and vegetables. It is usually served with freshly squeezed orange juice and Sandra's fluffy biscuits. Innkeeper Sandra Glenn or the Ogilvies will recommend local restaurants or prepare, with advance reservation, a fireside supper.

Coming home to Tennessee was a dream come true for the Ogilvies after they took early retirement. While living in other parts of the country, they bought several adjoining parcels of land until they had assembled what is now the farm.

"Wherever we lived over the years, we always called Tennessee home," says Anita. "When we started to renovate the old homeplace that came with the property, we wanted to do something of merit with the house . . . opening a country inn seemed like the best thing we could do with the property."

Dandridge

Mill Dale Farm

140 Mill Dale Road
Dandridge, TN 37725
423-397-3470, 800-767-3471

A B&B on an old farm welcomes guests

Innkeeper: Lucy C. Franklin. **Accommodations:** 3 rooms (all with private baths). **Rates:** $70. **Included:** Full country breakfast. **Payment:** Cash and checks. **Children:** Under 12 free with parents. **Pets:** Not allowed. **Smoking:** Allowed in designated areas. **Open:** Year-round.

➤ **In addition to eating, sleeping, and walking, the most popular pastime is sitting on the porch and listening to the rippling creeks. If one does yearn for more action, a swimming pool and three golf courses are nearby.**

Lucy Franklin and her late husband responded to the call to open their home to guests during the Knoxville World's Fair in 1982. They enjoyed it so much they decided to do it permanently about five years later. Entertaining was not a new experience to them; they had hosted numerous family get-togethers in the rural Dumplin' Valley community where their family has lived for generations. A Franklin family reunion may draw as many as 130 aunts, uncles, and cousins.

The farm originally contained about 300 acres, but with the sale of some acreage it is down to less than 50 acres. It is designated as a century farm because the land has been worked for more than a hundred years. The original farm had a gristmill, store, tannery, blacksmith shop, saw mill, creamery, and post office, plus out-buildings such as a barn, smokehouse, and springhouse. The grist-mill has been restored and is now used for a dwelling; the smoke-house is still in use.

The two-story farmhouse, with its wraparound porches, sits at the confluence of three creeks — Dumplin' Creek, Chaney Branch, and Franklin Branch. You have to park your car next to the barn and walk across the footbridge to the house. The house dates to 1843 and has had several additions during its history. Its freestanding elliptical staircase, put together with wooden pegs, and the cooking fireplace are its most distinctive features. The house has been in the family since 1860 and is filled with family antiques and heirlooms. The Franklins brought up their three children in the house. Lucy Franklin has renovated the house throughout.

Guests have plenty of space for hiking and walking and often follow their noses into the kitchen to find out what Lucy is cooking. She has a reputation for being one of the best cooks in East Tennessee. Her country breakfasts consist of bacon, sausage, or ham, eggs, biscuits, and all the trimmings. Lunch and dinner are not served at the inn, but several good restaurants are not far away.

Gallatin

The Hancock House

2144 Nashville Pike
Gallatin, TN 37066
615-452-8431
Fax: 615-452-8431
http://www.bbonline.com/hancock/

A spacious log home where the welcome mat is always out

Innkeeper: Roberta Hancock. **Accommodations:** 4 rooms (3 with private baths, 1 with shared bath) and 1 cabin (with private bath). **Rates:** $90–$200. **Included:** Continental or full country breakfast, afternoon tea and beverages, fruits in season. **Payment:** Major credit cards. **Children:** Check with innkeeper. **Pets:** Not allowed. **Smoking:** Allowed in designated areas. **Open:** Year-round.

➤ **The Hancock House, northeast of downtown Nashville, is a 25-minute drive (or less) from the Grand Ole Opry, the Hermitage, Music Row, the Parthenon, and other attractions.**

After pursuing lifetime careers and bringing up two children, Roberta Hancock and her husband decided it was time to do something else. She had taught school for twenty years; he was in the tobacco business. They decided to turn their fifteen-room log home into a bed-and-breakfast. Built around 1851, it is the only Colonial revival log house in Tennessee; it originally was a stagecoach stop and toll gate along the historic Avery Trace. The Hancocks also use a four-room log cabin, which has a kitchen and a private bath with a Jacuzzi, as a part of the inn.

All the guest rooms at the Hancock House have fireplaces, and telephone, television, and coffeemakers are available. The Bridal Suite and the Chamber Room have Jacuzzis. Guests have a choice of a Continental or a full country breakfast and are treated to afternoon tea and fresh fruit in season. The refrigerator is always stocked with cold drinks. The Hancocks also offer picnic baskets, receptions, parties, and gourmet dining by reservation. Entree options are chicken cooked in a variety of ways, beef tenderloin, and filet mignon. They can arrange golf tee times, horseback riding, private tours of country music stars' homes, tickets for the Grand Ole Opry and the Tennessee Performing Arts Center, and airport transportation.

Gatlinburg

Buckhorn Inn

2140 Tudor Mountain Road
Gatlinburg, TN 37738
423-436-4668
Fax: 423-436-5009
buckhorninn@aol.com

> **A mountain inn known for its great cuisine**

Innkeepers: John and Connie Burns. **Accommodations:** 6 rooms in the main inn, 4 cottages, 2 guest houses (all with private baths). **Rates:** $95–$275, plus $26 per person for dinner (optional). **Included:** Full breakfast. **Payment:** MasterCard, Visa. **Children:** 10 and older welcome. **Pets:** Not allowed. **Smoking:** Limited. **Open:** Year-round except Christmas.

➤ **The Buckhorn is located near the Great Smoky arts and crafts community, where more than one hundred artisans sell their work. The inn is about seven miles from bustling downtown Gatlinburg and one mile from the national park.**

Built in 1938, this well-seasoned inn has been serving guests for more than half a century. It is owned by Robert, Rachel, and Lindsay Young of Knoxville and managed by John and Connie Burns. The inn has many guests who return year after year to the low-key atmosphere.

The main inn is small and intimate, with activities centered around the great room, which features a library and Steinway piano at one end and a dining room at the other, with a sitting area and fireplace in the middle. This room opens onto a terrace, which offers great views of the Smokies, including Mount Le Conte. The guest rooms are small but comfortable. Young adventurers like sleeping in the water tower, now converted into a cozy bedroom. Unfortunately, the views are limited in some of the guest rooms. If you like privacy, try one of the cabins. Two have kitchenettes; two have refrigerators and coffeemakers. Many of the furnishings are original to the inn. Groups enjoy the Bebb Conference Center and guest house, which can accommodate up to twenty-five people.

The inn is situated on thirty-five wooded acres with a pond where ducks and geese dwell, so there's plenty of room to roam. There's a self-guided nature trail, and a keepsake booklet acquaints guests with the history of the property. The main activity at the Buckhorn is relaxing, but golf and hiking are options.

Breakfast and dinner are served in the dinner room, which is also open to the public by reservation. Breakfast, served every day between 8:00 and 9:30 A.M., features French toast and pancakes made with fruits and nuts; eggs with ham, sausage, or bacon; omelets; hash browns; Buckhorn scramble; the inn's home-mixed Mueslix; and "lighter than air" homemade biscuits. The inn offers six-course gourmet dinners every day but Sunday. Menus vary from week to week, but favorite entrées include blackened beef tournedos, pork tortilla rolls, osso buco, Hunan duck sauté, baked orange roughy with Cajun barbeque shrimp sauce, and slow-roasted beef tenderloin with marchand deVin sauce. Dinner is served by candlelight, and guests are asked to dress up a little — though jackets and ties are not required. Guests are welcome to bring their own alcoholic beverages. A sack lunch is available for $6.

Eight Gables Inn

219 North Mountain Trail
Gatlinburg, TN 37738
Tel. & Fax: 423-430-3344
800-279-5716
http://www.smokymtnmall.com

**A B&B at the foot of the
Great Smoky Mountains
National Park**

Innkeepers: Don and Kim Cason. **Accommodations:** 10 rooms (all with private baths). **Rates:** $99–$119, plus $15 for each additional person (lower rates in off-seasons). **Included:** Full breakfast, desserts, coffee bar. **Payment:** Major credit cards. **Children:** 12 and older welcome if prior arrangements are made. **Pets:** Not allowed. **Smoking:** Allowed on porch. **Open:** Year-round.

➤ **With its location between Pigeon Forge and Gatlinburg, Seven Gables is accessible to major attractions and activities, including music theaters, whitewater rafting, golf, hiking, shopping, and other pastimes.**

Tired of the corporate rat race, Don and Kim Carson decided to take a big leap and go into business for themselves so they would have more time to spend with their two children Amy and Jeremy. They became the official owners and innkeepers of Eight Gables Inn in the spring of 1995 after quitting their jobs in Dayton, Ohio, and selling practically everything they owned in order to buy the inn. (Both had worked in sales.)

Built by Helen Smith in 1991, the mountain retreat already had a AAA four diamond rating when they took over. During their first year of innkeeping they were able to retain the rating, as well as earn a certificate of merit for their participation in the Smoky Mountain Spring Beautification Program.

The inn takes its name from the eight gables that are the dominant architectural feature of the building, which also has a wraparound front porch. Guests enter the inn through the common room, where guests gather around the grand piano for sing-alongs. A staircase leads to the ten guest rooms, each beautifully decorated and offering views of the surrounding mountains. The innkeepers hope to build a small house for themselves and turn their current living quarters into a guest suite sometime in the future.

The Carsons serve a full breakfast, as well as desserts and coffee in the evening. They will also prepare dinner, given advance notice. The inn is available for weddings, reunions, receptions, and corporate seminars.

Hippensteal's Mountain View Inn

Grassy Branch Road
P.O. Box 707
Gatlinburg, TN 37738
423-436-5761, 800-527-8110

A romantic getaway in the Smokies

Innkeepers: Vern and Lisa Hippensteal. **Accommodations:** 11 rooms (all with whirlpool baths). **Rates:** $125. **Included:** Full breakfast. **Payment:** Major credit cards. **Children:** Welcome (one child permitted in bedroom with parents). **Pets:** Not allowed. **Smoking:** Allowed on verandahs only. **Open:** Year-round.

➤ **A professional artist, Vern Hippensteal sells his detailed paintings of the Smokies in more than eighty galleries around the country and conducts painting workshops and classes at the inn.**

At this mountaintop retreat in the heart of the Great Smokies, every room has a view of Mount Le Conte. Located near the Gatlinburg arts and crafts community off Buckhorn Road, about six miles from downtown, Hippensteal's Mountain View Inn is decorated thematically around Vern Hippensteal's watercolor landscapes of the mountains. Many of his works can be purchased at the inn, and he also has a gallery downtown.

Each guest room is named for the Hippensteal painting that serves as a focus for its decor — Winter's Lace, Spring's Arrival, Song of the Mountain. October Promise is special because it was painted specifically for the opening of the inn in the fall of 1990.

No detail has been overlooked in the inn, and every room is color-coordinated, with dark green, purple, and rose tones being the dominant colors. Vern's wife, Lisa, did most of the decorating. Each room has a balcony, queen-sized bed, whirlpool tub, fireplace that burns gas logs, and a view of the mountains.

In the dining room, the green and black cultured marble table-tops match the tile in the floor. The rose-colored wicker chairs in the dining room and the wicker furniture in the lobby are by Henry Link. An article that appeared in the *Washington Post* in 1993 named the inn "one of the twenty most romantic getaways in North America."

The Hippensteals serve breakfast only. Favorite dishes are sausage pies, cheese grits, and open-face cheese melts. Homebaked sweets are offered each evening, and soft drinks, coffee, and tea are always available to guests. Dinner is not served at the inn, but the Hippensteals will assist guests with dinner reservations in Gatlinburg.

Greeneville

General Morgan Inn & Conference Center

111 North Main Street
Greeneville, Tennessee 37743
423-787-1000, 800-223-2679
Fax: 423-787-1001

| A historic property now a new hotel |

General Manager: Wayne Smith. **Accommodations:** 52 rooms and suites (all with private baths). **Rates:** $79 and up. **Included:** Shoeshines, *USA Today,* data ports, terrycloth robes, hairdryers, turndown service. **Payment:** Major credit cards. **Children:** Welcome. **Pets:** Not allowed. **Smoking:** Smoking and non-smoking rooms. **Open:** Year-round.

➤ **Greeneville is known for its history. Within a few blocks of the hotel are the President Andrew Johnson Historic Site & Home, Old Harmony**

Graveyard, Dickson-Williams Mansion, and Nathanael Greene Museum. The Capitol Theatre for the Arts is one block south.

Opened in the summer of 1996, the General Morgan Inn & Conference Center is an excellent example of a public-private business venture. The $12 million historic landmark restoration project has transformed four old railroad hotels dating to the late 1800s and the property around them into a charming mixed-use project. Located in the National Register Historic District of Greeneville, the General Morgan Inn & Conference Center is affiliated with Grand Heritage Hotels International.

The full-service hotel offers fifty-two spacious rooms and suites, featuring high ceilings, restored moldings and woodwork, plus individual climate controls, color television, and dual-line telephones for fax or modem. Amenities in the luxurious marble bathrooms include hairdryers and terrycloth robes. Same-day laundry and dry cleaning, shoeshines, newspapers, valet parking, a restaurant, and lounge round out the list of the new property's many outstanding qualities. Brumley's restaurant — offering breakfast, lunch and dinner — specializes in southern and Continental cuisine. With business people in mind, the General Morgan also offers meeting space, convention services, and business concierge, including secretarial help, cellular phone rentals, copy machine and fax, postal and courier services.

Hotel guests may use all the facilities at the local YMCA, located one mile away. The center has an indoor swimming pool and gymnasium, Stairmasters, free weights, rowing machines, exercycles, and aerobics classes.

Jackson

Highland Place Bed & Breakfast

519 North Highland Avenue
Jackson, TN 38301
901-427-1472
Fax: 901-422-7994
http://www.bbonline.om/tn/highlandplace/

A luxurious B&B in the
Highland Avenue Historic
District

Innkeepers: Glenn and Janice Wall. **Accommodations:** 4 rooms (all with private baths). **Rates:** $75–$135. **Included:** Full breakfast. **Payment:** Major credit cards. **Children:** 12 and older welcome. **Pets:** Allowed. **Smoking:** Not allowed. **Open:** Year-round.

➤ **Janice Wall's cookbook is now in its fifth printing. She has been featured as the guest chef in *Southern Inns Bed & Breakfast* magazine and often gives cooking demonstrations at bookstores and tearooms.**

After spending many years planning and researching their "retirement" project, Glenn and Janice Wall decided to become innkeepers following retirement from Federal Express Corporation. Janice had already published a cookbook of her own recipes and given cooking demonstrations at local bookstores and tearooms. In the summer of 1992, they purchased Highland Place Bed and Breakfast, a thriving operation in Jackson's Highland Avenue Historic District. Three years later, the inn was selected as the West Tennessee Designer Showhouse.

The classic Revival Style brick home was built by Henry W. Louis in 1911 and has had a succession of owners who used it as a private residence. In 1978, Norman and Kay Rodriguez purchased what was then known as the "Hamilton-Butler Mansion" and returned it to its original grandeur after extensive renovations. One of the most outstanding rooms in the house is the library, which is paneled in cherry wood cut from the Louis farm. The house was converted into a B&B in 1989.

The Walls offer four luxurious guest rooms — The Louis Room, The Butler Suite, The Hamilton Suite (a favorite with honeymooners), and Rachel's Atrium Suite, the newest and most spacious. They serve a full family-style breakfast featuring Janice's prize-winning recipes. They will prepare picnic baskets and a private romantic dinner for two by prior arrangement. They continue to make improvements at the inn in order to serve the increasing number of business and corporate travelers who find their way to the inn, which is ideally suited for small gatherings.

Knoxville

Hyatt Regency Knoxville at Civic Coliseum

500 Hill Avenue, Southeast
Knoxville, TN 37915
423-637-1234
Fax: 423-522-5911

| An ultra-contemporary city hotel overlooking the river |

General Manager: Tom Mason. **Accommodations:** 362 rooms and 25 suites (all with private baths; some with wet bars). **Rates:** $89–$140. **Included:** Use of amenities, parking. **Payment:** Major credit cards. **Children:** Welcome. **Pets:** Allowed. **Smoking:** Smoking and nonsmoking rooms. **Open:** Year-round.

➤ **The hotel has been compared to one of the Tennessee Valley Authority dams and to a typewriter, and when the city staged the World's Fair in 1982, the Hyatt was right in style.**

At the Hyatt Regency Knoxville, you have the best view of the city, the Tennessee River, and Volunteer Landing, a revitalization of Knoxville's riverfront. In fact, from a distance the building looks like an Aztec temple, its triangular shape rising eleven stories. Built in 1971, the hotel was patterned after the Hyatt Regency Atlanta.

Inside, the atrium lobby soars the full height and stretches the entire length of the building, creating a vast space. Located here are the hotel's lounges and restaurants — Spirits, the Country Garden Restaurant (offering three meals a day), and the Knuckles Sports Bar with large TVs and pool tables. In-room dining is also available 24 hours a day.

Many guest rooms face the Tennessee River, but the rooms on the second, third, and fourth levels have a view of the city. The arrangement and decor of the rooms are similar to what one finds in many corporate hotels.

Boasting the largest ballroom in Tennessee (11,480 square feet), the Hyatt Regency has served the city well as a business and convention hotel because of its proximity to the Knoxville Civic Auditorium and Coliseum and the University of Tennessee. Business plan rooms include a fax machine and self-help office for $15 extra. Guests with busy schedules appreciate the hotel's express check-in and check-out. The hotel has an outdoor pool, sauna, and health club.

Loudon

The Mason Place Bed & Breakfast

600 Commerce Street
Loudon, TN 37774
423-458-3921
http://www.checkthenet.com/travel/mason.htm

A bed-and-breakfast antebellum inn impeccable in its decor and service

Innkeepers: Bob and Donna Siewert. **Accommodations:** 5 rooms (all with private baths). **Rates:** $96–$120. **Included:** Full breakfast; beverages, snacks, desserts. **Payment:** MasterCard, Visa. **Children:** Not appropriate. **Pets:** Not allowed. **Smoking:** Not allowed. **Open:** Year-round.

➤ **Though Captain Mason was a Northern sympathizer, his contractor sided with the South and placed the stars and bars of the Confederate flag in the upstairs porch railings.**

An east Tennessee showplace in Loudon near the Tennessee River, this classic Greek Revival home has been painstakingly restored by owners Bob and Donna Siewert, who purchased it at an auction. Originally the home stood amid a 1,200-acre plantation and remained in the possession of the same family for five generations. (Only three acres of the plantation remain.)

Construction on the 7,000-square-foot home for Thomas Jefferson Mason, a riverboat captain and politician, began in 1861. The plans called for it to be built of bricks that had been made by slaves, but when the Civil War broke out, the bricks were shipped to Fort Hill. Left without building materials, Captain Mason ordered heart pine from Georgia and continued with the building. The house was completed in 1865. The property was occupied by both Northern and Southern troops, and artifacts are still being found.

Donna and Bob, who are natives of Michigan, spent four and a half years restoring and furnishing the house. Now retired, Bob was a mechanical engineer and Donna was a registered nurse. In 1990, they received an Outstanding Restoration award from the East Tennessee Development District. The inn is listed on the National Register of Historic Places and has been featured in *Country Inns* magazine.

Guests have five rooms to choose from, all furnished in beautiful period antiques and decorated in Louis Nichole wallpapers. Each room has a gas-log fireplace. The restored smokehouse, located near the swimming pool, is very romantic, with its wood-burning fireplace, brick walls and floors, tin bathtub, and real featherbed. The Siewerts enjoy getting to know their guests and often have breakfast with them. Breakfast is an elegant affair, with candles, crystal, and china, and guests often linger for conversation.

There's plenty of space to roam at the Mason Place — about three acres of gardens and lawns with a gazebo, Grecian swimming pool, and wisteria-covered arbor.

Embassy Suites Memphis

1022 South Shady Grove Road
Memphis, TN 38120
901-684-1777, 800-EMBASSY
Fax: 901-685-8185

> **A hotel that's setting standards**

General Manager: David Ditto. **Accommodations:** 220 deluxe suites (all with private baths, wet bars, and refrigerators). **Rates:** $94–$149. **Included:** Full breakfast, manager's reception. **Payment:** Major credit cards. **Children:** Free with parents. **Pets:** Check with hotel. **Smoking:** Smoking and nonsmoking suites. **Open:** Year-round.

➤ **Attention to guests' needs is very important here; the hotel has won the chain's Top Ten Award for customer service several times.**

Though Embassy Suites is a chain, this hotel, a Memphis City Beautiful Award winner, is anything but typical. Every guest stays in a two-room suite, which includes a living room, bedroom, a dining/work space, wet bar and refrigerator. Suites also feature sofa beds, ice makers, cooking facilities, microwaves, and exercise bicycles. Each room has a two-line telephone and a remote control color TV.

All the suites are clustered around the atrium, filled with plants and fountains. Guests use this area for check-in, meeting other guests, and dining. A cooked-to-order breakfast is included in the tariff, as well as the two-hour cocktail reception each evening. Lunch and dinner at Grisanti's Italian Restaurant are extra. Airport transportation, parking, and cable channels are complimentary. The hotel also offers valet/laundry service and express checkout.

Guests have access to a swimming pool, exercise room, and sauna. There is also a billiards room where you can challenge your business partner in a game of pool. The hotel, which is eleven miles from downtown Memphis, can accommodate small meetings.

The Peabody

149 Union Avenue
Memphis, TN 38103
901-529-4000, 800-PEABODY
Fax: 901-529-9600

> **A grand city hotel with many grand traditions**

Vice President and General Manager: Mohamad A. Hakimian. **Accommodations:** 468 rooms and 15 suites (all with private baths). **Rates:** Rooms: $160–310; suites: $595 and up. **Payment:** Major credit cards. **Children:** Welcome. **Pets:** Not allowed. **Smoking:** Smoking and nonsmoking rooms. **Open:** Year-round.

➤ **The author David Cohn described the hotel aptly in 1935 when he wrote, "The Mississippi Delta begins in the lobby of the Peabody Hotel and ends on Catfish Row in Vicksburg. The Peabody is the Paris Ritz, the Cairo Shepheard's, the London Savoy . . ." One story goes that Mississippians hope heaven will be like the lobby of the Peabody.**

Since the 1930s the famous Peabody ducks have entertained guests at "The South's Grand Hotel." Originally, the performance was a prank, but it was received so enthusiastically that it became a tradition at the hotel. Led by their trainer, the mallards leave their palatial penthouse on the Plantation Roof at 11 A.M. and ride the elevator to the lobby, where they make a grand entrance on a red carpet lined with camera-toting tourists and children sitting atop shoulders to get a better view.

Flashbulbs pop as the ducks parade to the Italian Travertine fountain in the middle of the grand lobby, where they do what most normal ducks do — splash in the water, preen themselves, and waddle around. Then, precisely at 5 P.M., they assume their regal position and parade, single file, to the elevator to retire for the evening. The ducks march to the sounds of John Philip Sousa's "King Cotton March," which adds to the happy and festive atmosphere. After four months of intensive performances, the flock retires to the farm and another takes its place. The ducks are world famous and have been on tour to promote the hotel. (Another group of performing mallards represents the sister hotel in Orlando, Florida.)

The Peabody ducks symbolize tradition, on which the hotel has built its excellent reputation and continues to thrive. Needless to say, service is a time-honored ritual. Guests at the hotel are pampered from the moment they enter the grand lobby, which is the center of activity, until they depart. Cordial bellmen, many of them old-timers at the Peabody, greet and escort guests to their rooms. VIP guests receive turndown service, complemented with "duck" chocolate mints on their pillows.

The hotel has four restaurants where guests congregate, including the informal Café Expresso, a combination of a New York deli and a Viennese pastry shop. Dux, known for its outstanding American cuisine and wine list, is also a favorite. Mallard's Bar & Grill offers casual dining and entertaining, as well as a pasta bar. Chez Philippe, the hotel's signature restaurant, features contemporary French cuisine. (Duck is not on the menu.)

Of course, the Peabody has a wonderfully rich history. Built by Colonel Robert C. Brinkley in 1869 and named for George Peabody, the hotel is synonymous with southern hospitality. The first structure was replaced by a finer building in 1925; it was completely refurbished and restored to its original grandeur by its present owners, the Belz family, in 1981. A National Historic Landmark, the fourteen-story hotel has hosted such notables as Presidents Andrew Jackson, William McKinley, and Harry Truman; Confederate Generals Nathan Bedford Forrest and Jubal Early; writer William Faulkner; and aviator Charles Lindbergh. A piano that belonged to composer Francis Scott Key is displayed on the mezzanine.

The Peabody's spacious guest rooms are elegantly furnished and well stocked with amenities. Each of the "Romeo and Juliet" townhouse suites features a fireplace and marble staircase leading to a balcony overlooking the two-story living room and master bedroom — perfect for honeymoons and anniversaries. Guests enjoy a lavish health club and indoor heated pool. Also available are a steam room, aerobics, Nautilus, sauna, massage, and tanning. The Peabody Athletic Club has a full-time director.

In addition to the meeting and banquet rooms, the third floor of the hotel is the Peabody Executive Conference Center, designed to accommodate smaller VIP meetings. Two full-time conference coordinators are on hand to cater to the needs of groups. The aristocratic Continental Ballroom remains a favorite spot for gatherings of Memphis elite. The historic Skyway, one of the city's hottest nightspots, presents an art deco supper club and spotlights what's often called the best Sunday brunch in the Delta. The Plantation Roof, also a great gathering spot, offers an open-air panorama of the city and the Mississippi River. It also holds the Peabody Duck Palace.

The Peabody is a member of Preferred Hotels Worldwide and the National Trust for Historic Preservation's Historic Hotels of America. The downtown hotel is within walking distance of famous Beale Street, "the home of the blues," and the Mississippi River, where riverboats dock. It is also close to Cook Convention Center.

Talbot Heirs Guesthouse

99 South Second Street
Memphis, TN 38103
901-527-9772, 800-955-3956
Fax: 901-527-3700
reservations@talbothouse.com
http://www.talbothouse.com

A city guest house with personal service

Innkeepers: Phil and Jamie Baker and Bruce Bolthouse. **Accommodations:** 9 suites (all with private baths and fully equipped kitchens). **Rates:** $150–$250. **Included:** Breakfast items, fresh flowers, beverages, exercise equipment. **Payment:** Major credit cards. **Children:** Welcome. **Pets:** Not allowed. **Smoking:** Allowed. **Open:** Year-round.

➤ **"What we have tried to do is create an aesthetically pleasing, highly personal environment and to provide sincere, gracious service. We have kept our signage very minimal in order to keep an intimate, private atmosphere.... Our guests often leave handwritten personal thank you notes upon leaving." — Jamie Baker**

Comfort, not luxury, is the watchword at Talbot Heirs Guesthouse, a unique lodging that opened in downtown Memphis across from the Peabody in early 1996. Opened by Phil and Jamie Baker, the guesthouse offers nine suites, designed to give travelers a feeling of home. Both dislike hotels and shun them whenever possible when they travel; they each gave up their positions in high finance when they opened the guesthouse.

The Bakers took the name of the guest house from the legal description of the building — Talbot Heirs Subdivision. They chose a former apartment building for their new business venture and did all the decorating, using furnishings they felt would be comfortable and inviting, along with original artwork. Each suite, measuring 400 to 1,000 square feet in area, has a personality all its own. Room 6, for example, features a Tennessee marble floor with plantation shutters, a fainting couch with an overstuffed chair, and a separate bedroom with a Gothic iron bed. Each suite has a fully equipped kitchen that's designed for guests to prepare simple meals in; all the fixings for a cold breakfast are provided. Some guests fax their grocery lists to the front desk in advance so they'll have food in the refrigerator when they arrive.

"Each guest room is a collection of new contemporary furnishings, Oriental rugs, china, crystal, flea market finds, and lots of iron furniture that has been fabricated from manhole covers, old fencing, and old gates," says Jamie. "We have laid slate tile, hardwood floors, and heart of pine pickled floors. . . . We uncovered and refurbished the Tennessee pink marble that is original to the building. . . . It is truly a unique, eclectic, exciting property."

The guest house offer a number of services that are of interest to business travelers — fax machine, VCR, exercise machine, and conference facilities. The innkeepers are always on call to serve the needs of guests.

Monteagle

Adams-Edgeworth Inn

Monteagle Assembly
Monteagle, TN 37356
931-924-4000
Fax: 931-924-3236

| An elegant B&B in a Chautauqua setting |

Innkeepers: David and Wendy Adams. **Accommodations:** 13 rooms (all with private baths). **Rates:** $75–$195, plus additional charge for dinner. **Included:** Full breakfast. **Payment:** American Express, MasterCard, Visa. **Children:** Check with innkeepers. **Pets:** Not allowed. **Smoking:** Allowed on verandahs. **Open:** Year-round.

➤ **Monteagle was called the Chautauqua of the South because it was
patterned after the original Chautauqua in New York.**

Monteagle seems to have a certain magnetism to it. Descendants
of the first generation who sought the cool temperatures of the
Cumberland Plateau, the intellectual and religious stimulation,
and genteel way of life are still coming to the small Victorian village. They remember it as a happy place where they spent the
summers of their childhood with grandparents, aunts, uncles, cousins, and friends.

Wendy and David Adams, who operate the Adams-Edgeworth
Inn, were drawn to Monteagle because of their family ties. David's
father used to summer in nearby Beersheba Springs, and his mother
owned a cottage here. They were shopping for an inn and this one
happened to be for sale. At the time David was working in corporate finance and Wendy was director of development for the Atlanta Opera.

After finalizing their purchase in late 1990, they refurbished the
inn completely. The outside was given a fresh coat of white paint,
and the inside was furnished in antiques that had been in the family for years, as well as priceless works of art and other pieces they
had acquired in their travels throughout the world. As the daughter
of Benjamin H. Oehlert, who had served as ambassador to Pakistan,
Wendy acquired some wonderful things, including her father's official Wedgwood china, which now graces the table at the inn. The
result is an eclectic mix of antiques in an elegant Victorian setting.

The Edgeworth Inn, one of 161 Victorian structures that survives
today, actually dates to 1896 and is on the National Register of
Historic Places. (It was made into a B&B in 1977.) It was originally
a boarding house that served Monteagle's many visitors. The
unique village had been established in 1882 as the Monteagle Sunday School Assembly by a committee of southern gentlemen. It
was founded on the same principles as the one in Chautauqa, New
York, and assembly programs featured hymns, lectures, evening
prayers, excursions, socials, tennis, and swimming. Parents could
bring their children to Monteagle and turn them loose, never fear-
ing they would be harmed in the safe environment.

Though Monteagle went through some difficult years, especially
during World War I, World War II, and the Depression (losing some
buildings to fire), it has survived as a quiet, picturesque village. It
has not wavered much from the original concept, and in 1993 the
Chautauqua Network Conference met here. For eight weeks of the
summer there are scheduled programs for which there is a fee.

Guests who make their way to the Adams-Edgeworth Inn are not disappointed. It's a place where they can slow down and take stock of things, relax and unwind, make new friends. Accommodations at the inn are luxurious. Guests sleep on custom-made mattresses in four-poster beds under handmade quilts and down comforters. They are free to take long, hot showers in the steam room. A full breakfast, served in the formal dining room or the garden, comes with the room, and a four-course gourmet dinner is available upon request. An evening might begin with smoked salmon on Russian black bread and a fresh garden salad with Brie cheese, followed by raspberry sorbet and an entrée such as baked salmon in lemon chive sauce, served with vegetables. The meal might then be topped off with a delicious dessert and coffee. Often a guitarist or pianist is invited to play. The area also boasts several restaurants for those who want to eat elsewhere. Picnic lunches can also be arranged.

Guests may use the golf cart or bicycles to get around town, but many enjoy the extensive pathways and hiking trails around the village. Tennis, croquet, and swimming are other recreational options. The Adamses have an extensive library that guests enjoy, and the wide porches with their rockers are ideal for relaxing. Guests also enjoy browsing for gifts in the Window Shop on one end of the porch. The Adamses have sponsored seminars on a variety of subjects, including cooking, tennis, and stress, and have hosted murder mystery weekends. Other diversions such as Sewanee University of the South and the Jack Daniels and George Dickel distilleries are nearby.

Monterey

The Garden Inn

1400 Bee Rock Road
Monterey, TN 38574
931-839-1400
Fax: 931-839-1410
hinton@multipro.com
http: www.bbonline.com/tn/gardeninn/

A beautiful old setting is
the ideal spot for a brand
new inn

Innkeepers: Dickie and Stephanie Hinton. **Accommodations:** 11 rooms (all with private baths, some accessible to the disabled). **Rates:** $110–$155. **Included:** Full breakfast, desserts. **Payment:** Major credit cards. **Children:** 12 and older welcome. **Pets:** Not allowed. **Smoking:** Not allowed. **Open:** Year-round.

➤ **The inn is located near a number of state parks and attractions, including the Big South Fork National River and Recreation Area; Dale Hollow and Center Hill Lakes; and Cumberland Mountain, Fall Creek Falls, Rock Island, and Standing Stone state parks.**

The Garden Inn, on the edge of the Cumberland Plateau, off Interstate 40 between Knoxville and Nashville, opened in the spring of 1996. The inn occupies land that used to be a KOA campground. and its beautiful natural setting is really breathtaking. Just a few steps from the front door is Bee Rock, a towering overlook that offers a panoramic view of Calfkiller Valley. You can also see Stamps Hollow from the outdoor deck. And the gardens are filled with lovely blossoms, fruits and herbs, including blackberries, blueberries, raspberries, grapes, and other sweet smells.

When Dickie Hinton, an ordained Methodist minister, suffered a heart attack in 1994, he and his wife Stephanie, a professional chemist, decided to go into innkeeping. They chose to build a brand new inn rather than renovate an old building. They also enlisted the services of Bob Harwood of Wood Designs, Inc., who put a simulated mountain stream into the design of the inn and configured all the rooms so they would have a view of either the garden or the surrounding mountains. The Hintons used handcrafted cherry and walnut furniture and quilt patterns in the decor. From the start, they included their daughter Corey in their plans.

The inn has eleven guest rooms. Three of the rooms have whirlpool tubs; two, gas fireplaces. Guests at the inn are treated to a full breakfast in the dining room and evening desserts. The inn is an ideal spot for weddings, receptions, and conferences.

Nashville

Opryland Hotel

2800 Opryland Drive
Nashville, TN 37214
615-889-1000
Fax: 615-871-7741

A luxury hotel in the country music capital offering great entertainment

General Manager: Joe Henry. **Accommodations:** 2,883 rooms, more than 200 suites. **Rates:** $209–$3,500. **Payment:** Major credit cards. **Children:** Welcome. **Pets:** Allowed for disabled guests. **Smoking:** Allowed. **Open:** Year-round.

➤ **As wonderful as all the trappings are, Opryland Hotel's biggest selling feature is its friendly, courteous staff. Employees are hospitable without being phony; their smiles are genuine and the hellos sincere. They go out of their way to address you by name.**

From the balcony of Room 54128 you have a ringside seat for the Dancing Waters light, laser, water fountain, and music show, featuring pianist Vince Cardell, who performs magic from his perch high over the two-acre indoor garden called the Cascades. Lights, lasers, and water fountains are orchestrated in perfect timing with the music, which Nashville's Liberace performs two times each evening. (He is one of many stars and entertainers you will see at the hotel.)

You can sleep with the windows open in rooms facing the Cascades, the adjacent Conservatory (another two-acre indoor garden) or the new 4.5 acre Delta and think you're in Hawaii, as the waterfalls and fountains lull you into dream world. Actually, the place has a Disney aura to it, but it is unique in every way.

The Opryland Hotel is itself something of a dream. It was designed by Earl Swensson to represent "people architecture," his term for a new form that encourages interaction between a building and its users. Built in 1977, the hotel has been expanded three times — in 1983, 1988, and 1996. The newest addition — the Delta — is a subtropical garden reminiscent of the lower Mississippi River region. Under its soaring glass are several buildings, including Beauregard's Restaurant, which resembles an antebellum mansion.

Inside the hotel are a more than a dozen restaurants, thirty shops, ten lounges and a veritable art gallery of pieces all created by Tennesseeans. Be sure to see the giant mural that depicts Nashville and its citizens. Rooms are tastefully decorated with coordinating fabrics in draperies, bedspreads, and upholstered chairs and furnished in traditional mahogany.

Guests move freely in the spacious public areas. The hotel is large enough that you receive a map upon arrival. Each building dissolves into another, so the hallways seem to go into infinity. Everything you might need is contained within the hotel. (One departing guest said on leaving that he had not been outside the hotel in five days.) There are shops and more shops (selling everything from fine jewelry to western wear to souvenirs), a revolving lounge, and diverse restaurants (Beauregard's, Cascades, Rachel's Kitchen, the Veranda, Old Hickory, and Caffe Avanti and Ristoranti Volore). The hotel has three swimming pools, a health club, and a golf course — the eighteen-hole Springhouse Golf Club. Nashville city tours, which visit places such as Ryman Auditorium, the Country Music Hall of Fame, and country music stars' homes, leave from the hotel.

The hotel caters to meetings and conventions, but it seems like a leisure-oriented resort. The Ryman Exhibit Hall, named for Ryman Auditorium where the Grand Ole Opry played for thirty-one years, is one of the nation's largest single-level, self-contained exhibition hotel facilities, with 289,000 square feet.

Live entertainment is abundant at the hotel. At the heart of the operation is the Grand Ole Opry, the world's longest running radio show. It is broadcast every Friday and Saturday night of the year, and a matinee series increases your opportunities to see shows in the spring, summer, and fall. The Opry cast ranges from Hall of

Famers such as Little Jimmy Dickens to current superstars such as Garth Brooks, Alan Jackson, Vince Gill, Ricky Skaggs, and Patty Loveless. Broadcasts are live on WSM-AM (650) and are complete with spot commercials. Acquaintance with a performer or an Opry official may get you a seat on the stage right behind the spotlight. Since the Opry first went on the air in 1925 as the WSM Barn Dance, the show has never missed a Saturday night broadcast.

The Opry Plaza area of the resort is open all year, and it boasts two of Nashville's top museums — the Grand Ole Opry Museum and the Roy Acuff/Minnie Pearl Museum. Starwalk, a collection of handprints in concrete markers, celebrates Nashvillians who have won Grammy Awards. Admission to all is free.

Union Station Hotel

1001 Broadway
Nashville, TN 37203
615-726-1001, 800-331-2123
Fax: 615-248-3554

A former train station turned luxury hotel

Owner: Grand Heritage Hotels. **General Manager:** Jim McRae. **Accommodations:** 110 rooms and 14 suites (all with private baths). **Rates:** $149-$295. **Payment:** Major credit cards. **Children:** Welcome. **Pets:** Allowed with deposit. **Smoking:** Smoking and nonsmoking rooms. **Open:** Year-round.

➤ **Union Station features 24-karat gold leaf on the decorative friezes of the lobby, original tile floors, mahogany and brass accents, and the time-treasured wall clock, by which passengers once set their watches.**

Thousands of travelers have been reunited with friends and loved ones within the passages of this former railroad station, a 1900 Richardsonian Romanesque limestone building topped with gables and a clock tower and known for its magnificent vaulted stained glass ceiling. It has been restored beyond the beauty of its original grandeur.

Guest rooms have been carved out of the vast space of the building, and some even look like showrooms through the big arched window enclosures. (Privacy is guaranteed, however, by the use of heavy draperies.) During the hotel's most recent renovation two meeting rooms were added and carpeting, draperies, and upholstery were replaced throughout the hotel. On the concierge level rooms and amenities were upgraded.

The hotel has two outstanding restaurants — the Broadway Bistro, offering American cuisine, and Arthur's, Nashville's only four-star restaurant, which features such delights as roast rack of spring lamb, pinwheels of salmon royale, and tournedos of beef. There's also a shop in the lobby where you can buy coffee, soft drinks, and mouth-watering chocolate chip cookies. The hotel can accommodate small groups in rooms that still hold yesteryear's charms.

Newport

Christopher Place — An Intimate Resort

1500 Pinnacles Way
Newport, TN 37821
423-623-6555, 800-595-9441
Fax: 423-613-4771
TheBestINN@aol.com

An opulent mountain estate and country inn

Innkeeper: Drew Ogle. **Accommodations:** 9 rooms and suites (all with private baths, some with whirlpool tubs and fireplaces). **Rates:** $150–$300. **Included:** Full breakfast, afternoon tea, use of all facilities. **Payment:** American Express, MasterCard, Visa. **Children:** 12 and older welcome. **Pets:** Not allowed. **Smoking:** Allowed on porches and verandahs. **Open:** Year-round.

➤ **English Mountain (elevation 4,000 feet) sits on the fringe of the Great Smoky Mountains National Park. In the nineteenth century, some of the nation's elite, including President Theodore Roosevelt, came here to the Glen Alpine Springs Hotel, a fifty-room structure surrounded by fifty guest cottages, to enjoy the beauty of the mountains and to drink from the mineral springs. According to Indian legend, the springs had miraculous healing powers. The hotel was lost to fire in 1902.**

Drew Ogle, a professional pianist, returned home to East Tennessee in 1990 to go into the hospitality business. On many evenings he can be found at the piano sharing songs and memories with guests. He was trained in the classics and studied musical theater in college, but his real love is big band music.

Now in his mid-twenties, Drew is equally talented as the owner/innkeeper of Christopher Place, having learned all about the tourism business while growing up in Gatlinburg. He purchased the grand home from the FDIC and then renovated it over a nine-month period before opening it to the public in 1995. The original owner lost the million-dollar house in the late 1980s during the collapse of the Butcher banking empire in Tennessee, and it sat empty for several years. Originally called the Pinnacle, the 3-story, 14,000-square-foot structure has twin chimneys, a slate roof, dormers, front columns, and colonnades extending in opposite directions from the main house to two guest cottages. (It also has an elevator.)

The mansion, located on English Mountain, has always drawn stares, but now people ooh and aah over it more than ever. The eclectic decor of the opulent mountain estate — resplendent with richly colored fabrics, wallpapers, original works by local artists, and coordinating furniture and accessories — ranges from traditional to rustic to whimsical. The estate is ideal for quiet, romantic weekends, weddings, parties, or corporate meetings. *Country Inns* awarded Christopher Place first prize for Stargazer, a crimson room featuring Waverly and Currant fabrics and Star Gazer wallpaper, accented with gold sunbursts. AAA gave it a four-diamond rating. Honeymooners often opt for the Roman Holiday Room, which features a king-sized iron bed, a wood-burning fireplace, a whirlpool for two, and a panoramic view of the mountains.

Drew serves guests a full breakfast and afternoon tea. Lunch and dinner are available by reservation at an additional charge. Guests are free to explore the surrounding 200 acres, enjoy a game of billiards, play tennis, go for a swim, look for wildlife through the telescope on the rocker-lined verandah, work out in the exercise room, or relax by the fireplace in the library. Max, the Maltese of the mansion, welcomes attention from guests, of course.

Pikeville

Fall Creek Falls Bed & Breakfast Inn

Route 3, Box 298B
Pikeville, TN 37367
423-881-5494
Fax: 423-881-5040
http://www.bbonline.com/tn/fallcreek/

| **A beautiful inn on the Cumberland Plateau** |

Innkeepers: Doug and Rita Pruett. **Accommodations:** 7 rooms and 1 suite (all with private baths). **Rates:** $70–$115 (off-season rates available). **Included:** Full gourmet breakfast, homemade cookies, and beverages. **Payment:** Major credit cards. **Children:** 8 and older welcome (one at time). **Pets:** Not allowed. **Smoking:** Not allowed. **Open:** February–early January.

➤ **Nearby Fall Creek Falls State Park is known for its beautiful waterfalls, the highest being Fall Creek Falls, which drops 256 feet.**

Set amid forty acres in the Cumberland Plateau region is Fall Creek Falls Bed & Breakfast Inn, a retreat where you can quickly forget about the cares of the world. The inn is a dream come true for Rita Pruett, whose husband Doug also shares her enthusiasm for entertaining overnight guests. It has been featured in *Country Magazine* and *Tennessee Magazine*.

The Pruetts purchased the property near Fall Creek Falls State Resort Park in 1978 and built their inn a few years later. Doug, a licensed building contractor for twenty years before he retired, put his knowledge and expertise to work during the construction. He built the five-bedroom wing and laid the white pickled oak flooring throughout the house. Doug is also a gourmet cook, and guests rave about his breakfast menus, which include pecan waffles with homemade apple cider syrup and eggs Benedict. Breakfasts are served in the dining room on individual tables set with fine china, crystal, and silver.

The inn has eight guest rooms, each decorated in a Victorian or country theme using local crafts as accents. Some of the rooms are named for mothers and grandmothers in Doug and Rita's families — Ruby Belle, Pearl Melissa, Paunee Elizabeth, Jenny Lynn, and Catherine Evelia. The Sweetheart Room and the Wild Rose Suite, favorites with romancers, have heart-shaped whirlpool tubs.

After a full breakfast, you may retire to the sun room or wander down a nature trail and look for wildflowers or wildlife. If you feel more energetic, you may hike one of the many trails in the state resort park nearby that has the same name as the inn. Here you'll see some spectacular scenery, including several different waterfalls. The highest, at 276 feet, is Fall Creek Falls. Another option is golf at the park's 18-hole, par 72, championship course, named one of the top twenty-five public golf courses in America by *Golf Digest*. Other recreational possibilities are horseback riding, fishing, swimming, and all kinds of boating (from canoes to electric motors). But you may be perfectly content to relax at the inn.

Both Rita and Doug are very active in the community. A lifelong resident of the area and a former insurance agent and branch manager, she is currently president of the Van Buren County/Spencer Chamber of Commerce, president-elect of the Van Buren County Industrial Board and serves on the board of the Upper Cumberland Tourism Association (which encompasses fourteen counties). She also teaches seminars on innkeeping. He belongs to the Fall Creek Falls Community Action Group and serves as a volunteer fireman.

Fall Creek Falls Inn and
Fall Creek Falls State Resort Park

Route 3
Pikeville, TN 37367-9803
423-881-5241
800-421-6683 (information only)
Fax: 423-881-5008

**An award-winning resort
that offers many amenities**

Owner: State of Tennessee. **General Manager:** John Fonville. **Accommodations:** 71 rooms (all with private baths) and 1 suite in the inn (with private bath and kitchenette); 20 two-bedroom cabins (all with private baths, fireplaces, and fully equipped kitchens). **Rates:** Inn rooms: $62 weekdays, $65 weekends; cabins: $70 weekdays, $90 weekends. Additional: Recreational fees. **Included:** Coffee. **Payment:** American Express, MasterCard, Visa. **Children:** 15 and under free with parents. **Pets:** Not allowed. **Smoking:** Allowed. **Open:** Inn: January–mid-December; cabins: year-round.

➤ **Fall Creek Falls Inn, Tennessee's premier resort park, was named one of America's 30 Favorite Family Resorts by *Better Homes and Gardens* in 1993.**

As the highest waterfall east of the Rocky Mountains, Fall Creek Falls dramatically plunges 256 feet into a pool at the base of a gorge. And this isn't all the state resort park in central Tennessee has to offer — there are three other waterfalls, sparkling streams, gorges, timberlands, and scenic vistas.

Fall Creek Falls State Resort Park is a complete resort catering to groups and families. It offers every recreational amenity you can dream of — including an 18-hole championship golf course that was named one of the top 25 public courses in America by *Golf Digest*, horseback riding, and paved bicycle paths. You can swim in the Olympic-size swimming pool, enjoy canoeing or pedal boating, go fishing, or hike through the gorges and along the streams and lake-shore of the park. (A naturalist is on duty during the summer.) The park also has a store and launderette, located along with the information center and park headquarters in the Village Green Complex.

The main congregating area in the park is the inn, where the meeting room and dining room are located. The inn also includes a recreation room, shuffleboard, recreation equipment, an exercise/fitness room, and games. Each room has a private balcony overlooking the lake. The ten fisherman cabins are just as plush as the inn rooms, with everything you need for light housekeeping, including cooking utensils and linens. (You can fish from your private porch.) In addition, there are ten land-side cabins that overlook the lake; two of them are accessible to the disabled. Additional fishing cabins are currently under construction.

Groups of up to 104 can be accommodated in the dormitory-like coed lodge; another lodge can handle 110 people. Both include a meeting room and a kitchen. The park staff will assist groups in setting up their meetings and provide whatever services are needed.

Roan Mountain

Roan Mountain State Resort Park

Route 1, Box 236
Roan Mountain, TN 37687
423-772-3303 or 423-772-3314
800-250-8620

A mountain hideaway in the woods with all the amenities

Owner: State of Tennessee. **Accommodations:** 28 cabins (all with private baths and fully equipped kitchens). **Rates:** $102 per night or $ 617 for six nights. **Included:** Taxes and all recreational amenities. **Payment:** American Express, MasterCard, Visa. **Children:** Welcome. **Pets:** Not allowed. **Smoking:** Allowed. **Open:** Year-round.

➤ **There's a naturalist on duty in the park and a full schedule of special events featuring cloggers, storytelling, musical concerts, trout tournaments, bird walks, and wildflower tours.**

The top of 6,285-foot Roan Mountain looks like a winter scene on a Christmas card, its evergreen trees and thick rhododendron laden with heavy flakes of snow. You'll be putting yourself in the picture if you go cross-country skiing or bobsledding. (Bring your own equipment.) If the weather is iffy, you might use the trails in the park in the valley, about ten miles from the mountaintop. Snowfall occurs between November and March. When it isn't snowing, the mountaintop can be just as beautiful and enjoyable. A great temptation is to hike a portion of the Appalachian Trail that crosses the mountain.

Roan Mountain State Park, located at the base of the mountain, offers many exciting adventures besides skiing and hiking. During the summer it's an ideal place for swimming, picnicking, and playing horseshoes, badminton, and volleyball. The park's historic buildings offer insight into early life in these mountains. The Dave Miller Homestead — including the main house and several outbuildings — dates to 1870. An old iron mine is located on one of the trails near the visitor center, which features a gristmill and a mining exhibit.

The accommodations at Roan Mountain State Park are comfortable. Cabins are constructed of wood siding with cedar-shake shingles, stone chimneys, and large front porches, where you can sit in rocking chairs and look at the mountains. They're fully furnished, with buck stoves and complete kitchens. All have sleeping lofts. None has a phone or television set, however. If you want a break from the kitchen, you may eat in the park restaurant, but it is open sporadically.

Rogersville

Hale Springs Inn

Town Square
Rogersville, TN 37857
423-272-5171

> **A 19th-century inn, home of a retired sea captain**

Innkeepers: Captain and Mrs. Carl Netherland-Brown, Sue Livesay, and Bill Testerman. **Accommodations:** 8 rooms and 2 suites (all with private baths).

Rates: $40–$70. **Included:** Continental breakfast. **Payment:** American Express, MasterCard, Visa. **Children:** Welcome. **Pets:** Not allowed. **Smoking:** Not allowed. **Open:** Year-round.

➤ **Rogersville has more than thirty-five designated historic sites, some of them more than two hundred years old. The Netherland-Browns are always glad to point out places to see; they also give guests a self-guided walking-tour map of the town.**

As the former master of the *S.S. Bahama Star,* Captain Carl Netherland-Brown and his wife, Janet, have seen the world, but the place they have chosen to hang their hats in retirement is the Hale Springs Inn in Rogersville, one of Tennessee's most historic towns (dating to 1786). Born in the Volunteer State, the captain moved to Florida and went to sea at an early age. He is descended from the Netherlands, associated the Netherlands Inn in Kingsport, Tennessee.

The Netherland-Browns restored the three-story Federal-style brick inn between 1982 and 1988, adding private bathrooms, new wiring, and new heating and air conditioning. Recently, they created a beautiful formal garden, including a gazebo. They have also restored the family home, Rosemont, and the McKinney law office in Rogersville.

Built by John McKinney in the heart of town as a stagecoach stop in 1824 during frontier days, the inn was considered grand for its time. It was originally called McKinney's Tavern, and it was used for a time during the Civil War by Union soldiers. The present name was adopted in 1884 when the hotel became associated with Hale Springs Resort, about 15 miles away. Hale Springs Inn is the oldest continuously operating inn in the state.

The inn features very large guest rooms with high ceilings and working fireplaces. All are furnished in valuable antiques, some dating to the early 1800s. The Jackson Suite, named for President Andrew Jackson, who spent the night here in 1832, is the most popular room. It features a four-poster canopy bed, large sitting area, and fireplace, and it overlooks Main Street and the courtyard. Presidents Johnson and Polk also visited the inn and have rooms named for them. The Mollie Gray Suite, another favorite, is decorated in rosy hues.

The dining room, reminiscent of a Colonial tavern, has two fireplaces. It was added in 1987 in the area of the original tavern, and it's open to the public for lunch and dinner. Here guests dine on such gourmet delights as prime rib of beef with Yorkshire pudding, shrimp scampi, and breast of chicken Alfredo, all served in a candlelight atmosphere by waitresses in pioneer costumes. Guests may bring their own wine. Breakfasts at the inn are Continental and include cereals, home-baked breads, fruits, juices, and other beverages.

Rugby

Grey Gables Bed & Breakfast

Highway 52, P.O. Box 52
Rugby, TN 37733
423-628-5252
Fax: 423-628-5252

A family-owned Victorian B&B that's dedicated to guests

Innkeepers: Bill and Linda Brooks Jones. **Accommodations:** 8 rooms (4 with private baths, 4 with shared baths). **Rates:** $95. **Included:** Full breakfast. **Children:** Welcome. **Pets:** Not allowed. **Smoking:** Allowed on porches. **Open:** Year-round.

➤ **The Joneses also operate the historic Brooks General Store, previously owned by Linda's grandfather. It served as Rugby's commercial center for decades, and today is not only an operating store but something of an attraction. Customers sit around the potbellied stove, get their mail at the post office in the corner, and shop for necessities and crafts.**

This bed-and-breakfast inn has been a family affair from the beginning, with owners Bill and Linda Brooks Jones and their children doing most of the work themselves — from the design and construction of the house to the cooking and cleaning. They moved back to their roots after spending several years in St. Louis, Missouri. The innkeepers make every effort to offer a "Victorian England in Rural America Experience" at the inn with the ambiance, food, and hospitality.

Grey Gables was dedicated in 1990, though its architectural style is Victorian in keeping with historic Rugby, an English-like village of the 1880s. The house is furnished with Victorian antiques and family pieces that are original to the area. The two-story clapboard structure, with verandah extending across the entire front (ninety feet), sits in the middle of thirty-two acres. Guests step into the Victorian age when they enter through the stained glass door. In the entryway is a hall tree that served as a backdrop for Linda's parents' wedding many years ago, as well as other pieces that have special stories. Family pictures are scattered throughout the inn, and sometimes you can match a piece of furniture with the person who owned it. Each room has a different look, but all bear Linda's special touch. There are eight bedrooms, each appropriately named to fit its decor — the Victorian Room, the Rugby Room, and Aunt Nell's Room are a few.

A full breakfast and dinner are included in the room rate at Grey Gables. Dinner includes a salad, entrée, two vegetables, homemade rolls, dessert, and beverage. Lunch and high tea, served on special occasions, are a bit extra. (Linda knows all about high tea; she worked in an English tea room in St. Louis.) Recipes used at the inn are featured in a cookbook, *The Table at Grey Gables*. No alcoholic beverages are available at the inn, but guests may bring their own.

The Joneses stage special events such as hunt dinners, wildflower programs, pig roasts, and other interesting activities throughout the year. Daughters Taryn, Teresa, Tiffany, son Tim and daughter-in-law Kathy have all pitched in to make Grey Gables a success.

Newbury House at Historic Rugby

Highway 52, P.O. Box 8
Rugby, TN 37733
423-628-2441
Fax: 423-628-2266
RugbyTn@Highland.net

> An English experiment that
> survives as a hospitality
> center

Owner: Historic Rugby. **Accommodations:** 6 rooms (2 with private baths, 4 with shared bath) and 2 cottages (with private baths). **Rates:** $60–$72. **Included:** Full breakfast. **Payment:** MasterCard, Visa. **Children:** 12 and older welcome in inn; any age in cottages. **Pets:** Not allowed. **Smoking:** Allowed on verandahs. **Open:** Year-round.

➤ **The utopian society lasted a decade, its residents halfheartedly dabbling in farming and handicrafts while zealously pursuing cultural and recreational pursuits. Many dressed for afternoon tea every day.**

Take a step back into history in this English village in the Cumberland Mountains near the Big South Fork National Recreation Area. It was established as a cooperative, class-free society for Britain's sons of gentry by Thomas Hughes, social reformer and author of *Tom Brown's Schooldays,* in 1880.

The town consisted of more than 70 buildings, including the Tabard Inn, which borrowed its name from Chaucer's *Canterbury Tales.* It burned in 1884. Seventeen of the buildings — including the Episcopal Church, library, schoolhouse, bookshop, and Thomas Hughes's home — survived, however, and have been preserved for posterity, thanks to the efforts of Historic Rugby. Visitors may tour the public buildings daily.

Newbury House, the town's first boarding house, dating to 1880, and Pioneer House, dubbed the Asylum by early residents, are used today as lodgings. Perey Cottage is a reconstruction.

The Victorian-style Newbury House, a ten-room structure built by Otis Brown in the mansard style, offers many of the features of the old Tabard Inn. Guests are treated to a full breakfast each morning and can enjoy afternoon tea in the parlor. Pioneer House offers three guest rooms and a fully equipped kitchen. Many visitors have their meals at Harrow Road Café, a new structure that conforms to Rugby's historic architecture and serves Cumberland-Plateau home cooking and dishes from the British Isles, including fish and chips and Welsh rarebit.

Savannah

Ross House Bed & Breakfast

504 Main Street
Savannah, TN 38372
Mailing address:
P.O. Box 398
Savannah, TN 38372
901-925-3974, 800-467-3174
Fax: 901-925-4472
jnonros@centuryinter.net

An original family home offers an original experience

Innkeepers: John and Harriet Ross. **Accommodations:** 2 suites (each with a private bath and sitting room). **Rates:** $75–$100. **Included:** Full breakfast. **Payment:** Major credit cards. **Children:** 10 and older welcome. **Pets:** Not allowed. **Smoking:** Not allowed. **Open:** Year-round.

➤   **Union General Ulysses S. Grant and Confederate General Albert S. Johnston met in a major conflict at Shiloh. The cemetery contains 3,854 graves.**

A lifetime of memories and memorabilia is shared with guests at this elegant bed-and-breakfast inn in the heart of Savannah. The neoclassical home of the late Elijah W. Ross and his wife Nellie Williams Ross has been restored by their grandson, John Ross, and his wife Harriet. A third-generation attorney who practices law next door, John Ross decided in 1990 to restore the house according to the U.S. Department of Interior standards.

   On the National Register of Historic Places, the house was designed by architect Hubert T. McGee and built in 1908. The brick home has a two-story portico with Ionic columns and pilasters and a wraparound porch with columns and pilasters. The metal shingle roof is original.

Practically everything in the house is original — not only the walls and flooring but the furniture, handmade quilts, photographs, china, toys, books, paintings, records, letters, and clothing. (The Ross' daughters Christina and Elizabeth have had a wonderful time trying on the vintage clothing that belonged to their great-grandmother and great-aunt.) Everything in the house has been left intact, but the Rosses have given the house a new look with fresh coats of paint in historical colors. The woodwork and the fireplaces remain in their original condition. The restoration of the home as a B&B, according to Mr. Ross, is his way of preserving the house and sharing it with others. The Rosses live just a few doors from the inn in a more modern house, but they are always on call.

Guests have the full run of the house, including the kitchen and laundry. The refrigerator is always stocked with cold beverages and snacks. The Rosses serve a full breakfast and keep a collection of menus from local restaurants on hand.

With their keen interest in history, the Rosses are always happy to direct guests to the Tennessee River Museum in town and Shiloh National Military Park. Queen Haley, the grandmother of Alex Haley and the central character in the television mini-series *Queen*, is buried in Savannah. Another area attraction is Pickwick Landing State Resort Park.

Sevierville

Blue Mountain Mist Country Inn — Shagonage

1811 Pullen Road
Sevierville, TN 37862
423-428-2335, 800-497-2335

> **A Victorian mountain inn
> surrounded by mountains**

Innkeepers: Norman and Sarah Ball. **Accommodations:** 11 rooms (all with private baths, 2 with Jacuzzis), 1 suite (with private bath), and 5 cottages (with private baths and kitchenettes). **Rates:** $90–$140. **Included:** Full country breakfast, evening refreshments. **Payment:** MasterCard, Visa. **Children:** Well-behaved children welcome. **Pets:** Not allowed. **Smoking:** Allowed on porches. **Open:** Year-round.

➤ **From the wraparound porch of Shagonage (a Cherokee word meaning blue smoke), you have a ringside seat for Mother Nature's command performance.**

Blue Mountain Mist Country Inn is only a five-minute ride from Dollywood and only twenty minutes from Gatlinburg, the gateway to the Great Smoky Mountains National Park, but it's light-years away from the plastic strip of souvenir shops and attractions that stretches for miles down U.S. 331 and 441.

July days begin with the pink glow of dawn over the rim of the surrounding mountains and end with the blazing orange of sunset over the darkening shadows. During the height of the day, white daisies and blue bachelor buttons dance in the rolling green meadows amid the bailed hay. After dusk the cicadas and the bullfrogs that live in the lily pond out front join in a symphonic chorus, as the lightning signals the approach of a thunderstorm. The scene shifts with each passing moment and season — as summer turns to autumn, autumn turns to winter, winter to spring, spring to summer.

The porch is a great place for sipping morning coffee, playing a game of checkers with newfound friends, or watching the stars at night. You can sit in the white rocking chairs and get into a good book, sit close to your sweetheart on the porch swing, or relax in the hammock, as Little Bear, the family dog, keeps you company. The inside of the inn is just as entertaining. There are puzzles to work, books to enjoy, and music to listen to.

Norman and Sarah Ball, educators by profession, built the Victorian charmer on her family's 60-acre farm in 1987, following their visit to an inn in Charleston, South Carolina. He designed the 12-bedroom, 12-bath, 2-story inn with lots of windows and large public areas, including television and conference rooms in the basement. Inn rooms are named for communities in the area — Elkmont, White Oak Flats, Ramsey's Cascades, Chimney Tops, and others. Some of the bedrooms have clawfoot tubs. Rainbow Falls, a favorite with honeymooners, features stained glass by Chuck Ottolini, a local artist.

Behind the main inn in the woods are five country cottages. Perfect for romantic getaways, they feature Jacuzzis for two, fireplaces, porch swings, and queen-sized beds. Each is furnished in a country theme and has all the modern conveniences, including a kitchenette, television and VCR, grill, and picnic table. Cottage residents may have a breakfast basket delivered to their door or join other guests for breakfast in the inn.

Sarah, who retired from teaching to devote full time to the inn and her family, decorated the inn with antiques and family heirlooms. The friendship quilt hanging in the Greenbrier Room includes the names of many family members. Her parents, Estel and Ruth Ownby, enjoy visiting with the guests and reminiscing about the good old days before the national park was created. The Balls have two grown children, Misty and Eric, and a son Jason who still lives at home.

The atmosphere at Blue Mountain Mist is casual and relaxed, and judging from the comments written in the word books in each room, guests have a nice time here. They are welcome to help themselves to lemonade and cookies at any hour of the day. A full country breakfast, which might consist of fruit, eggs, sausage, bacon, cheese grits, sausage gravy, homemade biscuits, butter, jams, and jellies, is served family-style at 8:30 in the sunny dining room. Then guests are free to pitch horseshoes, play badminton, take a walk, or explore the nearby towns.

The Balls frequently host corporate meetings, weddings, and parties. They do not serve dinner, but can recommend restaurants in the area. In the evening they serve dessert, coffee, and other nonalcoholic drinks.

Von Bryan Inn

2402 Hatcher Mountain Road
Sevierville, TN 37862
423-453-9832, 800-633-1459

A mountaintop lodge in the Smokies

Innkeepers: D.J. and Jo Ann Vaughn. **Accommodations:** 6 rooms and 1 chalet (all with private baths, 2 with whirlpools); 2-night minimum in chalet. **Rates:** $90–$180. **Included:** Full breakfast, afternoon refreshments. **Payment:** Major credit cards. **Children:** 10 and older welcome in inn; all ages welcome in chalet. **Pets:** Not allowed. **Smoking:** Allowed outside. **Open:** Year-round.

➤ **The 2,100-foot elevation is ideal for viewing the surrounding giant mountains that soar over 6,000 feet. The Vaughns provide a telescope for close-up views.**

Everyone gets a room with a view at the Von Bryan Inn on top of Hatcher's Mountain, and that's why D.J. and Jo Ann Vaughn moved here. They had conducted an exhaustive two-year search, and when they spied this inn, they knew immediately that it was the spot they'd been looking for. Others, including Dolly Parton and T.

J. Sheppard, had eyed the prized mountaintop, too, but the Vaughns became the owners.

Luckily, the sprawling two-story home and guest chalet, built as a private retreat, could easily be converted into a bed-and-breakfast. With 6,100 square feet, guests certainly have plenty of room. The Vaughns have furnished the inn with antiques and quilts, giving it a warm, cozy feeling. Honeymooners usually prefer the romantic Red Bud Room with its cherry-red whirlpool tub, while families and couples traveling together like the Dogwood Suite, a chalet with three bedrooms, two baths, kitchen, and wraparound deck. Other rooms are the Tulip Poplar Room, featuring a queen canopy bed; the Sweet Gum Room; the White Oak Room, furnished in wicker; the Blue Spruce Room, which has two antique brass double beds; and the Garden Room, with its reading loft and steam shower surrounded by windows.

Guests enjoy congregating in the great room, with its lofty cathedral ceiling and large fireplace made of stacked stone. The spacious upstairs sitting room, offering spectacular views of the mountains, serves as a quiet retreat. Often guests wander into the kitchen where D.J., Jo Ann, or their two sons, David and Patrick, are preparing meals. A full breakfast (meat, eggs, homemade breads, juice, fruit, and coffee) is served; it is included in the rate, as are the afternoon refreshments. The Vaughns often share recipes with guests.

There is plenty to do on top of Hatcher's Mountain, from relaxing in the hammock to taking a plunge in the pool to going for a hike. The Vaughns often stage cooking classes, guided hikes, progressive dinners, and tours of the area. And if anyone cares to leave the mountaintop, attractions abound in Sevierville, Pigeon Forge, and Gatlinburg.

Walland

The Inn at Blackberry Farm

1417 West Millers Cove Road
Walland, TN 37886
423-984-8166, 800-862-7610
Fax: 423-983-5708

> A luxurious mountain inn
> that fits the bill for
> individuals and groups

Innkeepers: Brian Lee. **General Manager:** John Fleer. **Accommodations:** 26 rooms and 16 suites (all with private baths). **Rates:** $295–$1,845 (2-night minimum anytime; 3-night minimum in October and during holiday weekends). **Included:** Three gourmet meals, snacks and beverages, afternoon tea, turndown service, recreational equipment. **Payment:** American Express, MasterCard, Visa. **Children:** 10 and older welcome. **Pets:** Not allowed. **Smoking:** Allowed on verandah. **Open:** Year-round.

> ➤ **The most popular pastime at the inn requires little effort — looking at the mountains from the terrace — but more active options include hiking, jogging, bicycling, fishing, swimming, croquet, shuffle-board, and tennis.**

You can certainly get lost in this quiet, elegant inn, which is surrounded by 1,100 acres and the Great Smoky Mountains National Park. Designed by Barbara McMurray of Knoxville and built in 1939 of wood, stone, slate, and glass, the inn today is as inviting today as it ever was. It is located in the foothills in the woods overlooking a clearing, far from the traffic of Pigeon Forge and Gatlinburg. The nearest town is Walland, five miles away, and the Knoxville airport is about a twenty-minute ride.

Kreis and Sandy Beall, who purchased the property in 1976, remodeled the Main House, added the Guest House, and opened the inn to guests in 1990. To accommodate more guests, eight Holly Glade Cottages offering sixteen private suites were recently added at a cost of nearly $5 million. A fully stocked pantry and soothing whirlpool bath await guests in each cottage, along with a king-size bed and a spacious sitting area with custom-made furniture. The Chestnut and Oak Cottages, housing a gift shop, meeting rooms, fitness facility, and a club room were completed in late 1997.

Guests at the inn sleep in luxurious rooms with mountain views, and no expense has been spared in decorating. Mrs. Beall has used tons of polished floral print in the matching draperies and bedspreads. Each bed is covered with a down mattress pad and comforter — ideal for the cool nights in the mountains. Nightly turndown service is a tradition. The public rooms — which feature large windows that frame the scenery, wood paneling, and hardwood floors — are also exquisitely decorated, with overstuffed chairs and sofas and Oriental rugs, accented with original art, fine prints, and decorative pieces.

The dining room, with its many windows that bring the outdoors inside, is a perfect setting for elegant dining. Each set menu planned by Chef John Fleer, a graduate of the Culinary Institute of American in New York, is exciting. He has developed Blackberry's acclaimed "Foothills Cuisine," with multi-course dinners, seasonally oriented lunches, and a choice of hearty or light breakfasts. He says his creations "wander the line between refined and rustic, borrowing from both haute cuisine and country foods." Brunch is served on Sunday and tea every afternoon. Snacks are available throughout the day and evening. Special culinary weekends and holiday menus are presented several times a year.

Guests may enjoy swimming, tennis, hiking, biking, shuffleboard, horseshoes, croquet, and badminton. Fly fishing from two stocked, private ponds and from Hesse Creek is also an option. Group instruction and private lessons are available from Orvis-accredited instructions, and the gift shop is sanctioned and stocked by Orvis.

The inn has received numerous awards, including Mobil's four stars and AAA's four diamonds. It is a member of Relais & Chateaux and was recently named one of the top five inns in America by *Zagat Survey.*

Reservation Services and Innkeepers' Associations

Reservation Services

If you're interested in staying in places not normally advertised, you might want to use a reservation service. These organizations act as clearinghouses and liaisons—agents if you will—for private homeowners who want to rent out rooms, apartments, or condos without having to hang out a sign or advertise. Reservation services usually screen the properties and make sure they meet certain criteria. The services cost you nothing extra, but agents get a certain percentage of the room rate from the homeowners.

Innkeepers' associations have been formed in several states to ensure that high standards are maintained in the industry. They are not in the business of providing reservations services but often publish free directories listing the inns that have qualified for membership.

Arkansas

Bed and Breakfast Reservation Services and Tourist Accommodations
11 Singleton
Eureka Springs, AR 72632
501-253-9111 or 800-833-3394

Owner: Barbara Gavron. **Lodging:** Restored and new Victorian homes and honeymoon cottages in the historic district of Eureka Springs. (Owner also operates an inn apprenticeship program.)

Arkansas and Ozarks Bed & Breakfast Reservation Service
White River Landing, Inc.
HC 79, Box 330-A
Calico Rock, AR 72519
870-297-4197 or 800-233-2777

Coordinators: Ken and Lynn Griffin. **Lodging:** Contemporary homes, log cabins, historic lodges, and Victorian homes in Calico Rock, Gassville, Hardy, Heber Springs, Ozark, Mammoth Springs, Norfolk, Rogers, Yellville, and other locations in the Ozarks. Well-traveled and well-informed hosts offer unusual decor, gourmet breakfasts, hot tubs, private patios, musical instruments, and memorable stays.

Georgia

Bed & Breakfast Atlanta
1801 Piedmont Avenue NE, Suite 208
Atlanta, GA 0324
770-875-0525 or 800-96-PEACH
Fax: 770-875-9672
http://www.bedandbreakfastatlanta.com

Owner: James Demer. **Lodging:** Carefully selected and inspected homes, guest cottages, and inns in Atlanta and suburban communities within easy access of major expressways and the public transportation system.

R.S.V.P. Georgia and Savannah Bed & Breakfast Reservation Service
611 East 56th Street
Savannah, GA 31405
912-232-7787 or 800-729-7787

Lodging: Bed-and-breakfast inns, ocean suites, private carriage houses in Savannah, Charleston, Macon, Atlanta, and Brunswick.

Kentucky

Bluegrass Bed & Breakfast Reservation Service
2964 McCracken Pike
Versailles, KY 40383
606-873-3208

Contact: Betsy Pratt. **Lodging:** This service offers lodging in homes in and around Lexington, Kentucky Horse Park, Shakertown, Frankfort, and Louisville.

Louisiana

Bed & Breakfast Travel
8211 Goodwood Boulevard, Suite F
Baton Rouge, LA 70806
504-923-2337 or 800-926-4320
Fax: 504-923-2374
bnbtarvel@aol.com

Owners: Judy Young. **Lodging:** Bed-and-breakfasts throughout the South, including Louisiana, Mississippi, and parts of Alabama.

New Orleans Bed & Breakfast & Accommodations
P.O. Box 8163
New Orleans, LA 70182
504-838-0071
Fax: 504-838-0140
Bed-and-breakfasts in the New Orleans area.

Mississippi

Natchez Pilgrimage Tours
P.O. Box 347
Natchez, MS 39120
601-446-6631 or 800-647-6742

Lodging: Antebellum and Victorian homes in and around Natchez, including country plantations and pre–Civil War mansions.

South Carolina

Charleston Society Bed & Breakfast
84 Murray Boulevard
Charleston, SC 29401
803-723-4948

Lodging: Carriage houses and historic homes in Historic Charleston.

Historic Charleston Bed and Breakfast
60 Broad Street
Charleston, SC 29401
803-722-6606 or 800-743-3583
Fax: 803-722-9589

Owner: Carolyn Fairey. **Lodging:** Eighteenth- and nineteenth-century Charleston homes and carriage houses. Gardens, patios, fireplaces, Jacuzzis, and off-street parking are a few of the enticements offered in private homes. Service is also linked to Savannah, Georgia, and other cities in South Carolina.

Tennessee

Bed and Breakfast About Tennessee
P.O. Box 110227
Nashville, TN 37222
615-331-5244 or 800-458-2621

Coordinator: Freda Odom

Worldwide

Bed & Breakfast Reservation Services World-Wide, Inc.
P.O. Box 14841
Baton Rouge, LA 70898-4841
Tel. 504-336-4035; Fax: 504-343-0672
Susan M1052@AOL.com or ssmorris@ix.netcom.com
http://www.classifree.com/travel/bbww

Executive Director: Susan Morris. A bed-and-breakfast worldwide trade association and reservation service, with listings all over the world, including the South.

Innkeepers' Associations

Bed & Breakfast Association of Alabama
P.O. Box 707
Montgomery, AL 36101
This organization publishes a directory of B&Bs in Alabama.

Bed & Breakfast Association of Arkansas
P.O. Box 6381
Hot Springs, AR 71902
501-868-8905

Contact: Linda Westergard

Independent Innkeepers' Association
P.O. Box 150
Marshall, MI 49068
616-781-0970 or 800-344-5244
Fax: 616-789-0393

Executive Director: Norman D. Kinney. Organized in 1972 by Norman T. Simpson, "the father of country inn travel," the association publishes an annual directory of more than 250 guest accommodations in the United States, Canada, and the United Kingdom ($8.95, including postage and handling).

North Carolina Bed & Breakfast Association
P.O. Box 1077
Asheville, NC 28802
800-849-5392
Fax: 281-403-9335
ncbbi@bbonline.com

Contact: Bob Delong

South Carolina Bed & Breakfast Association
P.O. Box 1275
Columbia, SC 29151-1275
803-423-5407

Contact: Tom Griggs

Recommended Reading

We recommend the following books as excellent sources of information on sightseeing, restaurants, and regional history, as well as specialized activities such as fishing and hiking.

General

Annual Travel Guides of the American Automobile Association: Alabama, Louisiana, Mississippi; Arkansas, Kansas, Missouri, Oklahoma; Georgia, North Carolina, South Carolina; Kentucky, Tennessee. American Automobile Association. $8.95 each. Detailed guides on where to go, what to see, where to stay, and places to dine. AAA also publishes maps that accompany the guides.

Blue Ridge Mountain Pleasures: An A–Z Guide to North Georgia, Western North Carolina, and the Upcountry of South Carolina. Donald Wenberg. Globe Pequot Press, paperback, $12.95. A guide to auctions, crafts, gemstones, and other pleasures of the Blue Ridge Mountains.

Cruising Guide to the Northern Gulf Coast: Florida, Alabama, Mississippi, Louisiana. Claiborne S. Young. Pelican Publishing Company, paperback, $23.95. A definitive book on marinas, shoreside attractions, water depths, and other information on the coastal areas of northern Florida, Alabama, Mississippi, and Louisiana.

Discovering Dixie: Along the Magnolia Trail. The Day-by-Day Travel Guide to the Best of the Deep South. Richard Lewis Polese. Adventure Road Series, Ocean Tree Books, $9.95. A personal account of the author's journey through Alabama, the Carolinas, Florida, Georgia, Mississippi, Louisiana, and Tennessee.

Encyclopedia of Southern Culture. A ten-year project involving more than eight hundred writers and scholars offers an extraordinary portrait of one of the nation's richest cultural landscapes. Edited by Reagan Wilson and William Ferris, with a foreword by Alex Haley. University of North Carolina Press, $59.95.

Fishing the Southeast Coast. Donald Mullis. Sandlapper Publishing, paperback, $9.95; hardcover, $16.95. Gives an in-depth view of southern saltwater fishing areas from Morehead City, North Carolina, to the Georgia Sea Islands.

Fodor's Travel Guide: The South. Random House, $14.95. A basic reference guide to the southern states.

Frommer's Dollarwise Guide to the Southeast and New Orleans. Susan Poole. Prentice Hall Press, $13.95. A highly personal and selective guide to the most visited regions of Virginia, North Carolina, South Carolina, Florida Panhandle, the Gulf Coast of Alabama, and Mississippi. The last three chapters are devoted to New Orleans.

Golfing in the Carolinas. William Price Fox. John F. Blair Publisher, $39.95. Writer-in-residence at the University of South Carolina, the author has chosen fifty golf courses in the Carolinas that he considers to be the best.

Insight Guide to the Old South. Martha Zenfell (editor/producer) and Lyle Lawon (photographer). APA Productions, Inc., paperback, $22.95. Just off the press, this brand new guidebook covering the southern states of Virginia, Kentucky, North Carolina, South Carolina and Tennessee was written in a narrative form by regional writers. It includes compelling, full-color photographs, special essays on southerners, southern crafts, southern cooking, the Civil War, the Black South, and other topics. Travel tips, including recommended hotels/motels, restaurants, and attractions, plus color maps, make this guidebook a current and useful reference.

Mobil Travel Guides: The Mid-Atlantic, The Southeast, The Southwest, and South Central. Prentice Hall Press, $10.95 each. Tips on attractions, lodgings, and restaurants.

Modern Southern Reader. Edited by Ben Forkner and Patrick Samway. Peachtree Publishers, paperback, $23.95; hardcover $35.95. Major stories, drama, poetry, essays, interviews, and reminiscences from the 20th-century South.

A New Reader of the Old South. Edited by Ben Forkner and Patrick Samway. Peachtree Publishers, paperback, $19.95; hardcover, $35.95. Major stories, tales, slave narratives, diaries, essays, travelogues, poetry, and songs from 1820 to 1920.

Southern Lighthouses: Chesapeake Bay to the Gulf of Mexico. Bruce Roberts and Ray Jones. Globe Pequot Press, paperback, $16.95. Descriptions of forty-six lighthouses, plus maps and details on how to visit them.

Alabama

Alabama: A Guide to the Deep South. Works Progress Administration Federal Writers' Project staff. Omnigraphics, Inc., $55. A 1991 reprint of a monumental work completed by the WPA in 1941.

Alabama Lodging Guide. Alabama Bureau of Tourism and Travel, free. The state tourism office's official lodging guide contains listings of hotels, motels, and bed-and-breakfast inns. Call 800-ALABAMA for a copy.

Alabama on My Mind. Wayne Greenhaw. Sycamore Press, $11.95. Contains stories about the people, politics, and history of Alabama, as well as ghost stories.

Alabama: One Big Front Porch. Kathryn Tucker Windham. University of Alabama Press, reprinted in 1991, paperback, $14.95. A collection of stories — a southern blend of exaggeration, humor, pathos, folklore, romanticism, and family history — you might hear on the front porch of any Alabama home.

Alabama: Travel Guide. Alabama Bureau of Tourism and Travel, free. The state tourism office's official travel guide includes information on attractions, maps, and a travel information section. Call 800-ALABAMA for a copy.

The Best Quick Trips. Lynn Edge. *The Birmingham News.* $9.95. A travel book on Alabama that's a compilation of fifty-two of the author's weekly travel columns from *The Birmingham News.*

Arkansas

The American Spa. Dee Brown. Rose Publishing Company, $14.95. The life and times of the resort city of Hot Springs and its national park as told by a noted author and historian.

Arkansas. Henry S. Ashmore. The States and the Nation Series. Norton Publishers, $14.95. A historical and political summary of the state by the editor of the *Arkansas Gazette* at the time of the Little Rock crisis. Produced during the Bicentennial.

Arkansas: Its Land and People. Matt Bradley. Little Rock Museum of Science and History, $55. A lavish coffee table photographic essay by one of the state's finest photographers.

Arkansas Roadsides: A Guidebook for the State. Bill Earngey. East Mountain Productions, $9.95. A town-by-town look at Arkansas with linear maps.

The Buffalo River Country. Kenneth L. Smith. Ozark Society Books, $11.95. A detailed guide to the Buffalo National River.

Historical Atlas of Arkansas. Gerald T. Hanson and Carl H. Moneyhon. University of Oklahoma Press, $29.95. Maps of natural regions, soil, surface water, and temperature patterns are followed by settlement patterns showing relationships among geography, people, and technology.

A Living History of the Ozarks. Phyllis Rossiter. Pelican Publishing Company, paperback, $11.95. A guide to the region through landmarks and sites that offer clues to the intriguing history of the Ozarks.

The Roads of Arkansas. Dee Brown. Shearer Publishing, $12.95. Detailed section maps of the state.

The Smithsonian Guide to Historic America Series: Texas, Oklahoma, Arkansas. Alice Gordon and Jerry Camarillo Dunn, Jr., and Mel White. Stewart, Tabori, and Chang, $18.95. Brief histories of each state followed by detailed descriptions of historic sites.

Georgia

Atlanta Restaurant Guide. Bill Cutler and Christiane Lauterbach. Pelican Publishing Company, $7.95. Candid reviews of more than two hundred of Atlanta's best and most interesting restaurants.

Authorized Commemorative Editions of Atlanta's Official Olympic Bid Books. Volume 1. Welcome to a Brave and Beautiful City. Volume II. Atlanta: City of Dreams. Peachtree Publishers, $17.95 each. Official guides to the 1996 Olympics.

Classic Atlanta: Landmarks of the Atlanta Spirit. Text by William R. Mitchell, Jr., photography by Van Jones Martin. Peachtree Publishers, hardcover, $60. An elegant pictorial history of the architecture of this great southern city. This book documents, investigates, criticizes, and celebrates the architecture of Atlanta with fresh scholarship, intriguing archival photographs and drawings, and exquisite contemporary color photography.

Georgia at Its Best. Jeanne and Harry Harmon. Rutledge Hill Press, paperback, $12.95. One of the best general guidebooks to the state.

Georgia Off the Beaten Path. Bill Schemmel. Globe Pequot Press, paperback, $8.95. One of the state's outstanding writers takes you to little-known places in Georgia.

Georgia: The WPA Guide to Its Towns and Countryside. Federal Writers Project of the Works Progress Administration staff, with an introduction by Phinizy Spalding. University of South Carolina Press, 1990, $16.95. Reprint of the 1940 classic produced by the WPA.

Georgia's Historic Restaurants and Their Recipes. Dawn O'Brien and Jean Spaugh. John F. Blair Publisher, $12.95. This book highlights Georgia's historic restaurants and includes some of their recipes.

Journal of a Residence on a Georgia Plantation in 1838–1839. Frances Anne Kemble, edited and with an introduction by John A. Scott. University of Georgia Press, $11.95. The wife of plantation owner Pierce Butler gives her perspective and opposition to slavery as she views it firsthand while living on a Sea Island plantation.

A Marmac Guide to Atlanta. Bill Schemmel and Mary McDonald. Pelican Publishing Company, paperback, $8.95. The guide highlights transportation, lodging, restaurants, shopping, nightlife, sightseeing, and day and weekend trips.

Weekend Escapes from Atlanta, Nashville, Knoxville, Montgomery, Columbia, Macon, and Columbus. Edited by Mike Michaelson. Rand McNally. Outlines day trips from several southern cities.

Kentucky

Kentucky: A Guide to the Bluegrass State. Works Progress Administration, Federal Writers' Project staff. Omnigraphics, Inc., $55. A 1991 reprint of a WPA classic.

Kentucky Gems Series: Kentucky Handbook, Kentucky Tidbits, Kentucky Governors, 120 Kentucky Counties, Kentucky Shrines. Robert A. Powell. Kentucky Images Publishers, $2.65–$3.25 each. A very popular, inexpensive series that is one of the best resources on the Bluegrass State.

Kentucky Official Vacation Guide. Kentucky Travel. Everything you need to know about traveling in Kentucky is contained in this booklet. Call 800-225-TRIP for a free copy.

Sketches of Kentucky. Robert A. Powell. Kentucky Images Publishers, $23.25. A coffee table edition of historical pen-and-ink sketches, printed in buffalo brown ink on natural ivory paper, with accompanying text, covering the commonwealth of Kentucky.

Pleasant Hill and Its Shakers. Thomas D. Clark and F. Gerald Ham. Pleasant Hill Press, paperback, $4.95; hardcover, $10.00. Associated with the restoration of Pleasant Hill since the early 1960s and using his knowledge of F. Gerald Ham's writings, the author narrates the story of the Shakers with knowledge, warmth, humor, and dramatic animation.

Louisiana

Cajun Country Guide. Macon Fry. Pelican Publishing Company, paperback, $8.95. An in-depth study focusing on attractions unique to the Cajun country of southern Louisiana, this guidebook highlights various regions and gives a directory of sights, sounds, and flavors.

A History Lover's Guide to Louisiana. Mary Ann Wells. Quail Ridge Press, $12.95. The author guides readers through some of Louisiana's most exotic travel opportunities.

Louisiana Off the Beaten Path: A Guide to Unique Places. Gay N. Martin. Globe Pequot Press, $8.95. With the state motto Louisiana — as American as crawfish pie, Louisiana promises anything but the usual, and with this book as your companion, you're in for a can't-miss good time.

Louisiana Plantation Homes: The Grace and Grandeur. Joseph Arrigo, with photographs by Dick Dietrich. Voyageur Press, $19.95. The histories of thirty-four of Louisiana's plantation homes.

Louisiana Proud. Volumes I, II, and III. Andrew M. Smith, Sr. Louisiana Proud Press, $19.95 each. The author has traveled Louisiana from border to border photographing its landmarks, both the famous and the not-so-famous. He shares his collection through handsome pen-and-ink illustrations and a historical text written in an informal prose style.

Louisiana Tour Guide. Louisiana Travel Promotion Association. Details every traveler needs to know while traveling in Louisiana are included in this guide. Write to Tour Guide, P.O. Box 3988, Baton Rouge, LA 70821-3988 for a free copy or check the Louisiana website — http://www.louisianatravel.com.

The Majesty of the Felicianas. Text by Lee Malone, photographs by Paul Malone. Pelican Publishing Company, hardcover, $15.95. The Malones capture the startling beauty of the old homes of the Felicianas through words and pictures.

The Majesty of New Orleans. Photographs by Paul Malone, text by Lee Malone. Pelican Publishing Company, hardcover, $17.95. A look at the architecture, courtyards and patios, ironwork, and cemeteries that make the city of New Orleans the fascinating place it is today.

A Marmac Guide to New Orleans. Beth S. Cary and Liz B. McCarthy, edited by Cecilia Casrill Dartez. Paperback, $8.95. A detailed guide to the city and surrounding areas.

The Majesty of the River Road. Text by Lee Malone, photographs by Paul Malone. Pelican Publishing Company, hardcover, $15.95. Captures in words and pictures the charm and splendor of the palatial homes along the Mississippi River between Baton Rouge and New Orleans.

New Orleans Official Visitors Guide. New Orleans Metropolitan Convention and Visitors Bureau, Inc. Activities, dining, maps, shopping, and sightseeing are featured in this guide, Call 504-566-5011 for a free copy or check the Bureau's web site — http://www.nawlins.com.

Old New Orleans: Walking Tours of the French Quarter. Stanley Clisby Arthur, edited by Susan Cole Dore. Pelican Publishing Company, paperback, $8.95. Originally published in 1936, the book offers interesting insight into old New Orleans traditions, romances, social life, and intrigues.

The Pelican Guide to Gardens in Louisiana. Joyce LeBlanc, edited by Susan Cole Dore. Pelican Publishing Company, $7.95. The lush, tropical climate of Louisiana provides a perfect setting for some of America's most enchanting garden spots.

The Pelican Guide to Louisiana. Mary Ann Sternberg. Pelican Publishing Company, $6.95. This comprehensive, up-to-date guide to Louisiana leads tourists and residents alike on an eye-opening tour of the many and diverse attractions that characterize the Pelican State.

The Pelican Guide to the Louisiana Capitol. Ellen Roy Jolly and James Calhoun. Pelican Publishing Company, $6.95. A guide to the capitol's history, art, and architecture.

The Pelican Guide to Plantation Homes of Louisiana. Edited by Susan Cole Dore. Pelican Publishing Company, paperback, $7.95. Brief sketches and photographs of more than 250 architecturally and historically significant homes in Louisiana.

Plantations of Louisiana. Jess DeHart. Pelican Publishing Company, $12.95. A basic guide to the history and architecture of Louisiana plantations.

Romantic New Orleans. Text by Deirdre Stanforth, photographs by Louis Reens. Pelican Publishing Company, paperback, $9.95. Offers an insider's tour of New Orleans' neighborhoods, homes, food, music, and festivals.

Mississippi

The Majesty of Natchez. Reid Smith and John Owens. Pelican Publishing Company, $12.95. One of the most comprehensive guides to the antebellum homes of Natchez.

Mississippi. Text by Bern Keating, photographs by Frances Keating. University Press of Mississippi. This written survey of Mississippi is accompanied by superb full-color photographs.

Mississippi: The WPA Guide to the Magnolia State. Federal Writers' Project staff, with an introduction by Robert S. McElvaine. University Press, paperback, $15.95; hardcover, $35. A 1991 reprint of the 1938 WPA classic.

The Pelican Guide to Old Homes of Mississippi. Volume I. Natchez and the South. Volume II. Columbus and the North. Helen Kerr Kemp, edited by Susan Cole Dore. Pelican Publishing Company, paperback, $7.95 each. Volume I explores the architecturally and historically significant houses of southern Mississippi; Volume II is a guide to cities and towns in northern Mississippi.

Pilgrimage: A Tale of Old Natchez. Louise Wilbourn Collier. St. Luke's Press, $14.95. A bittersweet saga of one family's struggle to survive the devastation of the Civil War and the subsequent cultural and social changes that inundated their way of life.

The South's Warmest Welcome — Mississippi (state guide). CMississippi Department of Economic and Community Development, Division of Tourism Development. Call 800-WARMEST for a free copy.

Tours and Temples Along the Mississippi. Edited by David H. Dye and Cheryl Anne Cox. Paperback, $22.95. An overview of the most advanced native North American culture at the time of the European contact.

North Carolina

Charlotte: Nothing Could Be Finer. Doug Mayes. (Photography editing by Nancy Stanfield; corporate profiles by Doug Morrison.) Towery Publishing Company's Urban Tapestry Series, 1996. Hardcover. $44.95. Written by the "Dean of TV Newscasters in the Carolinas," this coffee-table book on the Queen City is not only easy reading but a beautiful portrayal of Charlotte, a New South city.

Country Roads of North Carolina. Glenn Morris. Country Roads Press. Paperback. $9.95. The author takes you down country roads of his home states — roads which meander through wonderful parks and country towns from the mountains to the shore.

Cruising Guide to Coastal North Carolina. Claiborne S. Young. John F. Blair Publisher, paperback, $17.95. A sailor's bible for the North Carolina coast, this book contains maps, charts, and photographs plus tidbits on local lore and suggested restaurants.

The Great Dismal Swamp. Bland Simpson. University of North Carolina Press, hardcover, $16.95. The author mixes personal experience, travel, narrative, oral history, and natural history to produce this portrait of the Great Dismal Swamp and its people.

Islands, Capes, and Sounds: The North Carolina Coast. Thomas J. Schoenbaum. John F. Blair Publisher, $12.95. A general history of eastern North Carolina and a layperson's guide to environmental issues.

North Carolina Beaches — A Guide to Coastal Areas. Glenn Morris. The University of North Carolina Press, paperback, $16.95. The book offers a north-to-south, island-by-island, beach-by-beach tour of public sites along the coast. It includes maps and charts and covers national seashores, state parks, public beaches, wildlife refuges, historic sites, fishing piers, lighthouses, ferries, museums, and other sites.

The North Carolina Gazetteer. William S. Powell. University of North Carolina Press, paperback, $13.95. This directory to North Carolina contains more than 20,000 entries on history and on the geography of towns, cities, and counties across the state.

The North Carolina One-Day Trip Book. Jane Ockers-hausen. EPM Publications, $11.95. A passport to North Carolina organized by seven geographic regions. This book can be used to plan any type of vacation, and it's delightful reading on a state that is diverse in history and geography.

North Carolina Travel Guide. North Carolina Travel and Tourism Division, paperback, free. This guide divides the state into ten regions. Each section includes a description of the region and a discussion of "where to go." Call 1-800-VISIT-NC for a copy.

North Carolina Traveler. Ginny Turner. Vantana Press, $9.95. Offers facts and insights that will serve as a guide to the best of the Tar Heel state. Suggests destinations to suit every budget and interest.

North Carolina's Historic Restaurants and Their Recipes. Dawn O'Brien. John F. Blair Publisher, hardcover, $14.95. This revised edition includes thirteen new restaurants and more than fifty new recipes, plus pen-and-ink drawings.

Ocracoke Portrait. Ann S. Ehringhaus. John F. Blair Publisher, paperback, $13.95; hardcover, $21.95. After spending eight years photographing this island off the North Carolina coast, the author has put together sixty-four duotone photographs and included comments from residents and tourists.

The Outer Banks. Anthony Bailey. Farrar, Straus, and Giroux, hardcover, $18.95. Combines the author's personal experiences, natural and local history, and people during his month-long visit to the state on its 400th anniversary.

State Parks of North Carolina. Walter C. Biggs, Jr., and James F. Parnell. John F. Blair Publisher, paperback, $14.95. This comprehensive guide to the state's 27 parks, plus several recreation areas and nature areas, also includes maps and information on nearby points of interest.

Touring the Western North Carolina Backroads. Carolyn Sakowski. John F. Blair Publisher, paperback, $14.95. The book's 21 tours cover the entire mountain region of western North Carolina and provide opportunities for seeing unspoiled landscapes and pastoral scenes as well as learning about its history.

WPA Guide to the Old North State. Works Progress Administration, Federal Writers' Project. University of South Carolina Press, paperback, $17.95; hardcover, $39.95. A 1989 reprint of a WPA classic.

South Carolina

The Best of Charleston: A Guide to the City's Hospitality. Sara Pitzner. University of South Carolina Press.

Cruising Guide to Coastal South Carolina. Claiborne S. Young. John F. Blair Publisher, paperback, $17.95. The only guide devoted exclusively to the state's waterways, the book contains maps, charts, photographs, and local history.

South Carolina Trails. Allen deHart. Globe Pequot Press, paperback, $12.95. Describes more than 500 miles of the state's best trails for hiking, bicycling, and equestrian activities.

South Carolina Vacation Guide. South Carolina Department of Parks, Recreation, and Tourism, free.

South Carolina: WPA Guide to the Palmetto State. Works Progress Administration Federal Writers' Project, with a new introduction by Walter B. Edgar. Paperback, $16.95; hardcover, $34.95. Includes all major cities at the time the guide was written during the Depression, plus updated guide, appendix, and introduction.

South Carolina's Historic Restaurants and Their Recipes. Dawn O'Brien and Karen Mulford. John F. Blair Publisher, $12.95. One of a series of seven books on historic restaurants, this one highlights those in the Palmetto state.

Touring the Coastal South Carolina Backroads. Nancy Rhyne. John F. Blair Publisher, $14.95. A detailed guidebook to places on the South Carolina Coast that are off the beaten path.

A Traveler's Guide to South Carolina. Sara Pitzner. University of South Carolina Press.

Tennessee

Dining in Historic Tennessee: A Restaurant Guide with Recipes. Marty Goddard. McClanaan Publishing House, $14. Old sights and historic restaurants with their best recipes.

Gatlinburg: Places of Discovery. Lou Harshaw. Greenburg Publishing, $8.95. A fascinating guide to the gateway of the Great Smoky Mountains.

Natural Wonders of Tennessee — A Guide to Parks, Preserves, & Wild Places. Ardi Lawrence and H. Lea Lawrence. Country Roads Press, paperback, $9.95. This guide will lead you deep into Tennessee's parks, forest, and reserves — to areas most vacationers miss — and serve as your companion as you explore fragile ecosystems, wildlife and bird sanctuaries, and other "green" places.

The Scots-Irish in the Hills of Tennessee. Billy Kennedy. 1995. Paperback, $14.95. Written by an Ulsterman, this is the chronicle of a pioneer people and their role in the opening of the American frontier.

Tennessee. Wilma Dykeman. W. W. Norton, $14.95. An overview of Tennessee history.

Tennessee: Off the Beaten Path. Tim O'Brien. Globe Pequot Press, $8.95. A naturalist's guide featuring little and hard-to-reach places.

Tennessee Trails. Evan Means. Tennessee Trails Association, Globe Pequot Press, $9.95. A hiking guide to the Smokies.

What's What

Airport on Premises

Arkansas
Gaston's White River Resort, 63
Kentucky
Lake Barkley State Resort Park, 181

Antiques Shop on Premises

Louisiana
Portiers Prairie Cajun Inn and Gift Boutique, 243
Mississippi
The Redbud Inn, 297
North Carolina
Miss Betty's Bed & Breakfast Inn, 422
South Carolina
Laurel Hill Plantation Bed & Breakfast Inn, 493
Wade-Beckham House, 442

Art Gallery on Premises

Mississippi
Who's Inn?, 309

Beach

Alabama
Marriott's Grand Hotel, 28
The Original Romar House, 25
Perdido Beach Resort, 27
Twin Pines Resort and Conference Center, 32

Bicycling

Billiards

Birding

Boating

Book Tours

Business Travelers

Tennessee
Christopher Place, 548
Embassy Suites Memphis, 536
Hyatt Regency Knoxville at Civic Coliseum, 532
The Hancock House, 524
Highland Place Bed & Breakfast, 531
The Inn at Blackberry Farm, 566
The Peabody, 537
Radisson Read House Hotel and Suites, 520

Carriage Rides

Georgia
Inn Scarlett's Footsteps: A Plantation, 113
Melhana — The Grand Plantation Resort, 130
Louisiana
Portiers Prairie Cajun Inn and Gift Boutique, 243
North Carolina
Pinehurst Resort & Country Club, 389

Children's Programs

Alabama
Marriott's Grand Hotel, 28
Perdido Beach Resort, 27
Georgia
Brasstown Valley Resort, 132
Callaway Gardens, 126
The Cloister, 165
The Ritz-Carlton Buckhead, 103
Kentucky
Marriott's Griffin Gate Resort, 198
North Carolina
High Hampton Inn, 346
Hound Ears Club, 340
South Carolina
Disney's Hilton Head Island Resort, 487

Craft Center

Arkansas
The Ozark Folk Center, 77
Georgia
Brasstown Valley Resort, 132
Kentucky
The Doctor's Inn of Berea, 180
Mammoth Cave Hotel/Lodge-Cottages, 203
North Carolina
The Grove Park Inn Resort, 334
High Hampton Inn, 346
South Carolina
Crowne Plaza Resort, Hilton Head Island, 486
Tennessee
Buckhorn Inn, 526
Hippensteal's Mountain View Inn, 528

Croquet

Arkansas
Johnson House Bed & Breakfast, 62
Queen Wilhelmina Lodge, 72
Georgia
The Cloister, 165
North Carolina
Eseeola Lodge, 357
Fearrington House, 391
High Hampton Inn, 346
Pinehurst Resort & Country Club, 389
Richmond Hill Inn and Conference Center, 336
The Swag, 370
Tennessee
Christopher Place, 548

Cross-Country Skiing

Tennessee
Roan Mountain State Resort Park, 553

Downhill Skiing

North Carolina
Cataloochee Ranch, 358
Hound Ears Club, 340

European Spa

Georgia
Chateau Elan, 106

Farm Destination

South Carolina
Sunrise Farm, 451

Film Library

Alabama
Blue Shadows Bed & Breakfast, 18
Georgia
Parrott-Camp-Soucy Home and Gardens, 124

Fishing

Alabama
Bay Breeze, 14
Blue Shadows Bed & Breakfast Guest House, 18
The Governor's House, 34
Lake Guntersville State Park Lodge & Convention Center, 20
Marriott's Grand Hotel, 28
Perdido Beach Resort, 27
Twin Pines Resort and Conference Center, 32
Arkansas
Buffalo Outdoor Center, 79
Gaston's White River Resort, 63
Pinnacle Vista Lodge, 69
Georgia
Brasstown Valley Resort, 132

Fitness Center

Gambling

Gardens

Golf

Gourmet Dining

Access for the Disabled

Hiking

Historic Sites

Horseback Riding

South Carolina
Brasington House Bed & Breakfast, 472
Cassina Point Plantation, 482
Middleton Inn at Middleton Place, 476
Nicholls-Crook Plantation House B&B, 456
1790 House, 484
Villa de la Fontaine Bed & Breakfast, 480
Wade-Beckham House, 442

Hunting

Georgia
The Lodge at Cabin Bluff, 147
Melhana — The Grand Plantation Resort, 130

Kitchen or Cooking Facilities

Alabama
DeSoto State Park Resort, 17
Lake Guntersville State Park Lodge & Convention Center, 20
Georgia
Callaway Gardens, 126
Helendorf River Inn & Towers, 118
Shellmont Bed & Breakfast, 104
Kentucky
Cumberland Falls State Resort Park, 182
Log Cabin Bed & Breakfast, 187
North Carolina
Hemlock Inn, 343
High Hampton Inn, 346
Innisfree Inn, 352
Mountain Brook, 364
South Carolina
Disney's Hilton Head Island Resort, 487
Litchfield Plantation Country Inn, 498
Sunrise Farm, 451
Tennessee
Blue Mountain Mist Country Inn—Shagonage, 562
Christopher Place, 548
Embassy Suites Memphis, 536
Newbury House at Historic Rugby, 558
Roan Mountain State Resort Park, 553

Limousine About Town

Georgia
Atlanta Grand Hyatt, 97
Louisiana
Melrose Mansion, 258
North Carolina
The Biltmore Greensboro Hotel, 387

Massage Therapy

Georgia
Chateau Elan, 106
The Cloister, 165
Melhana — The Grand Plantation Resort, 130
Renaissance Waverly Hotel, 100
Kentucky
Marriott's Griffin Gate Resort, 198
Mississippi
The Mockingbird Inn Bed & Breakfast, 314
Silver Star Resort & Casino, 312
North Carolina
High Hampton Inn, 346
The Orchard Inn, 363
The Panes, 344

Murder Mysteries

Arkansas
Dairy Hollow House, 51
The Empress of Little Rock, 66
Georgia
Glen-Ella Springs Inn & Conference Center, 110
South Carolina
The Inn at Merridun, 454
TwoSuns Inn Bed & Breakfast, 470
Tennessee
Adams-Edgeworth Inn, 540

Musical Performances

Arkansas
The Inn at Mountain View, 75
The Ozark Folk Center, 77
Tennessee
Christopher Place, 548

Nature Programs

Alabama
DeSoto State Park Resort, 17
Lake Guntersville State Park Lodge & Convention Center, 20
Arkansas
Gaston's White River Resort, 63
Queen Wilhelmina Lodge, 72
Georgia
Callaway Gardens, 126
Greyfield Inn, 142
Little St. Simons Island, 148
The Lodge at Cabin Bluff, 147
Kentucky
Cumberland Falls State Resort Park, 182
Lake Barkley State Resort Park, 181
Louisiana
Butler Greenwood B&B, 267
Mississippi
Canemount Plantation, 298
North Carolina
Bald Head Island, 406
Balsam Mountain Inn, 338
High Hampton Inn, 346
The Swag, 370
South Carolina
Disney's Hilton Head Island Resort, 487
Tennessee
Fall Creek Falls Inn and Fall Creek Falls State Resort Park, 552

Near University or College

Alabama
Auburn University Hotel & Conference Center, 10
Kentucky
Boone Tavern Hotel of Berea College, 178
The Doctor's Inn of Berea, 180
North Carolina
Washington Duke Inn & Golf Club, 385

Outdoor Hot Tub

Alabama
The Original Romar House, 25
Arkansas
Dairy Hollow House, 51
Georgia
Foley House Inn, 154
The Gastonian, 155
Magnolia Place Inn, 159
Presidents' Quarters, 162
Louisiana
The House on Bayou Road, 255
North Carolina
Mountain Brook, 364
Tennessee
Blue Mountain Mist Country Inn—Shagonage, 562

Paddle Wheel Excursions

Kentucky
Shaker Village of Pleasant Hill, 193
Louisiana
The Delta Queen, 252
Tennessee
Opryland Hotel, 544

Pets Allowed

Alabama
Radisson Suite Hotel, 22
Arkansas
The Edwardian Inn, 56
Georgia
Presidents' Quarters (kennels available), 162
Kentucky
Boone Tavern Hotel of Berea College, 178
Log Cabin Bed & Breakfast, 187
The Seelbach Hotel, 202
Louisiana
Bois des Chênes Inn, 245

Racquetball

North Carolina
The Swag, 370

Rafting/Canoeing

Arkansas
Buffalo Outdoor Center, 79
Georgia
The Lodge at Cabin Bluff, 147

Sailing

Georgia
Brunswick Manor, 140
North Carolina
The Inn at St. Thomas Court, 421

Spa Services

Georgia
Brasstown Valley Resort, 132
Chateau Elan, 106
Melhana — The Grand Plantation Resort, 130
Mississippi
Silver Star Resort & Casino, 312
North Carolina
The Panes, 344

Swamp/River Tours

Georgia
Open Gates Bed & Breakfast, 143
Louisiana
Bois des Chênes Inn, 245
Country Oaks Guesthouse, 241
Maison de Saizan, 264
South Carolina
Disney's Hilton Head Island Resort, 487

Swimming

Alabama
Auburn University Hotel & Conference Center, 10
Lake Guntersville State Park Lodge & Convention Center, 20
Huntsville Marriott, 21
Perdido Beach Resort, 27
Radisson Suite Hotel, 22
Twin Pines Resort and Conference Center (lake), 32
Arkansas
Gaston's White River Resort, 63
Margland Bed & Breakfast Inns, 78
The Ozark Folk Center, 77
Scott Valley Resort & Guest Ranch, 73
Georgia
Atlanta Grand Hyatt, 97
Brasstown Valley Resort, 132
Callaway Gardens, 126
Chateau Elan, 106

Tennis

Theater

Train Rides

Trap- and Skeet Shooting

Water Skiing

Winery

Index